EIGHTH EDITION

EXTRAORDINARY GROUPS

An Examination of Unconventional Lifestyles

EIGHTH EDITION

EXTRAORDINARY GROUPS

**An Examination of
Unconventional Lifestyles**

RICHARD T. SCHAEFER
DePaul University
and
WILLIAM W. ZELLNER

WORTH PUBLISHERS

Grateful acknowledgment is given for permission to reprint the photos on the following pages: **page 4:** Three Lions/Hulton Archive/Getty Images; **page 46:** Bettmann/Corbis; **page 88:** AP Photo/Corrado Giambalvo; **page 128:** age fotostock/SuperStock; **page 162:** Peter Stackpole/Time Life Pictures/Getty Images; **page 202:** Tim Thompson/Corbis; **page 248:** Robert Maass/Corbis; **page 280:** Peter Horree/Alamy

Publisher: Catherine Woods
Acquisitions Editor: Sarah Berger
Marketing Manager: Amy Shefferd
Photo Editor: Patricia Marx
Art Director: Babs Reingold
Senior Designer, Cover Designer: Kevin Kall
Associate Managing Editor: Tracey Kuehn
Project Editor: Carol O'Connell, Graphic World Publishing Services
Production Manager: Barbara Anne Seixas
Composition: Graphic World Inc.
Printing and Binding: RR Donnelley
Cover Photo: Steven Hunt/Image Bank

ISBN-13: 978-0-7167-7034-3
ISBN-10: 0-7167-7034-2

Printed in the United States of America

First printing

Worth Publishers
41 Madison Avenue
New York, NY 10010
www.worthpublishers.com

To the memory of
William W. Zellner,
a teacher and a scholar

CONTENTS

3   THE GYPSIES   89

4   CHRISTIAN SCIENTISTS   129

PREFACE

Now in its eighth edition, *Extraordinary Groups* has had a most gratifying history. Written by sociologists, using and illustrating sociological principles, the book has also been adopted in various other social science courses, including anthropology, religion, history, and psychology. This interdisciplinary approach is one reason the book has been used in hundreds of colleges and universities, a number that continues to grow.

Another reason for the book's appeal is that it is descriptive and explanatory rather than analytical. True, the description is interwoven with basic sociological concepts, but systematic analysis and inductive reasoning have been left to the discretion of the instructor.

The eighth edition of *Extraordinary Groups* contains a number of significant changes; indeed, every chapter has been revised and updated. All chapters have been reworked to be read without reference to extended intext quotations. More significantly, the chapters have been updated to reflect the latest events and scholarship. For example, the new light with which the nation sees the Amish following the horrific killings at the Pennsylvania Amish school in 2006 are considered. The most recent legal battles experienced by the Christian Scientists are included. The author's own experiences with Father Divine Movement including a personal interview with Mother Divine in 2005 are now a part of this edition.

The most obvious change since the seventh edition is the addition of several pedagogical features. Each chapter now begins with an opening image and includes a timeline to better guide the reader to gaining an overall historical picture of each group. Throughout each chapter key terms are highlighted and then are listed at the end of each chapter. At the end of each chapter has been added a listing of several websites with more information relevant to that chapter's extraordinary group. At the end of this book is now a comprehensive listing of key terms with full definitions.

There is also the addition of a chapter on the Church of Scientology. This is a truly new extraordinary group, which has only developed within the last seventy years. Unlike all the other groups, it is not derived from any existing religious group and is not a part of the Christian, Judeo, or Islam traditions. Also Scientology, which many dispute can even be considered a religion, is best known by its Hollywood adherents and as founded by L. Ron Hubbard, who previous to his development of Scientology was best known for his science fiction writings.

Every effort has been made in this edition by the author to maintain the creative and scholarly voices that have been behind the productive publication of *Extraordinary Groups*. The first edition was written by William S. Kephart, long-time professor of sociology at the University of Pennsylvania. Fortunately for tens of thousands of college students, Bill Zellner matched Kephart's passion for groups engaged in unconventional lifestyles, becoming a co-author with Kephart starting in the fourth edition. I knew Bill Zellner both as an undergraduate and graduate student when I taught at Western Illinois University, where he attended in the latter 1970s. He kept *Extraordinary Groups* alive and fresh for another three editions over a decade.

Acknowledgments

Over the years, the various editions of *Extraordinary Groups* have been strengthened by the thoughtful and perceptive comments of a number of reviewers. I appreciate the reviewers who offered their thoughts: T. John Alexander (Houston Baptist University), Douglas C. Bachtel (University of Georgia), Antonio A. Chiareli (Union University), Karen B. Martin (Great Basin College), Fred C. Pampel (University of Colorado), and Dennis L. Peck (University of Alabama).

Richard T. Schaefer
schaeferrt@aol.com
www.schaefersociology.net

ABOUT THE AUTHORS

Richard T. Schaefer obtained his M.A. and Ph.D. in sociology from the University of Chicago. His continuing interest in race relations led him to write his master's thesis on the membership of the Ku Klux Klan and his doctoral thesis on racial prejudice and race relations in Great Britain. Schaefer is author of *Racial and Ethnic Groups* (Eleventh Edition), *Race and Ethnicity in the United States* (Third Edition), *Sociology* (Eleventh Edition), *Sociology: A Brief Introduction* (Sixth Edition), and *Sociology Matters* (Fourth Edition). His articles and book reviews have appeared in many journals, including *American Journal of Sociology, Phylon: A Review of Race and Culture, Contemporary Sociology, Sociology and Social Research, Sociological Quarterly,* and *Teaching Sociology.* He has served as president of both the Illinois Sociological Association and the Midwest Sociological Society. In recognition of his achievements in undergraduate teaching, he was named Vincent de Paul Professor of Sociology in 2004.

William W. Zellner was professor of sociology at East Central University in Ada, Oklahoma. He attended Lafayette College, Missouri Valley College, Moravian College, and Millikin University, earning his B.A. and M.A. at Western Illinois University. His doctoral work was completed at South Dakota State University.

Zellner was author of numerous articles, essays, and books, including *Countercultures: A Sociological Analysis,* and *Sects, Cults, and Spiritual Communities: A Sociological Analysis* (co-edited with Marc Petrowky). He was past president of the Oklahoma Sociological Association, and three times past president of the Association for the Scientific Study of Religion, Southwest. He also served as chairman of an award-winning nine-county community action agency. He had been designated as a resource person for the United States Information Agency to foreign journalists interested in American religious sects and cults. In 1996, he launched his college's inaugural faculty lecture series with the topic "Overview of Countercultures and Extraordinary Groups." He passed away in 2003 shortly after the last edition he authored was available to welcoming readers, students, and instructors.

INTRODUCTION

America is a land of fascinating cultural diversity. Scores of various ethnic groups, hundreds of different religious sects and denominations—the toal seems almost inexhaustible. Indeed, it is the tremendous range of associational groups that sets America apart from most other societies.

Out of the multitude of different culture-groups that have appeared on the American scene, we have chosen eight for inclusion in the present volume:

The Old Order Amish	The Father Divine Movement
The Oneida Community	The Mormons
The Gypsies	The Jehovah's Witnesses
The Church of Christ, Scientist	The Church of Scientology

All of these groups are important in their own right. Just as liberally educated persons should have some knowledge of other times and other places, they should also have an awareness of the subcultural diversity within their own society. The only question to be asked is this: Why were these particular groups chosen, rather than others? The answer is threefold.

Sociological Illustration

The first—and most important—reason pertains to sociological illustration. The groups were selected because they illustrate major sociological principles in concrete form. Let us look at some examples.

As used by sociologists, the term primary group refers to a small, face-to-face group whose members share experiences, confide in one another, lend mutual support and understanding, and so on. These primary-group needs, as they are called, are deep-seated. They are characteristic of human beings everywhere. In most societies, the basic primary group is the family, and insofar as the personality structure of children is concerned, sociologists feel that the family has a lasting influence.

It stands to reason, therefore, that any culture or subculture attempting to eliminate the family must provide an alternative social mechanism for the satisfaction of primary-group needs. The Oneida Community is a good case in point.

In their attempt to create a utopian society, the Oneidans dispensed entirely with marriage, family, and parental child rearing. All males were permitted to have sexual relations with all females, and all children were

1

raised communally. Undue affection between parents and children—or between a particular man and a particular woman—was severely censured. And because the Oneida community lasted for some fifty years, with a total membership running well into the hundreds, the methods used to promote group solidarity were obviously effective.

Oneidans were all housed under one roof—the Mansion House—a building designed specifically to promote feelings of togetherness. Members ate in a common dining hall and held meetings in a community meeting hall. Activities such as smoking, drinking, and card playing were prohibited, because they were considered to be individualistic or anti-group. Conversely, musical presentations, theatricals, and other group activities were strongly encouraged.

In their day-to-day living, Oneidans totally rejected the concept of private property. They shared their material possessions, their wealth, their mates, and their children. Members held both a common economic philosophy and a common theology. So strong was their we-feeling that they were able to satisfy primary-group needs despite the large size of their community.

Let us look at one more example: *definition of the situation*. As W. I. Thomas, who coined the term, put it, "What men define as real is real in its consequences." And the Old Order Amish provide an excellent illustration, for they have defined the automobile as a threat to their social equilibrium—and they are acting accordingly.

Many permissive changes have taken place among the Amish, but one "contraption" remains taboo: the automobile. Members are not permitted to own them. And despite a variety of pressures, the Amish church has not yielded on this point—and probably never will.

The Old Order Amish have a close-knit family life. They are wedded to the soil, to the church community, and to the horse and buggy. And they feel that the auto would tend to disrupt their methodical and slow-paced way of life.

True, the Amish may be wrong in their judgment. The automobile might not bring with it the feared after effects. But that is irrelevant. They have already defined the situation, and they can hardly change the definition without also changing their entire social perspective.

Other sociological illustrations would include *culture conflict* among the Mormon polygamists; *social control* in the Gypsy community; *cultural theme,* as exemplified by the Father Divine movement; *gender role,* as illustrated by Mary Baker Eddy; *alienation; assimilation; conspicuous consumption; sanctions; folkways and mores; charisma; ethnocentrism; level of aspiration; values; and manifest and latent function.*

Various chapters in *Extraordinary Groups* contain a number of these sociological concepts around which are woven the threads and cultural fabric of the group in question. By associating the concept with the group of groups involved, the student is thus aided in the learning process.

Diversity

Although we could have selected groups that were fairly similar to each other, such as many of the counterculture communes that materialized between 1965 and 1975, we felt that—in terms of liberal arts values—diversity was much more rewarding. Accordingly, we chose groups that were markedly different from each other.

The Oneidans adhered to a system of strict economic communism, whereas the Mormons believe just as strongly in free enterprise. The Amish are a rural group and the Father Divine movement is urban. Unlike the centuries of history of the Amish, the Church of Scientology is totally a creation of the last seventy years. The groups vary in their outreach. Scientologists make their literature freely available, operate numerous information centers, and make effective use of its voluminous Internet site. The Jehovah's Witnesses and the Mormons gain members through proselytizing, whereas the Amish are content to let God increase their numbers.

Interest

The third and final reason for choosing these particular groups was simply that they are interesting. This we know, because many of the accounts in *Extraordinary Groups* were based on personal experience. For example, author Zellner was born and raised in Pennsylvania, and his fascination and conversations with the Old Order Amish have spanned many decades. Schaefer conducted fieldwork at primary retreat of the Father Divine Movement and met with Mother Divine on two occasions.

Our interest in the Oneida Community also goes back many years; in fact, a number of the surviving members were actually interviewed, as well as their descendants. Talks with the Christian Scientists were most rewarding. A representative of the church met with one of Schaefer's classes, answering their many questions about medical care. Interviews and association with Jehovah's Witnesses were also quite revealing.

We wish we could say that our relationship with the Gypsies was similarly rewarding, but—no pun intended—it was not in the cards. Both physically and conversationally, Gypsies are elusive. A good many of the interviews were out-and-out failures. Fortunately, a few of the interviewees were cooperative. Also, some invaluable fieldwork on the part of other investigators was available.

Sociological principles are not difficult to learn. The trick is to make them meaningful in keeping with the best traditions of a liberal education. And we do hope that a study of the following "extraordinary groups" will result in a meaningful grasp of the subject. Also, in terms of the cultural diversity mentioned earlier, a consideration of these groups may permit us to feel a little less smug about our own way of life.

CHAPTER ONE

THE OLD ORDER AMISH

- Early History
- "... A Peculiar People"
- The Amish Farmstead
- Leisure and Recreation
- Religious Customs
- Sanctions

- Courtship and Marriage
- The Amish Family System
- Education
- Challenges Facing the Amish
- The Future

The Amish are descendants of the sixteenth-century Swiss Anabaptists. *Anabaptists* is a general term that was applied to those who rejected infant baptism practiced by Roman Catholics and early Protestants. They advocated "believer" baptism or, in other words, baptism by consenting adults, which was a crime in the sixteenth century. Many of the Swiss Anabaptists came to be known as Mennonites because of the strong leadership of Menno Simons. In this sense, the Amish are a branch of the Mennonites, and the two groups have much in common, especially in a historical sense.[1]

Menno Simons was born in 1492 in the Netherlands. He was ordained a Roman Catholic priest, but broke with the church and eventually formed his own movement. His teachings included separation of church and state, adult baptism, and refusal to bear arms or take oaths. He died in 1561.

Although space does not permit an analysis of Menno Simons's theological and secular beliefs, one point should be mentioned. He was a firm believer in the **Meidung**—the shunning or avoidance of excommunicated members. It was the *Meidung* controversy that eventually led to the formation of the Amish.

---

[1]Interestingly, the Amish called themselves Amish-Mennonites until World War II. To file as conscientious objectors (the Amish will not go to war for any reason), they had to fill out a card. They were told by government officials "that they could not write down two religious names, so they dropped the name Mennonites and have been known simply as the Amish ever since." Richard Ammon, *Growing Up Amish* (New York: Atheneum, 1989), p. 17.

Early History

Jacob Amman was a Mennonite preacher. Little is known of his early life, although he seems to have been born in Switzerland in 1656. He rose rapidly in the church hierarchy, and soon became a respected leader. From all accounts, he was a stern and righteous man—not unlike an Old Testament prophet—journeying from place to place, admonishing, exhorting, dutifully defending the faith.

What distressed him most was the fact that some Mennonite leaders were not enforcing the *Meidung*. One thing led to another, factions developed, and in 1693 it became obvious that the *Meidung* controversy was irreconcilable. Those who believed in the ban joined Amman's group and became known as the Amish. The others stayed within the larger Mennonite fold.

When the two groups came to the United States, the schism persisted, as it does to this day. The *Meidung* itself, moreover, remains a key concept. In fact, it would be no exaggeration to say that the *Meidung* is the heart of the Amish system of social control. Details will be discussed in a later section.

What do the present-day Amish think of Jacob Amman? Some members contend that he was overly harsh in both his views and his implementation, although others defend his actions as necessary—given the temper of the times. He is certainly not a revered leader. Indeed, many of the Old Order Amish evidence little knowledge of—or interest in—Jacob Amman.

The reason is not hard to find. Amman was a strong leader with strong convictions, qualities that the Amish tend to de-emphasize. The Old Order Amish are devout believers in humility, brotherly love, group discussion, and consensus, and they are suspicious of those with leadership aspirations. Little wonder that their attitude toward Amman is one of ambivalence. Still, it is questionable whether the Amish would have survived as a separate group had it not been for the strong hand and unbending will of Jacob Amman.

The Amish began emigrating from Switzerland and Germany to the American colonies about 1710. They settled on land that would eventually become Pennsylvania, where William Penn was committed to a colony of religious toleration. The Amish as well as Quakers and Mennonites were welcomed.[2]

---

[2]For a comprehensive discussion of this early American period, see John A. Hostetler, *Amish Society* (Baltimore: Johns Hopkins University Press, 1980), pp. 54–64. For a look at Amish history and lifeways from an Amish perspective, see Hostetler, *Amish Roots: A Treasury of History, Wisdom, and Lore* (Baltimore: Johns Hopkins University Press, 1989). Included are more than 150 short articles written mostly by the Amish for in-group consumption. Also see Paton Yoder, *Tradition and Transition: Amish Mennonites and Old Order Amish 1800–1900* (Scottdale, PA: Herald Press, 1991).

The focus in this history and the chapter is the Old Order Amish, who are the conservative wing of Amish. Beginning in the 1860s, other groups broke away that have tended to be a bit more liberal, such as relaxation of certain behavioral standards or having separate churches rather than devotional meetings in homes.

Although they faced the usual hazards encountered by American colonists, the followers of Jacob Amman found an almost matchless opportunity for agricultural development. Climate, soil, rainfall, and topography were excellent. Best of all, the land was cheap and seemed to be in almost limitless supply. The Old Order Amish had come upon a farmer's dream, and they proceeded to make the most of it.

They grew and prospered, from a relatively small number of families in the 1700s to thousands in the 1800s. Indeed, the "almost limitless" supply of land in Pennsylvania eventually turned out to be anything but limitless, and to form new settlements the Amish were forced to migrate to other regions. Today there are settlements in no fewer than twenty-eight states. Of the more than 180,000 Old Order Amish, however, the majority live in Ohio, Pennsylvania, and Indiana. (See the Timeline.)

The Old Amish Order

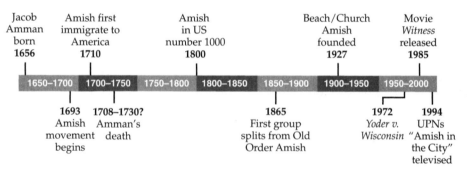

| Jacob Amman born 1656 | Amish first immigrate to America 1710 | | Amish in US number 1000 1800 | | Beach/Church Amish founded 1927 | Movie *Witness* released 1985 |

1650–1700 | 1700–1750 | 1750–1800 | 1800–1850 | 1850–1900 | 1900–1950 | 1950–2000

| 1693 Amish movement begins | 1708–1730? Amman's death | | 1865 First group splits from Old Order Amish | | 1972 *Yoder v. Wisconsin* | 1994 UPNs "Amish in the City" televised |

The Old Order Amish also have a number of communities in Canada, Central America, and South America. Paradoxically, there are no Amish in Europe, their original homeland.

Although the secular and religious practices of the Amish show many similarities no matter where they live, there are also some significant regional differences. And although we will try to present a more or less generalized account, special attention will be given to the Amish of Lancaster County, Pennsylvania, one of the oldest, largest—and certainly one of the most interesting—of all the Amish groups.[3]

---

[3]Readers familiar with Lancaster County will recognize the picturesque names of towns and villages in Amishland: Intercourse, Smoketown, Leola, White Horse, Compass, Bird-in-Hand, Beartow Gap, Mascot, Paradise, and others.

"... A Peculiar People"

In their olden attire and horse and buggy, the Old Order Amish appear to be driving out of yesterday. Actually, they are more than simply old-fashioned. Conservatism is part of their religion, and as such it permeates their entire life. The Amish recognize they stand apart from the general population. For generations, they have referred to the non-Amish as the **English** or **Englishers.**

The followers of Jacob Amman believe in a literal interpretation of the Bible and rely heavily on the statement, "But ye are a chosen generation, a royal priesthood, an holy nation, a peculiar people" (1 Peter 2:9). And because they have been specifically chosen by God, the Amish take great pains to stay "apart" from the world at large. They do this not only by living apart, but by rejecting so many of the standard components of modern civilization: automobiles, radio and television, high school and college, movies, air conditioning, jewelry and cosmetics, life insurance, cameras, musical instruments. The list goes on and on.

This is not to say that the Old Order Amish reject all change. As will be shown later, some of the changes have been fairly far-reaching.[4] But in general, the followers of Jacob Amman resist converting to what they believe to be harmful worldly ways.

Appearance and Apparel   Sociologists often use the term **in-group,** which refers to a group or category to which people feel they belong, in contrast to the **out-group,** a group to which people feel they do not belong. An in-group is generally characterized by the loyalty, like-mindedness, and compatibility of its constituents. Members refer to the in-group as "we," and to the out-group as "they." For the Amish, wearing apparel is one of the most distinguishing features of the in-group.

Men's hats—probably the most characteristic feature of their attire—are of low crown and wide brim; smaller models are worn by the youngsters. Coats are without collars or lapels, and almost always include a vest. (An Amishman and his vest are not easily parted.) Wire hook-and-eye fasteners are used on suit coats and vests.

Amish men's trousers deserve special mention, because (1) they never have creases or cuffs; (2) they are always worn with suspenders (belts are taboo); and (3) most are without zippered or buttoned flies. Instead, the

[4]Stephen Scott and Kenneth Pellman, *Living without Electricity* (Intercourse, PA: Good Books, 1990).

flap or "broadfall" type is used.[5] Also, with the exception of their shirts, Amish men's attire is predominantly black.

Following the biblical injunction, Amish women keep their heads covered at all times. Cosmetics and makeup, of course, are prohibited at all times. Dresses are of a solid color—blues and purples are quite common—with (variable) long skirts and aprons. In public, women also wear shawls and capes.

For Amish women, stockings must be black, and shoes are the black, low-heeled variety. Interestingly enough, in recent years young boys and girls have taken to wearing jogging shoes. In fact, the two most popular forms of footwear for the youngsters are jogging shoes and bare feet! For both sexes, all jewelry (including the wedding ring) is taboo, because whatever is worn is presumed to be functional. An ornamental exception might be the Amishman's beard, though this does have recognition value: prior to marriage young men are clean-shaven, whereas married men are required to let their beards grow. Mustaches—which in the European period were associated with the military—are completely taboo.[6]

Amish males wear their hair long, unparted, in a Dutch bob, with the necessary trimming done at home. Amish females also have their own special hairdo, both cutting and curling being forbidden. (Shaving their legs and plucking their eyebrows are also taboo.) Their hair braiding is distinctively Amish, however, and a classroom of twenty Amish girls—all with identical hairstyles—is an unusual sight for an outsider to behold!

The Old Order Amish are quite cognizant of the fact that they look different, and they have no intention of changing. On the contrary, their "difference" makes them feel close to one another and accentuates the ingroup feeling.

Some observers believe that, because the Amish are thrifty, they deliberately use clothing that never goes out of style. This is not the reason, however. True, the followers of Jacob Amman are indeed thrifty. With the exception of shoes, stockings, and hats, they make nearly all their own

[5]"When fly closures for pants were introduced in the 1820s," writes Scott, "some considered them indecent. In 1830, the *Gentlemen's Magazine of Fashion* pronounced the fly 'an indelicate and disgusting fashion.' While the larger society eventually accepted this feature, many plain people did not." Among the plain people were the Old Order Amish. See Stephen Scott, *Why Do They Dress That Way?* (Intercourse, PA: Good Books, 1986), p. 114.

Zellner was once given a workshirt and trousers by an ex-Amishman. Going to the bathroom requires a measure of planning. The trousers, flapped much like navy bell-bottoms, have seven buttons and snaps to undo. The gray shirt has wire hook-and-eye fasteners.

[6]The Amish sometimes appear inconsistent in their prohibitions. Thus, wristwatches are forbidden whereas pocket watches are permitted. Sometimes there is a good reason for the seeming inconsistency, and the Amish are well aware of the explanation. At other times, the answer would likely be, "It has always been so."

clothing. They also wear their clothes until they are literally worn out. But the basic reason they will not change styles is that they consider such change to be worldly—and worldliness has negative connotations.

General Lifestyle   It was Thorstein Veblen, one of the early giants of sociology, who first used the term **conspicuous consumption,** by which he meant the tendency to gain attention through the overt display of one's wealth. But whereas such display might be expected on the part of many Americans, it has no place in the Amish community. Their homes, for example, some of which have surprisingly modern features, would never contain elaborate furniture or fancy wallpaper. Clothes, as we have seen, are plain and functional, and neither sex will wear adornments of any kind.

With their emphasis on humility, the Old Order Amish dislike all types of public recognition. Pride, in fact, is considered a cardinal sin. As a consequence, actions that are more or less commonplace in society at large are seldom encountered in Amishland. Boasting is rare. Having one's portrait painted or picture taken is prohibited; indeed, cameras are completely taboo. Such behavior would be considered a sign of self-aggrandizement.[7]

Bicycles, motorcycles, and automobiles are strictly *verboten* in the Lancaster County settlement, and any adult who bought one would be subjected to severe group pressures. The automobile is the best-known case in point, and—as will be shown—the Amish lifestyle is strongly influenced by their being a horse-type rather than an automobile-type culture.

The Old Order Amish are a slow-tempo community. They value such traits as obedience, modesty, and submission, rather than mobility and competitiveness.[8] The hustle and bustle that characterize so much of the society of the English will not be found in Amishland. Seeing an adult Amish person in a hurry would be rather unusual!

In their business ventures, the Amish follow a fairly conservative route. They have no interest in stocks, bonds, or other forms of "speculation." They are staunch believers in private enterprise, however, and will take out mortgages, borrow money from banks, and use checking accounts. Banks consider them excellent customers and excellent credit risks.

The followers of Jacob Amman have no strong interest in politics. Although they do vote—in local more than in national elections—voter

---

[7]For readers who appreciate a mystery, here is one with no immediate answer. The followers of Jacob Amman do not own cameras, and are dead set against having their pictures taken. Yet, on the basis of postcards, brochures, pamphlets, newspapers, magazines, and books, the Amish may well be the most photographed group in America!

[8]For a discussion of Amish personality, see Hostetler, *Amish Society,* pp. 185–89, 333ff; and Donald Kraybill, *The Riddle of Amish Culture* (Baltimore: Johns Hopkins University Press, 1989), pp. 24–25.

turnout is relatively low. Hostetler reports that when they register, most do so as Republicans.[9] The Amish themselves have never held a major office of any kind, for a good reason: the church would not permit it.

The Old Order Amish tend to reject various forms of commercial insurance, including life insurance. However, they do have a fairly comprehensive network of mutual-aid organizations and self-help programs, some of which involve monetary assessments. A sick farmer can count on his fields being tended, and even harvested, by his neighbors.

Medicine and Health   Should an Amish family's barn burn down, up to a hundred neighbors will gather, and in a day or two raise a new barn. Barn raisings have attracted nationwide publicity, but Amish construction skills are sometimes put to good use in erecting other kinds of less publicized buildings.

For example, in the late 1980s a young pediatrician, Holmes Morton, discovered that a genetic disease, glutaric aciduria, disproportionately affects Amish and Mennonite children in Lancaster County. According to Frank Allen, the disease "strikes suddenly and with devastating results, attacking the liver and nervous system, including the brain. Many victims lapse into comas and die within 48 hours. Most of those who survive the initial episode suffer progressive paralysis. Until Dr. Morton came along, the disease had never been correctly diagnosed in the community."[10]

In his efforts to buy building materials to establish a clinic and diagnostic equipment, Dr. Morton attempted to take out a second mortgage on his home. But that wasn't necessary. On November 19, 1990, the *Wall Street Journal*, hearing of Morton's efforts, printed a front-page article telling of his dream.

Donations were not solicited; nevertheless, more than 250 readers from thirty-seven states chose to contribute to the project. Two of the donors gave $100,000. Hewlett-Packard Corporation donated diagnostic equipment valued at $85,000. And an Amish farmer donated three prime acres of Lancaster County farmland for a building site.

On a rainy Saturday in late November 1990, more than one hundred Amish met within a mile of the barn raised for the movie *Witness*, and had their first Amish clinic-raising.

The clinic has become home for the latest in gene therapy, a relatively new medical field. It appears that the Amish have a higher rate of inherited diseases than most communities. Amish in the United States are all

[9]Hostetler, *Amish Society,* p. 253.
[10]Frank Allen, "Farm Folks Gather in Strasburg, Pa., against a Plague: Raising High the Roof Beams of Holmes Morton's Clinic Begins to Fulfill a Dream," *Wall Street Journal,* November 19, 1990, p. A1.

descended from just 47 families. Since 1989, Morton's clinic has become one of the most advanced gene research clinics in the country.[11]

In the spring of 1991, the *Philadelphia Inquirer* reported that an Amish child had died from a genetic defect that crippled his immune system. The condition was treatable, but the drug "cost $2,200 a treatment, not counting laboratory tests and periodic hospitalizations. Altogether, the cost of therapy would have been $190,000 a year, probably for life."[12] Ultimately, the manufacturer that produces the drug offered it without charge, but the family refused. They did not feel that it was fair to ask the community to contribute $70,000 a year toward required therapy.

At one time the Amish were reluctant to patronize doctors and hospitals at all, and some members still refuse to do so. In early 1991, for example, four hundred cases of rubella (German measles) had been reported in six Pennsylvania counties, as well as in other Amish settlements. During the previous year, there were only 1,093 such cases reported for the entire United States.[13]

Nevertheless, despite some reluctance to use doctors and hospitals, most Amish now use medical facilities when the situation calls for it. The majority of Amish women, though, have their babies at home, delivered by a midwife.[14]

During March 1990, after criminal charges were brought against an uncertified midwife, legislation was introduced in Harrisburg to allow midwifery without credentials. The "plain people," not ordinarily disposed to political involvement, gathered at the state capitol in support of the legislation. Afraid that the state would intrude on their centuries-old childbearing practices, more than five hundred Amish and Mennonites attended the rally. They carried signs but said little. Nevertheless, one Amish farmer told a reporter that two of his children were delivered by midwives, and the other was born in a hospital. He further said that "I would never go to the hospital again. It is so much more relaxed to do it at home and it's a lot cheaper. We don't have any bright lights or fancy trim or any TVs. When we go into the hospital we feel strange."[15]

---

[11] Kate Rudder, "Genomics in Amish Country," posted July 23, 2004, on Genome News Network. Accessed February 9, 2005 (www.genomenewsnetwork.org).

[12] Donald C. Drake, "A Deadly Illness, a Choice for Amish," *Philadelphia Inquirer,* March 20, 1991.

[13] "Rubella Breaks Out in Amish Communities," *New York Times,* March 26, 1991.

[14] See Penny Armstrong and Sheryl Feldman, *A Midwife's Story* (New York: Arbor House, 1986). See also Carol Morello, "Embattled Midwife to the Amish," *Philadelphia Inquirer,* July 23, 1989.

[15] Steven Ochs, "Amish, Mennonites Rally for Midwife Bill," *Allentown Morning Call,* March 13, 1990. In an interview with Pennsylvania House member Leonard Gruppo, Maurice Zellner determined that the medical profession, led by the Pennsylvania Midwives Association, fought to kill the bill. It died in committee. Under current law certified midwives must complete a course to practice outside of hospitals. According to Gruppo, most Amish midwives do not qualify under the law.

Sadly, even the Amish with their conservative, rural lifestyle are not exempt from AIDS. Lancaster County ranks seventh in Pennsylvania in the number of AIDS cases reported. One preacher told Larry Lewis of the *Philadelphia Inquirer*, "We are not perfect. There is some premarital sex in the sect, probably a small amount of drug use, and some sexual straying."[16] He went on to say that he even knew of an older member of the community who had visited prostitutes at the county seat.

It should be mentioned, in connection with medicine and health, that the Old Order Amish are conservative in death as well as in life. Their funerals are plain: no flowers, no metal caskets, no music, no decorations, no mourning bands, no crepe. Most districts permit embalming, but a few do not. There are no Amish undertakers, however, and even funeral parlors are taboo. The wooden coffin is made by an Amish carpenter, services are held at home, and an Amish bishop presides. The olden custom of holding a wake—sitting up all night around the body of the deceased—is still practiced in most areas.

Amish cemeteries are startlingly plain. There are no flowers, no decorations, no elaborate tombstones, and no mausoleums. In fact, there is not even a caretaker, so that the graves sometimes have a run-down look. In general, the only handmade signs are small, uniform headstones, with the name and dates of the deceased—no scrolls, epitaphs, or other inscriptions. Most Amish cemeteries are off the beaten track. For the most part, they are—or were—part of an Amish farmer's land, and there is no charge for the use of burial lots.

As might be imagined, the entire cost of an Amish funeral and burial is only a fraction of that normally spent by the English (non-Amish).

The Amish Farmstead

Amish life revolves around the home—literally as well as figuratively. Most inhabitants of Amishland are born at home, they work at or near home, and they socialize at home. Most of their clothing is homemade, and nearly all their meals are eaten at home. Church services are held at one home or another. The Old Order Amish also marry at home, and—as a most fitting finale—their funeral services are held at home.

"Home," however, has a special meaning, for the followers of Jacob Amman are predominantly a rural people, and their traditional dwelling can best be described as a farmstead. Indeed, for most of the Amish in the United States, farm and home tend to be synonymous, a feeling that complements their religious philosophy.

[16]Larry Lewis, "The Reality of AIDS Touches Even the Amish: The Sect's Relative Isolation Cannot Shield It from the Pervasive Disease," *Philadelphia Inquirer*, April 12, 1992, p. B1.

Amish farms are acknowledged to be among the best in the world. In addition to fairly extensive crop acreage, their holdings often consist of large, well-kept houses and barns, stables, springhouses, silos, sheds, and storehouses. And, because the Amish community maintains no homes for the aged, a farmstead may include two, three, or even four generations. Additions are made to the farmhouse as needed. The presence of so many oldsters on the farm, of course, serves as a self-perpetuating conservative influence. At any rate, it is little wonder that some of the larger Amish farms have the appearance of miniature villages.

Basic to the Amish agricultural system is the fact that they do not employ tractors in the field. Whereas such a handicap might seem almost insurmountable to other farmers, the Amish try to turn it to their advantage. True, by using a team of horses instead of a tractor, the Amish farmer spends more time in covering less ground. However, he does not mind hard work. He has ample free labor in the form of his sons. He saves money by not having to buy and replace tractors. And his horses supply him with a rich source of natural fertilizer. As one Amish farmer is reported to have said, "When you put gasoline in a tractor, all you get out is smoke!"

Aside from tractors, the Amish do use a variety of up-to-date farm machinery: sprayers, cultivators, binders, balers, and haymaking equipment. Gasoline engines are permitted, and often a stationary tractor is used as a source of power.

Agricultural failure is infrequent, for the Amish farmer is a master of his trade. He understands the soil, his crops, and his dairy herds, and he loves his work. His farm products are choice, and he is able to sell them for top dollar. And although he may buy food on the open market, much of what he and his family eat is homegrown. In view of present-day food prices, this is a real advantage. Farming also supplies the Amishman with one of his chief topics of conversation.

Economic Develeopment   Until the late 1960s, church members could be excommunicated for being employed in other than agricultural pursuits. This is not the case today. Although farming is their chief occupation, not all Amish are farmers, either because of choice or lack of cultivatable land. Now their work is much more diversified. Although you will not find Amish computer programmers, there are Amish engaged as blacksmiths, harness makers, buggy repairers, and carpenters. Non-Amish often hire these craftspeople as well.

The movement by the Amish into other occupations is sometimes a source of tension with larger society, or the English. As long as the Amish remained totally apart from dominant society in the United States, they experienced little hostility. As they entered the larger economic sector, however, intergroup tensions developed in the form of growing prejudice. The Amish today may underbid their competitors. The Amish entry into the commercial marketplace has also strained the church's traditional teaching on litigation and insurance, both of which are to be avoided. Mutual assistance has been the historical path taken, but that does not always mesh well with the modern businessperson. After legal action taken on their behalf, Amish businesses typically have been allowed to be exempt from paying Social Security and workers' compensation, another sore point with English competitors.

The Amish entrepreneur represents an interesting variation of the typical ethnic businessperson one might encounter in a Chinatown, for example. Research on ethnic businesses often cites discrimination against minorities and immigrants as a prime force prodding the development of minority enterprises. The Amish are a very different case because their own restrictions on education, factory work, and certain occupations have propelled them into becoming small business owners. However, class differences are largely absent among the Old Order Amish.

In many of the above instances the jobs are only temporary, to be held until the Amishman can procure a suitable farm of his own. In many other cases, however, the jobs become more or less permanent. This is especially true in the Lancaster County area, where there has been a serious "land squeeze" for some time.

The Amish have become extremely successful with their new businesses. Pennsylvania State University has concluded a study of Amish businesses reporting that "of all Amish small businesses in Lancaster, 60 percent were started after 1980; more than 20 percent have annual sales between $50,000 to $100,000, while 14 percent boast sales of more than $500,000. More surprising, still, there is about a 5 percent failure-rate; the national average is closer to 65 percent."[17]

Interestingly, Kraybill puts the number of businesses managed by women at about 20 percent. The *Wall Street Journal* notes that "In their new role, Amish working women must grapple with child-care issues made all the more pressing by their continuing preference for relatively large families. At the same time, they must teach themselves leadership skills often shunned in their male-dominated homes."[18]

Kraybill further notes that "Lancaster County attracts more than 5 million tourists a year. Yet, only 30 percent of Amish small businesses target tourism. Most are exclusively supported by the Amish community."[19]

The question that must be asked is this: Does not the emphasis on farming and farm-related occupations have a stultifying effect on those whose aptitudes and talents lie elsewhere? After all, an impressive array of occupations

---

[17]W. Sean Roberts and Vince Leclair, "Pennsylvania's Amish Add Small Businesses to Farming," *Christian Science Monitor,* November 9, 1995, vol. 87, p. 9. Also see "An Amish Exception," *The Economist,* February 7, 2004, p. 33.

[18]Timothy Aeppel, "More Amish Women Are Tending to Business," *Wall Street Journal,* February 8, 1996, p. B1.

[19]Roberts and Leclair, "Pennsylvania's Amish Add Small Businesses to Farming," p. 9.

is closed to the followers of Jacob Amman: medicine, law, dentistry, higher education, optometry, veterinary medicine, banking, finance, the military and the police, acting, music, professional athletics, politics and government work, corporate positions, and so on. The list is indeed a mighty one.

Amish Homes   Describing the typical Amish home of the twenty-first century is not easy. In addition to the usual regional and district variations, the "generational" factor must be considered. Homes of the younger Amish may be noticeably different from those of their parents' generation.

Like the farm, the traditional Amish home is well kept and well run. It is plain, lacking in many of the modern conveniences, in good repair, and solid as an oak. (It needs to be, for untold generations of the same family will live there.)

Most of these houses are fairly large, for several reasons. The Amish have a high birthrate, and at any given time there are likely to be a number of children living at home. Also, Amish farmers tend to retire early in life, and they usually turn the house over to one of their sons while they themselves live in the adjoining *Grossdawdy House*. And finally, as will be shown later, the Old Order Amish have no church buildings. Their home is their church, and services are held on a rotating basis. Houses, therefore, must be large enough to seat the congregation.

In the traditional Amish home, rooms are large, particularly the kitchen, where huge quantities of food are cooked and served. (There is no dining room.) Throughout the house, furnishings tend to be functional, though not drab. The Amish religion does not forbid the use of color. Walls are often light blue, dishes purple. Articles such as bed coverings and towels can be almost any color. Outside the house, there is likely to be a lawn and a flower garden. Fences, walls, posts, and landmarks may also be brightly colored.

Although they love colors, the followers of Jacob Amman do not believe in mixing them. Wearing apparel, fences, posts, buggies—all are of solid colors only. Plaids, stripes, and prints are considered too fancy. For this reason, contrary to popular impression, the Amish never put hex signs on their barns.[20]

Newer Amish houses differ from the traditional variety in a number of ways. They tend to be smaller, and many do not have a "farmhouse" appearance at all. In fact, except for such items as no electrical wiring and the lack of curtains, they often look much like non-Amish houses. In the matter of modern appliances and equipment, the differences between "traditional" and "new" are even more significant.[21]

---

[20]Zellner, who grew up in Northampton County, Pennsylvania, says that hex signs are a product of his Pennsylvania Dutch heritage. A variety of signs are sold to bring good fortune or ward off evil spirits. Amish never have used them.

[21]In the Clarita, Oklahoma, community the bishop lives in a mobile home with no utilities attached to it.

The Amish have never permitted their members to use electricity furnished by public power lines. The church has been unyielding on this point, and the prohibition has served to restrict the kinds of devices and appliances available to members. Over the years, however, the followers of Jacob Amman have come up with some rather interesting alternatives: bottled gas, batteries, small generators, air pressure, gasoline motors, hydraulic power. The net result has been a variety of modern devices that have become available to the Amish, not only in their homes, but in their barns, workshops, stores, and offices.[22]

In addition to a fashionable exterior, for example, the contemporary Amish home in Lancaster County is likely to have modern plumbing and bathroom facilities, attractive flooring and cabinet work, and a moderately up-to-date kitchen. The latter would include a washing machine, stove, and refrigerator, all powered by one of the nonelectrical sources mentioned above.

The Pace of Change   How significant are the foregoing changes? There is no denying that the Lancaster County Amish have experienced some meaningful alterations, both in their home life and in their employment. Although the reasons may be complicated, many of the changes and modifications have acted as a safety valve; that is, they have given members some necessary leeway, denial of which might have caused internal dissension.

At the same time, the above-mentioned modernization should not obscure the larger picture: *resistance to change* is still one of the hallmarks of Amish society. A majority of all Amish remain in farming and farm-related occupations. Amishland remains a basically agricultural community.

Amish homes in the Lancaster area, furthermore, though surprisingly modern in certain respects, are without electricity. There are no light bulbs, illumination being provided by oil lamps or gas-pressured lanterns. And the list of prohibitions remains long: dishwashers, clothes dryers, microwaves, blenders, freezers, central heating, vacuum cleaners, air conditioning, power mowers, bicycles, toasters, hair dryers, radios, television—all are taboo.[23]

Which parts of modernity will be accepted by the Amish and which will not is difficult to ascertain. When they do change, the change is usually well thought out, with the community assisting the bishop in the decision-making process. Recently, many devout Amish have become avid rollerbladers—a shock to most outsiders.

Sam Stoltzfus, an Amish historian, says, "In-line skates are permissible . . . because they are seen as a newer version of roller skates, a cousin

---

[22]See the discussion in Kraybill, *Riddle of Amish Culture,* pp. 150–64.
[23]Kraybill, *Riddle of Amish Culture,* pp. 150–64.

of the ice skate and an improvement over the leg-powered scooter—all long used by the Amish."[24]

There is little indication, therefore, that change in the Amish lifestyle will get out of hand. The "land squeeze," forcing more of the Amish into nonfarm occupations, will doubtless continue, but only in certain areas. Regional differences in conservatism may undergo modification. The Lancaster County settlement, for instance, was at one time among the more conservative groups, but this is no longer true. In both their population growth and their own distinctive quality of life, however, they continue to thrive.

Leisure and Recreation

The followers of Jacob Amman work hard; indeed, it is difficult to see how any group could work harder. Recreation and leisure are another matter, however, for in these spheres they have somewhat restricted options. There are a number of reasons for this.

To begin with, the typical Amish farmer and his wife have a limited amount of leisure time. For the husband, the prohibition on tractors means that fieldwork is laborious and time-consuming. And because his wife is denied the use of so many electrical appliances, a number of her routine chores—particularly food preparation—must be done largely by hand.

Also, the Amish do not have a wide range of interests. Except for necessary business trips, they tend to stay away from cities. They feel that city life epitomizes worldliness, and worldliness is linked with wickedness. But this means that the Old Order Amish effectively cut themselves off from much of the cultural life of the English. They do not attend operas, ballets, or concerts. They do not patronize movies or stage shows. They do not go to art exhibits. Generally speaking, they seldom dine out—nor do they go to bars or nightclubs. Attendance at sporting events is strictly *verboten*.

At home, the followers of Jacob Amman are similarly restricted in their choice of activities. They do not have television, radio, or stereo. They do not dance, play cards, or attend cocktail parties. They have no pianos or other musical instruments. They are not particularly interested in popular magazines or novels. They are not even permitted that great American invention, the telephone! However, they are permitted to use pay telephones, which abound in Amishland. Also, depending on the district, phones may be found in Amish shops.

The Amish community does not celebrate most American holidays. Memorial Day, Halloween, Labor Day, Veterans Day, Lincoln's and

---

[24]David W. Chen, "Amish Going Modern, Sort of, About Skating," *New York Times*, August 11, 1996, sec. 1, p. 10.

Washington's birthdays, the Fourth of July—all are ignored. Christmas and Easter are celebrated, although the emphasis is religious rather than secular. Christmas does not involve a Christmas tree, lights, mistletoe, decorations, cards, or Santa Claus. All work is suspended, however, and the children are given presents.

The Ban on Autos   Another restrictive factor—one of the most striking, in terms of leisure and recreation—is the Amish ban on automobile ownership. The ban is unequivocal, although it is permissible to ride in someone else's car. It is also acceptable to take a bus or taxicab.

Several reasons have been suggested for the ownership ban. It has been pointed out that horses are mentioned in the Bible. It is said that automobiles—and their maintenance—are expensive compared to the horse and buggy. The matter of fertilizer (or lack of it) has already been mentioned. Although these factors may be contributory, they do not comprise the real reason. The real reason is that the Old Order Amish feel that automobile ownership would disrupt their entire way of life.

When automobiles first became popular in the 1920s, they were expensive and unreliable. They were, nevertheless, a major invention, and represented a sharp break with the more traditional forms of transportation. Accordingly, they were rejected by both the Amish and the majority of Mennonites. But whereas most Mennonite groups eventually lifted the ban, the Amish community refused to budge, a position they have held to this day.

The followers of Jacob Amman have come under heavy pressure to permit the ownership of automobiles. Horseshoes make grooves in the road, and in a number of areas grooved roads are commonplace. More important, modern highways are dangerous, and buggies have been smashed by oncoming cars, especially at night. State laws require lights on moving vehicles, and the Amish have had to install night lights, powered by under-the-seat batteries. Pressures for automobile ownership have become so great that occasionally an Amish family will leave the church and join the Beachy Amish, a more liberal (but much smaller) group that permits its members to own and drive automobiles.

The ban on cars is one of the key factors that others and the Amish themselves consider important to maintaining Amish identity. Most will suffer great inconvenience and expense to insure their Amishness if the need arises.

For years, some observers have predicted that it would only be a matter of time before the followers of Jacob Amman converted to autos, but the predictions have not come true. They probably never will either, and the reason is based on a long-recognized sociological principle.

Many years ago, W. I. Thomas—one of the founding fathers of sociology—hit upon the concept **definition of the situation.** Stated simply, this means that a social situation is whatever it is defined to be by the participants. In Thomas's own words, "What men define as real is real in its consequences." The point is that the Old Order Amish have defined the automobile as a threat to their social equilibrium, and they are acting accordingly.

Both individually and collectively, the Amish are wedded to the soil, to the church community, and to the horse and buggy. The automobile would represent a far-reaching and detrimental change. True, the followers of Jacob Amman may be wrong in their judgment. The auto might not bring with it the feared aftereffects. But that is irrelevant. The Amish have already defined the situation, and they can hardly change the definition without also changing their entire social perspective.

Relative Deprivation   The automobile aside, there does appear to be an imbalance in Amishland; that is, there seems to be an overabundance of work and a scarcity of leisure and recreation. As a consequence, are the Amish not disgruntled? Have they no desire to lead fuller lives?

The answer is no. A large majority of Amish people have no desire whatsoever to lead any other kind of life. They do engage in leisure activities, but even if they did not, it is doubtful whether their outlook would be appreciably dampened. The fact is that they believe wholeheartedly in the simple, uncomplicated, slow-paced way of life, and neither hard work nor the lack of many conveniences disturbs them.

One of the reasons for this can be explained by **relative deprivation,** another concept widely employed by sociologists. Relative deprivation refers to the conscious feeling of a negative discrepancy between legitimate expectations and present actualities. According to this concept, people feel aggrieved not because of what they are deprived of in any absolute sense, but because of what they are deprived of in terms of their reference group.

An employee who receives a $3,000 raise would probably be satisfied if it were known that the amount was as high or higher than that received by others in the department. But if the employee discovered that most of the others had received larger increases, his or her morale would suffer accordingly. Similarly, students are generally satisfied with a B grade— until they learn that the majority of the class received As, with B being the lowest grade given.

Applied to the Amish community, relative deprivation explains a great deal. Most Amish are early risers, day in and day out. They work exceptionally hard, yet are not permitted to own such things as automobiles, television, and air conditioning. But the point is, the entire reference group—all of Amishland—is experiencing the same set of restrictions. A feeling of relative deprivation, therefore, is lacking.

The followers of Jacob Amman are anything but disgruntled. They lack certain conveniences, true, but they all accept this as the will of

God. They work hard, but because they generally love their work they do not consider this a burden. As a matter of fact, an Amish family has little trouble operating a 150- or 200-acre farm. The difficulty is not in running a large farm, but in finding a farm large enough to keep the family busy!

The Positive Side   Thus far, we have discussed the negative side of Amish recreation—things they do not do. But what *do* they do in this connection? Much of their social activity revolves around their home and their religion. Socializing—usually men with men and women with women—takes place both before and after church services. On Sunday evenings, the young people hold "singings," social gatherings that serve as a kind of adjunct to dating and courtship. Certain religious holidays afford opportunities for further socializing, and—as will be shown later—weddings are gala occasions.

Just plain visiting is one of the principal forms of entertainment in Amishland. Church services are held every other week, and on alternate Sundays many families visit (or are visited by) relatives or friends. In spite of some acknowledged restrictions, Amish life is far from somber.[25]

The followers of Jacob Amman are also fond of outings and picnics, and from the amount of food consumed on these occasions, eating should perhaps be classed as a recreational activity! The Amish have a special place in their hearts for animals of all kinds, and it is quite common to see an Amish family enjoying a day at a zoo.

Within their own homes, the Amish do some reading, though they are not a bookish group. They read the Bible, the *Ausbund* (the Amish hymnal), and *Martyrs Mirror,* the story of early Anabaptist persecutions. Farm journals are fairly common, and many families subscribe to local papers. Interestingly enough, there is one Amish newspaper, *The Budget,* put out by a non-Amish publisher.

The Old Order Amish occasionally play games, such as chess and checkers, and the youngsters engage in a variety of sports. Some men chew tobacco, and many districts—including those in Lancaster County—now permit smoking. And although drinking is frowned upon, individual Amish men are sometimes known to "take a nip." Generally speaking, the followers of Jacob Amman evidence a certain degree of tolerance toward drinking, at least on the part of the men.

---

[25]The Amish are not devoid of a sense of humor, and visiting days are often a time for storytelling. If you want to know why the Amish are "genetically bred to be cheap, closer to a dollar bill than George Washington," and for other stories, see Eli R. Beachy, *Tales from the Peoli Road: Wit and Humor of Very Real People, Who Just Happen to Be Amish* (Scottdale, PA: Herald Press, 1992).

Interest in Amish lifestyle is so great that authors and illustrators are beginning to produce children's books on the subject. For a fine example, see Patricia Polacco, *Just Plain Fancy* (New York: Bantam Doubleday Dell, 1990).

Religious Customs

Although outsiders are often unaware of it, the Old Order Amish have neither churches nor any kind of central church organization. They have no paid clergy, no missionaries, and no Sunday schools. Yet they are one of the most devout groups in America, and their decentralized church structure—which is simplicity itself—has been remarkably successful.

The Amish are organized into church districts, each district covering a certain geographical area and including a certain number of families. Membership varies, depending on region, but most districts in the United States probably average between 150 and 200 members, including children. When the figure exceeds this number the district usually divides—a fairly frequent occurrence, because the followers of Jacob Amman have always had a high birthrate.

Held in Amish homes on a rotating basis, the Sunday morning service lasts about three hours. Men and women sit separately, with men occupying the first few rows and women at the rear. (Each district has a set of benches, which are hauled to the designated house ahead of time.) The sermons—almost entirely in German—are quite lengthy, and it is not uncommon to see members start to squirm after the first hour or so, especially because the benches have no backs.

Inasmuch as the Old Order Amish do not permit musical instruments, it is sometimes thought that they prohibit singing, but this is not so. Hymns are an integral part of their Sunday service; in fact, their hymn-book—the *Ausbund*—was first published in 1564 and is the oldest hymnal used by any Protestant group. The hymns themselves—140 in number and written for the most part by Anabaptist prisoners—tell of great suffering and steadfastness. The amazing thing is that the tunes are handed down orally from one generation to the next, for the *Ausbund* has no written notes, only words.

The Clergy   Each Amish district is normally presided over by four clergymen: a bishop, two preachers, and a deacon. The bishop (*Volle Diener*, minister with full powers) is the spiritual head of the district. One could really say "spiritual and secular head," because in Amishland the two spheres tend to blend. In any case, the *Volle Diener* is the head man. He presides at weddings, funerals, baptisms, communion services, and excommunications. He also preaches, although this is not his main job. His main job is to prescribe and enforce the rules and otherwise hold the community together. And because the rules of the church are never written, they are—in point of fact—what the bishop says they are.

The two preachers (*Diener zum Buch*, minister of the Book) assist the bishop at ceremonial affairs such as communion and baptism. But their chief duties are delivering the Sunday sermons, leading the congregation in prayer, and interpreting the Bible. The preachers must be well versed in biblical authority and must be able to stand before the congregation and deliver their sermons without notes or books of any kind.

The deacon (*Armen Diener*, minister of the poor) also assists at the Sunday services and at ceremonial affairs. His chief duties, however, have to do with the day-to-day operation of the district. For example, the deacon serves as go-between during marriage arrangements, he obtains information about reported rule infractions, he tries to settle internal difficulties, he looks after families with problems, particularly those involving widows and orphans, and so on.

The four clergymen are not salaried. They must attend to their farms and their families like any other Amishman. And because the church has no property, no treasury, and no centralized administration, the four officers have their work cut out for them. Women, incidentally, are not eligible for the clergy.

If two or more districts are in "full fellowship" with one another—that is, if they agree on specific rules of conduct, mode of dress, allowable equipment, and so forth—they may exchange preachers on a given Sunday. If the districts are not in full fellowship, there is little or no contact between them. In some areas, such as Lancaster County, the bishops of the various districts meet twice a year to discuss church matters and iron out differences. But this is as close to a centralized church organization as the Amish ever get.

Chosen by Man and God   Old Order Amish clergy are always selected by a "combination of man and God"; that is, they are nominated by a vote of the adult congregation, but the "winner" is chosen by lot. More specifically, if a vacancy should occur in the rank of preacher, the congregation is asked to make nominations. Any member who gets at least three votes has his name entered in the lot. On the day of the selection, a number of Bibles are placed on a table, the number corresponding to the number of candidates. One of the Bibles contains a slip of paper with a biblical quotation. As the candidates walk by, each one selects a Bible, and whoever draws the Bible with the slip is the new preacher. He is thus believed to have been chosen by God.

This is the procedure followed for the selection of preachers and deacons. However, the Amish believe the bishops should have some prior experience, and when a vacancy occurs at this level, the selection is made directly by lot from among the preachers and deacons. Once selected, clergy of all ranks normally hold their positions for life. And although in many ways their jobs are thankless ones, most Amish clergymen apparently consider it an honor to have been chosen.

All the clergy are important; however, the bishop is the central figure, because it is he who determines the character of the district. Although outsiders may see little difference among the various Amish communities, the differences are indeed there, and the bishop is aware of them—down to the last detail. Trimming of the beard, design of women's shawls and aprons, type of hats and bonnets, gadgets on the buggy, tractor usage, house furnishings, barnyard and shop equipment—all come under the careful scrutiny of the *Volle Diener.*

It is easy to see why some Amish districts do not have full fellowship with their neighbors. In some districts, the buggies have gray tops; in others, black tops; in others, white tops; and in others, yellow tops. Districts vary in the tempo of their hymn singing. In some districts, men wear their hair at shoulder length; in others, the hair does not even cover the ears. The style of women's head coverings and the length of their skirts vary. Permissible items in the way of home furnishings also vary. And so on.

Bishop Elmer   Clear Brook is an Old Order Amish settlement in northern Indiana. As previously noted, the Amish have a slow and deliberate decision-making process. Sociologist Dachang Cong chronicled the process of removing a bishop from leadership in Clear Brook, an almost unheard of event.

In 1987, Clear Brook had a population of about 11,000 Amish living in sixty-five districts. By the mid-1980s, Bishop Elmer was already in his seventies. Some in his district were complaining that he was so set in his ways that he would not listen to them.

Cong notes that by 1986 "Kerosene refrigerators were adopted by many conservative districts that had previously sanctioned only ice boxes. A non-Amish man used to deliver ice to the Amish, but his service started to falter in 1985 and became unreliable in 1986. . . . [T]hose who wanted kerosene refrigerators exerted pressure on their clergy. One of their forceful arguments was that since the non-Amish use electric refrigerators and the Amish in the liberal districts use gas refrigerators, the adoption of kerosene refrigerators does not hurt either Amishness in general nor the particular conservatism of the conservative districts."[26]

In the summer of 1986, Bishop Elmer finally relented, reluctantly telling his district that they could now buy and use kerosene refrigerators.

After a few weeks Elmer found that he could not live with his decision. He told the families who had purchased refrigerators to dismantle them; they could no longer be used. More concerned about his indecisiveness than his unwillingness to change, some of his congregation began attending churches in other districts. Preachers from these districts then visited Elmer in an attempt to persuade him to take a more moderate stance on the

---

[26]Dachang Cong, "Amish Factionalism and Technological Change: A Case Study of Kerosene Refrigerators and Technology," *Ethnology* 31 (July 1992): 208.

refrigeration issue. Bishops from outside the area were selected to provide a balanced perspective. They found that Bishop Elmer was at fault. He was overly harsh, had not included the feelings of his followers in decision-making processes, and was inconsistent and unfair about the refrigerators.

The investigating team notified Elmer of their decision, but Elmer refused to repent. Ordinarily, Amish leaders are amenable to conciliatory efforts. The team of three then took the next step. More bishops from out of state were invited into the controversy. All found with the original tribunal.

Elmer was again offered the opportunity to submit to authority, and again he refused. During a March 1987 meeting, he was replaced as bishop. All attending "expressed their hope that Elmer would change so that he would be reinstated."[27]

Soon after Elmer's removal, kerosene refrigerators were approved in the district. Elmer and five other families established ties with an ultra-conservative district in southern Michigan.

"Temporary Visitors"   The followers of Jacob Amman believe strongly that they are only temporary visitors on earth, and that their principal duty is to prepare for the next world. The present world—and all that it connotes—is bad; hence, the Amish try to remain aloof from it. This explains why they insist on being "peculiar"; that is, dressing differently, acting differently, and living differently.

Like most other aspects of their lives, Amish theological beliefs are the essence of simplicity. Because they are on earth for only a short period, the Old Order Amish have little interest in improving the world or making it a better place to live in. Their entire orientation is otherworldly. They believe that the Word of God calls for self-denial and are quite content to make the necessary sacrifices. God, furthermore, is a personal, literal God, and the Bible is a literal transcription of His word. Also—and this is quite important—God is omnipotent. All things are ordered by Him, and nothing happens without His knowledge.

As for personal salvation, the Amish believe in eternal life, which involves a physical resurrection after death. The eternal life, however, may be spent in either heaven or hell, depending on how one lives during one's visit on earth. Members can expect to go to heaven if they follow the rules of the church, for by so doing they put themselves in God's hands.

Although there are no written rules, all the Amish know what is expected of them. Furthermore, there is always the Bible to turn to; in fact, a good many of their customs—including the *Meidung*—are based on specific biblical passages.

[27]Ibid, p. 210.

Sanctions

The term **sanctions** refers to rewards and punishments employed by a group to bring about desired behavior on the part of its members. Sanctions can thus be either positive or negative, and most groups— including the Old Order Amish—use both kinds. The Amish have been more successful than other groups, however, because of their religious and social organization.

Positive sanctions are quite similar to those used by other communities: membership privileges, group approval, clerical blessings, rites and rituals such as baptism and communion, opportunities for socializing, and, of course, the satisfaction of worshiping God with one's own people.

For *negative sanctions,* the followers of Jacob Amman employ a series of penalties or punishments ranging from the very mild to the very severe. The first step involves informal sanctions: gossip, ridicule, derision, and other manifestations of group disapproval. Such responses are used by groups everywhere, but each Amish community is a small, close-knit unit, and the operation of adverse opinion is particularly effective.

The next step is a formal admonition by one of the clergy. If the charge is fairly serious, the offender might be visited and admonished by both preacher and bishop. The errant member might also be asked to appear before the congregation at large—to confess his or her sin and ask for the group's forgiveness.

The *Meidung* The ultimate sanction is the imposition of the *Meidung,* also known as the "shunning" or "ban," but because of its severity, it is used only as a last resort. The followers of Jacob Amman have a strong religious orientation and a finely honed conscience—and the Amish community relies on this fact. Actions such as gossip, reprimand, and the employment of confession are usually sufficient to bring about conformity. The *Meidung* would be imposed only if a member were to leave the church, or marry an outsider, or break a major rule (such as buying an auto) without full repentance.

Although the *Meidung* is imposed by the bishop, he will not act without the unanimous support of the congregation. Generally speaking, however, the ban is total. No one in the district is permitted to associate with the errant party, including members of his or her own family. Even normal marital relations are forbidden. Should any member of the community ignore the *Meidung,* that person would also be placed under the ban. In fact, the *Meidung* is honored by all Amish districts, including those that are not in full fellowship with the district in question. There is no doubt that the ban is a mighty weapon. Jacob Amman intended it to be.

On the other hand, the ban is not irrevocable. If the shunned member admits the error of his or her ways—and asks forgiveness of the congregation—the *Meidung* will be lifted and the transgressor readmitted to the fold. No matter how serious the offense, the Amish never look upon someone under the ban as an enemy, but only as one who has erred. And although they are firm in their enforcement of the *Meidung*, the congregation will pray for the errant member to rectify his or her mistake.

Although imposition of the ban is infrequent, it is far from rare. Males are involved much more often than females, the young more frequently than the old. The *Meidung* would probably be imposed on young males more often were it not for the fact that baptism does not take place until the late teens. Prior to this time, young males are expected to be—and often are—somewhat on the wild side, and allowances are made for this fact.

Baptism changes things, of course, for this is the rite whereby the young person officially joins the church and makes the pledge of obedience. Once the pledge is made, the limits of tolerance are substantially reduced. More than one Amish youth has been subjected to the *Meidung* for behavior that, prior to baptism, had been tolerated.

Courtship and Marriage

As might be expected, Amish courtship and marriage patterns differ substantially from those of non-Amish society. Dating customs are dissimilar. There is no engagement or engagement ring. There is no fancy wedding. There is no traditional honeymoon, wherein the newlyweds have a chance to be by themselves. And both before and after marriage, a woman's place is firmly in the home. There is no such thing as a women's movement in Amishland. Although their connubial behavior does show some similarity to that of the larger society, the Amish tend to have their own way of doing things.

Dating Practices   Amish boys and girls are much more restricted in their courting activities than are the youth of other groups. For one thing, Amish youth work longer hours; hence, they have less time for "running around."[28] Also, Amish youngsters have a limited number of places to meet the opposite sex. They do not attend high school or college, so they are deprived of the chief rendezvous of American youth. They do not normally frequent fast-food places, shopping malls, movies, bars, dances,

---

[28]"Running around," or *rum springa*, is an Amish expression and seems to be one of the few terms the outside society has borrowed from them. Later we see, though, that *rum springa* has special social significance for the Amish.

rock concerts, summer resorts, and other recreational catchalls. Nor are their families permitted to have automobiles, which places a further limitation on their amorous activities.

Another restrictive factor has to do with the so-called endogamous provision. Anthropologists employ the term *endogamy* to denote marriage within the tribe or other social unit, in contrast to *exogamy,* or marriage outside the group. Sociologists use the terms with reference to broad groupings such as religion, race, nationality, and social class. But in contrast to the trend in society at large—where exogamous practices seem to be on the increase—the Old Order Amish remain strictly endogamous.

Amish parents forbid their young people to date the English. In fact, the only permissible dating is either within the district or between districts that have full fellowship with one another. Endogamy among the Amish, therefore, does serve to limit the number of eligible mates. In outlying districts, this limitation may present some problems.

Despite these factors, Amish dating and courtship are at least as successful as that practiced in society at large. Because Amish youth marry at about the same age as the English—women between twenty-one and twenty-three, men between twenty-two and twenty-five—both sexes have a fair amount of exposure to dating. In the process, most of them seem to enjoy themselves, and nearly all of them marry.

Amish courtship activities generally revolve around the "singings" held on Sunday nights. These usually take place at the same farm where that day's church services were held. Singings are run by the young people themselves and often involve participants from other districts. Refreshments are served, songs are sung, and there is always a good deal of banter, joking, and light conversation. If he has a date, the boy may bring her to the singing. If he does not, he tries to get one in the course of the evening, so that he may drive her home.

Should the girl permit the boy to drive her home, a dating situation may or may not develop, just as in the outside society. Unlike the larger society, however, Amish youth place less emphasis on romantic love and physical attractiveness, favoring instead those traits that will make for a successful family and community life: willingness to work, fondness for children, reliability, good-naturedness, and the like. The couple themselves, incidentally, tend to avoid any display of affection in public.

Once the couple decide to get married, the young man is required to visit the deacon and make his intentions known. The deacon then approaches the young woman's father and requests formal permission for the marriage. Permission is usually granted, for both sets of parents are probably well aware of developments and may already have started preparations for the wedding.

Marriage Weddings are the most gala occasions in Amishland, and in Lancaster County alone there are more than a hundred of them each year. Marriage is a major institution for the followers of Jacob Amman, and they go out of their way to emphasize this fact.

The announcement is first made by publishing the banns at a church service, usually two weeks before the wedding. Unless the abode is too small, the wedding is held at the home of the bride. June is not a popular month, as it comes in the midst of planting season. The large majority of Amish weddings take place in November and December, after harvest.

The ceremony itself is not elaborate, although it is rather long, as certain portions of the Old Testament are quoted verbatim. There are no bouquets or flowers of any kind. The bridal veil, maid of honor, best man, photographs, decorations, wedding march, or other music—all are missing, though there is a good deal of group singing.

The groom wears his Sunday suit, and the bride wears a white cape and white apron. (The only other time she will ever wear all white is after death—when she is laid out in a casket.) At the conclusion of the ceremony, no wedding rings are exchanged, nor do the couple kiss. The bishop says simply, "Now you can go; you are married folk."

Although the wedding ceremony is unpretentious, the meal that follows is a giant. Enormous quantities of food are prepared, for the entire district may be invited, plus assorted friends and relatives. It is not uncommon to find several hundred people in attendance. Some people, in fact, actually attend several weddings on the same day.[29]

To help in the preparation and serving of the food, women of the district volunteer their services. Kitchens are often large enough to accommodate several cooks at a time. If not, temporary kitchens may be set up. Guests are generally served in shifts.

When the festivities are over, the couple spend the first night of marriage in the house of the bride's parents. The following morning, after the newlyweds help clean the parents' house, it's off for a two- to three-month trip to the homes of wedding guests. Although for most young people the honeymoon is a vacation whose chief aim is privacy, among the Amish it is merely an extended series of visits with friends and relatives. As guests on the honeymoon circuit, the newlyweds receive a variety of wedding presents, usually in the form of practical gifts for the home.

After the honeymoon, the couple take their place in the community as husband and wife. If it is at all possible, they will settle down to the business of farming. If it is the youngest son who has married, he and his wife may live in his parents' home, gradually taking over both farming and

[29]Scott, *Amish Wedding,* p. 13.

household duties. Even in other instances, however, the young couple will try to live close by, in a house purchased (with considerable parental help) because of its proximity to the parental homestead.

The Amish Family System

There is an old saying in the Amish community that the young people should not move farther away "than you can see the smoke from their chimney." And it is true that a large majority of the Amish were born in the same county as their parents. Rarely will the Amish sell a farm out of the family. Moreover, about the only time an Amish breadwinner will move from the area is when there is no more land available, or when he has had a deep-seated rift with the bishop. As a result, the Amish family system tends to be perpetuated generation after generation, with little change. The church not only frowns on major change, but—should young couples get ideas—parents, grandparents, and assorted relatives are usually close enough to act as restraining influences.

The Amish family system is at once simple and effective. Both husbands and wives are conscientious workers. They take pride in their endeavors. They are known to be such excellent farmers and workers that outsiders often believe them to be quite wealthy. In a monetary sense this is not so, although many Amish do possess sizable holdings of extremely valuable land.

Because the farm is likely to be an Amish couple's daily concern, they usually have a large number of children to aid in the enterprise. As will be shown later, Amish youngsters are generally exempt from higher education, so that such things as compulsory school attendance laws and child labor laws have limited meaning. Consequently, unlike other children, Amish youngsters are considered to be economic assets. Families with ten or more children are far from uncommon; in fact, the average number of births per couple is around seven.

Role of Women   It is widely understood throughout Amishland that woman's place is in the home. Wives do not lack for kindness and respect—so long as they maintain their subordinate status. As the Amish see it, this duality is simply in keeping with God's wishes: "Man is the image and glory of God; but the woman is the glory of man" (1 Cor. 11:7).

To the outsider, it is readily apparent that the women's movement has no real place among the Old Order Amish. Men make the major decisions, both in the community and in the church. As was mentioned earlier, women are not eligible for the clergy. In addition to their usual household duties, women also perform such tasks as milking cows, mowing the lawn, gardening, and painting walls and fences. In some cases, women can be seen plowing and harvesting with a team of horses. Indications are, though, that Amish men rarely help out with household tasks such as washing dishes, preparing food, cleaning, and the like. This may be changing as women are entering cottage industries and businesses.

Although there are doubtless exceptions, Amish wives seem well adjusted to the patriarchal way of life. Their social roles are not only well defined, but are uniform throughout Amishland. Amish women realize that their English sisters have achieved a much greater degree of equality, yet there is little indication that they desire to change the traditional status quo. They have a substantial voice both in home management and in raising the children. They have an official vote in all church matters, including nominations for the clergy. And—perhaps most important— they have the inner comfort that comes from the knowledge that they are following God's word.

One final note. In any Amish gathering, it can be seen that men tend to associate with men, women with women. The men do not kiss their wives or utter words of endearment. From this, it might be inferred that Amish spouses have only moderate affection for one another, but this is hardly the case. What the followers of Jacob Amman object to is not affection itself but any *overt* display of affection. After all, the Amish are a conservative people, and the idea of kissing, fondling, or holding hands in public is distasteful. In private, they are doubtless as affectionate as any other group.

Family Names   The subject of Amish names is of special interest to genealogists because (1) the Amish themselves seldom marry outside the group, and (2) outsiders rarely marry into the group. And because the number of Amish families immigrating to America was small, most of the present membership can trace their genealogy back to the original families. Amish surnames are much the same today as they were in the 1700s.

Despite the many thousands of Amish in Lancaster County, a dozen or so surnames cover most of the group. In fact, four of the names— Stoltzfus, King, Fisher, and Beiler—account for nearly 60 percent of the households. (There is an oft-told story about the one-room Amish schoolhouse in which thirty-nine of the forty-eight pupils were named Stoltzfus!) Other common surnames include Lapp, Zook, Esh, Smucker, Glick, Riehl, Blank, and Petersheim. Oddly enough, there do not seem to be any Ammans among the Amish of Lancaster County—or elsewhere.

To add to the cognominal confusion, the Old Order Amish rely on the Bible for first names. For males, names like John, Amos, David, Jacob, Samuel, and Daniel are quite popular. For females, Mary, Annie, Katie, Sarah, Rebecca, and Lizzie predominate. Anyone who sends a letter to John Beiler or Mary Stoltzfus, with nothing more than a rural delivery address, is likely to create an interesting problem for the mail carrier.

Primacy of the Home   Although the Amish recognize the importance of the school, there is no doubt in anyone's mind that primary responsibility for the socialization of children falls on the parents. If a youngster has difficulty in school, it is the parents who are consulted. If a boy has trouble within the Amish community, the bishop will talk with the parents as well as with the boy. And if a young person runs afoul of the law, the congregation will sympathize with the parents.

Generally speaking, Amish child rearing embodies a mixture of permissive and restrictive philosophies. Infants are more or less pampered and are seldom alone. As soon as possible, they are fed at the family table and made to feel a part of the group. Relatives and friends shower them with attention. Children soon come to feel that they are welcome members of the community, which in fact they are.

As soon as infants learn to walk, they are subject to discipline and taught to respect authority. Although the Amish family is not authoritarian in structure, it is true that great stress is placed on obedience. This is not a contradiction. The obedience is presumed to be based on love rather than fear, on the assumption—unquestioned in Amishland—that parents know best. Spanking and other forms of corporal punishment are quite common, yet the youngsters harbor no resentment. They learn early that such actions are for their own good and are simply manifestations of parental love and wisdom.

Training at home tends to supplement that received at school. Acceptance of traditional values is encouraged, and inquisitiveness discouraged. Cooperativeness rather than competitiveness is emphasized. Children are conditioned to the view that they are all creatures of God, and that therefore they should have deep consideration for the feelings of others. They are reminded—over and over again—of the dangers and evils that lurk in the outside world.

Ogburn's Theory of Family Functions   A number of years ago, William F. Ogburn, a sociologist interested in the study of cultural change, made an interesting observation apropos of the American family. From the colonial period to the present, he said, the family has been characterized by a progressive *loss of functions.* He went on to list the declining functions as education, religion, protection, recreation, and the economic function. The thrust of his argument was that other institutions had taken over these functions. Thus, the function of religion, once centered in the home, had been taken over by the church. Education had become the province of the schools. Recreation had been usurped by commercialized ventures. The economic function had been lost because the family was no longer a producing unit— due largely to the fact that child labor laws and compulsory school laws prohibited children from working. Ogburn's conclusion was that, because of these declining functions, the American family had been weakened.

Some sociologists have accepted Ogburn's thesis, others have questioned it, and the issue is far from dead. Some feel that, although the family may have lost some functions, it has gained others.[30] The Old Order Amish add another dimension to the debate, for the functions that Ogburn claimed had disappeared from the mainstream of American family life are still being performed by the Amish family.

Economically, the Amish farm family is an effective producing unit. Education is still largely a family function, as is recreation. Even religious services are held in the home, and, of course, prayers play an integral part in the life of every Amish family.

The upshot is that in a functional sense the Amish family is a remarkably strong unit. This strength, moreover, is manifest in a number of other ways. Indeed, there is considerable evidence that the Old Order Amish maintain one of the most stable family systems in America. Their birthrate is exceptionally high and is unaffected by social or economic conditions. They have a low infant-mortality rate. Nearly everyone marries, and they seldom marry outside the group. Loss of membership is not a serious problem. Husband-wife-children units are wedded to the land and show strong family and group loyalty. Their farm-type economy has proved both durable and successful.

Illegitimacy and adultery are almost unheard of. Desertion is practically unknown, and no divorces have yet been reported.

Compared to the larger society, the Amish experience fewer problems with the young—and with the old. The youth are seldom in trouble with the law, and, as mentioned earlier, the oldsters are cared for by their own families, not public institutions. Orphans, widows, and other dependents are looked after by the community, and no Amish person has ever been on welfare.

One final point that should be mentioned in connection with the Amish family system is their kinship structure, for nothing like it—nothing remotely like it—exists among typical families in the United States. After all, around one-half of American couples do not even sustain their own marriage—they separate or get divorced. Of those who do stay together, one- or two-child families are the norm. As a consequence, the extended family—aunts, uncles, nieces, nephews, cousins—tends to be small in number and limited in function. In Amishland, the opposite is true. The family is clearly the heart of Amish society, and their large kin network functions as a vascular support system.

---

[30]See the discussion in Chapter 14 in Richard T. Schaefer, *Sociology*, 10th ed. (New York: McGraw-Hill, 2007) and William F. Ogburn and Clark Tibbitts, "The Family and Its Functions," pp. 661–708, in *Recent Social Trends in the United States*, edited by Research Committee on Social Trends (New York: McGraw-Hill, 1934).

Education

It is commonly believed that the Old Order Amish are against education, but this is not true. What they are against is the kind of education that would tend to alienate their young people and threaten their agrarian, conservative way of life. In Amishland, therefore, schooling is likely to mean reading, spelling, arithmetic, penmanship, and grammar—plus elements of geography, history, and hygiene.

Today, Amish parents are more than willing to have their youngsters attend school—provided it is an Amish school—for the first eight grades.[31] But beyond that they balk. They feel that the years fourteen to eighteen are critical, and they object to having their teenagers exposed to high-school worldliness. Over the years, the Amish community has refused to give in on this point.

In the late 1960s, Amish parents in Wisconsin were arrested and convicted for refusing to send their children to the local high school. After a series of legal battles, the case eventually reached the Supreme Court. In the landmark *Yoder v. Wisconsin* decision in 1972, the Court ruled 7–0 in favor of the Amish parents. Although acknowledging the state's justifiable interest in universal education, the Court declared that there were balancing factors, "such as those specifically protected by the Free Exercise Clause of the First Amendment, and the traditional interest of parents with respect to the religious upbringing of their children. . . ."

The Amish community continues to have school problems in a few states, but the 1972 Supreme Court decision has served to eliminate much of the ill feeling. Now, too, public opinion has swung to the side of the Amish. In Lancaster County, the Amish have worked out an accommodation with state officials on a variety of school-related matters. Any new problems will likely be handled in a similar vein.

The Amish School   Amish schools are a true reflection of the Amish people: unassuming, efficient, economical. There are no frills—no school newspaper, clubs, bands, athletic programs, dances, or class officers. The Old Order Amish have no nursery, preschool, or kindergarten programs; in fact, the large majority of their schools have but one room and one teacher. Average enrollment is about thirty.

Amish communities either build their own schools or purchase them from the state. If they are purchased, certain alterations are made, including the removal of all electrical fixtures. Amish school buildings are heated by wood or coal stoves, and generally do not have indoor toilets. But aside

---

[31]For a classic account of the Amish educational system, see John A. Hostetler and Gertrude Enders Huntington, *Children in Amish Society: Socialization and Community Education* (New York: Holt, Rinehart & Winston, 1971).

from differences in heating, lighting, and toilet facilities, the Amish school looks much the same as any other one-room school: blackboards, chalk, bolted desks, coat racks, posters and colorful pictures, paper and pencils, and—naturally—homemade artistry adorning the walls.

The Amish teacher, usually a young, unmarried woman, is quite different from her non-Amish counterpart. The typical American teacher is a college graduate who, by virtue of having taken specialized courses in education, has acquired a state-issued teaching certificate. The Amish teacher, by contrast, has not even been to high school, let alone college.

The followers of Jacob Amman are convinced that being a good teacher has no relationship to such things as college degrees and state-issued certificates. They feel, rather, that teaching is a kind of calling, and that the calling is a God-given attribute. The ideal Amish teacher is one who, by her very being, can convey to youngsters the Amish outlook on life. Accordingly, she should be well adjusted, religious, and totally committed to Amish principles.

Although there are exceptions, naturally, most Amish teachers are dedicated individuals. Although they do not attend high school, many of them take correspondence courses. They have their own teachers' association, attend yearly conferences, and subscribe to the Amish teachers' *Bulletin*. They are often required to serve without pay as teaching assistants for a year or so before being assigned schools of their own. And when they are given their own classrooms, they are willing to work at a very low rate of pay.

The Amish teacher is more than "just a teacher." She is also principal, janitor, nurse, custodian, playground supervisor, and disciplinarian. Although Amish children are better behaved than most, disciplinary problems do arise, in which case the teacher applies the usual antidotes: reprimands, lectures, admonitions, keeping children after school, and having them write their "sins" on the blackboard. For serious infractions—such as willful disobedience or leaving the schoolyard without permission—most Amish teachers will not hesitate to use corporal punishment.

Values   As used by sociologists, the term **value** refers to the collective conception of what is considered good, desirable, and proper—or bad, undesirable, and improper—in a culture. In fact, values are so basic to those who hold them that they tend to be accepted without question. Most people, furthermore, seem to feel more comfortable when they are in the company of those with a similar value system.

As much as anything else, it is the totality of values that sets one group apart from another, a point well illustrated by the Amish school. It is not simply curriculum and course content that differentiate the Amish school from the public school—it is values. Accuracy, for instance, receives much greater emphasis than speed. Memorization of facts and the learning of

(Amish) principles are considered more important than analytical thinking and inquisitiveness.

Amish children receive grades—from A to F—but at the same time they
are taught not to compete with one another for top marks. To the followers
of Jacob Amman, talent—like so many other things in this world—is God-
given; hence, it is no disgrace to be a slow learner. In their hierarchy of values, it is more important to do good and to treat others with kindness.[32]

To emphasize that all are alike in the eyes of God, children's dolls are
faceless: eyes, noses, mouths, fingers, and toes are missing. The proscription against dolls with features is also consistent in the Amish belief system with the Scriptures that ban making graven images.[33]

Amish schools are as much concerned with the children's moral development as they are with their mental prowess. Values such as right–wrong,
better–worse, good–bad are alluded to over and over again. It is this
repeated emphasis on morality—not only by the school but by the church,
the home, and the community—that serves to mold the individual's conscience. This fact was mentioned earlier and is worth repeating, for
although the threat of the *Meidung* undoubtedly keeps potential wrongdo-
ers in line, it is conscience that is a key element in Amish conformity.

Challenges Facing the Amish

All groups have social problems of one kind or another, and the Old Order
Amish are no exception. At the same time, the Amish do have a remarkable record in the "problems" area. Crime, corruption, poverty, divorce
and desertion, alcoholism, drug addiction, wife and child abuse—such
problems have a low incidence in Amishland. In fact, their low problem
rate makes the followers of Jacob Amman wonder what the school controversy was all about. More than one Amish person has said, in effect, "They
wanted us to send our youngsters to the consolidated public school and on
to high school—but they're the ones with the problems, not us. . . ."

Human nature being what it is, the fact that the Amish have relatively
few social problems does not make those that do occur any easier to solve.
On the contrary, a given problem may cause more anguish in Amishland
than in the larger society. At any rate, the following problems are singled
out not because they represent major disruptions, but because they are
recurrent headaches that the Amish must somehow learn to live with.

Adolescence   One of the more serious problems facing the Old Order
Amish is that of their teenage youth, boys in particular. The latter will
sometimes get drunk, become disrespectful, indulge in worldly activities

[32]See ibid., pp. 54–96.
[33]Susan Bender, *Plain and Simple: A Woman's Journey to the Amish* (New York:
HarperCollins, 1990), pp. 17–18.

(including buying a car), and otherwise persist in violating Amish mores. Even the girls are sometimes involved. As Kraybill puts it, "The rowdiness of Amish youth is an embarrassment to church leaders and a stigma in the larger community."[34]

The allure of the English world has led the Old Order Amish to routinize, almost accept, some worldly activities among their adolescents. Amish youth often test their subculture's boundaries during a period of discovery called **rum springa,** a term that means "running around." *Rum springa* is a common occurrence but is definitely not supported by the Amish religion. Amish young people attend barn dances where taboos like drinking, smoking, and driving cars are commonly broken. Parents often react by looking the other way, sometimes literally. For example, when they hear radio sounds from a barn or motorcycle entering their property in the middle of the night, they don't immediately investigate and punish their offspring. Instead, they pretend not to notice, secure in the comfort that their children almost always return to the traditions of the Amish lifestyle.

In 2004, UPN aired the ten-week long "Amish in the City" reality program featuring five Amish youths allegedly on *rum springa* moving in with six citywise young adults in Los Angeles. Critics on behalf of the Amish community noted that this exploitation showed how vulnerable that Amish are since no program would develop to try to show the conversion of Muslim or Orthodox Jewish youth.[35]

Threat of Modernization   Every decade brings a variety of new inventions and technological improvements to society at large, and the Amish must continually fight against the inroads. Automobiles, telephones, electric lights, tractors, radio and television—such things have taken their toll on the followers of Jacob Amman. Every Amish community knows of adult members who have left the fold because of what they felt were unnecessarily strict rules.

In several cases, entire congregations have seceded. Thus in 1927, an Amish bishop, Moses M. Beachy, led a movement away from the main body. As mentioned earlier, members of this group—known today as the Beachy or Church Amish—are permitted to own automobiles and certain other modern conveniences. In 1966, a group known as the New Order Amish began to form. The New Order have installed telephones, permit the use of electricity, and use tractor-drawn farm machinery.

If, as is so often the case, history repeats itself, the Old Order Amish will probably experience further schisms and secessions in the decades to come.

---

[34]Kraybill, *Riddle of Amish Culture,* p. 138.

[35]Bernard Weinraub, "UPN Show is called Insensitive to Amish," *New York Times,* March 4, 2004, pp. B1, B8.

Interestingly, Pennsylvania Amish have a unique link with modernity. Over the course of the past decade, prospectors have successfully drilled about 100 natural gas wells on their properties. They can't use it, but after much deliberation, decided they could sell it to the English. Bishop Andy J. Byler said, "I don't know what to think. They say they will get your gas whether or not you have a well because it will come up on the next well down the road, if it is not yours."[36] Byler already had a well on his farm. It was interesting to note that he had asked members of his community for permission to drill another well. Although he owned the land, he would not drill without the consent of his neighbors.

Annoyance of Tourism—Or Is It?   The Amish are a folk society whose way of life until very recently hinged on remaining apart from the rest of the world. For them the influx of tourists into Amishland represented an irritating problem. Today, however, there are a growing number of Amish who welcome tourism with open arms.

State tourism officials got a surprise when they hired a Virginia firm to study tourism in Pennsylvania. It was thought that the Pocono Mountains or the picturesque Allegheny National Forest would top the list. Instead, Amish country was the top draw. Outsiders still own most of the businesses in Amish country: motels, guest houses, restaurants, farmers' markets, country stores, handicraft outlets, antique sales, souvenir and novelty shops, discount operations, buggy rides, the list seems endless. Most Amish are content with farming and remain annoyed with tourists. But the Amish population is growing and land available to them is diminishing. As a consequence, many Amish are now catering to tourists in a variety of ways. Still, only a small fraction of the tourist dollars go to the Amish.[37]

Bus tours—as many as fifty a day—are especially obnoxious to the Amish community. Run by professional tour guides, the vehicles clog the narrow roads, block the horses and buggies, park in front of the schools and farms, and otherwise upset the daily routine. Also, the Old Order Amish are forbidden to have their pictures taken, but camera-wielding tourists often seem to laugh at the proscription.[38]

The media, as we saw with "Amish in the City," has not always been kind to the Amish. In 1985, the motion picture *Witness*, starring Harrison

---

[36]"Natural Gas Helps Amish: They Can't Use It But They Can Allow Wells to Be Drilled on Their Land," *Morning Call:* Allentown, PA, July 7, 1999.

[37]"Amish Country State's Top Tourist Attraction," *Morning Call:* Allentown, PA, June 2, 1999.

[38]A number of excellent pictorial accounts of Amish life have been published. Among them are Ruth Seitz and Blair Seitz, *Amish Ways* (Harrisburg, PA: R B Books, 1992); John Wasilchick, *Amish Life: A Portrait of Plain Living* (New York: Crescent Books, 1991); and Leslie Hauslein and Jerry Irwin, *The Amish: The Enduring Spirit* (Godalming, Surrey, England: Colour Library Books, 1990).

Ford and Kelly McGillis, was released. Filmed over a ten-week period in Lancaster County, the picture purports to show various episodes in the lifestyle of the Old Order Amish. The Amish themselves objected strongly to the film, feeling that it was an invasion of both their privacy and their religion. They were upset with the depiction of Amish being violent, even if provoked, and of a relationship between an Amish woman and an English man. Nevertheless, the film proved to be immensely popular at the box office. How many viewers were prompted to visit Amishland first-hand will never be known, but the number must have been substantial.

A few Amish families have left the area for quieter pastures. Others operate the hundreds of craft shops and produce stands that now dot the landscape. Some observers feel that large-scale tourism has tended to reinforce cultural identity among the Amish, but this is debatable. In any case, the Amish of Lancaster County are one of the largest tourist attractions in America, and the situation is not likely to change. In most other areas, fortunately, tourism is not nearly so pressing.

Government Intervention   As the nation grows, the web of government becomes more complicated, laws proliferate, bureaucracy increases, and the Amish, no less than other citizens, are confronted with a maze of regulations. The followers of Jacob Amman must now have their children vaccinated and inoculated. Amish dairy farmers have been forced to have their milk inspected according to government regulations. And, though outsiders may or may not be aware of it, the Amish must pay state and federal income taxes, property taxes, and sales taxes.

At one time or another the Old Order Amish have also had run-ins with government agencies regarding such issues as compulsory education, building codes, social security and Medicare, safety devices on buggies, zoning regulations, unemployment insurance, and military conscription.

The last issue—involving draft laws and compulsory military service— deserves special mention, for the Amish are pacifists in a literal sense. They will not fight *under any condition.* As Huntington points out, "All forms of retaliation to hostility are forbidden. An Amishman may not physically defend himself or his family even when attacked. He is taught to follow the New Testament of the Sermon on the Mount."[39]

It follows, of course, that the Old Order Amish will not serve in the armed forces or otherwise fight for their country. And because of their stand, they had some altercations with the authorities during both world wars. Generally, though, their position has been respected by the government. If they were to be drafted today, Amish youth would be allowed to perform alternative service as conscientious objectors.

[39]Huntington, "Amish Family," p. 382.

It would not be correct to say the Amish are apolitical. After the September 11, 2001, terrorist attack, Amish reported being confronted by English about their patriotism. Indeed, to many outsiders, the fact that Amish do not fly the flag seemed suspicious. While they are pacifist, they would declare they love their country and teach their children to respect the flag. In fact, these conservative values led the 2004 George W. Bush campaign to encourage Amish to get out and vote. While some church leaders still caution against voting, ultimately the church leaves voting up to the individual. However, for many Amish, voting may not be the highest priority. Election Day falls on a very popular day for weddings, and as one Pennsylvania Amish man said, "If I hitch my horse there at the wedding, there's no way I'm going to make it all the way back to vote."[40]

When all is said and done, nevertheless, there is no doubt that the followers of Jacob Amman often find government regulations both burdensome and obstructive. As the record shows, they have had more than their share of bureaucratic grief. And although they have thus far been able to hold their own, the Amish community never knows when trouble will strike again.

Vanishing Farmland: The Number-One Problem?   Many observers feel that the scarcity of farmland is the biggest problem facing the Amish today. Although there is no real shortage of land in the United States, good farmland is extremely scarce in some Amish communities. The reasons are rather obvious. The Old Order Amish are increasing much faster than the population at large, and because most Amish turn to farming, the supply of arable land in a given community tends to become exhausted.

As a further aggravation, the Amish must often bid for land not only against other farmers but against industrial and commercial developers. In Lancaster County, for instance, the price of land has become astronomical, with some tracts selling for as high as $11,000 an acre.

From the Amish point of view, what is the answer?

Aside from subdividing their farmland among one or more of their sons—clearly a limited solution—the followers of Jacob Amman have only two realistic choices. They can relocate or turn to nonfarming occupations. Over the past fifty years, relocation has not been favored.

Some have migrated across the country or even to Latin America. Although it now appears that the option to migrate is open, it does not appear that mass migration is on the immediate horizon. What is evident, however, is that the Amish have turned increasingly to other occupations.

[40]"Bus people," *The Economist*, October 16, 2004, p. 29.

At the present time, to repeat, an estimated 30 percent of married Amish men work in jobs other than farming.

Does this nonfarming trend pose any real danger to the Amish way of life? At a "Coping with Modernity" conference held in Pennsylvania in the late 1980s, more than one authority voiced genuine concern. In fact, both the Lancaster and Philadelphia papers carried similar headlines: "Off-Farm Jobs Threatening Amish Life."[41] Headlines aside, however, what does the future hold? In view of the various problems discussed in the preceding pages, is life in Amishland really threatened?

The Future

To begin with—and speaking generally—the followers of Jacob Amman are very good in the "problem-solving" area. Some critics have argued that the Amish will not survive in their present form, that they will be gobbled up by high-powered, industrialized society. The Amish, however, have outlasted their critics and in all likelihood will continue to do so.

The aforementioned social problems, although certainly real enough, are somewhat deceptive. The youth problem is actually not so serious as it sounds. True, more than a few of their young people misbehave, and a number even defect to other groups—but this process serves as another safety valve. The Amish know full well that their rules are strict and that certain individuals will be unable to conform. But by giving their young people a certain amount of leeway prior to baptism, it is felt that those who do join the church will prove to be loyal and conscientious members.

In practice, the safety-valve theory seems to work, because—overall— a small percentage of baptized members actually leave the fold. As a matter of record, the Amish population has shown spectacular growth: 5,000 in 1900; 33,000 in 1950; well over 150,000 today.

Tourism seems to be more of a chronic irritation than a major problem. And one way or another, the Old Order Amish have learned to live with it. In fact—ironically enough—although most of the tourist dollars go to the non-Amish, tourism does provide the Amish community with ever-increasing income.

Problems such as government intervention and the threat of modernization are evidently being taken in stride. It is true that the vanishing farmland has more or less forced some Amish men to take other jobs, and this transposition should not be minimized. It is important, however, to look at the *nature* of these jobs. In Lancaster County, for instance, the

[41]*Lancaster Intelligence Journal,* July 25, 1987; *Philadelphia Inquirer,* July 26, 1987.

Amish have not sought blanket entry into the outside job market. On the contrary, their choice of occupations has been highly selective.

As Kraybill points out, many of the men work in craft shops located on or adjacent to the farm. Married women who work—quilting, baking, craftwork—do so at home.[42] Amish men operate a wide array of shops and small businesses: cabinetry, plumbing, construction, hardware, butchering, machinery repair, masonry, upholstery, furniture, and a variety of retail stores. However, they generally reject factory work as being a bad influence. Indeed, more than 75 percent of those who work away from home are either self-employed or work for an Amish employer.[43]

The same author goes on to conclude that although a third of the Lancaster County Amish have left the farm, "they have not embraced modern work. Nonfarm work is, by and large, local, family-oriented, small-scale, and nestled in ethnic networks. The Amish have retained personal craftsmanship and job satisfaction, as well as a high degree of identity with, and control over, their products. Moreover, they also control the time, speed, and other conditions of their work."[44]

Conclusion   All things considered, the Amish would seem to have a promising future in America. They have handled their problems inimitably and, on the whole, successfully. In the process, they have managed to solidify their identity. Outlook on life, relation to God and the universe, theology, sex roles, clothing styles, love of the soil, separatism, frugality, humility, pacifism, industriousness, attitude toward education—in brief, the basic ingredients of "Amishness"—are much the same today as they always have been.

In the past, the Old Order Amish have sometimes been misunderstood, hassled, fined, and even jailed. Today, conversely, they tend to benefit from public opinion. Tourism has brought millions of Americans to the various Amish communities. And as people have come to see and learn about the Amish firsthand, they have also come to respect the Amish way of life. Consequently, in disputes with the government, an Amish community can often count on valuable public support.

Schoolyard shootings have received considerable national attention, but the Nickel Mines Amish school was in a category of its own. In October of 2006, a lone gunman came into the one-room Amish schoolhouse, killing five girls and wounding five others before turning the gun on himself. While the nation looked on to find no easy answers for the gunman's motive, it admired the compassion shown by the local Amish community. To the killer's family, they brought food, showed unconditional support, and invited the widow to their funerals to share in the grieving. The

[42]See Kraybill, *Riddle of Amish Culture*, pp. 197–98.
[43]Ibid., pp. 199–205.
[44]Ibid., p. 211.

schoolhouse was demolished four months later, and the surviving children attended a new schoolhouse built 200 yards from the old one.

As they look ahead, the Amish in general are quite optimistic, both in a secular and a sacred sense. The latter, of course, is the critical component, for the followers of Jacob Amman have placed themselves in God's hands—permanently—and they have absolutely no doubts about their future.

KEY TERMS

Conspicuous consumption, p. 10
Definition of the situation, p. 19
English (or Englishers), p. 8
In-group, p. 8
Meidung, p. 5

Out-group, p. 8
Relative deprivation, p. 20
Rum springa, p. 37
Sanction, p. 26
Value, p. 35

SOURCES ON THE WEB

www.amish.net
This site is intended to serve travelers touring Amish areas—particularly Pennsylvania, Ohio, and Indiana.

www.thirdway.com
The Third Way Café, produced by Mennonite Media, has information primarily on Mennonites, but covers the Amish as well.

http://holycrosslivonia.org/amish/
This site of the National Committee for Amish Religious Freedom seeks to defend the religious freedom of the Old Order Amish religion in the United States.

http://www.religioustolerance.org/amish.htm
The Canadian-based Ontario Consultants on Religious Tolerance offer general information on the Amish.

SELECTED READINGS

Altick, Richard D. *Remembering Lancaster.* Hamden, CT: Archon, 1991.
Ammon, Richard. *Growing Up Amish.* New York: Atheneum, 1989.

Armstrong, Penny, and Sheryl Feldman. *A Midwife's Story.* New York: Arbor House, 1986.

Beachy, Eli R. *Tales from the Peoli Road: Wit and Humor of Very Real People, Who Just Happen to Be Amish.* Scottdale, PA: Herald Press, 1992.

Bender, Sue. *Plain and Simple: A Woman's Journey to the Amish.* New York: Harper-Collins, 1990.

The Budget, Sugarcreek Budget Publications. (Weekly newspaper written by non-Amish covering the Amish/Mennonite communities throughout the Americas.)

Fisher, Sara, and Rachel Stahl. *The Amish School.* Intercourse, PA: Good Books, 1986.

Good, Merle, and Phyllis Good. *20 Most Asked Questions about the Amish and Mennonites.* Intercourse, PA: Good Books, 1995.

Hauslein, Leslie A., and Jerry Irwin. *The Amish: The Enduring Spirit.* Godalming, Surrey, England: Colour Library Books, 1990.

Hostetler, John A., *Amish Society.* Baltimore: Johns Hopkins University Press, 1980.

Hostetler, John A., ed. *Amish Roots: A Treasury of History, Wisdom and Lore.* Baltimore: Johns Hopkins University Press, 1989.

Hostetler, John A., and Gertrude Enders Huntington. *Children in Amish Society: Socialization and Community Education.* New York: Holt, Rinehart & Winston, 1971.

Huntington, Gertrude Enders. "The Amish Family." In *Ethnic Families in America,* edited by Charles Mindel, Robert Habenstein, and Roosevelt Wright, pp. 367–99. New York: Elsevier, 1988.

Kraybill, Donald. *The Puzzles of Amish Life.* Intercourse, PA: Good Books, 1990.

———. *The Riddle of Amish Culture.* rev. ed. Baltimore: Johns Hopkins University Press, 2001.

———. *The Amish and the State.* Baltimore: Johns Hopkins University Press, 2003.

Kraybill, Donald, and Steven M. Nolte. *Amish Enterprise: From Plow to Profit.* Baltimore: Johns Hopkins University Press, 1995.

Kuvlesky, William P. "Some Amish Move a Lot: The Old Order Amish in Texas." Paper presented at the meeting of the Southern Association of Agricultural Scientists, Nashville, TN, 1987.

Luthy, David. *The Amish in America: Settlements That Failed, 1840–1960.* Aylmer, Ontario: Pathway, 1986.

Morello, Carol. "Embattled Midwife to the Amish." *Philadelphia Inquirer,* July 23, 1989.

Schlabach, Theron F. *Peace, Faith Nation: Mennonites and Amish in Nineteenth-Century America.* Vol. 2 of *The Mennonite Experience in America.* Scottdale, PA: Herald Press, 1988.

Scott, Stephen. *Plain Buggies: Amish, Mennonite, and Brethren Horse-Drawn Transportation.* Intercourse, PA: Good Books, 1981.

———. *Why Do They Dress That Way?* Intercourse, PA: Good Books, 1986.

———. *The Amish Wedding and Other Special Occasions of the Old Order Communities.* Intercourse, PA: Good Books, 1988.

Seitz, Ruth, and Blair Seitz. *Amish Ways.* Harrisburg, PA: R B Books, 1991.

Smith, Elmer. *The Amish People.* New York: Exposition Press, 1958.

Smucker, Donovan E. *The Sociology of Mennonites, Hutterites, and Amish: A Bibliography with Annotations, Volume II 1977–1990.* Waterloo, Ontario, Canada: Wilfrid Laurier University Press, 1991.

Smucker, Mervin R. "How Amish Children View Themselves and Their Families: The Effectiveness of Amish Socialization." *Brethren Life and Thought* 33 (Summer 1988): 218–36.

Wasilchick, John V. *Amish Life: A Portrait of Plain Living.* New York: Crescent Books, 1992.

Weaver, J. Denny. *Becoming Anabaptist: The Origin and Significance of Sixteenth-Century Anabaptism.* Scottdale, PA: Herald Press, 1987.

Wittmer, Joe. *The Gentle People: Personal Reflections of Amish Life.* Minneapolis: Educational Media, 1990.

Yoder, Paton. *Tradition and Transition: Amish Mennonites and Old Order Amish 1800–1900.* Scottdale, PA: Herald Press, 1991.

CHAPTER TWO

THE ONEIDA COMMUNITY

Most readers are familiar with the term **culture,** which refers to the totality of learned, socially transmitted customs, knowledge, material objects, and behavior. People in a society, whether it be the United States or Bulgaria, share a common culture. Less familiar, probably, is the concept **subculture.** Subculture is a segment of society that shares a distinctive pattern of mores, folkways, and values that differs from the pattern of the larger society. Residents of a retirement community, a street gang, and members of a marching band are all examples of a subculture.

In this chapter, we will consider an extraordinary subculture, the Oneida community, sharing an unusual set of religious beliefs and following an individual with unusual personal magnetism, John Humphrey Noyes. He exercised what is referred to as **charismatic authority.** This refers to power made legitimate by a leader's exceptional personal or emotional appeal to his or her followers. Max Weber drew attention to this as a powerful form of authority that often allowed the leader to advocate dramatic changes in social behavior.[1]

Noyes was able to lead and inspire without relying on the established rules or traditions. He was an astute judge of character. He could "read"

---

[1]On charismatic authority, see Max Weber, *The Theory of Social and Economic Organization.* Translated by A. Henderson and T. Parsons (New York: Free Press, 1947, originally published 1913–1922).

his followers with uncanny accuracy, knowing when to praise and when to blame. He knew when—and to whom—to delegate authority. Noyes always knew the mood and temperament of his community. And Oneida was "the lengthened shadow of this one extraordinary man, reflecting his complex personality and concerns."[2]

On the one hand, as will be shown, Noyes was an original thinker, a sound judge of human nature, and an exceedingly versatile individual. On the other hand, he was capricious, unpredictable, and at times given to making errors in judgment. Little wonder that social historians have been hard pressed to depict the "real" John Humphrey Noyes.

Background

Unlike most of the other leaders discussed in the present volume, John Humphrey Noyes was of upper-class origin. His mother, Polly Hayes, was a cousin of Rutherford B. Hayes, the nineteenth president of the United States. His father was John Noyes, a U.S. congressman from Vermont and a successful businessman.

Not much is known about the boyhood of John Humphrey Noyes. One of eight children, he was born in 1811 at Brattleboro, Vermont. In 1821, his family moved to Putney, a small town ten miles to the north. Redhaired, freckled, and somewhat self-conscious about his appearance, he was noticeably shy around girls. With members of his own sex, however, he showed clear evidence of leadership. He entered Dartmouth at fifteen, a typical college age at that time, and was eventually elected to Phi Beta Kappa.

Upon graduation, Noyes worked as an apprentice in a New Hampshire law firm. However, it soon became obvious that he was not cut out to be a barrister, and he returned home to Putney. Up to that time, he certainly had no thoughts of founding a subculture, and he had probably never heard of a place called Oneida.

The early 1830s found the country caught up in a frenzy of religious rejuvenation, and, as luck would have it, a four-day revival was held in Putney in September 1831. Noyes attended, listened—and succumbed completely. To those who knew him, he suddenly seemed to come alive with ideas, spiritual enlightenment, and visions of eternal truth. Although religion had not heretofore been a major part of his life, it was obvious that he had found his calling. Henceforth he would devote himself to disseminating God's word. A few weeks later he enrolled in theological seminary—first at Andover, then at Yale Divinity School.

At Yale, Noyes acquired the reputation of being a radical, and although he was granted his license to preach in 1833, he was not a

---

[2]Lawrence Foster, *Women, Family and Utopia: Communal Experiments of the Shakers, the Oneida Community and the Mormons* (Syracuse, NY: Syracuse University Press, 1991), p. 77.

success. At one point, for example, he declared himself to be without sin—for which heresy he was called before the theological faculty. He refused to recant, whereupon he was denied ordination and his preaching license was revoked.

The Putney Association

Jobless, penniless, and now looked on as a religious oddity, John Humphrey Noyes did not appear to have much of a future, but there were several things in his favor. He was only twenty-three years old. He had an inner flame that was inextinguishable. He was already making a few converts, and soon he would make more. In an oft-quoted statement, he said, "I have taken away their license to sin, and they keep on sinning. So, though they have taken away my license to preach, I shall keep on preaching." Events were to prove the statement more prophetic than Noyes realized.

For the next few years he traveled through New York and New England, living on a shoestring and spreading the doctrine of **Perfectionism:** people could be without sin. Although the concept did not originate with him, Noyes's brand of Perfectionism was genuinely new. And while, over the years, he introduced a number of additions and refinements, his basic theological postulate remained unchanged: Christ had already returned to earth in a *second* coming—in A.D. 70—so that redemption or liberation from sin was an accomplished fact. Given the proper environment, therefore, man could lead a perfect, or sinless, life.

This was a radical notion, of course, and while he made some headway in spreading the gospel of Perfectionism, the existing churches turned a deaf ear to his teachings. Noyes returned home in 1836, sobered by his experience. He would spend the next dozen years in Putney, incorporating Perfectionism into the most radical social experiment America had ever seen.

Things started off innocently enough. Noyes's first converts in Putney were members of his own family: his sisters, Charlotte and Harriet, his brother, George, and his mother. (His father rejected the whole idea.) Other converts trickled in, one here, one there. In 1838, he married Harriet Holton, granddaughter of the lieutenant governor of Vermont. She not only was a convert but remained a loyal Perfectionist all her life. By 1844, however, adult membership was still only about two dozen, although other small groups of followers were scattered throughout New England.

During the early years, the Putney Perfectionists were not a communal organization. Members lived in individual houses and worked at individual jobs. They had resources; in fact, they were incorporated for $38,000, the money coming largely from the estate of Noyes's father. Gradually, they developed a type of social organization referred to as a **commune.**

The commune is a form of cooperative living where community assets are shared and individual ownership is discouraged. Communes are popularly associated with the "flower power" and hippies of the 1960s, but communes have a long history and continue to persist as an alternative lifestyle. Communism, in its pure theoretical version, takes it lead from communes with no inequality and no distinctions of social rank.

Communes are usually organized as everyone sharing equally in the decision-making just like they share equally in earthly possessions. But even before they adopted the communal style of life, one thing was clear: the Putneyites were not a democracy. John Humphrey Noyes was both the leader and the binding force. And while he often gave the impression of operating through discussion and persuasion rather than by proclamation, there was no doubt in anyone's mind—including his own—about who made the rules.

In 1844, the Putney Perfectionists adopted economic communism as a way of life. They commenced to share their work, their food, their living quarters, and their resources. Their children began to attend a communal school. And once every day, for a protracted period, they met together for Bible reading, theological discussion, and a sharing of religious experiences.

Following his marriage to Harriet Holton in 1838, Noyes fathered five children in six years. Unfortunately, all but one were stillborn, a fact that was to have utmost significance. The Perfectionist leader grieved deeply, not only for the lost children but for their mother. Was this to be woman's lot in life, to bear children year after year, whether or not they were wanted? To suffer, to mourn, to be kept out of the mainstream of daily activity—all because of nature's imperious call? He thought not, but what could be done about it?

The Shakers, another communal group of the time, had solved the problem—to their own satisfaction, at least—by practicing celibacy. Noyes rejected this rather drastic solution, although he realized that, whatever the answer was, it would have to include some sort of birth control. He finally hit upon the novel idea of *coitus reservatus,* or, as he called it, **male continence.** It was not necessary, he said, for a man to reach ejaculation during the sex act. With a little practice, he could enjoy sex relations without attaining the climax that might lead to conception.

In his widely quoted pamphlet *Male Continence,* published in 1872, Noyes had this to say:

> Now we insist that this whole process, up to the very moment of emission, is *voluntary,* entirely under the control of the moral faculty, and *can be stopped at any point.*
>
> In other words, the *motions* can be controlled or stopped at will, and it is only the *final crisis of emission* that is automatic or uncontrollable. . . . If you say that this is impossible, I answer that I *know* it is possible—nay, that it is easy. (pp. 7–8)

As it turned out, Noyes's contention was correct, at least insofar as the Perfectionists were concerned. Throughout the whole of the group's existence, *coitus reservatus* was used—and used successfully.

In 1846, the group began to share spouses. As might have been predicted, once the Perfectionists began the practice of spouse sharing, the word soon spread. Actually, there was never any attempt—then or later—to keep the matter a secret. In his numerous sojourns and talks, Noyes often alluded to the fact that his brand of communism involved sexual as well as economic sharing.

Nevertheless, to the citizens of Putney, right was right, and wrong was wrong—and sex outside of marriage was wrong. It was the 1840s, and marriage meant one man and one woman, joined in the sight of God and legally recorded in the town-hall registry. The followers of John Humphrey Noyes, quite obviously, not only were living in sin but were more or less flaunting the practice.

One thing led to another. Finally, irate citizens met in protest and demanded action. In October 1847—amidst rumors of mob violence—John Humphrey Noyes was indicted in Vermont by a grand jury on grounds of adultery. He was released, pending trial, on $2,000 bail. Had the trial been held, the Perfectionist leader would almost surely have been found guilty. However, after much soul-searching and discussion—and on the advice of his lawyer—Noyes fled to New York. As he explained it later, the reason for his flight from Vermont was not to escape justice, but to save his followers and others from the mob violence that was clearly imminent. Oddly enough, though he probably caused more shock and outrage than any other religious leader of his time (with the probable exception of Joseph Smith, founder of the Mormons), John Humphrey Noyes was never to stand trial for his unorthodox—and illegal—practices.

Oneida

All during his stay in Putney, Noyes had made periodic forays into the hinterland to gain converts. His various publications had helped to spread the word. By 1847, when the Perfectionists' sexual system became operative, the popular press was also giving John Humphrey Noyes and his followers a good deal of publicity. When Noyes left Putney, therefore, other Perfectionist centers—rather loosely organized—were available to him. One such spot was a fairly large tract of land along Oneida Creek in New York State. Their newly found "promised land" was also near the Canadian border, which could prove convenient in case of future prosecution.

Formerly a reservation belonging to the Oneida Indians and now the site of a sawmill, the property was owned by Jonathan Burt, an ardent follower of Noyes. Burt had come upon hard times and was quite willing to turn over his land to the Perfectionist cause. Noyes was attracted to the site and wasted no time in reassembling the little flock of Putneyites. Burt and his associates stayed on. Other small groups of followers joined them. They cleared land, made their own implements and furniture, and held discussions. Working as farmers, they were able to buy up adjoining properties. Before long, their Oneida holdings totaled nearly six hundred acres. And in spite of adverse conditions, membership continued to grow. By the end of the first year, 1848, there were eighty-seven persons living in the Community. A year later, the number had more than doubled! (See the Timeline.)

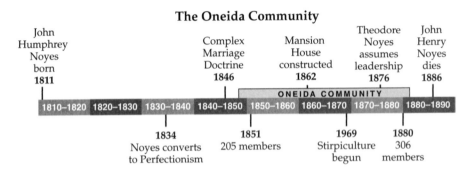

The Oneida Community

From the very beginning, the mission of the group was made crystal clear. With the help of Almighty God, as expressed through the person of John Humphrey Noyes, they were going to create a heaven on earth. Indeed, in his own words, Noyes had said, "God has sent me to cast up a highway across this chaos, and I am gathering out the stones and grading the track as fast as possible."[3] There was never any doubt about their utopian goal. Nor was there any doubt about how they were going to attain it.

The Mansion House   During their first winter at Oneida, the little group of Perfectionists lived in the existing dwellings: Jonathan Burt's homestead plus some abandoned Indian cabins. Top priority, however, was given to the construction of a communal home. John Humphrey Noyes believed that, in actual day-to-day living, true communism could best be achieved by having all members live under one roof. This was the way the Perfectionists lived throughout the rest of their existence.

In the summer of 1849, the first communal home was built. No one knows how it got the name Mansion House, but it was a wooden affair and was constructed by the entire Community. Membership grew so rapidly, though, that in 1862 the wooden structure was replaced by a brick building.

[3]Spencer Klaw, *Without Sin: The Life and Death of the Oneida Community* (New York: Penguin, 1993), p. 10.

In subsequent years, wings were added as needed, and the building still stands in its entirety. Noyes helped in the planning of both the original and the present building, and both were exceptionally well thought out.[4]

Although most adults had small rooms of their own, the building as a whole was designed to encourage a feeling of togetherness rather than separateness. To this end, *group facilities* predominated: a communal dining room, library, concert hall, recreation area, picnic grounds, and the like. It was in the Big Hall of the Mansion House that the regular evening meetings were held, and it was here that Noyes gave most of his widely quoted home talks.

Over the years, the Perfectionists developed a lively interest in the performing arts, and—although most of the talent was homegrown—they were able to organize such activities as symphony concerts, choral recitals, and Shakespearian plays. Occasionally, outside artists were invited to perform, but on a day-to-day basis the Community was more or less a closed group, with members seldom straying far from home.

Sociologically speaking, the Perfectionists' *reference behavior* related entirely to the group. The larger community, figuratively and literally, was considered to be "outside" and was usually referred to as "the World." It was this system of *integral closure,* sustained over several decades, that served as a primary solidifying force. And, of course, it was the Mansion House that made the system operable.

Today, the mansion house is a community center and senior citizens residence. There are 35 apartments, 8 guest rooms and a dining room. The building is owned by a not-for-profit museum, chartered as an educational organization. The building itself is a National Historic Landmark. The dining room and guest facilities are open to the public by reservation.[5]

Primary-Group Interaction

All of us have certain emotional needs: to talk, to be listened to, to socialize, to share experiences, to exchange banter, to elicit sympathy and understanding, and so on. These needs, for most people, are best satisfied

[4]During August 1993, Zellner had the opportunity to visit the Oneida Mansion House. Before an initial visit to any place, we all have expectations as to size, shape, general appearance, etc. I found the Mansion House larger than I had expected, certainly as large a house as I have ever seen. Individuals' rooms, on the other hand, were much smaller than I had envisioned, so small that a submariner would be uncomfortable in the setting. I should not have been surprised, however, as the focus was on group living, and people were expected to be around others most of the time, not alone in their rooms. The buildings and grounds were immaculately kept. For a virtual tour of the Mansion House, visit www.oneidacommunity.org.

[5]cf. Bruce M. Moseley, "Remembering Oneida's Past," *New York Times,* August 1, 1999, Sec 3, p. 18.

within the dimensions of a small, face-to-face group, such as the family, the clique, or the friendship circle. These groups are characterized by intimate, face-to-face association and cooperation. Sociologists refer to such groups, therefore, as **primary groups.** By contrast, **secondary groups**— such as the large corporation, the business firm, or the government bureau—are a formal, impersonal group in which there is little social intimacy or mutual understanding. For the most part, members tend not to relate to one another in an emotionally meaningful way.

With several hundred people living under one roof, the Oneidans had an interesting problem in human relations: how to enjoy the benefits of primary-group association in an organization that had already grown to secondary-group size? They had the advantage, naturally, of believing both in John Humphrey Noyes and in the tenets of Perfectionism, but these convictions alone would hardly account for the operational smoothness that prevailed.

Their success is explained by the fact that they worked out an amazingly effective system of interpersonal relationships. If it weren't that the discipline of sociology had not yet been envisioned, one would have thought that the Oneida Community had somehow gained access to a text in introductory sociology!

Practically everything the Perfectionists did was designed to play down the "I" in favor of the "we." Members ate together at a common dining table, worked together at common tasks, and played together in a variety of recreational pursuits. They shared their property. They shared their sexual partners. And they shared their children.

In their day-to-day activities, they were ever on guard against things that might become "antigroup." Thus, tea, coffee, and alcoholic beverages were taboo. At the dining table, pork products, including bacon and sausage, were never served; in fact, meat of any kind appeared infrequently. The Perfectionists reasoned that proclivities such as coffee drinking and meat eating might become habitual and hence distractive. By the same token, dancing was encouraged because it was a group activity, whereas smoking was prohibited because it was too individualistic.

From an outsider's view, some of the prohibitions seem excessive. An interviewer was told, for example, of an episode involving all the girl children. There were several large dolls that, like other material things in the Community, were shared. Around 1850, some kind soul thought it would be better if each of the little girls had a doll of her own, and this plan was put into effect. Unfortunately, it developed that the youngsters spent too much time with their dolls and not enough on household chores. Accordingly, on a specified date, all the girls joined hands in a circle around the stove, and one by one were persuaded to throw their dolls into the fire. From that time on, dolls were never allowed in the nursery.

Often overlooked is the fact that the religious practices of the Oneidans also served to reinforce primary-group association. It is true that the

Perfectionists dispensed with most of the formal aspects of religion. They maintained no church or chapel, held no prayer services, and had no paid clergy. Neither baptismal nor communion services were utilized. Because there was no marriage, there were no weddings. Death was played down, and there were no formal funeral arrangements. Christmas was not celebrated as a religious holiday, although in deference to outsiders, no work was performed on that day.

At the same time, religion was a central part of the Oneidans' daily lives. This was the whole point. Rather than have special religious celebrations or special days set aside for worship, the Perfectionists believed that every day should involve religious awareness. They were avid readers of the Bible and loved to discuss the various parables. They believed in Perfectionism. And they believed that by listening to John Humphrey Noyes—and following his teachings—they were listening to the voice of God.

The Big Hall   Every night, the Oneidans met in the Big Hall to combine the sacred and the secular. Women brought their sewing and knitting, and both sexes sat in groups around small tables. The program was conducted from in front of the stage by one of the senior members. A hymn was sung, passages from the Bible were read, and if he was present, Noyes would give one of his home talks. The talks themselves, involving as they did the secular application of Perfectionist theology, were one of the highlights of the evening—so much so that if Noyes was traveling, the talk was read by someone else. Also included in the nightly program were news and announcements, lectures, dancing, comments and suggestions by members of the audience, business reports, and so forth. The evening meetings can thus be seen as another means of promoting group solidarity. According to the weekly *Oneida Circular* of July 17, 1863, the meetings were "the most cherished part of our daily lives."

Noyes, incidentally, was no prude. He enjoyed entertainment and activities of all kinds, and encouraged his followers to do the same. Even on this point, however, he insisted on *group* involvement: a glee club rather than a soloist, a band or orchestra rather than a recital, a play or an operetta rather than a monologue, and so on.[6]

Although by modern standards such entertainment might seem rather tame, there is no doubt that the system worked. The Oneidans were clearly successful in their efforts to establish a primary- rather than a secondary-group atmosphere. They were also successful at preventing the development of a *culte du moi* in favor of an integrated and sustained we-feeling. Both in their conversation and their publications, "the family" was a constant reference point.

---

[6]John Humphrey Noyes played the violin vigorously in the Community's twenty-piece band, but, alas, a number of listeners observed, not well. Pictures of the all-male band show a wide variety of instruments, from clarinets to violas to snare drums.

One of the oft-told stories of the Community pertains to the time a visitor was shown through the Mansion House. "What is the fragrance I smell here in this house?" the stranger asked. The guide replied, "It must be the odor of crushed selfishness."

Decision Making

All organizations have a power structure and a decision-making process, and the Oneida Community was no exception. However, the Perfectionists had a special problem because (1) they were all housed under one roof, and (2) they were attempting to combine the social and the economic. They solved the problem by employing a combination of the democratic and the autocratic.

Committee Work   In keeping with their emphasis on group solidarity, the followers of John Humphrey Noyes might have been expected to arrive at decisions on a democratic basis. And in one sense, there was ample opportunity for discussion. The Community *Handbook,* for example, states that "In determining any course of action or policy, *unanimity* is always sought by committees, by the Business Board, and by the Community. All consider themselves as one party, and intend to act together or not at all. . . . If there are serious objections to any proposed measure, action is delayed until the objections are removed. The majority never go ahead leaving a grumbling minority behind" (p. 17).

True enough, but what these lines refer to were the day-to-day operational decisions. Major decisions, as well as Perfectionist doctrine and Community policy, were made by Noyes.

Rosabeth Moss Kanter, an authority on organizations, believes that *order* is a common characteristic of utopian communities. She states that "in contra-distinction to the larger society, which is seen as chaotic and uncoordinated, utopian communities are characterized by conscious planning and coordination. . . . Events follow a pattern. . . . A utopian often desires meaning and control, order and purpose, and he seeks these ends explicitly through his community."[7]

Order in the Oneida Community at the upper echelon was embodied in Noyes. And it was Noyes's intention that order in the lower echelons would be embodied in the committee system. Such was rarely the case.

On operational matters, members were indeed encouraged to speak out at the evening meetings. Moreover, there were a sufficient number of committees and departments to enable everyone to have a real voice in

---

[7]Rosabeth Moss Kanter, *Commitment and Community: Communes and Utopias in Sociological Perspective* (Cambridge, MA: Harvard University Press, 1973), p. 39.

the day-to-day management of the Community. In this respect, the trouble was not that members had insufficient authority, but that they had too much. There were no less than twenty-one standing committees and forty-eight different departments. Such things as heating, clothing, patent rights, photographs, haircutting, fruit preserving, furniture, music, dentistry, bedding, and painting all involved a committee or a department. There was even a department for "incidentals"!

The committees and committee heads met; departments and department heads met; the business board met. The Community itself met nightly. In a given thirty-day period, there were probably more managerial discussions in the Oneida Community than in any other organization of comparable size in the United States.

Ultimately, the Perfectionists wasted too much time thrashing out details and inaugurating meaningless change. In fact, change was almost an obsession with them. They changed the work schedule, the meal schedule, and the number of meals per day, discussing endlessly which foods to serve and which to prohibit. (The debate over whether to serve tea, for example, took several years. They finally decided to permit only a brew made from strawberry leaves.) The prohibition against smoking was also years in the making. The Perfectionists liked to change their jobs and their way of doing things. They even had a habit of changing their rooms.

The Central Members   Noyes was the acknowledged leader of the Community, ruling benevolently but firmly and basing his authority on divine inspiration. As his son Pierrepont put it, "The Community believed that his inspiration came down what he called the 'link and chain'—from God to Christ; from Christ to Paul; from Paul to John Humphrey Noyes; and by him made available to the Community."[8]

On their part, the Perfectionists were quite content with the arrangement. They acknowledged that Noyes was God's representative on earth. As a matter of fact, such acknowledgment was one of the preconditions for membership.

Nevertheless, Noyes was away a good part of the time, and in his absence important decisions had to be made—on some basis other than the twenty-one committees and forty-eight departments. The system employed was the utilization of "central members." These were a dozen or so men and women who more or less served as Noyes's deputies. They were all older, dedicated individuals, many of whom had been with John Humphrey Noyes at Putney.

This, then, was the leadership process: Noyes made the major decisions, with the cooperation of the central members. These decisions encompassed

[8]Pierrepont B. Noyes, *My Father's House: An Oneida Boyhood* (Gloucester, MA: Peter Smith, 1966), pp. 132–33.

economic policy, sexual matters, relations with the outside, admission of new members, childbearing and child rearing, and, of course, Perfectionist doctrine. Day-to-day operational details were handled by committees and departments, in consultation with the general membership.

The Oneida Community was hardly a model of functional efficiency. Yet the Perfectionists' system worked. Up to the very end, the Community functioned with scarcely a major quarrel. What they lost in operational efficiency, they gained in their primary-group associations and in their feelings of closeness to one another.

Role of Women

Because there were a number of divergent forces at work, the role of women must have presented something of a problem for the Perfectionists. On the one hand, they believed in equality. Concepts of rank and privilege were foreign to them; they were communists. On the other hand, in society at large, women held a clearly inferior position. They were generally excluded from higher education, from the professions, and from public office. All but the most routine jobs were closed to them. When the Oneida Community was founded in the spring of 1848, a wife had no legal control over her own personal property, and the right to vote was more than seventy years away. Indeed, the first Women's Rights Convention—at Seneca Falls, New York—had not yet been held.

To complicate matters, John Humphrey Noyes—in this sense, at least—was a product of his times, for he, too, believed in man's innate superiority over woman. They refused to acknowledge that, inherently, women were the equal of men. But as far as the allocation of jobs was concerned, the Community was ahead of society.

In practice, the Oneida women did work usually performed by women, but they also handled jobs that were normally reserved for men, such as being lathe operators. They did the cooking, washing, sewing, mending, and nursing, and were responsible for child care, but they also worked in various business and industrial departments. They held jobs in the library and on the Community newspaper. In a number of other areas, they worked side by side with the men. And they were well represented on the various committees, including that of the central members.[9]

There were a number of adult educational programs within the Community, and women as well as men were encouraged to take part.

---

[9]Marlyn Klee-Hartzell, "'Mingling the Sexes': The Gendered Organization of Work in the Oneida Community." *The Courier* 28 (Fall 1993) and Lawrence Foster, *Religion and Sexuality: Three American Communal Experiments of the Nineteenth Century* (New York: Oxford University Press, 1981).

Subject matter included mathematics, science, music, and foreign languages. At one time, the Perfectionists even discussed plans for establishing a university. And while the plans never materialized, there was no doubt that women would have been admitted to the same courses as men. The point is worth mentioning because at the time, in 1866, in all the United States only Oberlin College admitted women.

The New Attire   Male members of the Oneida Community dressed much like anybody else, but visitors were caught off guard when they first saw the women's attire. It was John Humphrey Noyes, never the one to accept a conventional practice if he could find an "improvement," who first pointed to the impracticality of the standard female attire. "Woman's dress is a standing lie," he wrote in the first annual report of the Community in 1848. "It proclaims that she is not a two-legged animal, but something like a churn, standing on castors!"

He went on to suggest a change: "The dress of children—frock and pantalettes—is in good taste, not perverted by the dictates of shame, and well adapted to free motion." Accordingly, three of the women embarked upon a daring stylistic venture. Following Noyes's suggestion, they proceeded to cut their skirts down to knee length and to use the cut-off material to fashion pantalettes, which reached to the ankle. After a demonstration and discussion at one of the evening meetings, the new garb was adopted forthwith. Thereafter, it was the only attire worn by the women of the Community.

In addition to short skirts and pantalettes, the Oneida women bobbed their hair. Their reasoning was that long hair took too long to fix and was not functional. The new style was quite satisfactory, although some outsiders thought the coiffure too brazen. Oddly enough, although the Oneida women first bobbed their hair in 1848, the custom was not introduced to the outside world until 1922. According to comments made in interviews, the distinctive appearance of the Oneida women was another factor that served to strengthen their we-feeling.

Membership and Secession

All groups face the problem of numbers. Some, like the Amish and Mormons, show fantastic rates of growth. Others, like the Father Divine Movement, lose members so rapidly that survival becomes a problem. The Oneida Community fell between these two extremes. Once they were fully established, their numbers remained fairly constant. Dissolution— in 1881—had nothing to do with loss of membership. In fact, the Perfectionists had much more trouble keeping people out than keeping them in.

What was the total membership of the Community? It depends on what is meant by "total." Available records indicate that at any given time, there were around three hundred members. When deaths and secessions are taken into consideration, total all-time membership was probably in the area of five hundred. There were roughly equal numbers of males and females, although there were somewhat more females at the older age levels.

At one time or another, there were seven branches, all under the leadership of John Humphrey Noyes. In addition to the main group at Oneida, there were smaller branches at Willow Place, New York; Cambridge, Vermont; Newark, New Jersey; Wallingford, Connecticut; New York City; and Putney, Vermont (reopened four years after Noyes departed). The branch at Wallingford, Connecticut—with about forty-five members—survived until the very end.

Except during the early Putney period, the Perfectionists did little or no active proselytizing. Yet they had no difficulty in attracting members. In some years, they received as many as two hundred applications. Over and over again, the *Oneida Daily Journal* reported requests for membership (evidently more male than female), but in most cases the applications were turned down.

The reason for the steady stream of membership applications is not hard to find. The Oneidans were a successful group—and word of their success traveled fast. Their own publications, as well as the popular press, afforded them wide coverage. Noyes himself journeyed and lectured extensively. And, of course, visitors to the Community could not help but be impressed by what they saw. The total number of visitors must have been staggering. The *Circular* reports that on one day—July 4, 1863—between 1,500 and 2,000 persons visited the Community.[10]

Applicants who were admitted were carefully screened, and once accepted they went through a probationary period for a year or so. The idea was to determine not only whether the newcomers could adjust to Community life, but whether they possessed the necessary devoutness. Over the years, most new members adjusted very well. Educational and recreational programs abounded, work was not excessive, and relations both within the Community and between the Community and the outside world were generally pleasant.

Unlike the Father Divine Movement, the Oneida Community was not primarily of lower- or working-class origin. They had more than their share of skilled artisans and (especially in later years) professionals. After the Perfectionists were on a solid footing, their ranks came to include any number of lawyers, dentists, doctors, teachers, engineers, accountants,

---

[10]Constance Noyes Robertson, ed., *Oneida Community: An Autobiography, 1851–1876* (Syracuse, NY: Syracuse University Press, 1970), p. 71.

ministers, and business managers. Also, many of the children born in the Community eventually went on to college and professional school.

Secession   While most of those who joined Oneida were satisfied with their decision, some were not. Each year a few individuals left—for a variety of reasons. Some were unable to adjust to the sharing of sexual partners. Others became discontented with the economic philosophy. Still others found themselves disturbed by Noyes's brand of Perfectionism.

In isolated cases, individuals joined for the wrong reason and soon became disillusioned. For example, from time to time Noyes would renounce orthodox medical treatment in favor of faith cures. He himself was alleged to have cured a woman who was both crippled and blind. Those whose hopes for a miracle cure were not fulfilled were natural candidates for secession.

In general, those who left the group were likely to be from the more recent additions. Veteran members seldom withdrew. The actual number of seceders is not known, but the figure was probably not high. Those who left were permitted to take with them whatever property they had brought, and those who had nothing were given a hundred dollars.

The Oneidans were not plagued with legal suits based on property rights. And unlike the Mormons, the Perfectionists seldom had to contend with apostates who spread untrue stories. In all the many decades of their existence, there were only two embarrassing experiences. One member, William Mills—for reasons that will be explained later—was asked to leave, refused, and had to be forcibly evicted. Another member, the highly unstable Charles Guiteau, left the Community in 1867 after a short stay. Fourteen years later, Oneidans were dismayed to learn that the same Charles Guiteau had assassinated President Garfield. (Guiteau himself was subsequently hanged.)

By and large, however, those who left did so with goodwill. A number of them actually came back and rejoined the Community. For the fact was that, on a day-to-day basis, the Oneidans were a happy group—more so, perhaps, than almost any of the other groups discussed in this book. In fact, Noyes taught that "unhappiness was, if not a sin, a serious deficiency."[11]

Even those who eventually voted to disband the Community had kind words and pleasant memories. The following remarks occurred during a personal interview: "I was too young to remember much. But as I grew older and asked my relatives about the Community days, their faces would light up. My own folks were 'come outers'; that is, they thought the thing had gone on long enough and weren't too sorry when the group broke up. But even they loved to talk about the 'old days' and how much

---

[11]Klaw, *Without Sin*, p. 7.

they missed them. They were wonderful people and they had wonderful times."

Mutual Criticism

One unusual technique used by the Perfectionists had an important bearing on high morale—and low secession. The technique was known as **mutual criticism,** and it deserves special mention for it was used by no other group. Mutual criticism refers to the practice of a member who was being reprimanded to be taken in front of either a committee or sometimes the whole community to be criticized for their action.

Mutual criticism apparently originated during Noyes's seminary days, when a group of students would meet regularly to assess one another's faults. The criticisms were carried on in a friendly but forthright manner, and all the participants—including Noyes—were pleased with the results. Response was so gratifying that Noyes instituted the practice at Putney. It was continued at Oneida and remained in effect throughout the whole of the Community's existence.

The technique of mutual criticism changed over the years. Sometimes the person involved simply stood up at the evening meeting and was criticized by each member of the group. As membership grew, however, the system proved unwieldy, and committees were appointed to conduct the criticism. Frequently Noyes added his own comments. But irrespective of the method, the goal remained the same: to bring about self-improvement through the testimony of impartial witnesses.

For certain members, understandably, criticism was traumatic. It is not easy for sensitive persons to listen to their own faults examined in public. A few Perfectionists, in fact, left the Community rather than submit to what they felt was unwarranted censure. The large majority, however, looked on the criticism not as a personal attack but as an impersonal expression of group opinion, an expression aimed at maximizing group morale.

Initially, mutual criticism involved those who were believed to be failing in the spiritual realm, or whose individuality was too pronounced. After the "treatment," they were expected to show some improvement. As Estlake, one of the Perfectionists, put it: "Mutual criticism is to the Community what ballast is to a ship."[12]

As time went on, however, the technique of mutual criticism came to be employed whenever a member genuinely desired self-improvement. In this instance, the person would volunteer, and although no records were

---

[12]Allan Estlake, *The Oneida Community: A Record of an Attempt to Carry Out the Principles of Christian Unselfishness and Scientific Race-Improvement* (London: George Redway, 1900), p. 58.

kept, mutual criticism evidently grew in popularity to the point where most sessions were voluntary. But voluntary or otherwise, the technique was effective.

All the Perfectionists were subject to mutual criticism, including the central members. The only exception was John Humphrey Noyes, who was never criticized by the Community. On occasion, however, he did undergo self-criticism.

Perhaps the most bizarre feature of mutual criticism was the fact that death did not necessarily put a stop to the process! Deceased members whose diaries or letters were found to be incriminating might find themselves being subjected *in absentia* to a "rousing criticism."

Aside from occasional excesses such as the above—and these were the exception rather than the rule—there is no doubt that mutual criticism was beneficial. It enhanced both individual morale and group cohesion. By its very nature, of course, most criticism was negative: it was aimed at revealing a person's faults. Noyes recognized this fact, and sporadic attempts were made at introducing "commendatory criticism," but the idea never took hold.

Economic Communism

One of the principal features of the Oneida Community was its total adherence to economic communism. From beginning to end, the Oneidans rejected all forms of personal wealth and private property. They never once had second thoughts about the correctness of their economic path.

Everything was jointly owned, including such things as clothes and children's toys. Pierrepont Noyes writes: "Throughout my childhood, the private ownership of anything seemed to me a crude artificiality to which an unenlightened Outside still clung. . . . For instance, we were keen for our favorite sleds, but it never occurred to me that I could possess a sled to the exclusion of the other boys. So it was with all Children's House property."[13]

On the subject of clothes, the same author states: "Going-away clothes for grown folks, as for children, were common property. Any man or woman preparing for a trip was fitted out with one of the suits kept in stock for that purpose."[14]

How did the Oneidans make out financially, in view of the fact that they were operating a communist economy in a capitalist society? The answer is, very well. Very well indeed, as we shall see. There are, however, some qualifications.

---

[13]Noyes, *My Father's House*, pp. 126–27.
[14]Ibid.

For the first ten years or so, the Community had more than their share of economic woes. Almost everything they tried seemed to fail. They started in agriculture, but although they had a number of experienced farmers in their midst, they somehow could not compete successfully in the open market. They next tried light manufacturing, turning out such products as outdoor furniture, baskets, slippers, and bags, to no avail. Then came commercialism, and the Perfectionists set about "peddling" such wares as silk thread, pins and needles, and preserved fruits and vegetables. Again they lost money.

A few of the lines showed a small profit, but overall, expenditures outstripped profits year after year. At one time, members agreed to sell their watches to reduce losses. In fact, if it had not been for the $108,000 brought in by those who joined the Community, the Oneidans would have gone bankrupt. They were losing an average of $4,000 a year.

They failed for several reasons. In some of their endeavors they lacked experience. In others, they had some unfortunate setbacks, such as a fire that destroyed supplies of goods. But the chief reason for their failure was that they were spread too thin: seven different branches in four different states. Accordingly, Noyes decided to retrench. All the branches were phased out except Oneida and Wallingford—with the bulk of the economic operation remaining at Oneida. As it turned out, this was a wise move. But there was a wiser one just around the corner.

Traps   In 1848, shortly after their founding, the Community admitted to membership one Sewell Newhouse. A north woods hunter and trapper, Newhouse was a legendary figure even before he joined the Perfectionists. More or less a loner, he knew every foot of the wilderness surrounding Oneida Lake. And he knew hunting and trapping. Around Oneida, his fame equaled that of Davy Crockett.

Aided by his prodigious strength, Newhouse made his own traps by using a blacksmith's forge, anvil, and hand punch. He made an excellent product and had no trouble selling his traps to local woodsmen. He had no real desire to make money or establish a business, however, and between sessions of trap making, he would invariably disappear into the north woods for a prolonged period.

Why Newhouse joined may have been a mystery, but his effect on the Community was indelible. At first, no one thought of using the traps as a basic Community product. Among other things, their manufacture involved a secret process of spring tempering, which Newhouse was reluctant to reveal. Under Noyes's patient prodding, however, Sewell Newhouse finally relented, and by the late 1850s the Oneida Community was turning out traps by the hundreds.

Demand for the product grew rapidly. To meet the orders that were pouring in, the Oneidans were forced to use assembly-line methods. In fact, whenever there was a deadline on a large order, the entire Community—including the children—would pitch in. And even this was not enough. By 1860, the Newhouse trap not only had become standard in the United States and Canada but was being used all over the world. Many professional trappers would use no other brand.

By this time, of course, the Perfectionists could not possibly handle all the orders themselves. They began to hire outside workers, the number eventually reaching several hundred. The trap factory, located near the Mansion House, developed into a typical industrial plant of the period. By the late 1860s, the Community was turning out close to 300,000 traps a year. During one record-breaking period, they actually manufactured over 22,000 traps in a single week.[15]

Interestingly enough, once they had "turned the corner" with the trap business, their other products—canned vegetables and preserved fruit, bags, silk thread—proved to be valuable sidelines. So, too, did their tourist business. As the fame of the Perfectionists grew, the number of visitors—with their admission fees—also grew.

Later on, in 1877, the Community began to manufacture silverware. Although there were some ups and downs, this business also proved successful. In 1881, when the Community disbanded, the industrial component was perpetuated under the name of Oneida Ltd. These silversmiths have grown and prospered, and their products are in wide use today.

It is often said that John Humphrey Noyes was the indispensable man insofar as the Perfectionists were concerned, an assertion that is doubtless true. Without him, there would have been no Community, and after he was gone the Community fell apart. But one question remains. How successful would Noyes have been if it hadn't been for a crusty old woodsman named Sewell Newhouse?[16]

Self-Sufficiency and Ethnocentrism   Once trap making had made their economic base secure, the Perfectionist brand of communism worked rather well. The Oneidans built their own home; made all their own clothes, including shoes; did their own laundry; raised their own food; and provided their own services. They did all these things, furthermore, at a remarkably low cost. The Community's *Annual Reports* indicate that the yearly expenditure for food was $24.00 per person, and the corresponding figure for clothing was $10.50![17]

---

[15]According to the *Oneida Community Daily Journal* of November 5, 1866, if it hadn't been for a mechanical defect, they would have been able to turn out 80,000 traps that week!

[16]A "Newhouse/Oneida" bear trap (eleven inches by thirty-six inches) was advertised in the October 1989 *Shotgun News* for $350. In February 2005, these traps were selling for $595 on eBay.

[17]*Bible Communism: A Compilation from the Annual Reports of the Oneida Association* (Brooklyn, NY: Oneida Circular, 1853), p. 16.

Like the Old Order Amish, the Oneida "family" performed functions that were disappearing from society at large. They provided their own recreation and their own religious services. They ran their own school, and—even though they practiced faith healing and krinopathy occasionally—they had their own doctors and dentists. The Perfectionists also had their own "social security benefits," which included child care, full employment, old-age assistance, and the like.

Functionally, economically, and socially, the Oneida Perfectionists were close to being a self-sufficient community. This self-sufficiency not only enhanced their in-group solidarity but also gave rise to ethnocentric feelings. Sociologically, **ethnocentrism** is the tendency to assume that one's own culture and way of life represent the norm or are superior to all others. The Oneidans were building the best traps. They were making money. Visitors were flocking to their doors, and there was a steady stream of new applications. Little wonder that John Humphrey Noyes and his followers felt that their way of life was superior to that found on the outside. As one of the members put it: "It was never, in our minds, an experiment. We believed we were living under a system which the whole world would sooner or later adopt."[18]

Sociality   What was there about life in the Oneida Community that attracted so many people? Oneidans were rarely alone. There was a caring atmosphere and a good feeling all around—lots of people to be with and talk to. Even their working arrangements reflected sociability. On a typical work day, Community members would rise between five and seven-thirty and proceed to the dining hall. Following breakfast, there was a short period of Bible reading, after which members would go to their assigned jobs in the trap factory, the mill, the farm, or elsewhere. A square board with pegs—each peg containing a member's name—was located near the library, and at a glance it was possible to tell each person's whereabouts. Dining hours changed over the years, but the Oneidans came to prefer a two-meal-a-day schedule, with dinner being served from three to four. After dinner there were adult classes in French, algebra, science, and other subjects, followed by the evening meeting. By nine or ten o'clock, most of the Community had retired.

While they were working, the Perfectionists liked to combine the social and the economic. Men and women worked side by side, and there was constant talking and laughing. During an interview, one former member made the following comments: "As children, we loved to visit the various departments they used to have: the laundry, the kitchen, the fruit cellar, the bakery, the dairy, the tailor shop. The thing is that small groups of people

---

[18]The statement was made by Pierrepont Noyes's mother-in-law, and is quoted in *My Father's House*, pp. 17–18.

worked side by side in most of these places, and they were able to talk with each other as they worked. It was this sort of thing, year after year, that gave rise to a kindred spirit."

While a certain amount of inefficiency was acknowledged, the Perfectionists were not idlers whose chief preoccupation was socializing. On the contrary, they were good workers. Their methods simply did not include regimentation, time clocks, quotas, and the like. As Robertson puts it, "From the beginning, the Community believed in work; not legally—that is, work forced upon the worker as a duty—but work freely chosen, as they said 'under inspiration.'"[19]

Work: A Cultural Theme   When there was work to be done, the Oneidans did it—without coercion. For the smaller projects, one of their most effective innovations was a cooperative enterprise known as the bee. "The bee was an ordinance exactly suited to Community life. One would be announced at dinner or perhaps on the bulletin board: 'A bee in the kitchen to pare apples'; or 'A bee to pick strawberries at five o'clock tomorrow morning'; or 'A bee in the Upper Sitting Room to sew bags.'"[20]

For the larger tasks—a building project, an influx of visitors, an important industrial order—a much larger proportion of the membership would turn out. All of the above, of course, was in addition to the daily work assignments. Generally speaking, while the Perfectionists never claimed to be a model of economic efficiency, their system worked.

Non-Oneidans often had difficulty in understanding just what made the Perfectionists so industrious, because there were no apparent work pressures of any kind. Similarly, some of those who joined the Community, expecting their duties would be easy, could not adjust to the energetic work pattern and soon resigned.

The economic aspects of the Community have been discussed in some detail, because most of the other sixty-odd communist experiments then under way in America failed because of economic difficulties. The followers of John Humphrey Noyes succeeded. Despite the fact that the accumulation of material wealth was not their primary concern, the Oneida Community—at the time it disbanded—was worth some $600,000. In 1881, this was no small amount.

Level of Living   On a day-to-day basis, the Perfectionists did not bask in luxury, but neither did they lead a Spartan existence. They ate well, in spite of their dietary prohibitions. They were amply clothed, although, like the Amish, there was no conspicuous consumption. If a man needed a suit, he would go to the Community tailor and—in accordance with a

[19]Robertson, *Oneida Community*, p. 47.
[20]Ibid., p. 103.

budgetary allotment—get measured for a new one. The same procedure was followed for other needs.

Noyes felt that Christian virtues such as humility and charity were best exemplified through common ownership. Throughout Oneida settlements, at least, there would be no rich, no poor; no masters, no slaves; no bosses, no underlings. Such a system, admittedly, constituted what sociologists call an **ideal type.** This construct developed by Max Weber is a model for evaluating specific types. The ideal type enables the sociologist to compare the actual situation with the conceptualized ideal. In this sense, the Oneidans, especially in the early years, came reasonably close to attaining their ideal of a commune governed by a common spiritual belief.

Members could, if they wished, travel or visit on the outside, but few availed themselves of the opportunity. There were too many attractions at home: recreation and entertainment, adult education, a well-stocked library, social and sexual privileges, opportunities for self-expression in the musical and performing arts, physical comforts (the Mansion House even included a Turkish bath)—all this in addition to the spiritual enlightenment provided by John Humphrey Noyes.

Even in the matter of work assignments, the Oneidans were given every consideration. There was no such thing as demeaning labor. Members were respected for the spirit with which they did their work rather than for the work itself. Menial tasks, such as cleaning and mending, were generally rotated. Special skills and abilities, on the other hand, were amply rewarded. Those with writing aptitude were assigned to the Community newspaper, those with a love for children worked in the children's department, and so on.

Complex Marriage

The world remembers the followers of John Humphrey Noyes not for their social or economic system, but for their practice of complex marriage. Right or wrong, just as the term *Mormon* brings to mind polygamy, so the term *Oneida* conjures up thoughts of the "advanced" sexual practices of the Community. It was Noyes himself who coined the phrase "free love," although because of adverse implications the phraseology was discarded in favor of **complex marriage.** Complex marriage is the state in which every man and every woman are married to each other. They could engage in sexual intercourse, but were not attached to one another as couples.

According to Noyes, it was natural for all men to love all women, and for all women to love all men. He felt that any social institution that flouted this truism was harmful to the human spirit. Romantic love—or "special love," as the Oneidans called it—was harmful because it was a selfish act. Monogamous marriage was harmful because it excluded others from sharing in connubial affection. The answer, obviously, was group marriage, and throughout the whole of their existence, this was what the Oneidans practiced.[21]

Over and over again, on both secular and religious grounds, John Humphrey Noyes criticized monogamy and extolled the virtues of complex marriage: "The human heart is capable of loving any number of times and any number of persons. This is the law of nature. There is no occasion to find fault with it. Variety is in the nature of things, as beautiful and as useful in love as in eating and drinking. . . . We need love as much as we need food and clothing, and God knows it; and if we trust Him for those things, why not for love?"[22]

Although he did not say it in so many words, Noyes hoped that the sharing of partners would serve as yet another element in the establishment of group solidarity. That he was able to succeed in this realm—despite the fact that the bulk of his followers had Puritan backgrounds—attests to his leadership capacity.

The system of complex marriage was relatively uncomplicated. Sexual relations were easy to arrange inasmuch as all the men and women lived in the Mansion House. If a man desired sexual intercourse with a particular woman, he simply asked her. If she consented, he would go to her room at bedtime and stay overnight. Once in a while, because of a shortage of single rooms, these arrangements were not practicable, in which case the couple could use one of the "social" rooms set aside for that purpose.

Sexual Regulations   Sex is never a simple matter (among humans, at least), and from the very beginning, complex marriage was ringed with prohibitions and restrictions. Other modifications arose over the years. By the early 1860s, a fairly elaborate set of regulations was in force, so that throughout most of the Community's existence, sexual relations were not nearly so "free" and all-encompassing as outsiders believed.

As early as Putney, Noyes taught that sex was not to be considered a "wifely duty," that is, something accepted by the female to satisfy the male. Noyes also went to great pains in his discourses to separate the "amative" (sex for pleasure) from the "propagative" (sex for reproduction) functions of sex. It was only when the two were separated, he said,

---

[21]Noyes, himself, may have had a "special love," Mary Cragin, the wife of one of his early followers. According to Foster, Mrs. Cragin was the first to inspire Noyes in the direction of complex marriage. Following her death in a boating accident in 1851, "Noyes proved almost inconsolable. For more than a year, nearly every issue of his newspaper contained fulsome tributes to her character, examples of her writing, and the like" (Foster, *Women, Family and Utopia*, p. 112).

[22]Quoted in Robert Parker, *Yankee Saint: John Humphrey Noyes and the Oneida Community* (New York: Putnam, 1935), pp. 182–83.

that the true goals of Perfectionism could be attained. In practice, this meant that men, through male continence, could have sexual intercourse up to, but not including, ejaculation. (Women, of course, could achieve sexual climax at any time.)

There were two exceptions to the nonejaculatory rule: (1) when the man was having intercourse with a woman who was past menopause, and (2) when a child was desired. Authorization for childbearing involved a special procedure and will be discussed in the following section. However, by permitting men to achieve ejaculation only with post-menopausal women, the Perfectionists not only were employing a novel method of birth control—effective, as it turned out—but were using an ingenious method of providing older women with sexual partners.

The *Handbook* also points up the desirability of courtship, and there is no doubt that in the Oneida Community sustained courtship was the order of the day. Men were eager to win the women's favor, so they acted accordingly. And the women evidently found it refreshing to be wooed by the men.

As in society at large, the men were apparently more enthusiastic than the women, at least in a strictly sexual connotation. The practice of having the man ask the woman for sexual relations, therefore, was soon replaced by a new system.

Use of a Go-between   Under the new system, the man would make his request known to a central member—usually an older woman—who in turn would pass on the request. In practice, the use of a go-between served a number of purposes. It spared the women—it was they who suggested the system—the embarrassment of having to voice a direct refusal or conjure up an excuse. As one of the interviewees said: "Sex relations in the Community were always voluntary. There was never any hint at coercion. But after they started using a go-between, it made things easier for everybody."

Employment of a go-between also gave the Community a measure of control over the sexual system. For example, the Perfectionists were ever on guard against two of their members falling in love—special love, as they called it. So if a particular couple were having too-frequent relations, the go-between would simply disallow further meetings between them. In the matter of procreation, too, it was important that the Community be able to establish paternity. And while this was not always possible, the go-between greatly facilitated the identification process.

The Oneidans considered sex to be a private matter. Aside from the particular go-between involved, "who was having relations with whom" never became common knowledge. Indeed, the subject itself was taboo. Public displays of affection, vulgarity of any kind, sexual discussions or innuendoes, immodest behavior—all were forbidden. During the many decades of their existence, the Perfectionists had but one unpleasant experience along these lines.

William Mills was accepted into the Community during the early 1860s. A rather vulgar person, it soon became obvious that he was a misfit. The women would have nothing to do with him. As a consequence, he started to cultivate the friendship of teenage girls. Breaking the Perfectionist taboo, Mills would discuss sexual matters openly with them, asking them about their amours and boasting of his own. The situation soon became intolerable, and he was asked to leave. He refused. The central members were in a quandary: from time to time others had been requested to leave, but none had ever refused. After several discussions, it was decided—in an almost literal sense—to take the bull by the horns. According to Robert Parker, "Mills found himself, one winter night, suddenly, unceremoniously, and horizontally propelled through an open window, and shot—harmlessly but ignominiously—into the depths of a snowdrift. It was the first and only forcible expulsion in the history of the community."[23]

In a burst of vituperation, Noyes said of Mills, "He is the representative of that species of parasites which works its way through the vitals of families and society by bare power of jackass-will and brazen effrontery, without lubrication of any kind except canting pretences of extraordinary piety."[24]

Taken collectively, the regulations concerning sex were designed to permit maximum freedom for the individual without jeopardizing the harmony of the group as a whole. This involved a delicate balance of rights and responsibilities, and Noyes was well aware of this fact. He strove mightily to keep sex "within bounds," and whenever there were excesses, he moved to correct them.

To take one example, the original procedure had been for the man to go to the woman's room and remain all night. Some of the women evidently complained that the practice was too "tiring," and Noyes saw to it that a change was made. Henceforth, the man would stay for an hour or so and then return to his own room. This was the procedure followed throughout most of the Community's existence.

Along these same lines, the Perfectionist leader constantly inveighed against the so-called fatiguing aspects of sexual intercourse. Instead of advocating *coitus reservatus* (that is, male continence), for instance, he could have endorsed *coitus interruptus*—both being equally effective as birth-control techniques. But Noyes was convinced that ejaculation had a debilitating effect on the male; hence, he preached against its danger.

---

[23]Parker, *Yankee Saint*, p. 223.

[24]Klaw, *Without Sin*, p. 13. Noyes could be quite colorful with words, if not just plain corny. Klaw cites as an example the following metaphor, "As a man is said to know a woman in sexual intercourse, why not speak of the telescope with which he penetrates her heavens, and seeks the star of her heart," *Without Sin*, p. 17.

He was also against *coitus interruptus* on theological grounds, because the practice is condemned in the Bible. That is, when Onan had intercourse with his deceased brother's wife, he refused to ejaculate in the natural fashion. Instead, he "spilled it on the ground, lest that he should give seed to his brother. And the thing which he did displeased the Lord" (Gen. 38:9–10).

Additionally, Noyes totally rejected all forms of contraception. For reasons best known to himself, he looked upon them as "machinations of the French" and refused even to consider them. To be acceptable, birth control had to include a strong element of (male) self-control.

Interestingly enough—and in spite of some rather questionable logic— John Humphrey Noyes's ideas about sex and birth control proved workable. His goal was to provide complex marriage with a spiritual base, and he apparently succeeded. Throughout the whole of the Community's existence, there were no elopements, no orgies, no exhibitionism. Nor was there any instance of homosexuality, sadism, masochism, or any other sexual activity that would have been considered reprehensible by the standards then current.

Ascending Fellowship   Complex marriage did pose one problem that Noyes went to great pains to solve: how to keep the older members of the Community from being bypassed in favor of the younger members. True, it was only with postmenopausal women that men were allowed to achieve ejaculation, but this restriction provided an inadequate answer to the problem. The real answer was to be found in the principle of **ascending fellowship**—the practice of older godly male members being in a special group called the Central Committee. They could pick a virgin of about the age fourteen for whom they were spiritually responsible.

According to the elaborate procedures of the principle of ascending fellowship, members were ranked from least to most perfect. Any follower who wished to improve, therefore, was advised to associate with someone higher on the spiritual scale. (Noyes taught that a high-ranking person would not in any way be downgraded by associating with a person of lower rank.) Because it took time and experience to achieve high spiritual rank, those at the upper end of the scale were nearly always the older, more mature members. It was these older Perfectionists, rather than the younger members, who were thus held up as the desirable partners.

How did this elaborate sexual system operate? Noyes's son Theodore in a 1892 letter offers this insight:

> But now to come closer, and take the bull fairly by the horns. In a society like the Community, the young and attractive women form the focus toward which all the social rays converge; and the arbiter to be truly one, must possess the confidence and to a certain extent the obedience of this circle of attractions and moreover, he must exercise his power by genuine

sexual attraction to a large extent. To quite a late period father filled this situation perfectly. He was a man of quite extraordinary attractiveness to
women, and he dominated them by his intellectual power and social
"magnetism" superadded to intense religious convictions to which young
women are very susceptible. The circle of young women he trained when
he was between 40 and 50 years of age, were by a large majority his devoted friends throughout the trouble which led to the dissolution [of the
Oneida Community between 1879 and 1881].

. . . I must suppose that as he grew older he lost some of his attractiveness,
and I know that he delegated the function [of initiating young women into
sexual intercourse] to younger men in several cases, but you can see that
this matter was of prime importance in the question of successorship and
that the lack of a suitable successor obliged him to continue as the social
center longer than would have otherwise been the case and so gave more
occasion for dissatisfaction.[25]

There is no doubt that age was shown great respect in the Community.
This is the way Noyes wanted it, and this is the way it was. In addition,
the fact that younger men were encouraged to have sexual relations with
older women served to strengthen the birth-control measures that were
used.

Complex Marriage: Unanswered Questions

Although the preceding pages give the broad outlines of the sexual system employed by the Perfectionists, a number of questions remain unan-
swered. To what extent did the women refuse sexual requests? Was a go-
between really used, or was this a formality that was easily bypassed? Did
women as well as men initiate sexual requests? Was not the factor of jealousy a problem? Did members have difficulty adjusting sexually to a
large number of different partners? Researchers have attempted to find
answers to these questions, but they have had only limited success. One
of the interviewees made the following points: "I grant the questions are
of sociological interest, but look at it from our view. If somebody came to
you and asked questions concerning the sex life of your parents and
grandparents, you'd have a tough time answering. The same with us.
When the old Community broke up, there was a natural reluctance to discuss sex. Former members didn't discuss their own sex lives, and naturally their children and grandchildren didn't pry."

[25]Private correspondence cited in Lawrence Foster, "Free Love in Utopia: How Complex
Marriage was Introduced in the Oneida Community," 2002 International Conference, Center
for Studies on New Religions, "Minority Religions, Social Change, and Freedom of
Conscience." Salt Lake City, June 2002.

During the decades of the Community's existence, many of the Oneidans were in the habit of keeping diaries. Diary keeping was evidently much more common in the nineteenth century than it is today. Some of the Perfectionists also accumulated bundles of personal letters. After the Community broke up, and as the members died over the years, the question arose as to what to do with all these documents.

Because so much of the material was of a personal and sexual nature, because names were named, and inasmuch as a number of the children and grandchildren were still living, it was decided to store all the old diaries, letters, and other personal documents in a specially constructed fireproof storage vault at Oneida, Ltd. The corporation, concerned about the sensitive nature of the material it was holding, decided to destroy the truckload of documents in the mid-1940s.[26]

While there is little doubt that the burned material would have shed much light on the sexual behavior of the Perfectionists, the action taken by the company is understandable. Oneida Ltd. is not in business to further the cause of sociological research, and regardless of how much the material might have benefited social scientists, there was always the possibility that the contents would have proved embarrassing to the company or to some of the direct descendants.

The diary-burning episode has been mentioned in some detail to show how difficult it is to answer sexual questions of the kind posed earlier. The interview information presented here should be thought of as a series of clues rather than as a set of definitive answers.

To what extent did the Oneida women refuse sexual requests? The company official who had examined some of the to-be-burned material reported that there was nothing therein to suggest a high refusal rate. Another male respondent stated that he had been informed by an old Community member that the man "had never been refused." One female interviewee felt that refusal was a problem "in some instances." Most of those interviewed, however, had no specific information to offer. The overall impression given is that female refusal was not a major issue, although it probably arose from time to time.

Was a go-between really used, or was this a formality that was easily bypassed? None of those interviewed had any direct evidence to offer. All that can be said is that there were no *reported* instances where the rule was broken. Because the matter was never raised by the Oneidans themselves, it is doubtful whether a real issue was involved. Given the religious orientation and esprit de corps of the members, there is every reason to suppose that the stipulated procedure was followed.

Did the Oneida women, as well as the men, initiate sexual requests? This question drew a generally negative answer from all the respondents. Several said they knew of some coquetry on the part of certain women,

---

[26]Lawrence Foster, *Free Love in Utopia* (Urbana: University Press, pp. x–xii, 2001).

but they had never heard of anything more direct. Two of the older female respondents stated that there was one known case where a woman went to a man and asked to have a child by him. In this instance, however, the implication is not clear, because the Perfectionists differentiated sharply between amative and procreative aspects of sex. All reports considered, it appears that the Oneida women were no more disposed to assume the role of active partner than were women in society at large.

Noyes himself constantly preached against the dangers of male jealousy. On one occasion, he remarked: "No matter what his other qualifications may be, if a man cannot love a woman and be happy seeing her loved by others, he is a selfish man, and his place is with the potsherds of the earth."[27] On another occasion—referring to a man who was becoming romantically involved with a particular woman—he said: "You do not love her, you love happiness."[28]

It is likely that male jealousy was at most a minor problem, though it did receive a certain amount of attention. Female jealousy was evidently no problem at all. It was not mentioned by any of those interviewed, nor, so far as could be ascertained, was the matter ever raised during the Community's existence.

Did the members of the Community have difficulty in adjusting sexually to a large number of different partners? The Oneidans were encouraged to have sex with a variety of partners but were not supposed to become emotionally involved with any of them. Respondents had little or nothing to report on this matter—which is unfortunate, because the question is an intriguing one.

Stirpiculture

Because John Humphrey Noyes had so many other "advanced" ideas about life on earth, it was predictable that he would not overlook the subject of children. His views on the matter, however, shocked even those who were used to his radicalism, and little wonder! Not since Plato's *Republic* had such utopian concepts been expounded. Noyes's plans, moreover—unlike those of the Greek philosopher—were more than just words on paper. He both preached them and put them into practice.

It will be remembered that Noyes introduced *coitus reservatus*, or male continence, to spare the Oneida women from being plagued with unwanted children—as they were in the world at large. He also felt that the Oneidans needed time to prove themselves—in both a financial and social sense—

[27]W. T. Hedden, "Communism in New York, 1848–1879," *American Scholar* 14 (Summer 1945): 287.

[28]Quoted in Raymond Lee Muncy, *Sex and Marriage in Utopian Communities* (Bloomington: Indiana University Press, 1973), p. 176.

before children were permitted. Accordingly, when the Community was founded, the Perfectionist leader announced that there would be no children until further notice. As it turned out, "further notice" stretched for a period of twenty years (1848–1868), during which time the prohibition remained in effect.

By the late 1860s, however, it was evident to both John Humphrey Noyes and the general membership that the ban should be lifted. There was much discussion within the Community, and the Perfectionists wondered when the announcement would be made and what form it would take. On his part, Noyes had given the matter a great deal of thought. He was ready to lift the ban on children, but he was not ready to endorse a system of uncontrolled births such as that found in the outside world.

John Humphrey Noyes read widely on the subject of propagation. He studied Francis Galton's works on hereditary improvement. He read Charles Darwin's *On the Origin of Species*. And the more he thought about it, the more he became convinced that a scientific breeding program could be adapted to the needs of the Oneida Community. Although the word *eugenics* was unknown—it was coined by Galton in 1883—eugenics was precisely what Noyes had in mind. In 1869, the Perfectionists embarked on their program, the first systematic attempt at eugenics in human history.

Eugenics is the study of human genetics and of methods to improve inherited characteristics. In recent years, eugenics has focused on genetic engineering and efforts to reduce certain inheritable diseases such as hemophilia. However, there is great controversy over the scope of even this aspect of genetic engineering, since it requires value judgments about what are undesirable human traits and what steps should be taken (e.g., terminating pregnancies in which fetuses show such genetic markers).

Eugenics in the popular mind often raises the horrors of some kind of Nazi experiment of creating a master race. While the Oneidans did not take on this magnitude, their selective breeding program was yet another very controversial aspect of the lifestyle practiced by the followers of John Humphrey Noyes.

Noyes called his selective breeding program **stirpiculture** (from the Latin *stirps*, meaning root, stock, or lineage), and from its inception there was no doubt about the goals, methods, or enthusiasm involved. The goal was crystal clear: biological improvement of the Oneida Community. In the words of the *Circular*: "Why should not beauty and noble grace of person and every other desirable quality of men and women, internal and external, be propagated and intensified beyond all former precedent by the application of the same scientific principles of breeding that produce such desirable results in the case of sheep, cattle, and horses?"[29]

---

[29]Quoted in Robertson, *Oneida Community*, p. 341. Martin Richards, "Perfecting People: Selective Breeding at the Oneida Community (1869–1879) and the Eugenics Movement," *New Genetics and Society* 23 (April 2004): 47–71.

The methods were also made explicit: only certain persons would be permitted to become parents. The selection would be made by a stirpiculture committee, headed by Noyes, and the committee's decision would be final. There would be no appeal. And even though this meant that the majority of Oneidans might never become parents, there was no objection from the membership. On the contrary, the Perfectionists endorsed every facet of the program.

At the start of the eugenics program, fifty-three women and thirty-eight men were chosen to be parents (stirpicults). Over the years others were added, so that eventually about one hundred members took part in the experiment. Approximately 80 percent of those who took part actually achieved parenthood. During the decade or so that the program was in effect, fifty-eight children were born, and four stillbirths.

There were also a dozen or so accidental conceptions. Despite their pledge, a few of the "unchosen" individuals did their best to achieve parenthood—with some success. For instance, there was a passage in one of the burned diaries in which a man—referring to his sexual encounter with a particular woman—said, "She tried to make me lose control." In general, though, both the men and women who were bypassed seem to have accepted their lot willingly enough.

The precise method of selection used by the stirpiculture committee was never revealed. Throughout most of its existence the committee was composed of central members, and presumably they judged applicants on the basis of physical and mental qualities. Most of the candidates applied as couples, although on occasion the committee suggested certain combinations.

While it was never explicitly stated, John Humphrey Noyes was undoubtedly the chief figure in the stirpiculture process. The concept was his, the committee was his, and it was he who served as chief judge and policymaker. The records show, for example, that the fathers were much older than the mothers, a fact that reflects the principle of ascending fellowship. Noyes felt strongly that the qualities necessary for fatherhood could only be acquired through age and experience. And while this was an erroneous, Lamarckian view, it was adhered to. In fact, a number of men in their sixties were chosen as stirpicults. Noyes himself fathered at least ten of the children, so that evidently he was not averse to self-selection. The principle of ascending fellowship was less applicable to women, naturally, because of the menopause factor.

What were the results of the stirpiculture program? Was it successful? Were the offspring really superior? Most observers thought so. During the entire program, no mentally or physically disabled children were ever born, no mothers ever lost. Compared with children on the outside, the Oneida youngsters had a markedly lower death rate. A number of them went on to achieve eminence in the business and professional worlds. Several wrote books. And nearly all of them, in turn, had children who were a credit to the Community. How much of the program's success was due to the eugenic factor will never be known, because the children presumably had a favorable environment *as well as* sound heredity.

Surprisingly few children were born in the stirpiculture program. In view of the high birthrate that prevailed in society at large, the fact that the stirpicults produced only fifty-eight live children is difficult to understand. *Coitus reservatus*, practiced by the Oneida males for so many years, may have had an unaccountable effect on their fertility, although this is probably a far-fetched explanation.

The most likely answer is that John Humphrey Noyes was fearful of the effects of multiple childbirth on the health of women. His own wife, in the pre-Oneida period, had had four stillbirths, and his outlook on life had been shaped by her experience. Nearly all the female stirpicults, for example, were authorized to have but one child. A handful had two children, and only two women had three. If there were other reasons for the Perfectionists' low birthrate, they have not come to light.

Child Rearing

According to Noyes's teachings, all adults were supposed to love all children and vice versa, and the entire program of Community child rearing was based on this philosophy. Excessive love between children and their own parents was called "stickiness" and was strongly discouraged.

In practice, Oneida children were anything but neglected. For the first fifteen months they were under the care of their own mothers. After that, the youngsters were moved to the Children's House, where they were raised communally. There they were taught to treat all Community adults as they would their own parents, and there they received their formal education. There too they were introduced to John Humphrey Noyes's brand of Perfectionism.

A fair amount of published material exists on the Community child-rearing program. Evidence indicates that the program was patently successful. The following question-and-answer session—although totally fictitious—is based on factual information. The answers are those a Community spokesman might have given, say, in the 1870s.

> Q. Where do the Oneida children live?
> A. In the Children's House. Originally this was a separate building. However, in 1870 a south wing was added to the Mansion House, and the children have been there ever since.
> Q. Do the youngsters have their own facilities?
> A. Yes. The south wing was designed with this in mind. The children have their own nursery, sleeping quarters, schoolrooms, playrooms, and so forth.

Q. Who is in charge of the children?

A. I suppose you could say the whole Community. But if you mean who is in charge of the Children's House, there are a dozen or more adults whose full-time job is looking after the youngsters.

Q. Are all these adults women?

A. No. Most of them are, but we do believe in having a show of male authority.

Q. What about the children's education?

A. They are taught the same subjects as other children. But they also receive an equal amount of on-the-job training in the various departments. And when we have a bee, they often join in like everybody else.

Q. Do you use outside teachers?

A. No, we have our own.

Q. Do the children like school?

A. Do children anywhere?

Q. How is their religious instruction handled?

A. They meet for an hour a day—in prayer, Bible reading, discussions of Perfectionism, confession of faults, and so forth.

Q. How do the children like this type of training? Is it effective?

A. The only thing they like about it is when the hour is over! At the same time, whether they like it or not, we think it is effective.

Q. Do they have their own dining facilities?

A. No. We believe in bringing them into the life of the Community as early as possible. After the age of two, they eat in the regular dining room. And after the age of ten, they are permitted to sit at the same tables as adults.

Q. Do the youngsters know who their real parents are?

A. Of course.

Q. Whose name do they take?

A. Their fathers'.

Q. Are they permitted to associate with their parents?

A. Oh, yes. They spend a certain amount of time with their parents every week. However, we try to get the children to think of all Oneida adults as their parents.

Q. Doesn't this work a hardship on the children? Isn't there a natural desire to establish a bond of personal affection?

A. Perhaps so. It depends on how a child is conditioned. We think that under our system, a young person gets more love and understanding than on the outside.

Q. It's hard to believe the Oneida youngsters don't yearn for their own parents.

A. Well, one little girl did. She would stand outside her mother's window and call to her, even though her mother wasn't supposed to answer. That was an exceptional case, however.

Q. And you contend that under the Perfectionist system, the children are happy?

A. We do. But why not ask them?

Q. Do you not have problems of discipline?

A. Of course, and both the adults and the children spend a good deal of time discussing the matter. On the whole—since we're a tightly knit group—we probably have fewer disciplinary problems than they do on the outside.

Q. There are reports that Oneida children are afraid of visitors. . . .

A. As a matter of fact, some of the younger children are. They usually grow out of it, but we're not entirely satisfied with that end of it.

Q. Are the adult members of the Community happy at being separated from their children?

A. Well, they knew the rules when they joined. However, they are not really separated. They have the love of their children and the pleasure of their company, without the day-to-day burden that plagues most parents.

Q. Is there any likelihood that the Perfectionists will ever change their system of child rearing?

A. None whatsoever. As far as we're concerned, the system has proved itself. It's here to stay.[30]

The End of the Road

All good things must come to an end—or at least, so it must have seemed to the Oneidans by the late 1870s. John Humphrey Noyes had been expounding his Perfectionist views for almost fifty years. Communal living—at both Putney and Oneida—had been successfully practiced for more than forty years. There was no doubt that, sociologically, the Perfectionists had established a genuine subculture. But now the currents were going against them. There was no single reason. The causes ran together like foam on the ocean. Nevertheless, the tide was inexorable.

Outside Pressures   By and large, outsiders who lived in the vicinity of Oneida were favorably disposed toward the Community. The Perfectionists were known to be honest, industrious, and law-abiding. Moreover, as time went on, Oneida was recognized as a growing source of employment. Unfortunately, as their fame grew, so did their "notoriety." Free love, complex marriage, scientific breeding—such things were more than nineteenth-century America could accept. And so the pressures grew—from isolated editorials and sermons in the 1860s to a concentrated barrage in the 1870s. Two of the attackers, in particular, are worthy of mention.

Anthony Comstock, self-appointed watchdog of American morals, was in a special position to hurt the Oneidans. A member of Congress from

---

[30]This hypothetical "Q & A" was developed by William Kephart, *Extraordinary Groups*, 1st ed. (St. Martin's Press, 1976).

New York, he sponsored the omnibus state law forbidding immoral works. He also organized the New York Society for the Suppression of Vice. Most important, in 1873 he persuaded Congress to enact a federal obscenity bill which, among other things, forbade the dissemination of all literature dealing with birth control. As fanatical a reformer as the country had ever seen, Comstock succeeded in tarring the Perfectionists with the brush of vice and obscenity. His followers found the Community an easy—and rather defenseless—target.

Less well known than Comstock, but even more effective, was Professor John Mears of Hamilton College. Whereas Comstock was against "obscenity" in any form, Mears's sole obsession was the Oneida Community. Week after week he wrote to the newspapers, gave public talks, and preached Sunday sermons—all against the "debaucheries" being practiced by John Humphrey Noyes and his followers.[31]

Methodists, Presbyterians, Baptists, Congregationalists—all took up the cry. Committees were appointed, conferences held, legal action demanded. Anthony Comstock's help was solicited. And while some editorials were fair, others joined in the diatribe against the Oneidans. Meanwhile, back at the Community . . .

Internal Pressures   All was not well. Dissent was not only in the air; it was stalking the corridors and invading the rooms. Behind closed doors, small groups of Perfectionists voiced their complaints. And while there is no doubt that outside pressures were a contributing factor, it was the internal dissension that really destroyed the Community.

To begin with, the nature of Perfectionism was changing. The deeply religious orientation gave way to an emphasis on social science, then in its infancy. Bible reading and sermons were superseded by talks on self-improvement and social engineering. Noyes himself seems to have initiated the trend, announcing in the *Circular* that that publication would no longer be a "strictly religious" paper.[32] While some in the Community went along with the change, others—particularly those in the older age groups—felt that the whole basis of their life was being violated.

Problems, too, were arising with the young people. Three in particular are worthy of mention: (1) Acceptance of John Humphrey Noyes as the ultimate authority came to be resented, especially by those who went to college and returned to live in the Community. Not unnaturally, they demanded a larger role in the decision-making process. (2) The principle of ascending fellowship began to be questioned. Young men and women objected to being paired off sexually with the older members. And (3) those

[31]Quoted in Parker, *Yankee Saint*, p. 268.
[32]Ibid., p. 274.

who failed to qualify for parenthood under the stirpiculture program took umbrage at the fact.

The Townerites   At the evening meeting of April 21, 1874, Noyes made an important announcement. (How important, even he did not realize.) Twelve new members—remnants of the defunct Free Love Society of Cleveland—were being admitted into the Community. Their leader was a minister-turned-lawyer, James W. Towner.

A man of some talent, Towner became a divisive force almost immediately. Those with complaints—a growing number, it seems—found him a ready listener. And although a majority of the Perfectionists remained loyal to John Humphrey Noyes, Towner succeeded in winning over a fair minority of the membership. In retrospect, he seems to have been a "shrewd operator" who was out to gain control of the Community for his own ends. While he failed in the attempt, he succeeded in dividing the Oneidans into two factions, Noyesites and Townerites.

The Townerites complained that Noyes was too autocratic, and they wanted an equal voice. While the entire story is much too long to relate here, an important part centered on a strictly sexual matter.[33]

According to the principle of ascending fellowship, young people were required to have their first sexual encounter with the older, more spiritual members of the Community. Noyes evidently reserved for himself the right to initiate the young girls, although as he grew older he sometimes delegated the authority to one of the central members. However, the Townerites questioned his authority to make the decision, and the controversy became bitter.

Although Noyes exercised the rights of "first husband" for many years, he did so only with girls who had reached menarche (first menstruation). The catch was that some of the girls reached menarche at a very early age—as low as ten in some instances, with a range of ten to eighteen, and an average age of thirteen.[34] The Perfectionist leader's exercise of first husband rights, therefore, provided the Townerites with a powerful weapon. If legal charges were brought, Noyes could be accused of statutory rape; in fact, Towner was rumored to be gathering evidence against the Perfectionist leader. Towner denied the allegation, but the argument continued.

Lack of Leadership   Where was John Humphrey Noyes all this time? As Comstock and Mears mounted their attacks, as internal dissension accelerated, as Towner succeeded in tearing the Community apart—what was the Perfectionist leader doing? Unbelievable as it may seem,

[33]For an excellent analysis of the controversy, see Constance Noyes Robertson, *Oneida Community: The Breakup, 1876–1881* (Syracuse, NY: Syracuse University Press, 1972).

[34]Ely van de Warker, "A Gynecological Study of the Oneida Community," *American Journal of Obstetrics and Disease of Women and Children* 17 (August 1884): 795.

the answer is: nothing. After battling all his life for what he believed in, John Humphrey Noyes—for no known reason—seemed to give up. He left the Community for extended periods of time, and even when he was there, he seemed to withdraw more and more from a position of active leadership. Little by little, the central members were permitted to make both operational and policy decisions. Unfortunately, they were not qualified to do so.

The Perfectionist leader not only withdrew from Community life, but the decisions he did make were disastrous. He permitted Towner to join, probably the worst decision of his entire career. He changed the Community's focus from the sacred to the secular—another misjudgment. And he made no provision for succession of leadership, other than to recommend his son Theodore for the job—still another bad decision. It was not only Noyes's spirit that waned, but his judgment as well.[35]

The Breakup   In 1877, Noyes resigned. One of his last acts was to appoint a committee to succeed him, headed by Theodore, who actually directed the Community for the next few years. But the group was too far gone to be saved by anyone—least of all by Theodore.

On June 22, 1879, John Humphrey Noyes left the Oneida Community, never to return. He left secretly in the middle of the night, aided by a few close friends. And he left for the same reason that he had fled Putney thirty-two years earlier: to escape the law.

Noyes felt that Mears or the Townerites were about to bring charges against him on grounds of statutory rape, and in view of his vulnerability he decided to leave New York State. Actually, he may have been overcautious. The Townerites could hardly have brought charges inasmuch as they were guilty of the same offense. And because Mears was exceedingly unpopular in the Community, he could hardly have gathered the necessary evidence. Nevertheless, Noyes left for Canada where—through emissaries—he kept in touch with Oneida.

In August, he sent word to the Community recommending that they abandon the practice of complex marriage. The recommendation satisfied both the Noyesites and the Townerites and passed without a dissenting voice. Shortly thereafter, a large number of monogamous marriages took place within the Community. Where it was possible, mothers married the fathers of their children. In the case of some of the younger women, Noyes more or less arranged the marriages.

For a while, the Oneidans continued to live communally, but it was clear to both insiders and outsiders that the end was imminent. Dissension prevailed. The aging Noyes remained more or less isolated in Canada. No new leader appeared. During 1880, plans for dissolution were discussed

---

[35]Theodore, a Harvard graduate, was a devout Darwinist who saw no reason to seek the creator. cf. Spencer Klaw, *Without Sin*, p. 225.

and approved, and on January 1, 1881, the Oneida Community officially ceased to exist.

The Aftermath

Although the group dissolved itself, it did not—in a literal sense—go out of business. For in spite of the wrangling and dissension mentioned above, the economic side of the Community held up surprisingly well: its net worth was $600,000. At the time of dissolution, a joint-stock company was formed—Oneida Ltd.—and the stock was apportioned among the members.

Like most business organizations, Oneida Ltd. has had its ups and downs. On the whole, however, the company has grown and prospered. For the first fifty years or so, the enterprise was managed—in whole or in part—by Pierrepont Noyes, a son of John Humphrey and an extremely able businessman. It was under his direction that the company phased out the traps and concentrated on silverware.

In 1960, P. T. Noyes—son of Pierrepont and grandson of John Humphrey—took over the presidency. And in 1967, the company was accepted for listing on the New York Stock Exchange with the simple designation "Oneida." Today it trades as an over-the-counter stock using the ticker symbol ONEI. During the late 1970s, the company diversified: copper wire and cooking utensils were added to the silverware lines. Today, Oneida Ltd. is a worldwide organization with thousands of employees.

The expanding global economy of the twentieth and twenty-first centuries has caused Oneida to refashion itself.[36] It has diversified to include glassware and decorative crystal. Manufacturing moved abroad and it operated only one production facility in the United States at Oneida, which was closed in 2005. Oneida was the last remaining stainless steel flatware manufacturer in the United States. This has left about 400 employees at administrative offices in Oneida. Yet it oversees sales of about $400 million annually, and continues to have high name identification among consumers in the flatware business.

What about the other phases of Community life following the breakup? A few members left the area entirely, never to return. A handful of the older members went to Canada, where they could be near their former leader. Towner's influence declined sharply, and a year after the breakup he and some twenty-five of his followers left for California. Many of them prospered, although they made no attempt to live communally. Towner eventually became a county court judge.

John Humphrey Noyes stayed in Canada with a few of the faithful. Most of his time was spent in Bible reading and—most likely—reminiscing. He

[36]Constance L. Hays, "Why The Keepers of Oneida Don't Care to Share The Table," June 20, 1999, Sec. 3, p. 1. Also see www.oneida.com and specifically at that site "Q & A—Sherrill Factory Announcement," accessed February 24, 2005.

died in 1886, at the age of seventy-four. He was buried at Oneida in the Community cemetery, his simple headstone identical to all the others.

Most of the ex-Perfectionists remained in the Oneida area. Some stayed on in the Mansion House, in private apartments. Others moved to nearby houses. The majority of the men retained their positions with Oneida Ltd., many becoming officers, a pattern that has persisted down to the present. The Mansion House, over the years, served as a kind of social headquarters for the Oneidans and their descendants. While the social function today is minimal—an occasional wedding, a funeral, an anniversary celebration—the building is still in excellent condition. It contains apartments, a dining hall, a library, a museum, and—if one knows where to look—some fascinating memories.

The Oneida Community: A Contemporary Assessment

Was Oneida a success or a failure, a rewarding venture or a waste of time? Was John Humphrey Noyes a genius, an egomaniac, or simply a religious eccentric? Writers collided over these questions a hundred years ago— when the Community was still in existence—and there is still disagreement. Perhaps there always will be.

In a sociological sense, the Perfectionists were anything but failures. They not only lived together, communally, for many decades, but developed an economic base that was strong enough to spawn a multimillion-dollar corporation. Furthermore, they were able to provide society at large with a genuinely new perspective.

As used by both anthropologists and sociologists, **cultural relativism** is the viewing of people's behavior from the perspective of their own culture. As a distinct subculture, the Oneida Community provides a good example of the significance of cultural relativism. That is, when the Community was flourishing, most Americans did not agree with the Perfectionist value system. Noyes's brand of communism, after all, had limited appeal. At the same time, it drove home to many Americans—firsthand—the realization that there were viable lifestyles other than their own.

This lesson is not lost even today. Students who read about the Oneida Perfectionists surely have a keener awareness of a completely different way of life even if we still consider it difficult to understand how hundreds of people came to accept the teachings of Noyes. Most of us show little willingness to relinquish personal property, renounce conjugal love, or reject parenthood. It certainly anticipated a time when sexual relationships could be discussed openly and raised the possibility that what is "proper" sexual behavior could be debated. Yet if one gives some serious thought to the Oneidans, their lifestyle becomes—if not attractive—at least understandable. Through understanding comes tolerance, the great lesson of cultural relativism.

KEY TERMS

Ascending fellowship, p. 72
Charismatic authority, p. 47
Commune, p. 49
Complex marriage, p. 68
Cultural relativism, p. 85
Culture, p. 47
Ethnocentrism, p. 66
Eugenics, p. 76

Ideal type, p. 68
Male continence, p. 50
Mutual criticism, p. 62
Perfectionism, p. 49
Primary group, p. 54
Secondary group, p. 54
Stirpiculture, p. 76
Subculture, p. 47

SOURCES ON THE WEB

www.oneidacommunity.org
Information aimed at tourists visiting the Mansion House of the Oneida
    Community.

http://library.syr.edu/digital/guides/o/OneidaCommunityCollection/
Syracuse University maintains the Oneida Community Collection and some of it
    is accessible online.

http://www.crjc.org/heritage/V04-1.htm
A detailed description of the Putney Village Historic District with numerous ref-
    erences to the Noyes family.

SELECTED READINGS

Burridge, Kenelm. *New Heaven, New Earth: A Study of Millenarian Activities.* New
    York: Schocken, 1969.
Carden, Maren Lockwood. *Oneida: Utopian Community to Modern Corporation.*
    Baltimore: Johns Hopkins University Press, 1969.
Cross, Whitney R. *The Burned-over District: The Social and Intellectual History of
    Enthusiastic Religion in Western New York 1800–1850.* Ithaca, NY: Cornell Univer-
    sity Press, 1950.
Dalsimer, Marlyn Hartzell. "Women and Family in the Oneida Community,
    1838–1881." Ph.D. diss., New York University, 1975.
Estlake, Allan. *The Oneida Community: A Record of an Attempt to Carry Out the Prin-
    ciples of Christian Unselfishness and Scientific Race-Improvement.* London: George
    Redway, 1900.

Fogarty, Robert. "Oneida: A Utopian Search for Religious Security." *Labor History* 14 (Spring 1973): 202–27.

———. *Special Love/Special Sex: An Oneida Community Diary.* Syracuse, NY: Syracuse University Press, 1994.

Foster, Lawrence. *Religion and Sexuality: Three American Communal Experiments of the Nineteenth Century.* New York: Oxford University Press, 1981.

———. *Women, Family and Utopia: Communal Experiments of the Shakers, the Oneida Community, and the Mormons.* Syracuse, NY: Syracuse University Press, 1991.

———, ed. *Free Love in Utopia: John Humphrey Noyes and the Origin of the Oneida Community.* Compiled by George Wallingford Noyes. Urbana: University of Illinois Press, 2001.

Handbook of the Oneida Community. Oneida, NY: Office of the Oneida Circular, 1875.

Hayden, Dolores. *Seven American Utopias: The Architecture of Communitarian Socialism, 1790–1975.* Cambridge, MA: MIT Press, 1976.

Kephart, William M. "Experimental Family Organization: An Historico-Cultural Report on the Oneida Community." *Marriage and Family Living* 25 (August 1963): 261–71.

———. *The Family, Society, and the Individual.* Boston: Houghton Mifflin, 1981.

Klaw, Spencer. *Without Sin: The Life and Death of the Oneida Community.* New York: Penguin, 1993.

Levine, Murray, and Barbara Benedict Bunker. *Mutual Criticism.* Syracuse, NY: Syracuse University Press, 1975.

Muncy, Raymond Lee. *Sex and Marriage in Utopian Communities.* Bloomington: Indiana University Press, 1973.

Nordhoff, Charles. *The Communistic Societies of the United States.* New York: Dover, 1966.

Noyes, Corinna Ackley. *Days of My Youth.* Oneida, NY: Oneida Ltd., 1960.

Noyes, George Wallingford. *John Humphrey Noyes: The Putney Community.* Syracuse, NY: Syracuse University Press, 1931.

Noyes, Hilda H., and George W. Noyes. *Male Continence.* Oneida, NY: Office of the Oneida Circular, 1872.

———. *Essay on Scientific Propagation.* Oneida, NY: Oneida Community, 1873.

———. "The Oneida Community Experiment in Stirpiculture." *Eugenics and the Family* 1 (1923): 374–86.

Noyes, Pierrepont B. *A Goodly Heritage.* New York: Holt, Rinehart & Winston, 1958.

———. *My Father's House: An Oneida Boyhood.* Gloucester, MA: Peter Smith, 1966.

Parker, Robert. *A Yankee Saint: John Humphrey Noyes and the Oneida Community.* New York: Putnam, 1935.

———, ed. *Oneida Community: An Autobiography, 1851–1876.* Syracuse, NY: Syracuse University Press, 1970.

Robertson, Constance Noyes. *Oneida Community Profiles.* Syracuse, NY: Syracuse University Press, 1977.

Thomas, Robert. *The Man Who Would Be Perfect: John Humphrey Noyes and the Utopian Impulse.* Philadelphia: University of Pennsylvania Press, 1977.

Wagner, Jon, ed. *Sex Roles in Contemporary American Communes.* Bloomington: Indiana University Press, 1982.

Walters, Ronald G. *American Reformers, 1815–1860.* New York: Hill & Wang, 1978.

CHAPTER THREE

THE GYPSIES

- Who Are the Gypsies?
- What Is the Origin of the Gypsies?
- Challenges to Studying the Rom
- *Marimé*
- Family and Social Organization
- Arranged Marriages and the Bride Price

- Economic Organization
- Quasi-Legal and Illegal Activities
- Lifestyle
- Social Control
- Prejudice and Discrimination
- Adaptability: The Rom Trademark
- The Future

Of all the groups discussed in the present volume, the Gypsies are the most "extraordinary." Even for experienced observers, their culture patterns are difficult to grasp. For the fact of the matter is that the Gypsies have a lifestyle that comes close to defying comprehension. The dust jacket of Peter Maas's controversial and widely read *King of the Gypsies*, for example, makes the following blurb claims:

> There are perhaps a million or more Gypsies in the United States—nobody knows exactly how many, not even the government. They no longer live in horse-drawn caravans on dusty roads; they live in cities, drive cars, have telephones and credit cards. Yet they do not go to school, neither read nor write, don't pay taxes, and keep themselves going by means of time-honored ruses and arrangements. Gypsies themselves recognize the contrast they make, and they are proud of it.[1]

Given the nature of modern journalism, can this statement be true? The answer is not a simple one, and each of the above points requires some explanation.

It is true that no one knows how many Gypsies there are in the United States. One million seems a reasonable estimate, but the real figure will probably never be known. Gypsies move about so much, many have so many different names and aliases, and are generally so secretive that

[1]Peter Maas, *King of the Gypsies* (New York: Viking, 1975).

pinpointing the numbers for a given city, let alone for the nation at large, is often difficult.[2]

Before proceeding further, we should directly address the term *Gypsies*. It is the term generally used to refer to the group, but is not one routinely accepted by the people. The Rom is the most neutral name of this extraordinary group who typically speak a distinctive language called *Romani* (or *Romany*). Many contemporary Rom, especially in Europe, have accepted *Traveler* to refer to themselves since Rom is sometimes reserved for only those who are traced to eastern or southern Europe. *Gypsy,* by contrast, was a name applied to them under the mistaken notion they were Egyptian in origin. However, we recognize that Rom is used only by those who specialize in the study of these fascinating people, so we will use Gypsy, but remind the reader of the proper use of Rom.

Who Are the Gypsies?

Gypsies live in cities and drive cars? Indeed they do. They are not likely to be found on farms or in the suburbs. They will not be found on the water. They are urban dwellers—towns and cities—and they reside in nearly all fifty states. At the same time, Gypsies are, and always have been, great travelers. They may be the greatest travelers the world has ever known. As we shall see, traveling serves as an integral part of the Gypsy lifestyle.

As for cars, Gypsies not only drive them but sometimes make their living repairing them. The days of horse-drawn wagons and caravans have long since gone, but Gypsies—as is their wont—have adapted remarkably well to motorized transportation. Indeed, despite the fact that they are a low-income group, Gypsies often drive Cadillacs.

Gypsies do not go to school? Not very often—and not for very long. They feel that formal education is not germane to their way of life and that the American school system would tend to assimilate their youngsters. **Assimilation** is the process through which a person forsakes his or her own cultural tradition to become part of a different culture.

Gypsies neither read nor write? True. A large portion of them are functionally illiterate. They cannot read or write their own language, Romany, for it is a spoken, rather than a written, tongue. The literacy situation is

---

[2]Ian F. Hancock, "American Roma: The Hidden Gypsy World," *Aperture* 144 (Summer 1996). Furthermore, there is no census data on Gypsies and only a few thousand volunteer they speak languages associated with them. The estimate of one million in the United States most recently appeared in Mary Beth Marklein, "European effort spotlight plight of the Roma." *USA Today,* February 2, 2005, p. 6A. Language data appear in the report "Languages Spoken, Census 2000" at www.census.gov.

improving, but so far progress has been slow. In spite of their self-imposed linguistic handicap, however, Gypsies have made a remarkable adaptation to their environment.

In urban United States, public school education has become more common. In fact, beginning in 1965, Roma became involved in creating school and Head Start programs to serve their people, first in San Francisco, then elsewhere, including Oregon and Washington State, then spreading eastward to Chicago and Baltimore.[3]

Gypsies do not pay taxes? Some observers would reply: "Not if they can help it." And it is true that many Gypsies do not pay property taxes because they have no taxable property. They often prefer to rent rather than to buy a dwelling place. Also, many Gypsies work irregularly and have low-paying jobs, so that their income taxes would be negligible. A fair number are on welfare. On the other hand, at least some Gypsies are moving into white-collar occupations, and their tax payments are probably commensurate with those of other white-collar workers.

Gypsies keep themselves going by means of time-honored ruses and arrangements? A complicated question, surely, but then the Gypsies are a complicated people. As is true of all ethnic groups, there are honest Gypsies and there are dishonest Gypsies. Unfortunately, however, many Gypsies continue to believe that all **gadje**[4] (non-Gypsies) are fair game. And more than occasionally this belief does culminate in ruses and petty swindles.

At the same time, Gypsy attitudes toward the *gadje* have been shaped by the *gadje* themselves. As will be shown, Gypsies have not been met with open arms by the various host countries. On the contrary, they have experienced near-universal prejudice and discrimination. There is no question that Gypsy enclaves everywhere are considered **countercultures.** As used by sociologists, the term refers to any group behavioral pattern that arises in opposition to the prevailing culture. Social distance studies in several countries, including the United States, simply confirm the obvious; namely, the Gypsies rank at the absolute bottom of the status scale.[5]

Through it all, the Gypsies have survived. Gypsies always survive. If they haven't exactly flourished, they have in many ways given a very

---

[3]Ian Hancock, "The Schooling of Romani Americans: An Overview." Paper read at the Second International Conference on the Psycholinguistic and Sociolinguistic Problems of Roma Children's Education in Europe, Varna, Bulgaria, May 27, 1992.

[4]Interestingly enough, the Gypsy language has not been standardized. Consequently, most of their terms have a variety of spellings. In the present account, spelling has been adapted to fit the pronunciation. For example, *gadje* is also written as *gazhé* and *gawjas*.

[5]Cited in Matt Salo and Sheila Salo, *The Kalderasha in Eastern Canada* (Ottawa: National Museums of Canada, 1977), p. 17.

good account of themselves. It is not easy to be a Gypsy. As one writer put it: "Only the fit need apply."[6] In the following pages, the full implications of this statement will become clear.

What Is the Origin of the Gypsies?

Like so many other aspects of their life, Gypsy origins are draped in mystery. As noted earlier, the Gypsies were mistakenly thought to have originated in Egypt. This was a belief that they themselves did little to discourage. In fact, some Gypsies still believe in their Egyptian roots, although it has now been rather well established that their original homeland was India. Romani, the Gypsy language, is thought to have its roots in Sanskrit—a classical language of India.

Exactly when the Gypsies left India—or what their status was—is still being debated. They have been variously described as being descended from the Criminal and Wandering Tribes, as being deported prisoners of war, and as being "a loose federation of nomadic tribes, possibly outside the Indian caste system entirely."[7] In his essay "American Roma: The Hidden Gypsy World," Ian F. Hancock contends that "a growing number of specialists believe that the Rom descended from a composite population of non-Aryan Indians, and possibly from African mercenaries (called Siddis) in India, assembled in the eleventh century into a military force to repel Islamic invasions."[8]

Whatever their class or caste origins, the Rom people most likely left India at different times—and from different areas—perhaps during the first few centuries A.D.[9] By the fifth century, they seem to have settled in and around Persia and Syria. And although their early migration patterns are anything but clear, Gypsies were reported in southeastern Europe (Greece, Hungary, Romania, Serbia) by the 1300s, and in western Europe (France, Germany, Italy, Holland, Switzerland, Spain) by the 1400s.[10] Hancock reports that the first Rom to come to America accompanied Columbus on his second voyage in 1498.[11] (See the Timetable.) Today there are Gypsies in practically every European country. They are also well estab-

---

[6]Rena C. Gropper, *Gypsies in the City* (Princeton, NJ: Darwin, 1975), p. 189.

[7]Donald Kenrick and Grattan Puxon, *Destiny of Europe's Gypsies* (New York: Basic Books, 1972), pp. 13–14.

[8]Hancock, "American Roma," p. 17.

[9]See the discussion in T. A. Acton, "The Social Construction of the Ethnic Identity of Commercial Nomadic Groups," in Joanne Grumet, ed., *Papers from the Fourth and Fifth Annual Meetings, Gypsy Lore Society, North American Chapter* (New York: Gypsy Lore Society, 1985), pp. 5–23.

[10]See Gropper, *Gypsies in the City*, pp. 1–16.

[11]Hancock, "American Roma," p. 20.

The Gypsies

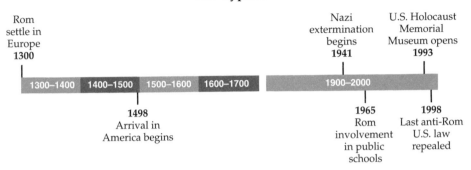

lished in North Africa, the Near East, South America, the United States, and Canada.

Some groups who are often thought of as Gypsies are not in fact true Gypsies, or Rom. These would include the Tinkers of Ireland and Scotland, and the Taters of Norway.[12] The Irish Tinkers, for example, are of Celtic origin, and they speak Shelte, a Celtic dialect.[13] In the present account, we are concerned only with the Rom.

As they spread throughout Europe, Gypsies came to be—above all else—travelers. "A Gypsy who does not keep on the move," wrote Block just prior to World War II, "is not a Gypsy."[14] Actually, the majority of Roma are sedentary Gypsies, or *Sinte*.

Nevertheless, *Sinte* or no *Sinte*, it was the horse-drawn wagons and gaily decorated caravans that seemed to strike a responsive chord in people of all ages. Jan Yoors, author of one of the most widely read books on Gypsy life, ran away as a young boy and lived for many years with a Gypsy group.[15] G. E. C. Webb, another writer, states that "for as long as I can remember, Gypsies have fascinated me. These dark-skinned strangers, indifferent to the rest of the world, mysterious in their comings and goings, traveling the roads with parades of highly colored raggedness, fired my imagination. I was curious about them and wanted to know more. But nobody, it seemed, could tell me more."[16]

---

[12]Frederik Barth, "The Social Organization of a Parish Group in Norway," in Farnham Rehfisch, ed., *Gypsies, Tinkers, and Other Travelers* (New York: Academic Press, 1975), pp. 285–89.

[13]For an interesting discussion, see George Gmelch, *The Irish Tinkers* (Prospect Heights, IL: Waveland Press, 1985).

[14]Martin Block, *Gypsies: Their Life and Their Customs* (New York: Appleton-Century, 1939), p. 1.

[15]Jan Yoors, *The Gypsies* (New York: Simon & Schuster, 1967).

[16]G. E. C. Webb, *Gypsies: The Secret People* (London: Jenkins, 1960), p. 9.

No combination of elements, however, could dampen the Gypsy spirit—or their fondness for bright colors, especially greens, yellows, and reds. As one effervescent Gypsy put it: "I wear bright beads and bright colors because we're a bright race. We don't like anything drab."[17]

The Gypsy Paradox   With their unusual lifestyle, there is no doubt that Gypsies fascinate the *gadje,* almost irrespective of the country involved. Novels, plays, operettas, movies, and songs have portrayed—and sometimes glorified—the romantic wanderings of the Gypsy vagabond. Popular pieces like "Gypsy Love Song" and "Play Gypsy, Dance Gypsy" have become part of the worldwide musical repertoire.

Yet side by side with the attraction and fascination have come harassment and persecution. This is the Gypsy paradox: attraction on the one hand, persecution on the other. The climax of persecution came during World War II, when the Nazis murdered about 600,000 Rom.

Despite worldwide persecution, however, the Gypsies have managed to survive. Gypsies always survive. As Gropper puts it: "For 500 years Gypsies have succeeded in being themselves against all odds, fiercely maintaining their identity in spite of persecution, prejudice, hatred, and cultural forces compelling them to change. We may have something to learn from them on how to survive in a drastically changing world."[18]

The Modern Period   Following World War II, urbanization and industrialization—together with population expansion—literally cramped the Gypsies' lifestyle. There was less and less room on the modern highway for horse-drawn caravans. Camping sites became harder to find, and the open countryside seemed to shrink. But—as always—the Gypsies adapted. Travel continued, albeit on a reduced scale. Caravans and wagons were replaced by automobiles, trucks, campers, and trailers. Somehow, by one method or another, the Rom managed to get by. And they did so without sacrificing their group identity or their freedom.

Their identity was not maintained without a price, however, for prejudice and harassment continued. Gypsy nomads were often hounded from one locale to another. The *Sinte,* or sedentary Rom—whose proportion tended to increase—were also met by hostility and discrimination. No Gypsies Allowed signs came more and more to be posted in public places.

The issue was hardly one-sided. From the view of local authorities, Gypsies were using community services without paying their share of the taxes. Indeed, they were viewed as not paying any taxes at all. Additionally, the Rom were perceived as dirty, they would not use indoor toilets, they lied, they cheated, and they stole. Sometimes the charges were true; often

[17]Quoted in Jeremy Sandford, *Gypsies* (London: Secker & Warburg, 1973), p. 13.
[18]Gropper, *Gypsies in the City,* p. 1.

they were unfounded. After all, when we are cheated, we say we are "gypped."

Fortunately, the Gypsies also had friends and supporters, and in a number of countries efforts were made to set up camping sites, establish housing facilities, provide legal assistance, and otherwise improve the lot of the Rom. By the 1970s, a number of national and international committees and councils had been organized—with Gypsy representation. The purpose of these groups has been not only to protect the interests of the Rom but to dispel stereotypes, combat false portrayals in the media, and act as a clearinghouse for information about Gypsies.

In 2005, eight central European states and a variety of international organizations launched the "Decade of Roma Inclusion." This declaration was to spearhead help but also to bring attention to the Rom as Europe's biggest and poorest minority.[19]

In some ways the Rom do indeed have a difficult life. Their relationship with the *gadje* often takes on the appearance of an interminable contest. At the same time, Gypsies often resist assimilation. They are demonstrably proud that they are Gypsies, an attitude that is unlikely to change.

How many Gypsies are there in the world today? Estimates vary from 9 to 15 million, with the latter figure probably being closer to the truth. (More than half are in Eastern Europe.) There is a general—though not unanimous—agreement that the Rom are divided into four tribes or nations **(natsiyi)**: the Lowara, Machwaya, Kalderasha, and Churara. While there are linguistic and cultural differences among the four *natsiyi,* surprisingly little has been written on this score.[20]

The United States   The first Gypsies to come to what is now the United States arrived in Virginia, Georgia, New Jersey, and Louisiana during the 1500s, although their fate remains unknown.[21] It is known that these early arrivals had been deported from various European countries—hardly an auspicious beginning. Significant numbers of the Rom, however, did not enter the United States until the 1880s and after.[22]

Up until the 1930s, the Rom followed their traditional traveling and camping patterns, replete with horse-drawn vehicles and colorful caravans. By the 1930s, though—as was true in Europe—the caravan had generally given way to motorized transportation.

[19]"Europe's Roma: Poor and Unloved," *Economist,* February 5,2005, p. 50, and David Magall, *Gypsy Identities 1500–2000: From Egipcycans and Moon-men to the Ethnic Romany* (London: Routledge, 2004).

[20]The figure of 15 million Roms was offered by Indian Prime Minister Indira Ghandi at the 1983 International Romani Festival in Chandigarh, India (see http://romani.org).

[21]Ian F. Hancock, "Gypsies," in Stephen Thernstrom, ed., *Harvard Encyclopedia of American Ethnic Groups* (Cambridge, MA: Harvard University Press, 1980), p. 441.

[22]Gropper, *Gypsies in the City,* p. 18.

The depression of the 1930s saw another significant event insofar as the Gypsies were concerned: the election of Franklin Roosevelt and the introduction of large-scale relief and welfare programs. To take advantage of the situation, the Rom began to flock to the large cities, such as Chicago and New York.[23]

The extent to which they stayed in the cities—and later in the smaller towns—depended on such things as economic opportunities, welfare practices, and degree of police harassment. And because all three of these factors changed from time to time, the Gypsy population in a given city often fluctuated. Nevertheless, the Rom were in the cities to stay, and today there is, for example, an estimated population of 50,000 Gypsies in Los Angeles and 200,000 in California.[24]

Challenges to Studying the Rom

> If you ask a dozen Gypsies the same question, you will probably get a dozen different answers. If you ask one Gypsy the same question a dozen times, you will still probably get a dozen different answers.
>
> —*Anonymous*

Although there are many versions, this adage contains more than a little truth. Gypsies live—and always have lived—in alien cultures. The boundaries between Rom and *gadje* are sharp, and the Rom have every intention of maintaining the sharpness. Deception, avoidance, misrepresentation, and lying are part of the Gypsies' arsenal, and they have had hundreds of years to perfect and embellish their defenses. In many ways, investigating the Rom is like trying to penetrate a secret society.

Perhaps the most formidable obstacle the researcher has to face is the avoidance syndrome. The Rom ordinarily do not mingle with the *gadje*; in fact, except for a possible visit to a fortune-teller, most Americans never come into contact with a Gypsy. Almost certainly they never see the inside of a Romani dwelling. Researchers face much the same problem. The fact that researchers are accredited university personnel means little to the Rom. Generally speaking, Gypsies have no intention of divulging their lifestyle and customs to social scientists or to anybody else.

Fortunately, we have some excellent American field studies, such as those by Anne Sutherland, Rena C. Gropper, and Isabel Fonseca.[25] These

---

[23]Ibid., p. 20.

[24]Myrna Oliver, "John Merino: Leader in L.A. Gypsy Council Dies," *Los Angeles Times,* August 14, 1995, p. A12.

[25]Anne Sutherland, *Gypsies: The Hidden Americans* (New York: Free Press, 1975); Gropper, *Gypsies in the City;* and Isabel Fonseca, *Bury Me Standing: The Gypsies and Their Journey* (New York: Alfred Knopf, 1995). This account of current-day Gypsy life in Eastern Europe helped to popularize a view of Gypsy identity (see Mayall, *Gypsy Identities,* pp. 33–35).

investigators not only are trained observers but spent several years among the Rom, learning the language and achieving a fair degree of acceptance. Yet even they experienced great difficulty in gaining repoire with their subjects.

There are difficulties that make it hard to *generalize* about Gypsy life. Practices of the Rom vary depending on their mobility patterns. Some Gypsies have lived in the same domicile for many years. Others move about constantly. Still others travel as the mood strikes them. And customs and lifestyle vary somewhat from one group to another.

Even if all Rom followed similar travel practices, their social structure would be difficult to analyze. Gypsies live in extended families, or **familiyi**, which form part of a larger kinship or cognatic group called the *vitsa*. The *vitsi*, in turn, are affiliated with one of the four tribes, or *natsiyi*: Lowara, Machwaya, Kalderasha, and Churara. The point is that many Gypsy customs may vary from one *familia* to the next, and from one *vitsa* to the next, making it hard, again, to generalize.

One final factor complicates the study of American Rom: their customs often depend on their country of origin. The Romnichals (English Gypsies), for instance, differ from the Boyash (Romanian), and both groups are culturally different from the Arxentina (Gypsies from Argentina and Brazil).[26]

In brief, the Rom in the United States do not present a uniform culture pattern. Because of their kinship structure, their social and economic organization, their geographical mobility, and their nationality differences, it would be difficult to generalize about Gypsies even if they were cooperative—which they are not. (And even the "cooperative" Gypsies pose a problem for the researcher. The Rom often have a working knowledge of their own particular group—but no other. Very few Gypsies have anything like a broad view or a historical picture of their own people.)

Marimé

Central to any understanding of the Rom is their concept of *marimé*. It is *marimé* that is the key to their avoidance of the *gadje,* and it is *marimé* that serves as a powerful instrument of social control.

Marimé means defilement or pollution, and as used by the Gypsies it is both an object and a concept. And because there is really no comparable term used by non-Gypsies, it is sometimes difficult for the latter to comprehend the meaning. "*Marimé*," writes Miller, "extends to all areas of Rom life, underwriting a hygienic attitude toward the world. . . . Lines are drawn between Gypsy and non-Gypsy, the clean and the unclean, health

---

[26]See the discussion in Marcel Cortiade, "Distance between Romani Dialects," *Newsletter of the Gypsy Lore Society, North American Chapter* 8 (Spring 1985): 1ff.

and disease, the good and the bad, all of which are made obvious and visible through the offices of ritual avoidance."[27]

The most striking aspects of *marimé* have to do with the demarcation of the human body. The upper parts, particularly the head and the mouth, are looked upon as pure and clean. The lower portions, especially the genital and anal regions, are considered *marimé*. As the Rom see it, the upper and lower halves of the body must not "mix" in any way, and objects that come into contact with one half must not come into contact with the other.

There are countless examples of this hygienic-ritualistic separation. Ronald Lee, who is himself a Gypsy, writes that "you can't wash clothes, dishes, and babies in the same pan, and every Gypsy has his own eating utensils, towels, and soap. Other dishes and utensils are set aside for guests, and still others for pregnant women. Certain towels are for the face, and others for the nether regions—and there are different colored soaps in the sink, each with an allotted function."[28]

Marimé apparently originated in the early caravan period, when—for hygienic purposes—it was imperative that certain areas of the camp be set aside for cooking, cleaning, washing, taking care of body functions, and the like. Also, within the close confines of the wagons and tents, it was important that rules pertaining to sex be carefully spelled out and enforced. As is so often the case, however, over the years the various hygienic and sexual taboos expanded.[29]

Gropper states that "a woman is *marimé* during and after childbirth, and during her monthly period. . . . A *marimé* woman may not cook or serve food to men. She may not step over anything belonging to a man or allow her skirts to touch his things. Women's clothing must be washed separately from men's."[30]

Even such a natural phenomenon as urination may cause difficulties for the Rom. "One old lady called off a visit to a friend because she was indisposed and felt it would be too embarrassing to urinate frequently. Men often go outside to urinate rather than do so in their own homes, especially if guests are present."[31]

Interestingly and—given their conception of *marimé*—quite logically, Gypsy women attach shame to the legs rather than the breasts. Sutherland points out that it is shameful for a woman to have too much leg exposed, and that women who wear short skirts are expected to cover them with a

---

[27]Carol Miller, "American Rom and the Ideology of Defilement," in Rehfisch, ed., *Gypsies*, p. 41.

[28]Ronald Lee, *Goddam Gypsy: An Autobiographical Novel* (Montreal: Tundra, 1971), pp. 29–30.

[29]Miller, "American Rom," p. 42. See also Elwood Trigg, *Gypsy Demons and Divinities* (Secaucus, NJ: Citadel, 1973), p. 64.

[30]Gropper, *Gypsies in the City*, pp. 92–93.

[31]Sutherland, *Hidden Americans*, p. 266.

sweater when they sit. On the other hand, "Women use their brassieres as their pocketbooks, and it is quite common for a man, whether he be the husband, son, father, or unrelated, to reach into her brassiere to get cigarettes or money. When women greet each other after a certain absence, they squeeze each other's breasts. They will also squeeze the breasts to show appreciation of a witty story or joke."[32]

Marimé vs. Melalo   Mention should be made of the distinction between *marimé* and *melalo*. *Marimé* is pollution or defilement, as just described. **Melalo** simply means dirty, or as Lee describes it, "dirty with honest dirt."[33] Someone who has not had a bath would be *melalo,* but not *marimé*. Hands that are dirty because of manual labor would be *melalo* rather than *marimé*—although they would be *marimé* if they had touched the genitals.

In actual practice, Gypsies tend to wash their hands many times a day—because they may have touched any number of objects or organs that are *marimé*. Miller states that "a working Rom also washes his face and hands whenever he feels his luck leaving him during the day; he washes again upon returning from his work."[34]

The distinction between *marimé* and *melalo* explains why a Gypsy domicile often appears dirty to a non-Gypsy—and vice versa. Some Rom dwelling places, for example, are anything but spic and span. Food scraps, cigarette butts, paper, wrappings—all may be thrown on the floor, presumably to be swept out later. Such a condition is not *marimé* so long as the proper rules of body hygiene, food preparation, and so forth are followed. As one writer puts it: "Americans tend to be shocked at visible dirt, but Gypsies abhor invisible pollution."[35]

The *Gadje*: Definition of the Situation   Not all of the *natsiyi* follow the same rules and procedures regarding *marimé*. There are also some variations among family groups within the same *natsia*. The Salos note that families who follow a strict observance pattern have a higher status than those who tend to be lax.[36] But there is one point on which all true Rom are agreed: the *gadje* are *marimé*. Miller writes as follows:

> The *gadje* are conceived as a different race whose main value is economic, and whose *raison d'être* is to trouble the Rom. The major offense of the *gadje*, the one offense that the Rom can never forgive, is their propensity to defilement. *Gadje* confuse the critical distinction between the pure and the impure. They are observed in situations which the Rom regard as compromising: forgetting

[32]Ibid., p. 264.
[33]Lee, *Goddam Gypsy*, p. 244.
[34]Miller, "American Rom," p. 47.
[35]Gropper, *Gypsies in the City*, p. 91.
[36]Salo and Salo, *Kalderasha*, p. 115.

to wash in public bathrooms; eating with the fork that they rescued from the floor of the restaurant; washing face towels and tablecloths with underwear at the laundromat; relaxing with their feet resting on the top of the table.

Because they do not protect the upper half of the body, the *gadje* are construed as *marimé* all over, head to foot. This condition, according to Rom belief, invites and spreads contagious disease. Rom tend to think of all illness and physical disability as communicable, and treat them accordingly.[37]

Because the *gadje* are *marimé*, relations with them are severely limited. In fact, Sutherland states that "interaction with the *gadje* is restricted to economic exploitation and political manipulation. Social relations in the sense of friendship, mutual aid, and equality are not appropriate."[38] The same author goes on to say that "not only the person of non-Gypsies but items that come into contact with them are *marimé*. Any time a Rom is forced to use *gadje* places or to be in contact with large numbers of *gadje* (for example, in a job, hospital, welfare office, school), he is in constant danger of pollution. Public toilets are particularly *marimé* places, and some Rom go to the extent of using paper towels to turn faucets and open doors."[39]

The reader may recall that in the chapter on the Amish the concept *definition of the situation* was used; that is, "What men define as real is real in its consequences." And just as the Amish have defined the automobile as a threat to their social equilibrium, so the Gypsies have defined the *gadje* as *marimé*.

Barrier to Assimilation   Do not the various rules and prohibitions involved in *marimé* impose a hardship on the Rom? In one sense, the answer is yes. The urban world, the Gypsies' major habitat, is seen as "pervasively *marimé*, filled with items and surfaces that are subject to use and reuse by careless *gadje*, polluted, diseased, and therefore dangerous."[40] To avoid the danger, Gypsies must take any number of daily precautions—and there is no doubt that these precautions are time consuming and burdensome. Little wonder, as Miller points out, that "the home is the final bastion of defense against defilement, and the only place that the Rom feel altogether at ease."[41]

At the same time, *marimé* serves as an extremely effective barrier to assimilation. The so-called melting pot in America has boiled unevenly, with some groups being assimilated much faster than others. The Gypsies, of course, would fall at the lower end of any assimilation scale—which is just where they want to be. As the Rom see it, assimilation would be tantamount to group extinction.

[37]Miller, "American Rom," pp. 45–46.
[38]Sutherland, *Hidden Americans*, p. 258.
[39]Ibid., p. 259.
[40]Miller, "American Rom," p. 47.
[41]Ibid.

Nowhere is this resistance to assimilation more apparent than in their attitude toward the *gadje*. The belief that the *gadje* are *marimé* not only serves as a barrier to assimilation but acts as an ever-present sustainer of pride and self-respect. In fact, so pervasive is their negative attitude toward the *gadje* that Gypsies will not assimilate even after death! Nemeth's analysis of cemetery plots and tombstones revealed that the Rom attempt "to maintain distance in the graveyard between themselves and non-Gypsies, and between themselves and outcasts from their own society."[42]

Some Gypsiologists, however, believe that the rules pertaining to *marimé* are softening. The Salos, in their study of Canadian Rom, found this to be the case.[43] In most areas of the United States, however, *marimé* still seems to be a potent force. When an older Gypsy woman was asked whether she felt that *marimé* was weakening, she shrugged and said: "Maybe. I hope not. Some of the young kids don't know it, but it's what holds us together."

Family and Social Organization

Gypsies maintain a rather complicated form of social organization, and it is sometimes difficult to unravel the various kinship and community networks. It will simplify matters, however, if two points are kept in mind:

1. Gypsies are not loners. Their lives are spent in the company of other Gypsies. In fact, the term *individual Gypsy* is almost a play on words. In most of their communities, there are no single-person households, and no households of childless newlywed couples.[44]
2. The Rom are living in an alien culture, and they generally have little intention of assimilating. They are keenly aware of their position, and they are determined to keep an ever-clear line between the *gadje* and themselves. Their social organization is designed to enhance the process of *boundary maintenance*.

The *Familia*   The heart of Gypsy culture is the *familia*. As Yoors points out: "The inner cohesion and solidarity of the Gypsy community lies in the strong family ties—which are their basic and only constant unit."[45]

The **familia,** however, is much larger and more complex than the American nuclear family. Whereas the latter is generally thought of as a

[42]David Nemeth, "Gypsy Taskmasters, Gentile Slaves," in Matt T. Salo, ed., *The American Kalderasha: Gypsies in the New World* (Hackettstown, NJ: Gypsy Lore Society, 1981), p. 31.
[43]Salo and Salo, *Kalderasha*, pp. 128–29.
[44]Ibid., p. 39.
[45]Yoors, *Gypsies*, p. 5.

husband-wife-children unit, the *familia* includes spouses, unmarried children, married sons and their wives and children, plus other assorted relatives and adopted youngsters. And because Gypsy couples often have six or more children, the *familia* may easily total thirty to forty members.[46] By the same token, because in many ways the Gypsy world is a man's world, the male head of the *familia* may wield considerable power.

The *familia*, then, appears to be an extended family, but it is actually more than that: it functions as an extended family. Members live together (or close by); they often work together; they trust and protect one another; they celebrate holidays together; they take care of the sick and the aged; they bury the dead. The *familia*, in brief, is close to being a self-sufficient unit. One of the few functions it does not perform is that of matrimony, because marriages between first cousins are frowned upon.

Although the Rom believe in private property and free enterprise, ownership is often thought of in terms of the *familia* rather than the individual. Traditionally, as Clebert notes, "the essential nucleus of the Gypsy organization is the family. Authority is held by the father. . . . [P]roperty belongs to the family and not to the individual. But the family is not limited to the father, mother, and children. It includes aunts, uncles, and cousins."[47]

The *familia* is particularly effective as a *supportive institution*. Whether the problem is economic, social, political, or medical, the various family members unite in their efforts to provide aid. Should a police official, social worker, inspector, tax collector, or any other unwelcome *gadjo* appear on the scene, the intruder will be met with formidable—and generally effective—opposition. Should a family member fall ill, the *familia* will spare no expense in obtaining professional help, especially if it is a serious illness.

As hospital personnel can attest, a full-blown *familia* on the premises creates something of a problem. The Salos write that "illness, especially a terminal illness, requires the supportive presence at the hospital of the entire extended family. Hospitals often balk at the consequent waiting-room crowds."[48]

The very structure of the *familia*, of course, creates some problems—housing and otherwise. Landlords do not take kindly to rentals involving a dozen or more persons. Noise, sanitation disposal, complaints by neighbors—all must be reckoned with. Also, by virtue of its size, the *familia* is cumbersome. It is one thing for a Gypsy couple to pack up and move; it is quite another for a large *familia* to "hit the road." And because the Rom obviously like to travel, the extended family presents a mobility problem.

[46]For an interesting account of the *familia*, see Gropper, *Gypsies in the City*, pp. 60–66.
[47]Clebert, *Gypsies*, p. 129.
[48]Salo and Salo, *Kalderasha*, p. 19.

The *familia* has functional as well as structural problems. Disagreements and conflicts are bound to occur. Jealousies do arise. Living arrangements are sometimes felt to be unsatisfactory. In her study of Philadelphia Gypsies, Coker found that "there is constant slandering; rumors are started, and attacks and counterattacks are made. Most of the rumors involve sex. Some reflect on the morals of young girls, implying that they are dating non-Gypsy men, or, as a particularly vicious accusation, that they are going out with Negroes."[49]

Despite the problems involved, the Rom show few signs of abandoning the *familia*. On the contrary, they seem to thrive on it. In some cases, the size of the extended family has been reduced. In others, the married sons may form their own households. Nevertheless, the *familia* continues to be the center of the Gypsy world. As long as the *gadje* are seen in an adversary context, the *familia* will remain the Gypsies' principal bastion of security.

Most Rom have converted to the religion of their host countries, which would typically mean some aspect of Christianity or Islam. These formal religious affiliations are supplemented by the traditional beliefs of *Marimé*.

The Vitsa   Whereas the *familia* can be thought of as an extended family, and a broader *familiyi*, the **vitsa** is a kin group made up of a number of *familiyi*. Some Gypsiologists refer to the *vitsa* as a clan or a band, but the important point is that the Rom think of it as a *unit of identity*. Members of the highly publicized Bimbalesti *vitsa*, for example, would identify with one another—feel a kindred relationship—even though they might all come together very infrequently.

Vitsi (plural of *vitsa*) vary in size from a few *familiyi* to a hundred or more households. Members of a smaller *vitsa* may live near one another and operate as a functioning group. The Rom have large families, however, and most *vitsi* tend to grow. The majority of American *vitsi*, therefore, function as a group on only two occasions: at a Gypsy court *(kris)* and at a death feast *(pomana)*, especially where the deceased has been a respected elder.[50]

After a certain point, a *vitsa* may simply become too large, whereupon a split often takes place, usually along sibling or cousin lines. Sutherland cites the Minesti as an example of a large *vitsa* that has recently divided into several smaller *vitsi*.[51] The head of the *vitsa*, incidentally, is generally a respected male elder, although leadership problems do arise—and may be another reason for a *vitsa* to split.

---

[49]Gulbun Coker, "Romany Rye in Philadelphia: A Sequel," *Southwestern Journal of Anthropology* 22 (1966): 98. See also Gropper, *Gypsies in the City*, pp. 60–66.
[50]Sutherland, *Hidden Americans*, pp. 82–83.
[51]Ibid., p. 194.

Gypsies identify themselves—and other Rom—by their *vitsa* affiliation and by the liberal use of nicknames. However, they also have one or more names that are used in dealing with the *gadje*. These *gadje* names, according to Clark, are often popular American names such as John, George, and Miller.

> The *gadjo* may find a John George, George John, Miller John, John Miller, Miller George, and George Miller. He may even find a Gypsy named Johnny John or Miller Miller. But he probably won't find the John George Miller he is looking for unless the man wants to be found.
>
> The Rom deny that this is done deliberately to confuse the *gadje*. With a broad smile, a Gypsy explained that these were just nice names and everybody liked them.[52]

Arranged Marriages and the Bride Price

Gypsies are one of the few groups in America who follow the olden custom of arranged marriages. Indeed, such marriages seem to be a cornerstone of the Rom the world over. Matrimony is important to Gypsies, and they are reluctant to place their young people in Cupid's hands. This is not to say that the young are forced into marriage. Although Romani marriages may be arranged, the parents do not arbitrarily impose their will. However, parents do play a major role in the mate selection process, and the arrangements for the bride price, or *daro,* are entirely in their hands.

Gypsy culture stresses the importance of group rather than individual activity. And as Gropper observes, "Marriage for the Rom is quite definitely more than a union of husband and wife; it involves a lifetime alliance between two extended families."[53]

Arranged marriages normally include a **daro,** a payment by the groom's family to the bride's family. The actual figure varies from less than $1,000 to $10,000 or more. The higher the status of the young woman's *familia,* and the greater her personal attractiveness, the higher will be the asking price.

Although a *daro* of several thousand dollars is quite common, part of the money is spent on the wedding festivities. The money is also used to pay for the bride's trousseau, to furnish the couple with household equipment, and so on. Additionally, part of the money may be returned to the groom's father, "as a sign of good will."[54]

Weddings themselves are private in that they involve neither religious nor civil officiants. They are, in a very real sense, Gypsy weddings, and

[52]Marie Wynne Clark, "Vanishing Vagabonds: The American Gypsies," *Texas Quarterly* 10 (Summer 1967): 208.

[53]Gropper, *Gypsies in the City,* p. 86.

[54]Sutherland, *Hidden Americans,* p. 232.

are usually held in a rented hall. The festivities—involving ample food and drink—are fairly elaborate, and while formal invitations are not issued, all Gypsies in the community are welcome.[55]

The *daro* has traditionally served as a protection for the young wife. That is, if she should be mistreated by her husband or his *familia*, she can return home—whereupon the money might have to be forfeited.

Whether Gypsy wives are abused more than other wives is doubtful, but it is true that both sexes marry at a relatively young age. Marriages of eleven- and twelve-year-olds are known to occur, although the desired age range is between twelve and sixteen, and "not over 18 for a first marriage."[56] It seems likely, therefore, that many Gypsies are marrying under the legal age, although this fact would cause them no undue worry. The Rom are not overly concerned about marriage and divorce records, birth certificates, and other vital statistics.

While any two Rom can marry, most marriages involve partners from the same *natsia*. Young people are also encouraged to marry within the *vitsa*, provided the relationship is not that of first cousin or closer. The Rom feel that by having their youth marry someone in the same *vitsa*—a second cousin, for example—the prospects for a happy marriage will be increased. *Vitsa* members not only have blood ties, but follow the same customs, have the same *marimé* proscriptions, and so forth.

The *Bori* After the wedding, it is customary for the young wife to live with her husband's *familia*. She is now known as a **bori** and comes under the supervision of her mother-in-law, doing most of the housework.

Contrary to the culture pattern in the United States, Rom girls tend to be *older* than the boys they marry. As Sutherland explains, "It is important that the girl be older than the boy, since after marriage she must be able to perform her duties as a *bori* and make money for her husband; however, her husband need not take many responsibilities until he is fully mature."[57]

Despite the age difference, there is no doubt that many a *bori* has experienced genuine difficulties in adapting to her new role. More than occasionally, she simply gives up and returns to her own *familia*. In many instances, of course, the *bori* is treated well—as it is to everyone's advantage to have a smooth-running household.

The *bori,* naturally, is expected to bear children—lots of them. Birth-control measures apparently are not used. On the contrary, childless marriages are looked upon as a great misfortune.

Once in a great while gender roles are reversed, and the boy lives with the girl's *familia*. This situation might occur because the boy was unable to

[55]Gropper, *Gypsies in the City,* p. 158.
[56]Sutherland, *Hidden Americans,* p. 223.
[57]Sutherland, *Hidden Americans,* p. 223.

meet the bride price, or because he possessed some undesirable physical or mental trait. Such a person is called a "house Rom," and because he is under the domination of his parents-in-law, he loses the respect of the other men in the community.[58]

Changes in the System   Although arranged marriages and the *daro* remain integral parts of Gypsy culture, the system may not be so rigid as it once was. Like society at large, the Gypsy world is witnessing increased freedom on the part of its young people. The Salos note, for example, that at one time young Gypsies were not permitted to date without chaperones being present, a custom that is now often disregarded.

Parents are paying more heed to their children's wishes, and romantic love seems to be gaining in popularity. John Marks concludes that "parents still arrange the marriage, but now some young people fall in love whereas they used to marry without ever seeing each other beforehand."[59] Premarital chastity on the part of the young woman, however, has always been highly regarded—and it remains so.

Elopements are reported to be increasing, and some of the young men "are willing to defend their wives against their mothers."[60] Some adults are openly critical of the traditional marriage system, although others stoutly defend it. Thus far, the number of families that have actually dispensed with the *daro* is relatively small.

The "Passing" Question   In spite of the above changes, one Gypsy custom has remained unaltered: the prohibition against marriages with the *gadje*. Because the *gadje* are *marimé*, intermarriage with them is also *marimé*. To repeat, this is the Gypsy *definition of the situation*, and they show no signs of relenting on the issue.

Despite the prohibition, such marriages do take place—much to the chagrin of the Gypsy community. When they do occur, it is usually a marriage between a Gypsy man and a *gadji* (non-Gypsy woman). The frequency of such marriages is a matter of debate. In her study of Barvale, California, Sutherland found that Rom-*gadje* marriages comprised only 5.5 percent of all Gypsy marriages.[61]

Lauwagie maintains, however, that the Rom-*gadje* intermarriage rate must be fairly high, and that significant numbers of Gypsies are "passing"; that is, becoming part of the larger community. She argues that the Rom have a substantially higher birthrate than non-Gypsies, and that if a

[58]Sutherland, *Hidden Americans*, p. 175.
[59]Quoted in ibid., p. 219.
[60]Gropper, *Gypsies in the City*, p. 163.
[61]Sutherland, *Hidden Americans*, p. 248.

significant number of them did not pass every year, the Gypsy population would be much larger than it is at present.[62]

Economic Organization

Gypsies are not the world's best workers. They have traditionally been involved in marginal and irregular occupations: horse trading, scrap metal, fortune-telling, blacktopping (repairing driveways), auto-body repair, carnival work, and as musicians.

The Rom are quite willing to use banks, credit cards, charge accounts, and other appurtenances of a competitive economic system, but as a group they are loath to become involved in what they perceive to be the "rat race." Indeed, many Gypsies are quite adept at staying out of the race.

In his Chicago study, Polster found that the Gypsy men did not have steady jobs but worked only when they felt like it.[63] In their Canadian investigation, the Salos concluded that the Rom saw work as a necessity and not as a goal or way of life.[64] The same writers go on to say that "although the Gypsy is ingenious in adapting occupationally, the true commitment of each man is to earn the respect of his people. The pursuit of social prestige among his fellow Rom makes up a significant portion of his life. The Rom must be free to visit, gossip, politick, arrange marriages, and to undertake journeys connected with these activities. The earning of a livelihood is a secondary though necessary activity."[65]

The Rom face a number of economic and occupational handicaps. Many of their traditional pursuits have dried up. Horse trading has long been defunct. Metalwork, a traditional Gypsy standby (Kalderash actually means "coppersmith"), has largely been taken over by factory methods. Carnival work has been steadily reduced.

The Rom are also penalized by their lack of formal education, because all of the professional occupations require college and graduate training. And finally, a number of jobs—plumber, nurse, certain kinds of hotel and restaurant work—are off-limits to the Rom because of their *marimé* proscriptions.

All things considered, the wonder of it all is not that Gypsies have failed to climb the economic ladder, but that they have adapted as well

---

[62]Beverly Nagel Lauwagie, "Ethnic Boundaries in Modern States: *Romano Lavo-Lil* Revisited," *American Journal of Sociology* 85 (September 1979): 310–37.

[63]Gary Polster, "The Gypsies of Bunniton (South Chicago)," *Journal of Gypsy Lore Society* (January–April 1970): 142.

[64]Salo and Salo, *Kalderasha,* p. 73.

[65]Ibid., p. 93.

as they have. In fact, one could argue—as one writer does—that the Rom "fill a gap, albeit marginal, in the *gadje* system of production. They perform needed tasks, such as repair of shopping carts and seal-coating of driveways, that under usual economic conditions are too irregular or unprofitable to be attractive to larger, *gadje* economic enterprises."[66]

The *Kumpania* It is important to note that the Rom produce none of their own material needs. These must be procured from the *gadje*. And the procurement is often psychologically as well as materially rewarding: "Economic relationships of Rom with *gadje* are ideally exploitative. *Gadje* are by definition ignorant and foolish. The Rom value governing these relationships may be defined as 'living by one's wits.' The psychological satisfaction of 'putting one over' on the *gadje* is often, at least in anecdotal retrospect, valued even more highly than the actual profit made."[67]

According to Sutherland, "The *gadje* are the source of all livelihood, and with few exceptions the Rom establish relations with them only because of some economic or political motive."[68] The same author points out that economic relations among Gypsies are based on mutual aid, and that they consider it immoral to earn money from other Gypsies. The only legitimate source of income is the *gadje*, and "skill in extracting money from them is highly valued in Rom society."[69]

The economic unit in this "extraction" process is not the *familia* or the *vitsa*, but the *kumpania*, a unionlike organization composed of all male Gypsies living in a particular town or city. An effective *kumpania* would determine the number of blacktopping businesses or fortune-telling establishments to be permitted in the area, whether licensing or political protection was necessary, and so on. Such a *kumpania* would have the power to keep out unaffiliated *familiyi*. A loose *kumpania* would lack such power. *Familiyi* could come and go at will, making for an untenable social and economic situation.[70]

The *kumpania* takes on added meaning when seen from the vantage point of Gypsy culture. As part of their effort to maintain a sharp boundary between themselves and the *gadje*, the Rom avoid working with non-Gypsies. If necessary, they will accept employment in a factory or commercial establishment, but this is not their normal practice. Typically, Gypsies operate in terms of *wortacha*, small work units consisting of adult

[66]Beverly Nagel Lauwagie, "Explaining Gypsy Persistence: A Comparison of the Reactive Ethnicity and the Ecological Competition Perspectives," in Grumet, ed., *Papers*, p. 135.

[67]Matt T. Salo, "Kalderasha Economic Organization," in Salo, ed., *American Kalderasha*, p. 73.

[68]Sutherland, *Hidden Americans*, p. 65.

[69]Ibid.

[70]Ibid., pp. 34–35.

members of the same sex. Thus, two or three men might engage in black-topping or auto-body maintenance. Women might work in small-sized groups doing door-to-door selling or fortune-telling.

Quasi-Legal and Illegal Activities

Although most of the economic activities of the Rom are legal in nature, some are quasi-legal and others are clearly illegal. Blacktopping and sealing of driveways, for instance, are perfectly legal operations. But when the asphalt is laid at only one-third of the required thickness, and when the sealer has been surreptitiously diluted, the legality becomes questionable. Similarly, auto-body repair is legal, but if instead of actually removing the dents a thick coating of "paint and putty" is used, the practice is obviously unethical.

Fortune-Telling   Fortune-telling is a special case, for if there is one field that has been monopolized by the Rom, it is certainly fortune-telling. Indeed, the terms *Gypsy* and *fortune-teller* seem to go hand in hand—and with good reason.

> [A Rom] girl is expected to be a fortune-teller or reader and advisor, as early as thirteen or fourteen. Fortune-telling is regarded as an appropriate gender role and occupation among Gypsy women, and girls observe their mothers, aunts, and other female relatives performing this tradition every day.[71]

Fortune-telling is not a difficult occupation to learn, overhead expenses are negligible, and—depending on the location—business may be good. Clark cites the old Gypsy saying: "A fortune cannot be true unless silver changes hands."[72] And there have always been enough *gadje* who believe in this aphorism to make crystal gazing, palmistry, and card reading profitable ventures. For example, New York City police estimate that there are 200 fortune-telling establishments in the city, most of them run by Gypsies. Robin Pogrebin reports that ". . . some of them are operating legitimately, but scores of others are preying on vulnerable people hungry for psychic solace or metaphysical wisdom. Victims have paid out as much as $500,000 over an extended period of time . . . including a psychologist who was taken for $250,000.

The *Bujo*   On occasion, Gypsy fortune-tellers have been accused—and convicted—of flimflam, or *bujo*. The *bujo* is nothing more than a swindle,

---

[71]Ruth E. Andersen, "Symbolism, Symbiosis, and Survival: Roles of Young Women of the Kalderasha in Philadelphia," in Salo, ed., *American Kalderasha*, pp. 16–17.
[72]Clark, "Vanishing Vagabonds," p. 205.

whereby a gullible customer is cheated out of a goodly portion of his or her savings. One common ruse is called "switch the bag." In this instance, a bag of fake money or cut-up paper is substituted for a bag of real cash—which the customer had brought to the fortune-telling parlor in order to have the evil spirits or curse removed. (In Romany, *bujo* means "bag.")

According to the New York police, *bujo* swindles in excess of $100,000 have occurred. There are some Gypsy fortune-tellers "with a hundred or more arrests on their record."[73] Obviously, these are unusual cases; in fact, many Rom frown on the *bujo* because it causes bad community relations and is likely to bring police action.

At the same time, the *bujo* has occurred often enough to cause many areas to outlaw fortune-telling. Many major cities in the United States, as well as most Canadian regions, have banned fortune-telling. Some observers feel that the illegalization of fortune-telling may be the Gypsies' biggest problem. (Interestingly enough, in 1985, the California Supreme Court, overruling a lower court decision, found that an ordinance prohibiting fortune-telling for profit violated the constitutional right to free speech.

Legalities aside, the Rom continue to ply their trade, even though they are somewhat restricted in many areas. They often pose as "readers" and "advisors" rather than as seers. And this, in turn, may necessitate a measure of police "cooperation." But by one method or another, the Gypsies survive. Gypsies always survive.

Other Illegal Activities   What about other types of crime—robbery, burglary, rape, murder, and so on—are the Gypsies not involved in these, also? The answer is yes and no. They are seldom involved in crimes of violence, such as assault, mugging, rape, and murder. Stealing is another matter, however, and the police are likely to have strong feelings on the subject. Because Gypsies tend to commit crimes in novel ways, some twenty police officers across the United States have become specialists in Gypsy crime.

The blunt fact is that law-enforcement officers who come in contact with them believe that an undue proportion of American Gypsies are engaged in theft. Hancock says that such thinking is as ridiculous as thinking that most every Gypsy is a gifted fiddler.[74] District attorneys and prosecutors are likely to take a similarly dim view of the Rom, for it is both difficult and exasperating to try to send Gypsies to jail. To the Rom, time spent in prison means breaking a variety of *marimé* proscriptions. Consequently, an individual Gypsy will go to almost any length to avoid an actual jail sentence.

[73]Joseph Mitchell, "The Beautiful Flower: Daniel J. Campion," *New Yorker,* June 4, 1955, p. 46.
[74]Hancock, "American Roma," p. 17.

Lifestyle

Although generalizing about the lifestyle of any people is difficult, the Rom do have certain culture traits that set them apart from other groups. At or near the top of the list—and a trait that has been alluded to several times in the present account—is the Gypsies' indomitable love of freedom.

The Rom do not like to be tied down—by schools, businesses, material possessions, community affairs, financial obligations, or any other social or economic encumbrance. Their lifestyle reflects this predilection, and they are quite proud of it. Gypsies also associate freedom with fresh air and sunshine, a belief that goes back to the days of the caravan. In this earlier period, the Rom linked illness and diseases with closed spaces. Fresh air was believed to be a cure-all.

Travel and Mobility   Nowhere is the Gypsy love of freedom more apparent than in their fondness for travel. The Rom may no longer be nomads, but they remain a highly mobile people.[75] One important reason for their mobility is the economic factor. While many Rom have a home base, job opportunities may arise elsewhere. Roofing, auto-body repair, carnival work, summer harvesting—all may require periodic travel. In at least some cases, overseas journeys are involved. The Salos report that "the dispersion of the Rom, coupled with an efficient system of communication provided by the *gadje,* allows them to be aware of economic conditions far afield. Some of the Canadian Gypsies have contacts in or first-hand knowledge of conditions in Ireland, Wales, England, Belgium, France, Yugoslavia, Greece, the United States (including Hawaii), Mexico, Australia, and South Africa."[76]

The Rom also travel for social reasons: to visit friends and family, to find a *bori* (bride), to celebrate Gypsy holidays, to attend weddings and death feasts. Illness is a special category, and Gypsies will travel long distances to be with a sick relative.

Predictably, the Rom frequently travel for tactical reasons: to avoid the police, social workers, school authorities, landlords, and the like. This sort of travel—coupled with their aforementioned name changes—makes it exceedingly difficult for the authorities to track down and identify "wanted" Gypsies. In fact, during their travels, the Rom often pass themselves off as non-Gypsies.[77]

---

[75]Ronald Lee, "Gypsies in Canada," *Journal of Gypsy Lore Society* (January–April 1967): 38–39.

[76]Salo and Salo, *Kalderasha*, p. 76.

[77]Carol Silverman, "Everyday Drama: Impression Management of Urban Gypsies," in Matt T. Salo, ed., *Urban Anthropology, Special Issue* 11 (Fall–Winter 1982): 382.

A final reason for travel—and an important one—is simply that Gypsies like to move about. It makes them feel better, both physically and mentally. The Rom associate traveling with health and good luck, and regard settling down as associated with sickness and bad luck.[78]

The Life Cycle   Gypsy children arrive in large numbers, and they are welcomed not only by their *familia* but by the entire Gypsy community. Although they are supposed to show respect for their parents, youngsters are pampered. As John Kearney points out, the maxim "Children should be seen and not heard" was surely never coined by a Gypsy.[79] Corporal punishment is used sparingly—and reluctantly. A Romani child is the center of attention, at least until the next one comes along.

In many ways, Gypsy children are treated like miniature adults—with many of the same rights. Their wishes are respected in much the same manner as those of adults.[80] Subservience and timidity are not highly regarded by the Rom—and children are encouraged to speak up.

Gypsy children also spend much more time in adult company than do their non-Gypsy counterparts. This would almost have to be the case, because the Rom do not have much faith in formal education. While some government-funded Gypsy schools have been set up in various parts of the country, the Gypsy child's real training comes either at home or in what has been called "participatory education."[81] From the age of eight or nine, boys accompany their fathers on various work assignments, whereas the girls engage in household activities and start to observe fortune-telling routines.[82]

Although aggressiveness in children may be encouraged, adolescents—boys in particular—often need no encouragement. Like teenagers the world over, Romani youth do cause problems. They misbehave, they are disrespectful, they sometimes mingle with the *gadje*. In fact, Clark believes that a major problem in the Gypsy world right now is their adolescents, "who want to be teenagers first, and Gypsies second."[83] In most cases, however, maturity seems to serve as a panacea—with no harmful aftereffects.

In Gypsy culture, both sexes tend to achieve higher status as they get older. A young man marries, matures, and has children. And as his children grow, "so does his status." When he is ready and able to marry his youngsters off, his position in the community is generally secure.

As he grows older, he will be expected to solve family problems and settle altercations. He also acts as a repository for Gypsy traditions and

[78]Sutherland, *Hidden Americans*, pp. 51–52.

[79]John Kearney, "Education and the Kalderasha," in Salo, ed., *American Kalderasha*, p. 48.

[80]Gropper, *Gypsies in the City*, p. 130.

[81]Barbara Adams, Judith Okely, David Morgan, and David Smith, *Gypsies and Government Policy in England* (London: Heinemann, 1975), p. 136.

[82]Gropper, *Gypsies in the City*, p. 138.

[83]Clark, "Vanishing Vagabonds," p. 165.

culture. He will spend increasing time and energy "on the affairs of the band rather than on those of his own immediate family. He is becoming an Old One and a Big Man."[84]

A parallel sequence is followed in the case of the Gypsy female. As a young girl she is expected to assist in the housework. Later on—when she marries and becomes a *bori*—she is under the domination of her mother-in-law. But as she ages and has children of her own, she achieves a measure of independence and her status rises accordingly.

In many Gypsy communities, it is the woman rather than the man who deals with outsiders—school officials, social workers, and the like. And if she is successful in this regard, her position in the community becomes one of respect. She, too, is looked upon as a repository of wisdom, especially when it comes to dealing with the *gadje*.

Both sexes look forward to becoming parents, and both look forward to having grandchildren. The latter, it is said, signify true independence, for now the Old Ones have both their children and their children's children to look after them.

Gender Roles   The Rom have sharply defined gender roles. Indeed, one Gypsiologist states that "the male-female division is the most fundamental in Rom society."[85] The gender roles, furthermore, are characterized by separateness. Whether the occasion is a Gypsy function or simply day-to-day activity within the *familia*, men tend to gather on one side of the room, women on the other. The Rom are great talkers, but unless a special situation arises, the conversation will probably not be a mixed one.[86]

This separateness extends even to the marital sphere. Except for having a sex partner and someone besides his mother to cater to his needs, the groom's lifestyle changes very little. "Gypsy marriage is not predicated on romantic love, and the Rom frown on any display of affection between husband and wife. The husband wants the wife to perform services for him, but he continues to spend much of his time with his brothers and cousins. Husband and wife rarely go out together."[87]

Occupationally, also, sex roles tend to be definitive. Women tell fortunes; men are responsible for the physical layout of the fortune-telling parlor. Women cook and take care of the household chores. Men are responsible for the acquisition and maintenance of transportation facilities. In many areas, the women bring in more money than the men. In fact, Mitchell claims that, economically, one Gypsy woman is worth ten

---

[84]Gropper, *Gypsies in the City,* p. 165.
[85]Sutherland, *Hidden Americans,* p. 149ff.
[86]Ibid.
[87]Gropper, *Gypsies in the City,* p. 88.

men.[88] And while this may be an exaggeration, the women's income seems to be steadier and more reliable than the men's. It is the men, nevertheless, who normally hold the positions of power in the *familia*, the *vitsa*, and the *kumpania*.

Social Control

Romaniya—not an easy term to define—refers to the Gypsy way of life and their view of the world. It embraces their moral codes, traditions, customs, rituals, and rules of behavior. In brief, as Hancock puts it, *romaniya* is what the Gypsies consider to be right and acceptable.[89] It is the glue that holds their society together.

Romaniya is not a set of written rules, however. It is, rather, a built-in aspect of Gypsy culture. And because it is not a written code, the Rom face two problems: (1) Who determines what is and what is not *romaniya?* and (2) How should those who knowingly or unknowingly fail to comply be handled? These questions raise the whole issue of social control.

As used by sociologists, **social control** refers to techniques and strategies for preventing deviant human behavior in any society. **Informal social control** refers to social control that is carried out casually by ordinary people through such means as laughter, smiles, and rituals. **Formal social control** is social control carried out by authorized agents, such as police officers, judges, school administrators, and employers. Sociologically, informal control is considered more important than formal control because it is used all the time to maintain social control, and the Gypsies are a good case in point. The Rom have dispensed almost entirely with formal controls and rely largely on the informal variety.

Gossip, ridicule, and wisecracks, for example, are highly effective because the Rom are a closed society. Individual members cannot escape into anonymity—as is often the case in society at large. In any Gypsy community, therefore, reports and rumors of aberrant behavior lose no time in making the rounds.

Leadership: The *Rom Baro*   In most groups, leadership serves as an important instrument of social control, but in this respect Gypsies are not so fortunate. The Rom are not known for their leadership qualities. For one thing, Gypsy leadership is a function of age; that is, the older one gets, the greater knowledge one has of *romaniya*—and knowledge of *romaniya* is a recognized source of power. Almost by definition, then, the Rom seldom have any young leaders.

---

[88]Mitchell, "Beautiful Flower," p. 54.
[89]Hancock, "Gypsies," p. 443.

Another drawback is the tendency for Gypsy leadership to be fragmented. Theoretically at least, each *familia*, each *vitsa*, and each *kumpania* has its own leader. And while there is some overlap—and some real harmony—there is also much bickering and infighting, especially when different *natsiyi* are involved.

Leadership starts in the *familia*, where the head is known as a *phuro*. As the *phuro* ages and as his *familia* grows in size and strength, his standing in the community—and his power—increase accordingly. Should his judgment prove sound, should he show genuine interest in the various members of his *familia*, and should he prove effective in his dealings with the *gadje*, the *phuro* might become the leader of the *vitsa* or of a *kumpania*. He would then be known as a *Rom Baro* or "Big Man."

The Big Man has a dual function: to provide help and services for his followers, and to serve as a liaison with the non-Gypsy community, especially in a political sense. A Big Man rules by persuasion and discussion rather than by coercion, and should his persuasive powers fail, he may be replaced. Also, should he be convicted of a crime, his tenure as a *Rom Baro* may be terminated.

Although there are any number of Big Men in the Gypsy world, there really is no "King of the Gypsies," even though certain individuals often make the claim in order to ingratiate themselves with local authorities. For example, Silverman writes that the "status of King or Queen is invoked when securing hospital rooms or visiting privileges in funeral homes. One informant said: 'Any Gypsy who enters a hospital is automatically a King. They get better treatment. . . . There's no such animal in the Gypsy race as a King. But you go to the newspaper morgues in New York and get old papers, and every time a Gypsy died he was King. There has got to be 1,000 Kings.'"[90]

The most famous (or infamous) American Gypsy leader in modern times was Tene Bimbo, *Rom Baro* of the Bimbulesti *vitsa*. Tene Bimbo pursued power from coast to coast, and in the process he was reportedly arrested 140 times—for everything from petty larceny to murder! "If there are any charges that have not been brought against Tene Bimbo," one newspaper reported, "it is probably just an oversight."[91]

Tene Bimbo died in 1969 at the age of eighty-five, and there has been no *Rom Baro* like him since that time—and there probably never will be. Although his descendants speak fondly of him, and liken him to a modern Robin Hood, most Gypsies are glad that he is no longer on the scene. They feel that he brought unwanted notoriety to the Rom and was responsible for a distorted view of the Gypsy world. (Peter Maas's *King of*

[90]Carol Silverman, "Negotiating 'Gypsiness': Strategy in Context," *Journal of American Folk-Lore* 101 (July–Sept. 1988): 261–75.
[91]Cited in Maas, *King of the Gypsies*, p. 4.

the Gypsies, mentioned earlier, was based on the struggle for power that erupted after Tene Bimbo's death.)

The most famous (or infamous) European Gypsy leader in modern times was Ion Cioaba who "proclaimed himself King of All Gypsies Everywhere but wielded most of his meager influence as a political gad-fly in his native Romania . . ."[92] He died in 1997 at the age of 62.

In 1992, he held a coronation ceremony attended by 5,000 Gypsies and a bemused press. At the ceremony, he wore a solid gold crown weighing 13 pounds. Because Gypsies do not regulate who can or can't be royalty, it took only a few months for a rival Gypsy to set himself up as Emperor of All Gypsies.

Robert Thomas described Cioaba as "a portly man who usually shunned traditional Gypsy costumes in favor of a blue business suit, became an outspoken advocate of Gypsy rights, although rarely with much success. For example, he demanded that Germany stop the deportation of Gypsies to Romania and he sought reparations for the thousands of Gypsies who died in the holocaust."[93]

***Marimé* as Social Control**   Although Gypsy leadership may or may not be an effective source of social control, *marimé* has traditionally been a powerful instrument. Indeed, it may just be the most important factor in keeping the Rom in line. The reason is not hard to find, for *marimé* is more than a simple declaration that a person or thing is polluted. A Gypsy who has been declared *marimé* is ostracized by the entire group. Other Rom will have nothing to do with him or her.

Within the confines of their own society, Gypsies are gregarious. They are never really alone. Practically all of their waking moments are spent in the company of other Rom. Talking, laughing, working, arguing, gossiping, and, most important perhaps, eating—all are considered group activities. To be declared *marimé*, therefore, effectively cuts a Gypsy off from the very roots of his existence. He brings shame not only upon himself but upon his family.

Sutherland writes that *marimé* "in the sense of being rejected from social intercourse with other Rom is the ultimate punishment in the Gypsy society, just as death is the ultimate punishment in other societies. For the period it lasts, *marimé* is social death."[94] A permanent *marimé* sentence is

[92]Robert Thomas Jr., "Ion Cioaba, 62, of Romania, Self-Styled King of All Gypsies Dies," *New York Times,* February 27, 1977, Sec. B, p. 10.

[93]Thomas, "Ion Cioaba," p. 10. Perhaps Cioaba and activists like him were more effective than previously supposed. It was announced that Germany had created a $1.7 billion fund to compensate victims of the holocaust. The settlement was pressed for by Jewish interest groups. Germany's chancellor, Gerhard Schröder, announced, however, that Gypsies would share in the fund.

[94]Sutherland, *Hidden Americans,* p. 98.

not only the most severe form of Gypsy punishment, but if there is no way to win reinstatement, the person involved may actually prefer to end his life by suicide.[95]

The *Kris Romani*   Fortunately for the Rom, *marimé* need not be permanent. Accused Gypsies have the right to a trial to determine whether they are guilty as charged. As used by the Rom, **kris** refers to their system of law and justice, for they do not generally use the legal system of the *gadje*.

The *kris* consists of a jury of adult Gypsies, presided over by an impartial judge. Certain judges, or *krisatora*, are known for their wisdom and objectivity and are in great demand.[96] No judge, however, will accept a case unless the litigants agree beforehand to abide by the verdict. In addition to allegations involving *marimé*, *kris* cases include disputes over the bride price, divorce suits, feuds between *vitsi*, allegations of cheating, and so on.

A *kris* is convened only for serious reasons, because Gypsy trials are time consuming—and expensive. Personnel may come from other parts of the country, and it may be necessary to use a rented hall. In a lengthy trial, "courtroom" supplies may include food and liquor, payment for which must be made by the guilty party.[97]

Because of these factors, a *kris* is not likely to be held until all other attempts at adjudication have failed. Ordinary disputes, for example, may be settled by the *Rom Baro* or by informal debate. And even if these efforts should fail, a *divano*—a public discussion by concerned adults—can be requested.

Is the *kris* an effective instrument of social control? It is hard to say. In most cases, probably yes—but there is a built-in weakness to the system. Presumably, the disputants agree beforehand to abide by the decision. If they do not, theoretically at least, they have no recourse but to leave the Gypsy world. In the last analysis, however, what can really be done with Gypsies who refuse to obey their own laws? As Acton observes, "It is difficult today for any Gypsy group larger than the extended family to exert effective sanctions on their members."[98] Yoors puts it as follows: "The *kris*, or collective will of the Rom, is a structure in flux. . . . The effectiveness of

[95]Gropper, *Gypsies in the City*, p. 100.

[96]In August 1995, John Merino, perhaps the best-known *krisatora*, died in Los Angeles. A third-generation California Gypsy, Merino headed a twelve-member *kris* that meets twice monthly to settle disputes. Merino, a real estate investor and manager, was also captain of the Hawthorn police reserves. He said he wanted his life to send a message "to my people that it is possible to remain a Rom within that rich culture and heritage and yet be accepted in American society." Merino had attended El Camino College. (Myrna Oliver, "John Merino: Leader in L.A. Gypsy Council Dies," *Los Angeles Times*, August 14, 1995, p. A12.)

[97]See the discussion in Gropper, *Gypsies in the City*, pp. 81–102.

[98]Thomas Acton, *Gypsy Politics and Social Change* (London: Routledge & Kegan Paul, 1974), p. 99.

the pronouncements of the judges depends essentially on the *acceptance of their decisions by the majority of the Rom.* There is no direct element of coercion to enforce the rule of law. The Rom have no police force, no jails, no executioners."[99]

Prejudice and Discrimination

Prejudice and discrimination are realities that virtually all Gypsies must learn to face—and live with. The sad fact is that the Rom have been persecuted in practically every country they have ever inhabited. As was mentioned, the Nazis murdered hundreds of thousands during World War II. Entire *vitsi* were wiped out. Furthermore, Kenrick and Puxon note that during the many months of the Nuremberg war crimes trial, not a single Gypsy was ever called as a witness![100] Nor was any monetary restitution ever made to the surviving Romani groups.

In 1979, President Carter formed the *U.S. Holocaust Memorial Council;* its purpose was to establish a lasting memorial to all those who suffered and died in Hitler's death camps. It was not until 1987 that a Gypsy was invited to sit on the sixty-five-member council. In a report from the commission to President Carter, "the word Gypsy appears just once, along with Poles, Soviet prisoners of war, Frenchmen, Serbs and Slavs as 'others,' in an appendix. The total number of Romani dead is now estimated to be some 600,000. While this amounts to a tenth of the number of Jewish victims, in terms of the genocide of an entire people, the proportions are nevertheless similar."[101]

Eventually when the U.S. Holocaust Memorial Museum opened in 1993, a Gypsy wagon found in Czechoslovakia was included, as well as a violin of a Gypsy musician who was executed by the Germans and a traditional Gypsy woman's dress. Initial concerns about ignoring the tragedy of the Roma were set aside by various references to the lost.[102]

Although the wholesale slaughter ceased with the downfall of Hitler, Gypsies' problems with prejudice and discrimination continue in both Western and Eastern Europe. Nevertheless, before the fall of the Berlin Wall, Communist bloc states provided a measure of protection for their Gypsy populations.

Since the fall of the Berlin Wall, Gypsies have, perhaps, suffered more than any other group in Europe. For example, in response to hostility in

[99]Yoors, *Gypsies*, p. 174. (Italics added.)

[100]Kenrick and Puxon, *Destiny of Europe's Gypsies*, p. 189.

[101]Ian F. Hancock, *The Pariah Syndrome: An Account of Gypsy Slavery and Persecution* (Ann Arbor, MI: Karoma, 1988), p. 81.

[102]Jeshajahu Weinberg and Rina Elieli, *The Holocaust Museum in Washington* (New York: Rizzoli, 1995).

Romania, many Gypsies did what Gypsies often do: they moved. Of the 91,000 Romanians seeking entrance into Germany during an eight-month period in 1991, a total of 91 percent were Gypsies. The total number choosing Germany as a destination now nears half a million.[103]

For the most part they are unwanted anyplace in Europe. They serve as scapegoats, often the victims of skinhead and neo-Nazi violence. Their homes are torched. They are occasionally murdered. Even in the Czech Republic, the state purported to have had the smoothest transition from a totalitarian to a democratic structure, significant anti-Gypsy sentiment exists.

While organized anti-Rom feeling has been limited in the United States, it has not been absent. In 1998, New Jersey repealed its anti-Rom law adopted in 1917. This is thought to be the last such measure on the books in the United States.[104]

Vaclav Havel, president of the Czech Republic, noted cogently, "I have often compared the condition of our society, of all societies that have rid themselves of Communism, to the post-penitentiary condition of someone released from prison." Havel added, "A person who was accustomed for many years to living under rigorous rules that prevented him from making his own decisions suffers from a kind of shock, which manifests itself in many ways. It is a sudden change, which brings new freedom and responsibilities, and many find it difficult to cope with [such freedom].

"They find themselves in a state of uncertainty, in which they tend to look for pseudo-certainties." Havel added, "One of those might be submerging themselves in a crowd, a community, and defining themselves in contrast to other communities."[105] And, of course, Gypsy communities are always found wanting. Such thinking is at the heart of what sociologists define as *ethnocentrism* (introduced in our consideration of the Oneida), the practice of negatively judging another culture by the standards of one's own culture.

Under Communism, the public could not openly express its vituperative anti-Gypsy sentiment. But freedom of speech—even, to a great extent, inflammatory speech—is allowed in an open society. It belongs to everyone, including right-wing extremists. Anyone can organize a street demonstration for working up hatred. Since 1990 at least three Gypsies have been murdered by skinheads.

Havel sees the Czech "Gypsy problem" as a litmus test. "I think in the Czech Republic we have created all the basic institutions of democracy—

---

[103]Zoltan D. Barany, "Living on the Edge: The East European Roma in Postcommunist Politics and Societies," *Slavic Review* 53 (Summer 1994): 340.

[104]"The Religion and Culture of the Roma," accessed February 17, 2005, at www. religioustolerance.org/roma.htm.

[105]Henry Kamm, "Gypsies Find No Welcome from Czechs," *New York Times*, December 8, 1993, p. A7 (N).

political parties, a parliament, elections. Now building a civil society, to promote a climate that would encourage people to act as citizens in the best sense of the word and drive out manifestations of intolerance even without a threat of repression [becomes important]."[106]

Gypsy hatred is evident everywhere. In one community, Czech citizens persuaded city government to build a 15-foot wall between their housing and a Gypsy settlement across the street. The mayor of Usti Nad Labem does not apologize for the decision (now on hold due to the intervention of civil rights groups). "This wall is about one group that obeys the laws of the Czech Republic and behaves according to good morals, and about a group that breaks these rules—doesn't pay rent, doesn't use proper hygiene and doesn't do anything right. . . . This is not a racial problem it is a problem of dealing with decent and indecent people."[107]

Jane Perlez tells of the plight of a Gypsy, Stefan Miko, who owns a small construction company in the Czech community of Rokycany. He "cannot go to any of the bars to have a beer. His teenage children are barred from a nearby disco, his 14-year-old son is afraid to start classes at a school for bricklayers for fear of being beaten up by skinheads." Miko is thinking about emigrating to Canada.

Canada has canceled visa requirements for Czech citizens. After a television documentary appeared on Czech TV showing Gypsies in Canada leading useful, productive lives, flights to Canada were booked up two months in advance. In response, Liana Janackova, mayor of Ostrava, said she would ease their way: "the city would pay $600 toward the air fare of every Gypsy who wanted to go to Canada, provided the departing family handed its apartment over to the city." She justified her offer by saying it would be cheaper to pay Gypsies to leave than to continue to pay welfare benefits.[108]

Davis Joyce, on the faculty of East Central University in Ada, Oklahoma, was in 1995 and 1996 Soros Professor of American History at Kossuth University in Debrecen, Hungary. Shortly after moving to Debrecen, he noticed an apartment dumpster covered with graffiti. Joyce, just beginning to develop a feel for the Hungarian language, was nevertheless able to discern that the graffiti said, in part, "Gypsy, go back to India."[109]

Isabel Fonseca, in Bury Me Standing, describes the life of a family in post-Communist Albania. "Artani, the only Duka with a job, went to work before first light. He collected the garbage of the capital, for which he was paid eight hundred leks, or eight dollars, a month. . . . He went

[106]Ibid.
[107]Jane Perlez, "A Wall Not Yet Built Casts The Shadow of Racism," New York Times, July 2, 1998, Sec. A, p. 4.
[108]Jane Perlez, "Boxed in by Bias, Czech Gypsies Look to Canada," New York Times, August 31, 1997, Sec. 1, p. 3.
[109]Zellner interview of Davis Joyce 12-22-1996.

mainly for something to do, to walk into town in the cool dawn, to get away from [his village]."[110]

In many countries, only a few jobs are deemed appropriate for lowly Gypsies, among them garbage collector. Perhaps the graffiti discovered by Joyce was put on the dumpster so that Gypsies would be sure to see it.

On another occasion, Joyce, walking in downtown Debrecen with a friend, noticed billboards and posters advertising a café entertainer. He asked his companion, ordinarily a sensitive person, if the entertainer was well-known in Hungary. "No," his friend was emphatic, "he's just a stinking Gypsy." Joyce was to learn that prejudice toward Gypsies was widespread in Hungary, rampant in every social class.

Despite an apparent national prejudice, Hungary is far more forward-thinking than most Eastern bloc countries in what all regard as their "Gypsy Problem." Hungarian social scientists see the plight of the Rom as one of a lack of proper education. They estimate that 73 to 74 percent of the Rom population is functionally illiterate. Nevertheless, they note that more and more Gypsy children are now completing the eighth grade.

Education beyond the eighth form can continue in three ways: skilled-worker training school, vocational secondary education school, or gymnasium (roughly equivalent to high school in the United States).[111]

About 16 percent of Gypsy children now graduate from skilled-worker training schools, but sociologists note that "the majority of the vocational schools provide occupational skills for jobs for which there has been no demand on the market for years and will not be in the foreseeable future. Even with the certificates it is practically impossible to find a job." Nearly half of all non-Gypsy children go on to secondary schools, compared with 3 percent of Gypsy children.[112]

Solutions proposed to solve the "Gypsy education problem" include providing a bonus to parents who demand that their children continue in school, and a law raising the school dropout age to eighteen.[113]

Barany writes of other problems associated with education that require consideration.

> Although there were significant variations in the east European communist states' approaches to the Rom, the goal was everywhere to transform them into "useful" members of those societies. Initially, at least, the communist regimes' notion of assimilation appeared to be as simple as the "application of a formula: (Gypsy) + (Socialist wage-labor) + (Housing) = (Hungarian worker) + (Gypsy folklore)."

[110]Fonseca, Bury Me Standing, p. 23.
[111]Gabor Havas, Gabor Kertesi, and Istvan Kemeny, "The Statistics of Deprivation: The Roma in Hungary," Hungarian Quarterly (Summer 1995): 69.
[112]Ibid., p. 69.
[113]Ibid., p. 78.

. . . The means to realize Romany assimilation were often carelessly chosen and insensitively implemented, and at times resulted in increased exclusion of the Rom. For instance, the complex reasons for the low educational level of the Rom were frequently ignored. Romany children did not have the opportunity to study in their native tongue; those children who could not speak the languages of the dominant populations were at an obvious disadvantage, one that many prejudiced teachers "remedied" by putting them into classes for retarded children or into segregated institutions. At school they were discriminated against by their peers and teachers alike. No wonder many left school early, especially since their parents rarely insisted that they stay.[114]

Ethnographer Peter Szuhay writes of the Gypsy stereotype:

It is generally held that the Gypsies are not overfond of work, and welfare assistance is said to be their other major source of income, be this state social security benefits or grants to the needy from local authorities. Their large families are also looked on as part of a scheme to get something for nothing. Remarks about lack of cleanliness are commonplace, as are those of noisiness. The peasants also object to the drinking habits of Gypsies and to their profligacy. They immediately drink the little income they have, or the welfare benefits they get, and cannot make their money last to the end of the month. But it also bothers peasants if a Gypsy proves to be successful, and they doubt the honest origin of any Gypsy property. They object to them being generous or free with their money, be it in the village inn, or at family feasts or church functions. (Sociologists note that *in-group* virtues, such as supporting churches, are often considered *out-group* vices.)[115]

Remove the word *Gypsy* from the above stereotype, and fill in the blank with a racial stock or ethnic group viewed in the same way by some members of your community. One stereotype seems to fit all. Sociologists call this *blaming the victim*. Blaming the victim is the portraying the problems of racial and ethnic minorities as their fault rather than recognizing society's responsibilities.[116]

American Gypsies, too, continue to face prejudice and discrimination. Some large cities—such as New York and Chicago—have special police assigned to the Rom. In smaller towns, sheriffs will often escort Gypsies to the county line, glad to be rid of them.[117]

Why does the persecution continue? Some observers contend that it is a matter of ethnic prejudice, similar to that experienced by African Americans, Latinos, and certain immigrant groups. Others, however, simply feel that the Rom are perceived as nonproductive troublemakers. As one police official put it, "They're nothing but economic parasites." The truth of the matter can

---

[114]Barany, "Living on the Edge," pp. 326–27.

[115]Peter Szuhay, "Arson on Gypsy Row," *Hungarian Quarterly* v36 (Summer 1995): 83.

[116]William Ryan, *Blaming the Victim*, rev. ed. (New York: Random House, 1976).

[117]On numerous occasions, managers of large discount stores in rural areas have told Schaefer they will telephone fellow managers at stores in nearby towns that "Gypsies are on the way."

be debated, but that is beside the point. If people *perceive* of Gypsies as non-productive dissidents, then unfortunately for all concerned, prejudice and discrimination might be looked on as justifiable retaliation.

Adaptability: The Rom Trademark

Whether the Rom spend much time thinking about the causes of discrimination is doubtful. Being realists, they expect it. And being Gypsies, they learn to live with it. In fact, being Gypsies, they learn to live with a great many things they do not like or agree with. This, indeed, is the Gypsies' trademark: adaptability.

In addition to coping with discrimination, Gypsies have also had to adapt to a vast panorama of social change. Times change, customs change, governments change—sometimes it seems that nothing is permanent—but whatever the transformation, the Rom seem to make the necessary adjustments. They adapt without losing their cultural identity.

Examples of their adaptation are numerous. Gypsies have never had their own religion. In all their wanderings and migrations, they have simply adapted to the religion—or religions—of the host country. The same is largely true of clothing styles, although as Polster observes, Gypsy women often do wear colorful outfits.[118] And aside from a seeming fondness for spicy dishes, the Rom adapt to the foods and cuisine of the country or area they are living in.

During the days of the caravan, Gypsy nomads camped outside the towns and cities—off the beaten track. When changing conditions forced them from the road, they took to the cities, where they have adapted rather well. Today, most of the American Rom are to be found in urban areas.

When horses were replaced by mechanized transportation, the Rom adapted. Instead of being horse traders, they learned auto-body repair and motor maintenance. When metalworking—long a Gypsy specialty—was superseded by factory-type technology, the Rom turned to roofing and blacktopping. When fortune-telling became illegal in various places, Gypsies became "readers" and "advisors." And when these latter efforts were challenged, the Rom resorted to bribery and police "cooperation."

Gypsies make no claim to being quality workers, or even to being industrious. But both in America and elsewhere they are versatile. *They adapt.* As one Gypsy remarked, "Put me down anywhere in the world, and I'll make a living."[119]

Some Gypsies manage to do well even when they are not "making a living." Despite their literacy handicap, and despite their unfamiliarity with

[118]Polster, "Gypsies of Bunniton," p. 139.
[119]Adams et al., *Gypsies and Government Policy,* p. 132.

(and disdain for) documentary records, they have learned to adapt to the welfare bureaucracy with—in many cases—remarkable results.

The Future

What does the future hold for the Rom in the United States? Not even a Gypsy with a crystal ball can tell. It is possible, nevertheless, to make some educated guesses.

To begin with, Gypsy activism will probably increase—somewhat. On the international scene, meetings such as the World Romani Congress have had some success in focusing attention on Gypsy problems. Two notable efforts resulted. Gypsies were included in billion dollar settlements with Swiss banks and German industries guilty of using slave labor during the holocaust. In the United States, the American Gypsy Organization and other groups have also been established. Such organizations cannot help but have a positive effect on Gypsy–*gadje* relations.[120]

At the same time, Gypsy activism has inherent limits. The American Rom are a low-profile group. They are often difficult to find, let alone activate! They have traditionally resorted to travel and avoidance rather than organization and demonstration. Mass protest, for example—often used by other minorities—would hardly strike a responsive chord in most Gypsy communities. Stranger things have happened, of course. Hoffman reports that in 1978, "British Gypsies threatened to block highways unless they received better treatment from local authorities." Whether Rom in the United States would employ such tactics is problematical.[121]

Looking ahead, the widespread illiteracy that has characterized the Rom will most likely be reduced—somewhat. Schools for Gypsy youngsters have been set up in California; Washington, D.C.; Philadelphia; Chicago; Seattle; and Camden, New Jersey; and the trend may continue. As Hancock points out, however, failures have thus far outnumbered successes, and "the majority of Gypsies remain opposed to schooling of any kind."[122]

Assuming that their illiteracy rate is reduced, the position of the Rom in the job market should also improve—somewhat. Even now, there are Gypsies to be found in white-collar and professional positions. Their number is relatively small, however, for the Rom have scarcely penetrated the realm of college and graduate education.

Still looking ahead, relations between the Rom and the *gadje* may improve—somewhat. In many ways, American Gypsies have cut them-

---

[120]See Hancock, "Gypsies," pp. 444–45.
[121]Paul Hoffman, "Here Come the Gypsies: Call Them Citizens," *New York Times,* April 30, 1978, p. E8.
[122]Hancock, "Gypsies," p. 444.

selves off from the economic rewards of the larger society. To partake of these rewards they will probably have to change their attitude toward the *gadje*, and the extent to which they will do this can only be conjectured.

The Rom may also soften the rules pertaining to *marimé*—somewhat. In certain Gypsy communities, these rules have already been softened, and if the trend continues, improvements in the relations with the larger society may be one of the by-products. At the same time, most Rom know full well that the concept of *marimé* lies at the heart of the Gypsy world. Without *marimé*, social control would be difficult to maintain. Whether any further erosion of the rules will occur, therefore, remains to be seen.

To sum up, any changes in the Gypsy way of life, or in *romaniya*, will be moderate rather than drastic. The Rom are keenly aware of what they are and who they are—and they are proud of it. And while they may make some changes that will improve their adaptation to the larger society, they will probably not become a functioning part of that society. They will not assimilate. They will not give up their unique identity. They will not renounce their culture. Thus, in all probability they will continue to feel the twin prongs of discrimination and harassment, albeit on a reduced scale.

Exactly how much change the Rom will allow—or what form these changes will take—is debatable. But one thing seems certain: the Gypsies will survive. Gypsies always survive.

KEY TERMS

Assimilation, p. 90
Bori, p. 105
Counterculture, p. 91
Daro, p. 104
Familia, p. 101
Familiyi, p. 97
Formal social control, p. 114
Gadje, p. 91

Informal social control, p. 114
Kris, p. 117
Marimé, p. 97
Melalo, p. 99
Natsiyi, p. 95
Romaniya, p. 114
Social control, p. 114
Vitsa, p. 103

SOURCES ON THE WEB

www.errc.org
The European Roma Rights Center based in Hungary is dedicated to combat anti-Roma discrimination and abuse.

http://romani.org
This website is dedicated to the Rom and their recognition as a people and as a nation.

http://www.gypsyloresociety.org
An international association of persons interested in Gypsy and Traveler Studies founded in Great Britain in 1888.

www.soros.org/initiatives/roma/links
A variety of Rom-related initiatives in Europe are outlined at this Web site.

SELECTED READINGS

Andersen, Ruth E. "Symbolism, Symbiosis, and Survival: Role of Young Women of the Kalderasha in Philadelphia." In *The American Kalderasha: Gypsies in the New World,* edited by Matt T. Salo, pp. 11–28. Hackettstown, NJ: Gypsy Lore Society, 1981.

Beck, Sam. "The Romanian Gypsy Problem." In *Papers from the Fourth and Fifth Annual Meetings, Gypsy Lore Society, North American Chapter,* edited by Joanne Grumet, pp. 100–109. New York: Gypsy Lore Society, 1985.

Clark, Marie Wynne. "Vanishing Vagabonds: The American Gypsies." *Texas Quarterly* 10 (Summer 1967): 204–10.

Clebert, Jean-Paul. *The Gypsies.* London: Vista, 1963.

Cortiade, Marcel. "Distance between Romani Dialects." *Newsletter of the Gypsy Lore Society, North American Chapter* 8 (Spring 1985): 1ff.

Dodds, Norman. *Gypsies, Didikois, and Other Travelers.* London: Johnson, 1976.

Fonseca, Isabel. *Bury Me Standing: The Gypsies and Their Journey.* New York: Knopf, 1995.

Friedman, Victor A. "Problems in the Codification of a Standard Romani Literary Language." In *Papers from the Fourth and Fifth Annual Meetings, Gypsy Lore Society, North American Chapter,* edited by Joanne Grumet, pp. 55–75. New York: Gypsy Lore Society, 1985.

Gmelch, George. *The Irish Tinkers.* Prospect Heights, IL: Waveland Press, 1985.

Gropper, Rena C. *Gypsies in the City.* Princeton, NJ: Darwin, 1975.

Hancock, Ian F. "Gypsies." In *Harvard Encyclopedia of American Ethnic Groups,* edited by Stephan Thernstrom, pp. 440–45. Cambridge, MA: Harvard University Press, 1980.

———. *The Pariah Syndrome: An Account of Gypsy Slavery and Persecution.* Ann Arbor, MI: Karoma, 1988.

Kearney, John. "Education and the Kalderasha." In *The American Kalderasha: Gypsies in the New World,* edited by Matt T. Salo, pp. 43–54. Hackettstown, NJ: Gypsy Lore Society, 1981.

Lee, Ronald. *Goddam Gypsy: An Autobiographical Novel.* Montreal: Tundra, 1971.

Lockwood, William G. "Balkan Gypsies: An Introduction." In *Papers from the Fourth and Fifth Annual Meetings, Gypsy Lore Society, North American Chapter,* edited by Joanne Grumet, pp. 91–99. New York: Gypsy Lore Society, 1985.

Maas, Peter. *King of the Gypsies.* New York: Viking, 1975.

Marre, Jeremy, and Hannah Charlton. *Beats of the Heart.* New York: Pantheon, 1985.

Mayall, David. *Gypsy Identities 1500–2000: From Egipcyans and Moon-men to the Ethnic Romany.* London: Routledge, 2004.

Nemeth, David. "Gypsy Taskmasters, Gentile Slaves." In *The American Kalderasha: Gypsies in the New World,* edited by Matt T. Salo, pp. 29–41. Hackettstown, NJ: Gypsy Lore Society, 1981.

Okely, Judith. *The Traveler Gypsies.* New York: Cambridge University Press, 1982.

Pippin, Roland N. "Community in Defiance of the Proscenium." In *The American Kalderasha: Gypsies in the New World,* edited by Matt T. Salo, pp. 99–133. Hackettstown, NJ: Gypsy Lore Society, 1981.

Polster, Gary. "The Gypsies of Bunniton (South Chicago)." *Journal of Gypsy Lore Society* (January–April 1970): 136–51.

Rehfisch, Farnham, ed. *Gypsies, Tinkers, and Other Travelers.* New York: Academic Press, 1975.

Salo, Matt T., ed., *The American Kalderasha: Gypsies in the New World.* Hackettstown, NJ: Gypsy Lore Society, 1981.

Salo, Matt, and Sheila Salo. *The Kalderasha in Eastern Canada.* Ottawa: National Museums of Canada, 1977.

Silverman, Carol. "Everyday Drama: Impression Management of Urban Gypsies." In Matt T. Salo, ed., *Urban Anthropology, Special Issue* 11 (Fall–Winter 1982): 377–98.

Sutherland, Anne. *Gypsies: The Hidden Americans.* New York: Free Press, 1975.

Tong, Diane. "Romani as Symbol: Sociolinguistic Strategies of the Gypsies of Thessaloniki." In *Papers from the Fourth and Fifth Annual Meetings, Gypsy Lore Society, North American Chapter,* edited by Joanne Grumet, pp. 179–87. New York: Gypsy Lore Society, 1985.

Yoors, Jan. *The Gypsies.* New York: Simon & Schuster, 1967.

———. *Crossing: A Journal of Survival and Resistance in World War II.* New York: Simon & Schuster, 1971.

———. *The Gypsies of Spain.* New York: Macmillan, 1974.

CHAPTER FOUR

CHRISTIAN SCIENTISTS

- Mary Baker Eddy
- Beginnings of Christian Science
- Early Critics
- Building the Mother Church and Other Institutions
- The *Christian Science Monitor*
- Mary Baker Eddy's Legacy
- Organization

- Church Roles
- Christian Scientists: Cult, Sect, or What?
- Who Are Christian Scientists?
- Contemporary Problems
- Spiritual Healing
- Finances and Membership
- The Future

During her lifetime, Mary Baker Eddy, the founder of Christian Science, was the most talked about, written about, religious leader in America.[1] Accounts of her life and works range from adoration to accusations of charlatanism and worse. How much was true and how much was fiction is difficult to determine. Her most active years, from the mid-nineteenth century through the first years of the twentieth century, coincided with the darkest era of muckraking journalism, a time when reporters rarely let facts get in the way of a good story. Based on little more than hearsay and gossip are accusations that Mary Baker Eddy was a prostitute, plagiarized her religious theory, and abetted her husband in a conspiracy to commit murder. None of these charges appear to be true.

What is true of Mary Baker Eddy is that she founded a church and successfully promoted a religious belief system that conflicted with the teachings of Calvinism, the dominant religious force in nineteenth-century New England. This led her to be denounced by the established churches. It also made her newsworthy. Attacked from both press and pulpit, Mary Baker Eddy was despised by many. As occurs with almost any "new" religion,

---

[1]Mary Baker Eddy wanted to call her church the Church of Christ but there already was a group by that name. Consequently, she added a comma and the word *Scientist* to make the official name, Church of Christ, Scientist. The church has become informally known as Christian Science by both members and nonmembers. We are using that accepted term, Christian Scientists, throughout this chapter.

the public was, for the most part, willing to accept anything sordid that was written or said about Christian Science's founder as true.

Not all of Mary Baker Eddy's critics were preachers and pressmen. Some were simply intellectual atheists. For them, religion was not rejected out-of-hand, but carefully thought through—and found wanting. Mark Twain (Samuel Clemens) was such a person. Although he found little merit in any religion, he particularly disliked Mary Baker Eddy and her teachings. In one of his books, he described her as "grasping, sordid, penurious, famishing for everything she sees—money, power, glory— vain, untruthful, jealous, despotic, arrogant, insolent, pitiless where thinkers and hypnotists are concerned, illiterate, shallow, incapable of reasoning outside of commercial lines, immeasurably selfish."[2]

Twain then went on to describe how her followers felt about her[3]—just the opposite of his own feelings! "Mrs. Eddy is patient, gentle, loving, compassionate, noble-hearted, unselfish, sinless, widely cultured, splendidly equipped mentally, a profound thinker, an able writer, a divine personage, an inspired messenger whose acts are dictated from the Throne, and whose every utterance is the Voice of God."[4]

Few people were ambivalent about Mary Baker Eddy. She inspired and expected great loyalty from her followers, while those not in her camp tended to view her as Mark Twain did. Oddly, however, there was no indication during the first fifty years of her life that her name would be indelibly etched in the annals of American religious history.

She also holds the distinction of one of the few *women* to found a new religious faith that continues to be practiced today. She led a remarkable life, as one biographer put it, "Conventional in her twenties, weak in her thirties, struggling in her forties, a social outcast in her fifties, indefatigable worker in her sixties, famous in her seventies, formidable in her eighties."[5]

Mary Baker Eddy

Born at Bow, New Hampshire, on July 16, 1821, Mary was the youngest of six children born to Mark and Abigail Baker. Although neither parent had the benefit of a formal education, both were well-read in the great literary works, philosophy, and religion.

---

[2]Mark Twain, *Christian Science* (New York: Collier & Son, 1907), p. 208.

[3]The most recent literature pro Christian Science is Jillian Gill's *Mary Baker Eddy* (Reading, MA: Preseus Books, 1998). A recent apostate literature is Caroline Fraser's *God's Perfect Child; Living and Dying in the Christian Science Church* (New York: Henry Holt, 1999).

[4]Twain, op. cit., pp. 208–9.

[5]Gill, *Mary Baker Eddy*, p. xvii.

In her book *Retrospection and Introspection,* Mary Baker Eddy describes her father as a strict, unbending Calvinist, concerned with the "final judgment day, the peril of endless punishment, and a God devoid of mercy to unbelievers."[6] She did not hold with her father's biblical interpretations, and the stress brought on by constant disagreement with him is said to have caused her excessive anxiety and worry. In fact, she was so overwrought as a child that a doctor recommended that she drop out of school.

The extent of her nervous disability is not known, but withdrawing a child from school, particularly a girl, required little explanation in the first part of the nineteenth century. Mary Baker's lack of formal education, however, does not mean that she was uneducated. With the help of a brother, Albert, a graduate of Dartmouth and a law partner of Franklin Pierce, Mary was well schooled in religion, philosophy, literature, and law.[7] Nevertheless, though she was to become a prolific writer, her literary style was adversely affected by her lack of formal education. The first editions of *Science and Health,* her Christian Science doctrinal writings, are full of errors. After the church was solidly established, professionals were hired to edit her manuscripts.

First Attempt at Marriage   Mary Baker was to marry three times. Her first marriage in 1843 to a struggling young businessman, George Washington Glover, lasted less than six months. By all accounts, it was a happy marriage. With her husband, she moved to Charleston, South Carolina, where he built and sold houses. Also on his business agenda was construction of a cathedral in Haiti. While gathering materials for the latter project, he contracted a fever and died within a few days.[8]

After her husband's death, Mary Glover returned to New Hampshire, pregnant and penniless. Her only child, George Jr., was born in her parent's home, but he did not remain there long. Mary's poor health, exacerbated by the death of her husband and the trip back to New Hampshire, left her unable to care for the child. A servant of the Bakers, Mahala Sanborn, was assigned the task of rearing George Jr. A bond developed between the two, and when Mahala married, her request to take the child with her was granted. Soon after, the only child that Mary Glover was

---

[6]Quoted in Charles S. Braden, *Christian Science Today* (Dallas: Southern Methodist University Press, 1958), p. 13.

[7]Albert Baker was elected to the New Hampshire House of Representatives at the age of twenty-nine, and served three one-year terms, in 1839, 1840, and 1841. He served as chairman of the judiciary committee in 1841, the year of his death. Franklin Pierce was the fourteenth president of the United States.

[8]Biographers with a negative slant claim that Mr. Glover was a wealthy slave owner. There is no evidence that this was so.

ever to bear moved to Minnesota with his adopted family. Contact with George Jr. thereafter was infrequent and usually unpleasant.

Living in her parents' home as an adult was not always easy for Mary. Abigail, her mother, often had to act as a buffer between her husband's pietism and Mary's less-than-enthusiastic acceptance of Calvinism. In *Historical Sketches,* a biography published by Christian Science, it is said that "of all the persons with whom Mary Baker Eddy came in contact, her mother must have affected her the most. She loved her mother devotedly, and they were together most of the time during the years which included the most impressionable part of the daughter's life."[9]

Except for brief periods, Mary lived with her parents until she was twenty-nine years old. Her mother passed away in 1849, and she stayed on with her father until he remarried a year later. Having no independent income and still in poor health, she moved in with a sister, Abigail Tilton. Thenceforth, she was to have little to do with her father.

Second Attempt at Marriage   In 1853, Mary married Dr. Daniel Patterson, a dentist and homeopathic practitioner.[10] The couple took up residence at Franklin, New Hampshire.

Church biographer Clifford Smith notes that "Patterson was a capable dentist, and popular socially, but as the future would prove he was deficient in other qualities essential to financial and marital success."[11] Perhaps Smith understated the case. The handsome dentist, simply put, was a ladies' man. His practice involved frequent professional visits to nearby communities. On these trips it was not uncommon for him to develop amorous liaisons. Apart from his infidelities, Patterson was a poor provider. On one occasion he convinced Mary to mortgage her personal possessions to invest in a sawmill at North Groton, New Hampshire. The venture lasted five years and ended in total failure. Creditors took everything: furniture, books, and a gold watch belonging to Mary.

After losing the sawmill, the Pattersons moved frequently, one step ahead of their creditors. Dr. Patterson resumed his dental career. Unfortunately, he also resumed his "professional trips." In fact, by 1866 Dr. Patterson had abandoned his wife completely. In 1873 Mary obtained a divorce and changed her name back to Glover.

---

[9]Clifford P. Smith, ed., *Historical Sketches* (Boston: Christian Science Publishing Society, 1941), p. 16.

[10]Homeopathy is a system of medical treatment based on the theory that disease can be cured by giving the sufferer small doses of drugs similar to the agent that caused the disease. Mary Baker Glover hoped that Dr. Patterson could treat her many illnesses with this method.

[11]Ibid., p. 44.

A Fall on the Ice   The following news item appeared in the *Lynn* (Massachusetts) *Reporter* on Saturday, February 6, 1866:

> Mrs. Mary Patterson of Swampscott fell upon the ice near the corner of Market and Oxford streets on Thursday evening and was severely injured. She was taken up in an insensible condition and carried into the residence of S. M. Bubier, Esq., nearby, where she was kindly cared for during the night. Dr. Cushing, who was called, found her injuries to be internal and of a severe nature, inducing spasms and intense suffering. She was removed to her home in Swampscott yesterday afternoon, though in a very critical condition.[12]

On the Sunday following her accident, a neighbor, fearing that Mary was near death, summoned a minister. While the neighbor waited at her bedside for the clergyman, Mary began reading her Bible. In time, she rose from her sickbed and announced herself free of pain. In later years, she was to recall that her reading of Matthew 9:2 led to her healing: "Arise, take up thy bed, and go unto thine house."[13]

For Mary, it was an awakening. Long interested in spiritual healing, she now laid claim to healing herself. With her recovery, "Christian Science" was born, together with the associated practice of spiritual healing.

"Science," as used by Mary in naming her new religion Christian Science, differs from today's understanding of the term. In her own words, "Science, properly understood, refers only to the laws of God and to His government and of the universe inclusive of man."[14] Stephen Gottschalk writes that Mary felt "that Christian Science was scientific because it provided a method or rule for demonstrating universal divine law."[15]

Beginnings of Christian Science

Following her accident on the ice, and now convinced of the soundness of her own spiritual healing, Mary Baker Glover (as she now preferred to be called) set out to convince others that spiritual healing was attainable.[16] But major obstacles had to be overcome, especially in the economic sphere. Shortly after her accident, Dr. Patterson "eloped" with the wife of

[12]Quoted in Norman Beasley, *The Cross and the Crown* (Boston: Little, Brown, 1952), p. 3.
[13]Ibid.
[14]Mary Baker Eddy, *Science and Health with Key to the Scriptures* (Boston: Christian Science Board of Directors, 1934), p. 128.
[15]Stephen Gottschalk, *The Emergence of Christian Science in American Religious Life* (Berkeley: University of California Press, 1973), p. 26.
[16]Mrs. Eddy would never use the name Patterson again. After her subsequent marriage to Asa Eddy, she sometimes referred to herself as Mary Baker Glover Eddy, Mary Baker G. Eddy, or, simply, Mary Baker Eddy.

a well-known resident of Lynn. And to add to her woes, her father died. Although a man of substantial means, he left her nothing.

Mary's sister Abigail Tilton again tried to rescue her. According to biographer E. Mary Ramsay, "Mrs. Tilton wrote to ask Mary to come and live next door to her, offering to build her a suitable house; but she attached a condition to this otherwise attractive proposal to which Mary could not agree. She must promise to attend the Tiltons' church and give up her theory of divine healing."[17]

Unwilling to give up her beliefs, Mary Baker Glover lived in boarding houses and in the homes of friends for the next four years, some providing room and board in exchange for her teachings. She was not welcome long in any one place because of her outspoken beliefs.

During the formative years of Christian Science, Mary was barely able to keep a roof over her head. Nevertheless, it was during these early years that she put her thoughts on paper, ultimately producing the doctrinal manual of the church, *Science and Health with Key to the Scriptures.*

As was her bent, she often allowed friends and fellow boarders to read her developing manuscripts. One interested reader was Hiram Crafts, a shoe factory employee, who was to become Mary's first serious student. After months of study, he advertised himself as a doctor, guaranteeing the return of fees if clients were unhappy with the results. Mr. Crafts was moderately successful in this venture.

In late 1867, Mary Baker Glover moved to Amesbury, Massachusetts, to the home of Mrs. Sarah Bagley, another student. While she was there, twenty-one-year-old Richard Kennedy, a distant relative of Sarah Bagley, took an interest in her teachings.

Two years later, Kennedy convinced Mary to move with him to Lynn, Massachusetts, and establish a healing practice. Biographer Norman Beasley describes the arrangement: "Kennedy proposed that they share equally in any income he might receive from his practice, in return for which he was to be given help with patients, and, also, was to receive continued instruction. Mary agreed to his proposition. It permitted her to spend time on a book that was beginning to take shape in her mind."[18]

Although the arrangement did not last long (two years), it was profitable for both partners. There was a steady stream of patients, and those healed were solicited to take courses in spiritual healing themselves. A class was announced, and a set fee of $300 established. The average worker during the 1870s earned less than $1,000 a year. But Beasley reminds us that "if three hundred dollars for a dozen lessons seems high, . . . it should not be forgotten that by this modest expenditure one could set himself up as a Doctor and

[17]E. Mary Ramsay, *Christian Science and Its Discoverer* (Boston: Christian Science Publishing Society, 1955), p. 52.
[18]Beasley, *The Cross and the Crown*, p. 22.

charge fees comparable to those of the orthodox medical practitioners of the day."[19] The tuition charges established Mary Baker Glover as a professional.

The partnership with Dr. Kennedy ended abruptly. In the process of his ministrations, Kennedy practiced manipulation, massaging the head and solar plexus of each client. Mary Baker Glover instructed her pupil to stop the practice, arguing that all healing flows from God, not from the fingers of the practitioner. Kennedy refused, and the partnership ended.

In the first edition of *Science and Health*, Mary Baker Glover wrote: "Sooner suffer a doctor infected with smallpox to be about you, than come under the treatment of one that manipulates his patients' heads, and is a traitor to science."[20] Laying on of the hands, as practiced in Pentecostal churches, has never been a part of Christian Science practice.

For three years following the break with Kennedy, Mary lived as she had before, in boarding houses and in the homes of students. In 1875 she used the money she had earned in her short association with Dr. Kennedy to buy a house of her own in Lynn. Although she was to move several times after that, it was always to a home that she owned. Her gypsylike existence of nearly thirty years was over.

Was Mary Baker Eddy a Charismatic?   The term *charisma* is used very broadly. We introduced the term in Chapter 2, to refer to the appeal that John Humphrey Noyes apparently had over his followers in the Oneida Community. Laypeople and the media alike are quick to use the term when describing a politician, rock musician, or movie star. By this they mean that the person in question is endowed with special abilities, setting him or her apart from ordinary mortals.

Max Weber, the giant of German sociology, had an altogether different understanding of the concept "charisma." While he did not deny that charismatic leaders could possess unique abilities, he recognized, too, that such persons could be quite ordinary. The criterion that sets such people apart from the bulk of humanity is that followers attribute super-human characteristics to them.

Most of Mary's early followers were from working-class backgrounds, and more than a few were attracted to her for only a very short time. Unlike Father Divine, whose following grew to enormous proportions after the death of one of his critics, Judge Lewis J. Smith (see Chapter 6), Mary seemed to lose one convert for every two she gained. Those who left, like Dr. Kennedy, could not or would not live up to the standards she had set. A trait common to the charismatic personality is "having all the answers." It was not possible to disagree with Mary on even minor issues and remain a close associate.

---

[19]Ibid., p. 27.
[20]Cited in Braden, *Christian Science Today*, p. 28.

Third Marriage   Once established in her own home, Mary surrounded herself with friends and students. Of all her students, none was as devoted as Asa Eddy, a sewing-machine salesman. After a short courtship, the two were married on New Year's Day, 1877 (see the Timeline). After his wife deemed him suitably trained, Eddy was the first to assume the title "Christian Science Practitioner."[21]

The Christian Scientists

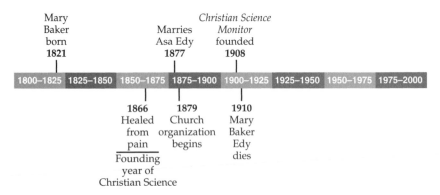

By all accounts, the marriage was a happy one, lasting until Asa Eddy's death in 1882. Much was made of his passing, especially in the press. If indeed spiritual healing was possible, why didn't she heal her husband? Indeed, if he himself was a practitioner, why didn't he heal himself?

The main thrust of Christian Science healing is rooted in the belief that "God created man minus a capacity for sickness and when [the recipient of healing] fully grasps that, he is exempt from it."[22] In other words, disease is part of the material world, a false world, and not part of God's spiritual world subject to God's love and divine law. The sole function of the practitioner is to heal with prayer.

Mary reported to the press that two factors contributed to her husband's demise. One, he had not asked for her help. She argued that healing without the consent of the sufferer is "promiscuous mental treatment." Therefore, she could not help him.

In the second place, she believed there was more than a possibility that her husband was the victim of "mental malpractice"—murdered! If spiritual thought transferred to a patient can produce positive effects, then the use of thought for evil purposes is also possible. Mary believed that a dis-

---

[21]*Christian Science Practitioner* is the term used today for a trained Christian Science healer. Before Asa Eddy adopted the title "practitioner," graduates of Mrs. Eddy's classes assumed the title "doctor."

[22]*Mary Baker Eddy's Christian Science* (Boston: Christian Science Publishing Society, 1990), p. 17.

affected student, Edward Arens, was responsible for her husband's death—that Arens had in fact murdered him with evil thoughts.

Although nothing ever came of the murder allegation, Mary Baker Eddy was experiencing a variety of other difficulties, especially from within the group.

Early Critics

Because of financial need, Mary's home in the beginning was also a boarding house. Students often chose to live in her residence while taking courses. As noted earlier, courses in Christian Science healing were expensive. Not all of her students were happy with her teachings, and some left her home embittered. Several of these students claimed that Mary Baker Eddy was not just prostituting the Bible but was guilty of prostitution in the meaner sense of the word. None of these allegations were ever substantiated. However, reports that she was contentious, sometimes rude, and tight with the dollar seem to be based on fact.

You will recall that Mark Twain labeled her "penurious" and "vain," with a hunger for "power and glory." Later biographers suggest that she may have suffered from megalomania, a mental disorder involving delusions associated with wealth and power. But it must be remembered that until she was well into her fifties, she had very little money, often living off the charity of others. Not wanting to fall into such circumstances again, she may have been overly cautious with money. With regard to the accusations of hungering for power and glory, it can be argued that she was zealously promoting a "religious discovery" she felt obligated to share with the world.

Also, critics may have punished Mary Baker Eddy for being a "public" woman. Women, during the period in question, acting outside the strongly colored, stereotyped images set for them by men, were often subjected to disapproval and scorn.

Gender Role Behavior   In spite of her success, Mary Baker Eddy faced a difficulty sometimes overlooked by historians: she operated outside the norms of what sociologists call expected *gender role* behavior. Gender roles are the expectations regarding the proper attitudes and activities of male and females. Gender roles come from learned behavior, and it is on the basis of this behavior that both the participant and society are able to act with reasonable smoothness. During Mary Baker Eddy's lifetime, gender role behavior was sharply defined. Men and women had quite different roles, particularly in the occupational sphere, and there was little overlapping. For example, the professions—medicine, dentistry, law, higher education, the clergy—were male provinces, and any female who sought admittance was thought suspect.

The clergy and medicine were entirely male, and the fact that Mary Baker Eddy was the head of her church and competed with medical practitioners was a major handicap. Feminist Jean McDonald notes that "it could not have . . . encouraged the professional security of either clergymen or physicians to find a woman of late middle age and highly 'unmanly' image invading the professional space of both groups simultaneously."[23]

Accusations of Plagiarism   Critics in Mary Baker Eddy's time often focused on the sources of Christian Science. Some argued that her concern with the unreality of the material world was borrowed from the Hindu religion. Others accused her of purloining the works of Hegel to form her concept of metaphysics.

The most serious charges leveled against her, however, were associated with visits to a mental healer in Portland, Maine, named Phineas Quimby. Prior to her accident on the ice, Mary Baker Eddy, in poor health, had experimented with a variety of cures. On the several occasions that she sought Dr. Quimby's help, they discussed mental healing, and apparently some of his practices became part of Christian Science practice.

The Quimby papers were published in 1921 and include this statement from George Quimby, the author's son, who despised Mary: "The religion which she [Mary Baker Eddy] teaches certainly is hers; for which I cannot be too thankful; for I should be loath to go down to my grave feeling that my father was in any way connected with Christian Science."[24]

It is probably as Charles Braden says: "It does not seem necessary to establish the particular source of Mary Baker Eddy's thought, whether it was completely original or dependent upon others. Eventually she did work out a system which, while it has many points of similarity to Quimby and other sources, is substantially different from all of them, and certainly goes far beyond what any of them dreamed of."[25]

Building the Mother Church and Other Institutions

No formal steps were taken toward establishing a church organization until 1879, thirteen years after Mary Baker Eddy's founding of Christian Science, some four years after the publication of her textbook, *Science and Health*. Prior to that time, meetings were held and students completed courses in "spiritual healing" in Mary Baker Eddy's home. Had it not been for the enmity of the dominant churches, their attacks, and the in-

---

[23]Jean A. McDonald, "Mary Baker Eddy and the Nineteenth-Century 'Public' Woman," *Journal of Feminist Studies in Religion* (Spring 1986): 91–92.

[24]Quoted in Beasley, *The Cross and the Crown,* p. 147.

[25]Braden, *Christian Science Today,* p. 35.

sistence of her students, Mary would probably not have agreed to a formal church organization.

In fact, Mary Baker Eddy's writings indicate a reluctance to establish a formal church. Braden notes that "to the end of her days she continued to republish, in *Miscellaneous Writings,* her *Journal* statement of 1892 that 'it is not indispensable to organize materially Christ's church,' that 'if this be done, let it be in concession to the period, and not as a perpetual, indispensable thing.'"[26] "Yet," Braden continues, "there is nowhere now any more centrally controlled religious organization than the church she founded."[27]

The Mother Church   In 1880, Mary Baker Eddy rented Hawthorne Hall in Boston to conduct religious services. In this prominent meeting place, long noted for attracting famous teachers and lecturers, she began to draw the well-to-do of Boston's society. Some came because they were interested in her religious theories, others because they were curious about the woman who was drawing so much public attention.

The meetings were held on Sundays at three in the afternoon to avoid conflict with services held in the established churches. So popular were these sessions that Hawthorne Hall's modest seating capacity of 236 was insufficient to accommodate the audiences, and Chickering Hall, with a seating capacity of some 500, was rented in 1885.

After several church reorganizations, Mary Baker Eddy, in 1893, wrote to fifty of her most devoted followers and asked that each make a Christmas donation of $1,000 for erecting a church building in Boston that would be known as the Mother Church. According to Braden, the building was "paid for in full, with a substantial surplus remaining over. . . . Dedicated in 1895, its marble inscription proclaims it *a testimonial to our beloved teacher, the Rev. Mary Baker Eddy.*"[28]

Inside the giant marble and granite building located in Boston's fashionable Back Bay district was a lavishly appointed "Mother's Room." The intent was that Mary Baker Eddy should have a suitable place to stay on her visits to the church. Ironically, although she was firmly in control of the church until her death in 1910, she visited the Mother Church only twice, staying overnight in the Mother's Room only once. The room was closed in 1908 following articles in the press written by Mark Twain ridiculing it as a shrine.

Massachusetts Metaphysical College   The impetus for building a worldwide organization may well have been the Massachusetts Metaphysical College. In 1881, predicated on a Massachusetts statute of 1874, Mary Baker Eddy sought and was granted a charter for establishing a college in

[26]Ibid., p. 42.
[27]Ibid., p. 43.
[28]Ibid., p. 54.

Boston with the privilege of granting degrees. The act was repealed in 1883, but the institution was not dissolved until 1889.

At the institute, Mary Baker Eddy, operating with a state license, attracted a sizable student following. The courses she chose to teach were pathology, ontology, therapeutics, moral science, and metaphysics—all with respect to their application to the treatment of diseases. The fees charged for courses were higher than those charged at Harvard University, just across the river.

Certainly, many of Mary Baker Eddy's students became successful practitioners, the $300 fee being returned many times over. As previously noted, during the latter part of the nineteenth century, licensing was not a problem. Christan Science practitioners could actually hang a shingle next door to a medical doctor and compete. Also, skeptics must remember that Christian Science practitioners did nothing *physically* to their patients. Medical doctors did, and, given the state of medical technology, many of their actions—including surgery—did more harm to their patients than good.

Practitioners' signs were beginning to appear everywhere: New York, Philadelphia, Chicago, Los Angeles. Some of Mary Baker Eddy's followers were establishing classes of their own, exponentially increasing the number of Christian Science followers. So great was the call for practitioners in Chicago, for example, that in 1884 Mary spent three weeks in that city teaching students the science of spiritual healing.

Students were encouraged to organize Christian Science Institutes as "soon as each could get as many as half a dozen students together. A number of these enterprises were launched throughout the country—though not always under the suggested name. The California Metaphysical College appeared in San Jose [in 1886]. In Chicago the Christian Science University was set up, and even in Boston itself the Academy of Christian Science was established."[29]

Despite Mary Baker Eddy's emphasis on organization and authority, Christian Science during this period was sometimes out of control. A number of those schooled as practitioners simply did not have enough training to act in accordance with Christian Science teachings. Others were unscrupulous and used Mary Baker Eddy and Christian Science to fill their pockets with fees.

The *Christian Science Monitor*

In 1908, two years before her death at age eighty-nine, Mary Baker Eddy summoned her board of directors and told them to establish a newspaper. There were already several in-house publications, among them the *Chris-*

[29]Braden, *Christian Science Today,* p. 46.

tian Science Journal and *Christian Science Sentinel,* but the new one was to be different. It was to benefit everyone, not just Christian Scientists. Mary Baker Eddy made it clear to her editorial staff from the outset that the purpose of the newspaper was to "injure no man, but to bless all mankind." The *Christian Science Monitor,* now nearly a hundred years old, remains faithful to that tradition.

Apparently, several factors contributed to the establishment of the *Monitor.* According to Gottschalk, "It was not until the founding of the *Monitor* that [Christian Scientists] found a practical form for involvement in social affairs."[30] Prior to the *Monitor,* Christian Science was oriented toward the personal and private. The *Monitor* "was an ideal vehicle for the expression of Christian Scientists' social concern. For it committed them to consciousness of human affairs but not to any particular involvement with them."[31]

A second reason for starting the *Monitor* was to promote what Mary Baker Eddy believed was needed reform in journalism. She was never to forgive the muckraking accounts of her life published in the yellow press, and the so-called Next Friends suit promoted by the *New York World* was anathema to her.[32]

In March 1997, Norm Bleichman, of the Committee on Publications for the Mother Church, stated that subscriptions to the *Monitor* were down, but noted that most print media nationally had suffered losses in recent years. He went on to say that the church now has a successful Web page.

Mary Baker Eddy's Legacy

Mary Baker Eddy believed in both heaven and hell, but for her, neither was a place. Each was a state of mind. She saw hell and the devil as lies, foreign to God and His truth. God, being infinitely good, could not use evil to condemn his people to death, pain, and suffering. The mind of man, she believed, was seduced and not in sync with the ultimate mind, the mind of God. The tendency for humankind to succumb to a tribal god and the erroneous belief that life exists in matter were the root causes of all human problems. Mary Baker Eddy believed that life could exist only in God's spiritual world, never in matter.

[30]Gottschalk, *Emergence of Christian Science,* p. 272.
[31]Ibid., p. 272.
[32]Articles printed in the *New York World* two years prior to her death prompted Mrs. Eddy's son, George, and more distant relatives, to ask a New Hampshire court to have her found incompetent and unable to handle her affairs. After lengthy hearings, the judge found Mrs. Eddy quite able to handle her affairs, and dismissed what had become known as the "Next Friends" suit. Next Friends is a legal term used in New Hampshire. Although suit was filed against Mary Baker Eddy, it was purportedly filed in her interest by her friends.

Many of Mary Baker Eddy's followers believed that she was the Messiah and would never die. Others argued that if she did die, she would be resurrected, as Jesus had been. Mary Baker Eddy ignored both assumptions, but had no qualms about telling her students that "God spoke through her." On December 4, 1910, at the age of eighty-nine, Mary Baker Eddy died of pneumonia.

At the time of her death, Christian Scientists was experiencing rapid growth. Estimates place it as having 65,717 members in 1906 and 202,098 by 1926.[33] Lending the movement credibility and prestige was the *Christian Science Monitor,* accepted as one of the finest newspapers in the country. But could the church survive without Mary Baker Eddy?

The Routinization of Charisma   Weber, in his study of charismatic leadership, argued that the disciples and staff of a charismatic leader differ from leaders in a bureaucratic system. A charismatic leader gains authority because of who they are. She or he is free to intervene whenever felt necessary. While this gives extraordinary power, it makes it very difficult for others to take on the leadership. By contrast, a bureaucracy or organization has elaborate procedures for succession.

It is obvious that leaders selected by Mary Baker Eddy in the early years of Christian Science fit the characteristics defined by Weber. Most were chosen because she believed them to be loyal to her and her theology, not because they were competent. Charisma, by nature, is unstable. It can exist in its pure form only so long as the charismatic leader is alive.

In other words, for an organization to survive after the charismatic leader's death or departure, charisma must in some way be perpetuated and made routine. For all practical purposes, Mary Baker Eddy—perhaps unintentionally—started such routinization before her death.

As her church grew and prospered, she found leaders capable of the challenge of a growing organization. No longer were members solely from New England's laboring class. The board of directors of the Mother Church soon consisted of skilled and talented people, as was the staff of the *Monitor.* As she grew older, Mary Baker Eddy, perhaps out of necessity, turned over much of the responsibility of these organizations to a professional staff, honest men and women capable of managing Christian Science.

Perhaps lending most to the routinization of charisma, however, was the *Manual.* From time to time, after the formation of the Mother Church, Mary Baker Eddy sent by-laws to the directors. In 1895 these by-laws were codified and became the *Church Manual.* During the fifteen years prior to her death, the *Manual* went through eighty-nine editions. One stipulation was that the *Manual* could not be revised without Mary Baker

---

[33]Membership data archived at adherents.com, accessed March 7, 2005.

Eddy's consent. As a consequence, Mary's final revision stands as the basic law of the church.

Under the circumstances, therefore, Mary Baker Eddy, in a sense, cannot die unless Christian Science dies. For example, "in April 1895, she sent down a by-law abolishing preaching from the pulpit, requiring that henceforth 'the Bible and *Science and Health with Key to the Scriptures* be the pastor on this planet of all the churches of the Christian Science denomination.'"[34] Hence, the words spoken in Christian Science churches today are still the words of Mary Baker Eddy.

Organization

Since Mrs. Eddy's death, the church has been run by a five-person board of directors. Today, the board is composed of three men and two women, although no gender-specific number is required in the *Manual*. There is no hierarchical structure beneath the board. There are many divisions with complex operations within Christian Science, but each is answerable directly to the board of directors.

Sociologists have long recognized that committee decision making is at best difficult, but that the optimal size for a decision-making committee is probably either five or seven persons. An even number allows for tie votes. When a committee gets too large, communication becomes difficult, factions develop, and the process is slowed.

The Christian Science Board is not elected by the general membership. When a member leaves the board, a replacement is selected by the sitting board members, thus insuring continuity of thought. Appointment to the board is for life, with the presidency rotated annually.

Branch Churches   An "official count" of churches or church membership is prohibited in the Christian Science *Manual*: "Christian Scientists shall not report for publication the number of the members of the Mother Church, nor that of the branch churches. According to the Scripture they shall turn away from personality and numbering the people."[35] This is still followed, and the Church posts it on the Web for all to see at www.christianscience.org/Manual.html. Nevertheless, a reasonable account is available. The *Christian Science Journal*, published monthly, lists the churches, and a simple count reveals that there are nearly 1,300 branches in the United States. Informed sources put the current membership at nearly 150,000 individuals.[36]

---

[34]Braden, *Christian Science Today,* pp. 55–56.

[35]Mary Baker Eddy, *Church Manual of the First Church of Christ, Scientist in Boston,* 89th ed. (Boston: The First Church of Christ, Scientist, 1936).

[36]Branches include "societies" and reflect the data in the March 2005 issue of *Christian Science Journal.*

The *Manual* is clear on what it takes to form a church:

A member of the Mother Church who obeys its By-Laws and is a loyal exemplary Christian Scientist working in the field is eligible to form a church. . . . A branch church . . . shall not be organized with less than sixteen loyal Christian Scientists, four of whom are members of the Mother Church. This membership shall include at least one active practitioner whose card is published in the list of practitioners in the *Christian Science Journal*.[37]

Christian Scientists meet twice weekly, Sunday morning and Wednesday evening. The Christian Science Board of Education in Boston provides uniform material for these sessions, in much the same way that Jehovah's Witnesses provide the religious material for their meetings. A major difference exists, however, between the Witnesses and the Christian Scientists in method of presentation. The Witnesses encourage discussion, albeit controlled, of the materials sent them; Christian Science prohibits any discussion. With the routinization of charisma, no interpretations of Mary Baker Eddy's words are allowed.

The following format, published in the *Manual,* is followed at all Sunday meetings:[38]

1. Hymn.
2. Reading a Scriptural Selection.
3. Silent prayer, followed by the audible repetition of the Lord's Prayer with its spiritual interpretation.
4. Hymn.
5. Announcing necessary notices.
6. Solo.
7. Reading the explanatory note on first leaf of *Quarterly*.
8. Announcing the subject of the Lesson-Sermon, and reading the Golden Text.
9. Reading the Scriptural Selection, entitled "Responsive Reading," alternately by the First Reader and the congregation.
10. Reading the Lesson-Sermon. (After the Second Reader reads the BIBLE references of the first Section of the Lesson, the First Reader makes the following announcement: "As announced in the explanatory note, I shall now read correlative passages from the Christian Science textbook, *Science and Health with Key to the Scriptures*, by Mary Baker Eddy.")
11. Collection.
12. Hymn.
13. Reading the Scientific Statement of Being, and the correlative SCRIPTURE according to I John 3:1–3.
14. Pronouncing Benediction.

The Wednesday evening meeting is orchestrated in much the same way as the Sunday service. One distinct difference, however, is the giving of

[37]Eddy, *Church Manual*, pp. 72–73.
[38]Ibid.

testimony. Item six on the Wednesday schedule calls for "experiences, testimonies, and remarks on Christian Science."[39] The testimony focuses on Christian Science healing through prayer. The *Journal,* written primarily for church members, and the *Sentinel,* written for a larger audience, include such testimony as well. Doubtless, spiritual healing will always be a dominant concern of the church.

Each church offers a Sunday school program for children and for youth under age twenty. Mary Baker Eddy defined the content of the Sunday school program, stipulating that the first lessons should focus on the Ten Commandments, the Lord's Prayer, and her interpretation of the Sermon on the Mount. The *Manual* states that "the instructions given by the children's teachers must not deviate from the absolute Christian Science contained in their textbook."[40]

In the foregoing paragraphs, reference has been made to the roles of practitioner and reader in the Church of Christ, Scientist. To comprehend the structure of the church, we must explore these roles, along with the roles of lecturer, teacher, and librarian.

Church Roles

There are five positions critical to the operations of the Christian Scientist on a day-to-day basis. They are practitioners, teachers, readers, librarians, and lecturers.

Practitioners As previously noted, to form a branch church, one of the founding members must be a practitioner. Because the church has no clergy, the practitioner is a lay member like everyone else. Robert Peel points out that "his ministry is not an office in a church structure. . . ."[41] The practitioner's ministrations are for anyone who seeks them—members of the general public as well as Christian Scientists. . . . He is not restricted to a local congregation in his ministry and is self-supported in the way that a general practitioner of medicine is—by his patients' payments."[42]

Peel goes on to say that not all of the practitioners' time is devoted to the healing of physical diseases, noting that much of their time is spent addressing the typical problems that most members of the clergy address: "emotional disturbances, family problems, questions of employment,

[39]Ibid.

[40]Ibid., pp. 62–63.

[41]It is specifically forbidden in the *Manual* (p. 74) for practitioners to have offices in the church.

[42]Robert Peel, "The Christian Science Practitioner," in *Christian Science: A Sourcebook of Contemporary Materials* (Boston: The Christian Science Publishing Society, 1990), pp. 137–41.

schooling, professional advancement, etc."[43] He further states that the "two classes of problems are too closely interrelated to be logically separable. The important thing is that the word *healing* be understood to apply to the whole spectrum of human sins, fears, griefs, wants, and ills."[44]

Any Christian Scientist in good standing for three years can become a practitioner by taking a short course and making application to the board of directors. The successful applicant must show a record of successful healings.[45] Testimonials should accompany the application form.

The Church of Christ, Scientist, also authorizes "nurses" trained in assisting in the spiritual recovery of patients. Some are employed by nursing homes that are run for Christian Scientists. Such nurses attend to the needs of patients in much the same way as medical nurses, except, of course, they do not have a medical background.

The *Journal* published in 2005 the names of about 2,000 practitioners and teachers. At mid-century, the healers had numbered more than 11,000. A distinction is made between special nurse and graduate nurse.[46]

Teachers   There are, today, approximately 200 teachers certified by the Christian Science Board of Education. The number who may be certified is limited by the board of directors, and has varied from time to time. To apply, a member must be loyal to the church and to the teachings of Mary Baker Eddy. Affidavits from a minimum of five members of the Mother Church attesting to moral character, loyalty, and the ability of the applicant to perform healing must accompany the application.

Before applying, the candidate is also required to complete a "primary" course of study and the church's "normal" course. Those who complete both courses may write C.S.B. (Bachelor of Christian Science) after their names.

After board certification, the new teacher is expected to establish "primary" classes. The *Manual* specifies that tuition should not exceed $100, and no more than thirty pupils may be enrolled. Only one class may be offered annually. There are twelve "primary" class sessions, each running three to four hours. When Mary Baker Eddy established the rule, $3,000 was a handsome annual income. The fee remains the same today because the *Manual* cannot be altered. Many full-time Christian Scientists earn their living by being both teachers and practitioners.

---

[43]Ibid., p. 139.

[44]Ibid.

[45]Healing in Christian Science is not confined to practitioners. An applicant must have demonstrated the ability to heal before applying for practitioner certification. Self-healing may be included on the resume.

[46]Philip Zaleski, "Thinking Made It So, for a While," *New York Times*, August 2, 1999, Sec. 7, p. 8

Interestingly, a few prospective teachers have lost their *primary course* credentials on application for the *normal course.* Braden explains:

> A candidate is disqualified if the teacher with whom he went through Primary class, however long ago, is not *currently* in favor with the Board. Here is something that goes quite beyond the loyalty of the person . . . who is applying. . . .
>
> Only by being "retaught" by a teacher in favor with the Board, . . . again paying a hundred-dollar fee, can the pupil return to the bought and worked-for privileged position of which he finds himself deprived through no fault of his own.[47]

The Mother Church argues that teachers found wanting impart faulty knowledge and thus weaken their students.

Readers   Each church has a first and second reader elected from the congregation. Readers in the branch churches must also be members of the Mother Church. The functions of the readers are spelled out in the *Manual:*

> They shall read understandingly and be well educated. They shall make no remarks explanatory of the LESSON-SERMON at any time, but they shall read all notices and remarks that may be printed in the Christian Science Quarterly.[48]

The next paragraphs in the *Manual* appear to be most interesting:

> It shall be the duty of every member of The Mother Church, who is a First Reader in a Church of Christ, Scientist, to enforce the discipline and by-laws of the church in which he is a Reader.
>
> The Church Reader shall not be a Leader, but he shall maintain the Tenets, Rules, and discipline of the Church. A Reader shall not be a President of a church.[49]

(One might well ask, however, whether it is possible to demand discipline and enforce the by-laws of an organization without being a leader.)

Readers and librarians are paid a stipend for their services. Moreover, they may hold other church positions such as teacher or practitioner, which, as stated earlier, generate income.

Librarians   A familiar sight across the nation is the Christian Science reading room, and there are now more than 2,400. An open Bible and the textbook *Science and Health* are on display, and racks are filled with Christian Science literature. The public is welcome. With few exceptions,

---

[47]Braden, *Christian Science Today,* p. 109.
[48]Eddy, *Church Manual,* p. 32.
[49]Ibid., pp. 32–33.

each church sponsors such a facility. Smaller churches near each other sometimes share sponsorship.

Librarians are appointed by the board of directors, and the *Manual* states that "he or she shall have no bad habits, shall have had experience in the Field [*sic*], shall be well educated, and a devout Christian Scientist."[50] Christian Science literature is sold in the reading rooms along with Bibles, Bible commentaries, and the like. To facilitate use of the libraries, some churches furnish child care providers.

Lecturers   Each year, the board of directors appoints official church speakers. Lectureship is an esteemed position in the church and is financially rewarding. Annually, each branch church is required to have one visit from a visiting speaker, the cost being borne by the branch church. The policy, established by Mrs. Eddy, is to "provide in lecture a true and just reply to public topics condemning Christian Science."[51]

The *Manual* requires that speakers provide a copy of proposed lectures to the clerk of the Mother Church before public presentation to avoid objectionable material. In this way, the board maintains control of what is said in public presentations. Church members are urged to invite non-Scientists to these meetings. Most lecturers are seasoned teachers or have had experience with the church Committee on Publications.

Christian Scientists: Cult, Sect, or What?

The collective nature of religion has led to many forms of religious association. In modern societies, religion has become increasingly formalized. Specific structures such as churches and synagogues have been constructed for religious worship; individuals have been trained for occupational roles within various fields. Sociologists find it useful to distinguish between four basic forms of organization: the ecclesia, the denomination, the sect, and the new religious movement, or cult. We can see differences among these four forms of organization in their size, power, degree of commitment expected from members, and historical ties to other faiths.

An **ecclesia** (plural, *ecclesiae*) is a religious organization that claims to include most or all members of a society and is recognized as the national or official religion. Since virtually everyone belongs to the faith, membership is by birth rather than conscious decision. Examples of ecclesiae include Islam in Saudi Arabia and Buddhism in Thailand.

A **denomination** is a large, organized religion that is not officially linked with the state or government. Like an ecclesia, it tends to have an

---

[50]Ibid., p. 63.
[51]Ibid., p. 93.

explicit set of beliefs, a defined system of authority, and a generally respected position in society. Denominations claim as members large segments of a population. Generally, children accept the denomination of their parents and give little thought to membership in other faith. Denominations also resemble ecclesiae in that they make few demands on members. However, there is a critical difference between these two forms of religious organization. Although the denomination is considered respectable and is not viewed as a challenge to the secular government, it lacks the official recognition of power held by an ecclesia.

The United States is home to a large number of denominations. Some Christian denominations in the United States, such as the Roman Catholics, Episcopalians, and Lutherans, are the outgrowth of ecclesiae established in Europe. New Christian denominations also emerged, including the Mormons and Christian Scientists, two groups considered in this book.

A **sect** can be defined as a relatively small religious group that has broken away from some other religious organization to renew what it considers the original vision of the faith.

Sects are fundamentally at odds with society and do not seek to become established national religions. Unlike ecclesiae and denominations, they require intensive commitments and demonstrations of belief by members. Partly owing to their outsider status, sects frequently exhibit a higher degree of religious fervor and loyalty than more established religious groups. Recruitment focuses mainly on adults, and acceptance comes through conversion.

Sects are often short-lived. Those that are able to survive may become less antagonistic to society over time and begin to resemble denominations. In a few instances, sects have been able to endure over several generations while remaining fairly separate from society. Sociologist J. Milton Yinger uses the term **established sect** to describe a religious group that is the outgrowth of a sect, yet remains isolated from society. The Hutterites, Jehovah's Witnesses, Seventh-Day Adventists, and Amish are contemporary examples of established sects in the United States.

Sects are difficult to distinguish from cults. A **cult** is generally a small, secretive religion or major innovation of an existing faith. Cults are similar to sects in that they tend to be small and are often viewed as less respectable than more established faiths. Unlike sects, however, cults normally do not result from schisms or breaks with established ecclesiae or denominations. Some cults, such as those focused on UFO sightings, may be totally unrelated to existing faiths. Even when a cult does accept certain fundamental tenets of a dominant faith—such as belief in Jesus as divine or Mohammad as a messenger of God—it will offer new revelations or insights to justify its claim of being a more advanced religion.

Like sects, cults may be transformed over time into other types of religious organizations. An example is the Christian Science Church, which began as a cult under the leadership of Mary Baker Eddy. Today, this church exhibits the characteristics of a denomination. In fact, most major religions, including Christianity, began as cults. So to answer the question, the Christian Science Church would be considered today neither a sect nor a cult, but a denomination.[52]

Who Are Christian Scientists?

Christian Scientists can be found in any city of any size. We see their clean, well-kept churches and reading rooms. They are our neighbors, classmates, coworkers. As Christian Science author DeWitt John puts it, the religion "comes to all sorts of people. It comes to the rich and poor, the talented and the simple, the old and the young, the pure and the impure, the sick and the well, the beautiful in character and those whose dispositions are scarred with ugliness. It comes to people of many races and many backgrounds."[53]

Indeed, Christian Scientists do come from every walk of life and every socioeconomic bracket. But is there a character type more common than others? From the beginning, Christian Science has attracted large numbers of white, urban, middle-class women. According to McDonald, "Women scholars have generally theorized that Eddy and other women of the period gravitated toward Christian Science, not for its theological worth but for its personal utility—because it satisfied their needs for status and power in a male-dominated society that largely closed off other avenues of achievement."[54]

The *Journal*, as previously noted, lists the names of practitioners. In his 1954 doctoral dissertation, Harold Pfautz published data from the *Journal* indicating that in every decade since 1900 female practitioners have far outnumbered male practitioners. In his final count in 1950 there were 7,786 female practitioners and 1,045 male practitioners. Of the total number, 6,546 lived in cities with a population of more than 100,000. Apparently, this trend continues. The December 1992 *Journal* lists 2,610 female practitioners and 453 male practitioners, most living in urban areas.

---

[52] James T. Richardson and Barend van Driel, "Journalists' Attitudes toward New Religious Movements," *Review of Religious Research* 39 (December 1997), pp. 116–36; Rodney Stark and William Sims Bainbridge, "Of Churches, Sects, and Cults: Preliminary Concepts for a Theory of Religious Movements," *Journal for the Scientific Study of Religion* 18 (June 1979): 117–31; and *The Future of Religion* (Berkeley: University of California Press, 1985). This section on religious organization is adapted from Richard T. Schaefer, *Sociology: A Brief Introduction*, 6th ed. (New York: McGraw-Hill, 2006), pp. 338-41.

[53] John, DeWitt, *The Christian Science Way of Life* (Englewood Cliffs, NJ: Prentice-Hall, 1962), p. 1.

[54] McDonald, "Nineteenth-Century 'Public Woman,'" p. 89.

Included in the ranks of Christian Science are notables, but unlike some faiths (notably Scientology), famous Christian Scientists do not make an issue of drawing attention to their affiliation. Celebrities have included Val Kilmer, Doris Day, Robert Duvall, Jean Stapleton, and Jean Harlow. Other notables include two astronauts, Guion Beford and Kathy Sullivan; Charles Percy, former U.S. senator from Illinois; and Paul Smucker, the businessman of jelly fame. Other former members include H. R. Haldeman and John Ehrlichman; both served as White House chief of staff during the Nixon administration.

Contemporary Problems

Extraordinary groups such as we are considering face challenges from within as well as from without. The Amish encounter opposition to their competition with local workers and struggle to find sufficient land. The Oneida had to withstand attacks on its lifestyle and unsuccessfully tried to maintain their cohesive identity. Christian Scientists also face challenges—from without is the issue of healing and from within is troubling finances and declining membership.

Spiritual Healing

As we have seen, Christian Science is unusual in its 150-year teaching and practice of a spiritual healing method through prayer alone. Christian Scientists are not antagonistic to medicine and often express respect for the work of medical practitioners, but argue it just is not best for them. Furthermore, they make their healing to Christian Science practitioners available to anyone who accepts the prayer-based ministry.

It would not be surprising to learn that as the church began to receive public notice, many in medicine and in the legal system are not very charitable about healing without reliance on "modern medicine."

One of the most persistent problems facing the church dates back to the formative years of Christian Science—the effectiveness of spiritual healing. In the early years, many suits were filed against Christian Science practitioners in both civil and criminal courts.

One of the most celebrated of the early cases involved Harold Frederic, an American novelist of some repute. Prior to his death in 1888, he had been treated by a Christian Science practitioner in London, England. Outraged, the *London Times* reported that "Christian Science is a dangerous importation, a rather naive product of a rather naive people."[55] The

---

[55]Cited in Beasley, *The Cross and the Crown*, p. 496.

newspaper concluded that the practitioner should be tried for murder—and he was.

It was learned during the trial that Frederic had gone to the practitioner in desperation, after medical doctors had deemed his case hopeless. The practitioner was acquitted. Nevertheless, considerable attention was given the incident in the American press, and during that period, legislation was passed in nearly every state to limit the practice of healing to graduates of medical schools.

Following Mary Baker Eddy's death, according to Damore, the Christian Science Board of Directors "imposed stricter standards for membership and practitioner authority, mindful of the unfortunate results accomplished by those early adherents who had seen 'healing' as a means of escaping the drudgery of factory work."[56] The board's efforts bore fruit. One by one, the states exempted Christian Science from compliance with licensing laws. Damore notes that in "1949 the Ohio legislature finally legalized the public practice of Christian Science, making it the last state to exempt practitioners from medical statutes."[57]

Does It Work?   Tens of thousands of Christian Scientists would argue that spiritual healing works. Semi-annually, the Church presents a Spiritual and Healing in Medicine conference jointly with the Harvard Medical School. In many respects, Christian Scientists find allies with other faiths that talk about prayer as a means to healing, but it is the exclusivity to prayer that makes Christian Science unique. At the conference, attendees are reminded of the thousands of testimonials to episodes of faith and healing. To further document the power of this spiritual system of self-care, experiences are cited from pediatricians, psychotherapists, and other medical doctors.[58]

Skeptics note the absence of any outside controlled experimental studies to validate the claims. Much more troublesome have been the lawsuits focusing on the deaths of Christian Scientists, especially the children of practicing members.

The Trial of Dorothy Sheridan   In 1967, Dorothy Sheridan, a thirty-year-old divorcée with two children, was head teacher at a nursery school in a village near Cape Cod, Massachusetts. She had belonged to the Christian Science Church for three years.

On February 24, her five-year-old daughter, Lisa, complained of being sick and was put to bed. The following day the child developed a high

[56]Leo Damore, *The Crime of Dorothy Sheridan* (South Yarmouth, MA: John Curley, 1978), pp. 236–37.

[57]Ibid., p. 238.

[58]Virginia Harris, "Spiritual Essence of the Writings of Mary Baker Eddy," 2002 Spiritual and Healing in Medicine conference. Accessed March 8, 2005, www.christianscience.org.

fever and heavy cough. A few days later, however, the child seemed to be over the crisis: the fever broke and the coughing stopped. During this period, Dorothy Sheridan had not called a doctor but had been in touch with a Christian Science practitioner.

After the apparent crisis, Lisa did not return to normal. She remained lethargic, had congestion, and evidenced difficulty in breathing. Concerned, Dorothy Sheridan called a second practitioner for help. The practitioner told her to continue praying in accordance with Christian Science teachings—that disease was the result of "mortal beliefs." The healing of a child is believed to be guided through the prayer and understanding of the parent.

After two weeks, with no treatment other than prayer, Lisa Sheridan died. An autopsy revealed that she died of pneumonia, the result of an apparently treatable infection. One lung had collapsed, and the other contained more than a quart of pus.

It is a common misconception that Christian Scientists cannot use the medical community under any circumstances. Mrs. Eddy herself wore glasses, had false teeth, and used morphine prescribed by a medical doctor for severe back pain. The church also permits the use of doctors for procedures defined as "mechanical," for example, the setting of broken bones and obstetrics. Today, in instances where there is a difference of opinion between Christian Science parents and medical authorities, the Church policy is to encourage cooperation with those authorities. The Church urges the reporting of communicable diseases, vaccination, and the provision of certified midwives or other medical attendants at childbirth as legally required.[59]

County prosecutors, convinced that Dorothy Sheridan was guilty of manslaughter, had difficulty framing a charge. No law in Massachusetts existed making it illegal to withhold medical attention from a sick child. It was finally decided, however, that the state of Massachusetts had a compelling interest in the welfare of children "threatened by a system of healing that depended upon prayer."[60]

Dorothy Sheridan was defended by counsel provided by the Mother Church.[61] After lengthy argument, the presiding judge charged the jury, stating: "Under common law, a parent has the duty to provide a minor, unemancipated child with the necessaries of life," concluding that "when needed to preserve life or health," medical attention is considered a necessity.[62]

[59]Danmore, *The Crime of Dorothy Sheridan*, p. 142.
[60]Ibid., p. 329.
[61]Estimates of the cost of Dorothy Sheridan's defense range up to $250,000.
[62]Cited in Danmore, *The Crime of Dorothy Sheridan*, p. 471.

The statute the indictment was based on used the term *physical care*. The defense was taken aback when the judge defined medical and physical care as one and the same, precluding other types of treatment. Nevertheless, most observers believed that Dorothy Sheridan would be acquitted, or that the trial would end in a hung jury. Dorothy Sheridan led an exemplary life. Hadn't she suffered enough with the loss of her child?

Ironically, the first vote cast in the jury room was nine to three for acquittal. But a restauranteur, a barber, and a homemaker held out for conviction, arguing that the defendant's acts were not reasonable, in keeping with community standards. Eventually, those who voted for acquittal were swayed, and Dorothy Sheridan was convicted.

Indeed, no one really wanted to punish Dorothy Sheridan; she had suffered enough. She was sentenced to five years probation, the only stipulation being that she seek medical attention for her remaining child, should the need arise.

Instead of appealing the case, the church worked through the Massachusetts legislature, urging the following language be amended to the general laws:

> A child shall not be deemed to be neglected or lack proper physical care for the sole reason that he is being provided remedial treatment by spiritual means alone in accordance with the tenets and practices of a recognized church or religious denomination by a duly-accredited practitioner thereof.[63]

Governor Francis Sargent signed the legislation, with the law taking effect in December 1971.

Legal Challenges Persist   In 1989, an eleven-year-old Minnesota boy, Ian Lundman, died of complications from diabetes. The child was not under the care of a physician. The child's natural father, Douglass Lundman, sued the Church of Christ, Scientist; the boy's mother, Kathleen McKown; and his stepfather, William McKown. Mario Tosto, a practitioner, and Quinna Giebellaus, a Christian Science nurse, were also sued.

A Minnesota District Court awarded Douglass Lundman $9 million in punitive damages, asserting that the Mother Church was culpable. The damages against the McKowns, Tosto, and Giebellaus amounted to $5.2 million. A state appeals court struck the punitive damage ruling against the church, in essence affirming the right to believe. The award against the practitioners was reduced to $1.5 million, in essence denying the right of believers to act on their beliefs.

In January 1996, the United States Supreme Court allowed the decision to stand without comment. In response, the *Christian Science Monitor*

---

[63]Cited in ibid., p. 562.

noted, "[The Court] . . . created a negative precedent for the practice of Christian Science, since it implicitly stated that freedom of belief does not extend to freedom of conduct."[64]

Michael McConnell, a University of Chicago professor who filed the appeal, stated that "it was the first civil damages award ever obtained against Christian Scientists for the death of a child."[65]

Despite occasional setbacks, both the health care industry and the courts have reached some degree of accommodation with the church. Health insurance carriers, such as Blue Cross–Blue Shield, provide coverage and pay Christian Science practitioners for their services. Skeptics argue that Christian Scientists are good risks because theirs is a healthy lifestyle. Smoking and drinking, for example, are grounds for banishment from the church. Apart from that, practitioners' fees are much lower than those charged by medical doctors, and hospitals are almost never used.

Until recently, Medicare and Medicaid paid claims for some Christian Science services. Practical nonmedical care, such as help with bathing, bandaging, and the use of sanitariums have qualified for reimbursement since the origin of these programs thirty years ago. Practitioners have never been paid for their services. The legislation, however, is limited to Christian Science services. Other churches that employ practical nonmedical care were not included in the bills.

A suit was filed against the government by an organization formed by Rita Swan, a former church member, whose 16-month-old son died of spinal meningitis in 1977 while in the care of Christian Science practitioners. CHILD (Child's Healthcare Is a Legal Duty) is committed to blocking federal monies going to such nonmedical health care. The case alleged that Christian Scientists were receiving special treatment from the government in violation of the Constitution. In August 1996, a federal judge in Minnesota agreed, ruling against both the Christian Science Church and the United States Justice Department, which had sided with the church.

In January 1997, the Justice Department changed its position. Janet Reno wrote that "the government has no compelling interest in confining payment for nonmedical nursing services to members of one faith. If Congress wished to provide parallel coverage universally for all persons who are religiously motivated to forgo traditional medical care, then the language of the [Medicare and Medicaid] provisions should have been crafted to embrace all faiths."[66]

[64]Robert Marquand, "Court Lets Stand Decision against Spiritual Healing," *Christian Science Monitor,* January 23, 1996, p. 3.

[65]Linda Greenhouse, "Christian Scientists Rebuffed in Ruling by Supreme Court," *New York Times,* January 23, 1996, p. 1.

[66]Warren Richey, "Church to Pursue Nursing-Care Suit," *Christian Science Monitor,* January 27, 1997.

Supporters from both within and outside the church saw this as a patient's choice in health care even when it was the parents making decisions about the nature of their children's course of treatment. In April 2001, the Supreme Court refused to hear the case allowing Medicare and Medicaid dollars to go to general supplies such as bandages, bedpans, feeding, and bathing. While opponents said the decision opened the door to quackery, a spokesman for the Mother Church saw the opinion as "a sect-neutral accommodation available to any person who is relying on a religious method of healing. . . . This is a victory for parents."[67]

In reviewing ten course cases beginning in 1980 through 2001 of children of Christian Science parents or guardians who died, three conclusions can be reached. First, in all the cases where conventional medical treatment were suspended, the parents were exonerated. Second, observers of these cases questioned whether Christian Science healing practices were being held to a standard medicine rarely faces. Third, in none of the recent cases has the Church been held liable since it does not direct the action taken by its followers.[68]

Finances and Membership

The 1990s were not a kind decade for the Christian Science Church. During this period, the public, not to mention the members, became aware of internal problems in the organization.

As was true in much of mass media, fascination grew in the Church over the "can't miss" opportunities in the expanding cable television market. Many at the distinguished *Christian Science Monitor* felt expansion into cable was coming at their expense. In 1988, three top editors of the *Christian Science Monitor* "quit to protect a massive scaling-back of the paper in size and staff so the church could donate more resources to television . . . church officials said they were merely keeping up with the times by expanding beyond their . . . newspaper . . . into television, shortwave, public radio, and a slick, monthly international news magazine."[69] The most costly of these ventures was the Monitor channel, a twenty-four-hour cable, advertiser-supported TV network. Hundreds of millions were

[67]Tanya Albert, "Supreme Court Upholds Pay to Christian Science Health Facilities," April 30, 2001. Accessed March 7, 2005, from amednews.com, of the American Medical Association.

[68]"The Church of Christ, Scientist," July 16, 2001. Accessed March 8, 2005, from www.religiousmovements.lib.virginia.edu/nms/chrissci.html.

[69]Steve Stecklow, "Church's Media Moves at Issue: A Burgeoning Network Sparks Dissent," *Philadelphia Inquirer*, October 14, 1991, p. A1.

spent on these projects, with $61.5 million coming from endowments and an employee pension fund.

More than a few church members feared that the move into television would bankrupt the church. Among that number were Robert Peel and Stephen Gottschalk, church leaders often cited in this text. Gottschalk resigned his position with the church in 1990, commenting that "the atmosphere of The Mother Church was so repressive that even the most constructively voiced criticism would be grounds for losing one's job."[70]

In March 1992, the chairman of the board stepped down, along with several other high officials. The Monitor channel was offered for sale. There were no bidders. On June 28, the board closed the cable operation with an estimated loss of $473 million. Monitor Radio survived the cable TV failure, but it too was offered for sale in April 1997.

During the summer of 1999, the World Times, publisher of the *World Paper,* a weekly newspaper, agreed to buy the Monitor news network for an undisclosed price: "the deal is contingent on enough stations that broadcast Monitor Radio agreeing to continue broadcasting the programs under the new ownership."[71]

Perhaps even more controversial than church media projects was the board's decision to publish Bliss Knapp's *The Destiny of the Mother Church.* Stecklow writes: "Knapp . . . and his family so much wanted the church to publish his book . . . that in their wills they offered the bulk of their multimillion-dollar estate as an incentive."[72]

The book, written in the early 1940s, labeled "incorrect literature" by the board until 1991, elevates Mary Baker Eddy to a status equal to Jesus. According to Knapp, Mary Baker Eddy's arrival as a religious figure was foretold by the biblical prophet Isaiah and that her work was "complimentary to that of Jesus Christ." Gottschalk notes that "when the *New York Herald* in 1895 asked her if she thought she was the second Christ, Mary Baker Eddy responded, 'Even the question shocks me. . . . To think or speak of me in any manner as a Christ, is sacrilegious. Such a statement would not only be false, but the absolute antipode of Christian Science.'"[73]

Church officials argue that the book would have been published whether or not a bequest was attached to it. Critics counterargue that the

[70]Ibid.

[71]"Tentative Accord to Sell Monitor Radio," *New York Times,* June 5, 1997, Sec D, p. 6, and Gill, *Helen Baker Eddy,* pp. xvi–xvii.

[72]Stecklow, "Church's Media Moves at Issue."

[73]Stephen Gottschalk, "Honesty, Blasphemy and the Destiny of the Mother Church," *Christian Century,* November 6, 1991, p. 1028. (Also see "Tumult in the Reading Rooms," *Time,* October 14, 1991, p. 57).

motive for publication was to help fund the media network, noting that Knapp completed his manuscript more than forty years ago. (Had the book not been published by 1993, the Knapps' will provided that the bulk of the estate would be divided between Stanford University and the Los Angeles Museum of Art. After publishing Knapp's book, to preclude legal complications with Stanford University and the Los Angeles Museum of Art, a settlement was reached. The Mother Church received 53 percent of the estate (valued at $92 million); the balance was divided between the university and the museum.[74]

In addition to media problems, the Church has been losing members. It had a documented 270,000 members in the mid-1930s and reported to have about 150,000 new members. The Church policy is not to release membership data. Another measure would be to look at its number of churches in the United States. Analysis of available data shows 1,829 in 1971; 1,450 in 1991; 1,204 in 1996; and 1,200 in 2005. Similarly, there were in terms of practitioners and teachers, 4,965 in 1971; 2,237 in 1991; 1,802 in 1996; and 1,304 in 2005. By both measures the Church appears to be experiencing a decline in membership. This clearly has to contribute to financial challenges that virtually any religious organization faces.[75]

The Future

On the record, church membership has been declining for years. While there may be a variety of reasons, two stand out. First, during earlier periods many women doubtless joined the movement in order to compete in a man's world. Today, this reason is much less pressing. In recent years, rather obviously, women have made substantial gains in nearly every field.

Second, confidence in the medical profession has increased greatly during recent decades. Advanced medical technology and physicians' competence are today more or less taken for granted. The upshot is that fewer people are attracted to "spiritual healing." And even those who believe in the healing power of prayer tend to join churches that believe in prayer, but also believe that God is the provider of physicians and medical treat-

[74]Stanford University News Service, August 23, 1992. Accessed March 8, 2005, from www.stanford.edu.

[75]Data assembled from adherents.com, accessed March 7, 2005; Stephen Barrett, "Christian Science Statistics: Practitioners, Teachers, and Churches in the United States." Accessed March 8, 2005, from www.quackwatch.org; and "Professional Services and Church Information Directory," *Christian Science Journal* (March 2005), pp. 762–86.

ment. Nevertheless, childhood socialization is powerful. Comedian Ellen Degeneres humorously notes:

> I was raised a Christian Scientist and we were taught that we could heal our bodies through prayer, that sickness was an illusion that could be defeated by the power of the spirit. Since my family were Christian Scientists, we probably saved a bundle: no aspirin, no medicine at all. I didn't take my first aspirin until I was in my teens and even now I feel a twinge of guilt when I go to the pharmacy—I feel as if I am in an opium den. (Though, to be fair, I've only been to an opium den twice and I was so stoned I barely remember what it was like.) We never had to buy any of that stuff. Also, we didn't need medical insurance. It would have been a waste of money because we never went to the hospital.[76]

Another aspect of the church militating against its recovery is the average age of its members. Stephen Gottschalk describes the church as aging, with difficulty attracting new members. Today, Christian Science is attempting to expand interest in the church by vigorously promoting *Science and Health with Key to the Scriptures.* Indeed, sales have risen dramatically. According to chairperson Virginia Harris, "people are searching for something other than 500 channels. We used to see 'God is dead' on the cover of *Time.* That is no longer where this country's thought is."[77]

In spite of these factors, Mary Baker Eddy's church may well survive, albeit with a much smaller membership. The church has retrenched. Following the media failure, nearly five hundred church employees, including media staff, were let go. The new board of directors is working with a balanced budget. And, who knows, perhaps the church will find a mechanism for increasing membership.

So—what will the outcome be? Cliché or not, only time will tell.

KEY TERMS

Cults, p. 149

Denomination, p. 148

Ecclesia, p. 148

Established sect, p. 149

Sects, p. 149

---

[76]Ellen Degeneres, *Ellen: My Point . . . And I Do Have One* (New York: Bantam Books, 1996), p. 128.

[77]Gustav Niebuhr, "Alternative Medicine's Rise Cheers Christian Scientists," *New York Times,* October 1, 1994, p. 30.

SOURCES ON THE WEB

www.tfccs.com
Official Web site of the Mother Church, the First Church of Christ Scientist in Boston, Massachusetts.

www.christianscience.org
The Church Web site offers access to official publications.

www.childrenshealthcare.org
This nonprofit national organization, Children's Healthcare Is a Legal Duty (CHILD), established in 1983, seeks to protect children from what it regards as abusive religious and cultural practices. The Christian Science Church spiritual healing is frequently targeted by CHILD.

SELECTED READINGS

Beasley, Norman. *The Cross and the Crown*. Boston: Little, Brown, 1952.
Braden, Charles S. *Christian Science Today: Power, Policy, Practice*. Dallas: Southern Methodist University Press, 1958.
Canham, Erwin D. *A Christian Scientist's Life*. Englewood Cliffs, NJ: Prentice-Hall, 1962.
Christian Science: A Sourcebook of Contemporary Materials. Boston: Christian Science Publishing Society, 1990.
Damore, Leo. *The Crime of Dorothy Sheridan*. South Yarmouth, MA: John Curley, 1978.
Eddy, Mary Baker. *Unity of Good and Other Writings*. Boston: Trustees under the Will of Mary Baker G. Eddy, 1919.
_____. *Science and Health with Key to the Scriptures*. Boston: Christian Science Board of Directors, 1934.
_____. *Church Manual of the First Church of Christ, Scientist in Boston, Massachusetts*, 89th ed. Boston: The First Church of Christ, Scientist, 1936.
Empirical Analysis of Medical Evidence in Christian Science Testimonies of Healing 1969–1988. Boston: First Church of Christ, Scientist, 1989.
Eustace, Herbert W. *Christian Science: Its Clear Correct Teaching and Complete Writings*. Berkeley, CA: Lederer, Street & Zeus, 1964.
Fraser, Caroline. *God's Perfect Child: Living and Dying in the Christian Science Church*. New York: Henry Holt, 1999.
Gill, Jillian. *Mary Baker Eddy*, Reading, MA: Preseus Books, 1998.
Gottschalk, Stephen. *The Emergence of Christian Science in American Religious Life*. Berkeley: University of California Press, 1973.
Haldeman, I. M. *Christian Science in the Light of Holy Scripture*. New York: Revell, 1909.

John, DeWitt. *The Christian Science Way of Life.* Englewood Cliffs, NJ: Prentice-Hall, 1962.

Johnsen, Thomas C. "Historical Consensus and Christian Science: The Career of a Manuscript Controversy." *New England Quarterly,* March 1980.

Peel, Robert. *Christian Science: Its Encounter with American Culture.* New York: Holt, 1958.

——. *Spiritual Healing in a Scientific Age.* New York: Harper & Row, 1988.

Ramsay, E. Mary. *Christian Science and Its Discoverer.* Boston: Christian Science Publishing Society, 1955.

Smith, Clifford P. *Historical Sketches.* Boston: Christian Science Publishing Society, 1941.

Twain, Mark. *Christian Science.* New York: Collier, 1907.

CHAPTER FIVE

THE FATHER DIVINE MOVEMENT

- The Communion Banquet
- The George Baker Story
- The New York City Period
- Name Game
- Sayville—The Turning Point
- Why They Joined
- The Economic Structure
- Social Organization and Nomenclature
- No Sex—No Marriage— No Family

- The Rewards
- Enemies and Defectors
- Scope and Operation of the Movement
- Mother Divine
- The Movement: Weaknesses and Strengths
- The Present Scene

The Rosebud led me to the study for my opportunity to meet the faith's leader. Reflecting the nationalistic pride of Peace Mission, the Rosebud was wearing a blue skirt, white blouse, and a red blazer embroidered with a large V—a uniform unchanged for over seventy years. When I asked her what the V stood for she said "virtue" or "victory." but I know that the letter originally stood for "virgin," since Rosebuds, the choir and communion attendants of the faith, take a lifelong pledge of celibacy.[1]

Within a few minutes I met Mother Divine, who, at age 80, makes a striking, handsome presence dressed in a white dress and speaking in a very engaging, alert demeanor. She was interested in knowing where I was from; upon learning that I was from Chicago, she recalled the woman who had led the Peace Mission there that had been closed now for a generation. She was pleased to know I was familiar with the teachings of Father Divine and said that they had ceased producing their publication *New Day* and were now reaching so many more through their Web site.

---

[1]Based on Schaefer's two meetings with Mother Divine and visit at Woodmont estate, Gladwyne, Pennsylvania, August 14, 2005.

One of the Rosebuds made sure I had a card with the site's address (www.libertynet.org/fdipmm/homepage.html), before I left the estate.

As I talked with her in the sunlit study of Father Divine, which has remained relatively undisturbed since his death in 1965, I noticed she sat in a chair next to his large oak desk—his desk chair and the his chair at the head of the table in the dining room are never sat in by anyone since his spirit remains with the faithful. Out the study windows I could see the Shrine to Life that I had earlier been allowed to enter in which the earthly remains of Father Divine are entombed in a crypt said to resemble the Ark of the Covenant—the chest that Christians say holds the Ten Commandments.

Later, elsewhere in the Woodmont mansion, I would talk to Mother Divine about a picture shows her on the occasion of an event very special to her. The Canadian-born woman who now leads the Peace Mission told me vividly how she recalled becoming a naturalized U.S. citizen in a special ceremony at nearby Valley Forge, Pennsylvania, as a part of the nation's Bicentennial Celebration. Again her recollections were always positive, with a sparkle in her eyes.

Not all the visitors were able to enter the Shrine through the doors called the "Portal of Life Eternal" much less be permitted to speak with Mother Divine. Those dressed with bare shoulders or women in short skirts or pants were kindly escorted around the mansion by a Rosebud, but went barely further than the Great Hall entrance, with its large picture of Father and Mother Divine. They were allowed to view the Shrine to Life only from the outside and at a distance of about a hundred yards.[2]

As the different Rosebuds showed me around the serene estate, it was difficult to think that I was at the headquarters of religious faith rather than immersed in an historical tour of a 32-room mansion dating back to 1892. The religious commitment among the five or so followers present was evident, and their continued devotion to Father Divine was palpable, but the energy of thousands followers coming together at one time as had occurred in the past was but a memory on this warm August afternoon in 2005.

The Peace Mission movement is extraordinary for a variety of reasons. Its founder and spiritual leader was a black man, Father Divine. Members of the Mission were very proud to be Americans and advanced the principles of democratic government, but they remained steadfastly antiwar, even during World War II. His followers in urban United States were primarily African American, but there was a substantial white membership—it was as unusual then as it is now to have a racially diverse following in any Christian denomination. At the height of the movement's success, he was more ardently praised and revered by his followers than any other religious leader in the United States. To those who believed, he was more than just an exalted person. He was, quite simply, God.

[2]A description of the Shrine to Life and limited interior photographs appear in D. Roger Howlett, *The Sculptures of Donald De Lue: Gods, Prophets, and Heroes* (Boston: David R. Godine, 1990), pp. 159–65.

Let's imagine what the scene might have been in one of the many Circle Mission churches across the United States in the 1950s when members of the Peace Mission Movement awaited the arrival of Father Divine.

The Communion Banquet

The U-shaped banquet table is decked in spotless linen, shining silverware, and fresh flowers. Each place setting includes a goblet with a cone-shaped napkin, in the center of which stands a small, bristling American flag. Just above the head table is a neon sign, FATHER DIVINE'S HOLY COMMUNION TABLE, and underneath the sign there are three large American flags. On the left wall is a felt banner with PEACE embroidered in large, even letters. On the right wall is a printed sign with the unsurpassable message: FATHER DIVINE IS GOD ALMIGHTY. All in all, it is a striking scene, and the 250 assembled guests—a mixture of blacks and whites—seem well aware of the fact.

The room itself vibrates with excitement and anticipation. Suddenly the tempo increases. There are several screams and shouts. From somewhere, a female voice rings out, "He's here! Father's here!" There is mass movement toward the doorway, where the curtains are parting. Then Father Divine—accompanied by Mother Divine on his right—breaks into the room with no uncertain step.

He is an African American man, short of stature, with smooth skin. His head is shiny bald, and while at the moment his face is impassive, his eyes are quick and penetrating. He wears jewelry: a diamond ring, an expensive-looking wristwatch, a gold chain across his vest, and two emblematic lapel buttons. Yet the overall effect is not one of pomp or flash. Father Divine's suit is dark and well cut, his tie is a conservative stripe, and his shoes are black.

Despite his diminutive size, it is apparent—to those present, at least—that he is a commanding personality. Every step of his buoyant walk, every gesture, every nod of his head brings gasps of delight from the onlookers. Several of the women jump high into the air.

Although Father Divine appears to be of indeterminate middle age, Mother Divine is clearly much younger. (She is his second wife, his first wife having died several years earlier.) A striking-looking white woman, Mother Divine is immaculately dressed. Almost a head taller than her husband, she gazes at him from time to time with genuine adoration. In addition to being his wife, she obviously is also one of his most devoted followers.

Together they make their way to the head table. Although the throng presses in closely, no one so much as touches Father. On his part, Father Divine seems to take the adulations for granted. Neither condescending nor overbearing, he acts with good-natured dignity and restraint. It is apparent that he is in command of the situation at all times.

Father and Mother Divine are seated, and because Father's feet do not reach the floor, a cushioned stool is placed under them. His followers return to their tables, and the noise subsides. The communion banquet is about to begin.

And what a banquet it is! A dozen different vegetables, roast beef, fried chicken, baked ham, roast turkey and duck, meat loaf, steak, cold cuts, spareribs, liver and bacon, four different kinds of bread, mixed salad with a choice of dressing, celery and olives, coffee, tea, and milk, and a variety of desserts, including layer cake, pie, pudding, fresh fruit, and great mounds of ice cream.

A corps of waitresses—immaculately clad in white—stand by, ready to help with the food. Each dish is first placed in front of Father Divine, who blesses it by touching the dish or adding a serving fork or spoon. The dishes are then passed on to the guests. The waitresses enthusiastically pour coffee, refill empty plates, help circulate the dishes, and otherwise encourage the diners to enjoy what Father Divine calls "the abundance of the fullness." (As we shall see, food has always played an important part in the Father Divine movement.)

With so many courses, so much food, and so many people, the serving and eating process takes a good deal of time—two and a half hours, to be exact. There is never a dull moment, however; in fact, there is so much happening that it is difficult to follow it all.

A thickset black woman suddenly jumps to her feet and thrusts both arms upward. "I was paralyzed!" she shouts in a throbbing voice. "No movement in the legs—none at all. And then I met you, Father, and you cured me. I am yours forever, Father, with true devotion!" She sits down and buries her head in her arms.

A middle-aged white woman stands up. "I had tuberculosis real bad. It was consumption. I coughed all day, and I coughed all night, and they told me I was a goner. Then you came into my life, Father, and made me well again overnight. I love you, Father, truly love you."

A thin black man with gray-white hair gets up slowly. "Before I was twenty, I was put in jail twice for stealing. Each time, I told the judge I didn't do it, but in my heart I knew I did. I was a bad boy, and I grew up to be a bad man. I set my neighbor's car on fire and never told nobody— till now. It was only when God came to me in the form of Father Divine that I was able to resolve myself. Thank you, Father."

Festivities   The Rosebuds, the women's choir, break into song at this point. They range in age from about ten to thirty-five, and all are dressed in red jackets and navy blue skirts.

There are approximately forty Rosebuds in the choir, and they sing their hearts out on every song. Their spirit is indomitable, inexhaustible. Although they are accompanied by a pianist, they have no sheet music to read. All their songs—dozens of them—are memorized. The words are original, although some of the songs are well-known melodies like "White Christmas" and "Anchors Aweigh."

During many of the songs the chorus is repeated, at which point the young women clap their hands and stamp their feet. When this happens, the audience joins in—and the chorus is likely to be repeated several more times. Unmistakably, the room is filled with happy singers. The only person not visibly affected is Father Divine himself, who acts as though the festivities were a routine part of his life. (Which indeed they are!)

Following the Rosebuds' songs, there are more confessions of sin and some additional tributes to Father Divine. One woman stands on a chair and shouts, "I love you, Father! Truly!" There is a chorus of agreement, after which individual testimonials are heard from all parts of the room.

"Blessed is the Lord!"

"I owe you everything, Father! Thank you, Father!"

"Bless his heavenly body!"

"Father Divine is *God Almighty!*"

At this point, the Lilybuds stand up and render a song. Dressed in attractive green jackets with white trim, the Lilybuds are an older version of the Rosebuds. There are perhaps fifty of them, and their ages seem to range from thirty-five up. Although they are not as vivacious as the Rosebuds, they do not lack enthusiasm. And their devotion to Father Divine is obviously unsurpassed. Their song has the ring of utmost sincerity.

> We want to be a real true Lilybud,
> Basking in our FATHER'S LOVE every day.
> We want to be a real true Lilybud,
> Obeying and doing what our precious FATHER says.

Now, for the first time, people are beginning to dance in the aisles. The dancing is unrehearsed, spontaneous, and individualistic. No two steps are alike, and no two people touch one another. Subdued at first, the movements and gesticulations accelerate as the evening wears on.

Following the Lilybuds' rendition, there is much shouting and applause, and then—as if led by an invisible cheerleader—the entire audience stands up and chants:

> Two, four, six, eight. Who do we appreciate?
> FATHER DIVINE! MOTHER DIVINE! Yea!

> One, two, three, four. Who are we for?
> Five, six, seven, eight. Who do we appreciate?
> FATHER DIVINE! MOTHER DIVINE! Yea!

Throughout the proceedings, Father Divine remains impassive. Much of his time has been spent in blessing the food plates and starting them on their way. Now he himself eats—slowly and sparingly. If he is impressed by the goings-on, he does not show it. He seems to look at no one in particular, and, with the exception of an occasional comment to Mother Divine, he is silent.

It is time now for a song from the Crusaders—the men's group. Although they include men of all ages, the Crusaders are a much smaller group than the Rosebuds or the Lilybuds. In fact, a large majority of those present, both uniformed and nonuniformed, are female. There are about fifteen Crusaders, and they are dressed in powder blue coats, white shirts, and dark trousers. They sing lustily and—like their predecessors—with obvious devotion.

> I want to love YOU, FATHER,
> A little bit more each day,
> I want to love YOU, FATHER,
> In all I do and say.
> For the wondrous works YOU do,
> For I know YOU'RE GOD ALMIGHTY,
> And I've given this heart to YOU!

At the end of the song, the audience erupts with an outburst of clapping and shouting. There are more testimonials and dances, and more of the women leap into the air. One oldster lies down across three chairs, sobbing uncontrollably. But all such behavior appears to be taken for granted by the group itself. There seems to be a tacit sequence of events, and if the activity is becoming more feverish, it is because the sequence dictates that the program is coming to a climax. And sure enough, there is a stirring at the head table. Father Divine is getting up to speak.

The Sermon   As Father Divine looks into the eyes of his followers, there are shouts of "God! God! God!"; "Peace, Father!"; "Thank you, dear one!"; "Hallelujah!"; "I love you, Father!"; "God Almighty!" Once he commences to speak, however, all noise stops. For the duration of his talk, the audience gives him their full attention.

As he speaks, twenty-five young female secretaries take up their notebooks and write down Father's words in shorthand. As a matter of fact, everything Father Divine says—sermons, discourses, speeches, interviews, extemporaneous remarks—is recorded by the ever-ready secretaries. Their shorthand is then transcribed and appears in *New Day*, the movement's biweekly newspaper, thus preserving Father Divine's words for posterity.

(The secretaries have always held a rather exalted position in the organization, because their work—when the movement was at its peak, at least—required them to stay close to Father Divine day in and day out. The secretaries include both black and white members, most of whom are ex-Rosebuds. Mother Divine had been both a Rosebud and a secretary.)

Father Divine speaks in a strong, resonant voice, with a distinctive tone quality. Though he starts slowly—almost methodically—his audience is spellbound from the very first word. The sermon itself is a combination of the practical and the profound, the esoteric and the absurd, yet his phrasing is such that it is often difficult to tell which is which.

Though we have Blessings unlimited economically, and though we have physical comfort and convenience for ourselves and for millions of others, yet back of all of it is IT, which said, "Let there be light, and there was light."

Back of all of it was, as it is, the same, that while on the water, as so to speak, invisible, and spoke into visibility the earth upon which we are living, the beginning of the material and economic things of life![3]

Several times during his sermon, Father Divine punctuates an affirmation with, "Aren't you glad!" And each time the audience answers with a resounding, "Yes, so glad!" or, "So glad, Lord!"

When the sermon is finished, there is a tumultuous burst of applause, and shouts of "So true, Father!"; "Thank you, Father!"; "Lord God Almighty!" People jump and whirl, and a number have tears in their eyes. Almost all are visibly moved. One woman clutches herself and screams, "I love you, sweetheart!" Another lies on the floor motionless, scarcely noticed by the others. An elderly man takes his cane and whacks it against the table as hard as he can, the vibrating silverware adding to the din.

In the midst of all the exuberance, the Rosebuds rise and sing one of their inimitable songs, and there is more stamping and clapping. Additional testimonials and confessions follow—and further expressions of adulation for Father. Then the Lilybuds rise and sing. Then the Crusaders. Genuine ecstasy. Genuine rapture. No doubt about it. Only Father Divine manages to take it all in stride. In a few minutes, he and Mother Divine—with their entourage of secretaries and others—will leave and, quite possibly, visit another of their "heavens," where a similar spectacle will unfold.

"God in a Body"   Although it may read like fiction, this description of a Father Divine communion banquet is based on fact. The foregoing scene is a composite picture of actual happenings. Father Divine died in 1965, and while the movement continues, the "enthusiasm" has been necessarily dampened. Nevertheless, while he was alive, he was a phenomenally successful leader.

Who was this man, this superman, this "God in a body"? When and where was he born? What was his youth like? When did he first aspire to be God? Whence cometh his financial support? How did his movement get to be worldwide in scope? Can it survive, now that "God" is no longer on earth?

Some of these questions are answerable; some—at the moment, at least—are not. From World War I to the present, the Father Divine story is traceable. It is far from complete, but the broad outlines are known. The period prior to World War I is the stickler. Here the picture is murky and tantalizing, and this is unfortunate. For if we knew the real origin and background

---

[3]Full texts of sermons such as this one were reprinted periodically in the *New Day* until the printing operation closed in 1992. The Divinites have a Web site, as Mother Divine told Schaefer in his August 14, 2005, interview.

of Father Divine the man, we would have a much better understanding of Father Divine in his role as a religious leader.

The George Baker Story

Relatively few books have been written about Father Divine, and most of them are out of date.[4] Moreover, the various accounts have been journalistic in nature, and some gross differences in reporting exist. In recent years, fortunately, there has been some scholarly interest in the subject, and during the 1980s and 1990s several revealing works have appeared.[5]

Although our knowledge of Father Divine's early years is admittedly spotty, it seems that there was once a man named George Baker. His date of birth has been reported as anywhere between 1860 and 1880, depending on who is doing the reporting. According to the most recent of these accounts, he was born in 1878 in Monkey Run, a black ghetto at the northern edge of Rockville, Maryland.

His parents were Nancy and George Baker Sr., two ex-slaves. Both were hard workers; in fact, as a house servant, Nancy was called on to work day and night. Unfortunately, her heavy schedule did not prevent her from gaining weight, and eventually "her obesity rendered her incapable of working."[6]

The episode is mentioned in some detail because it seems to have had a bearing on young George Baker's subsequent actions. Watts writes as follows: "One day not long after his mother died, George Baker vanished from Rockville. He fled the poverty and agony of Monkey Run, leaving behind relatives and friends puzzled over his disappearance. He rejected destitution, his obese mother, his struggling family, and the white racism that promised to imprison him in Monkey Run for life."[7]

---

[4]See Robert Allerton Parker, *The Incredible Messiah* (Boston: Little, Brown, 1937); John Hoshor, *God in a Rolls Royce: The Rise of Father Divine* (1936; reprint, Freeport, NY: Books for Libraries Press, 1971); Sarah Harris, *Father Divine: Holy Husband* (1953; reprint, New York: Macmillan, 1971). See also the series by St. Clair McKelway and A. J. Liebling, "Who Is This King of Glory?" *New Yorker*, June 13, 1936, pp. 21ff; June 20, 1936, pp. 22ff; and June 27, 1936, pp. 22ff. There have been hundreds of articles about Father Divine in publications such as *Time, Newsweek,* and the *New York Times*. The principal historical sources, however, seem to be those just cited.

[5]See Stephen Zwick, "The Father Divine Peace Mission Movement" (Senior Thesis: Princeton University, 1971); Roma Barnes, "Blessings Flowing Free: The Father Divine Peace Mission Movement in Harlem, New York City, 1932–1941" (Ph.D. diss., University of York, England, 1979); Kenneth E. Burnham, *God Comes to America: Father Divine and the Peace Mission Movement* (Boston: Lambeth, 1979); Jill Watts, *God, Harlem U.S.A.: The Father Divine Story* (Berkeley: University of California Press, 1992); and Robert Weisbrot, *Father Divine and the Struggle for Racial Equality* (Urbana: University of Illinois Press, 1983).

[6]Watts, *God, Harlem U.S.A.,* p. 6.

[7]Ibid., p. 12.

The Peace Mission offers little information about Father Divine's early life, viewing it largely irrelevant to his spiritual mission. They do emphatically deny his name was George Baker, and instead present his full name as Major Jealous Divine.

The whereabouts and activities of the man who would become Father Devine remain unknown for the next two or three years. There are isolated reports of his refusing to attend Jim Crow schools, of being jailed for riding in the "whites only" section of a trolley car, of being a Sunday school superintendent, and of spending six months on a chain gang. None of the accounts have been proved—or disproved. It is not until around 1900 that the various biographical accounts tend to converge.

By that year, George Baker had settled in Baltimore, working as a gardener during the day and as an assistant preacher at night and on Sundays. He was neither more nor less successful than other black ministers of the period who were forced to take outside jobs—until fate intervened one Sunday morning in 1907, in the form of one Samuel Morris.

Although reports differ on how the two men met, the meeting itself had a profound and lasting effect on George Baker. Samuel Morris rejected the usual hellfire-and-damnation approach to salvation and instead taught that God dwells within every person. One report has it that Morris proclaimed himself to be God and, upon being evicted from the church where he was preaching, was befriended by George Baker. Another report makes no mention of this episode but states simply that Baker was drawn to the religious philosophy of Samuel Morris, returning "again and again" to hear him preach.

In any case, it may have been at this time that George Baker caught the idea of becoming God. Prior to his association with Morris, his sermons had given no inkling of heavenly aspirations, but by 1907 he seems to have become intertwined—apparently forever—with the Deity.

Although the details at this point are not clear, Samuel Morris and George Baker evidently worked out an arrangement whereby they shared the godship. Also, at this time, both men apparently changed their names (or were "reborn"). Samuel Morris was henceforth known as Father Jehovia, and George Baker became known as the Messenger.

In 1908 they were joined by a third man, John Hickerson, a tall, African American minister with an imposing voice. Not to be outdone by his companions, Reverend Hickerson also adopted a more spiritual name, St. John the Vine. Although Father Jehovia (Samuel Morris) seems to have been number one, the three men were somehow able to share their divinity, and for the next several years they were as flamboyant a preaching team as the area had ever seen.

The Messenger   In 1912 the triumvirate broke up. Presumably, they were no longer willing to share their divine authority, and in any case they went their separate ways. St. John the Vine Hickerson traveled to New York City, where he founded his own church. Father Jehovia passed from the picture and for all intents and purposes was never heard from again. The Messenger (George Baker) turned southward, gained some converts, and—if we can believe his biographers—ran into a pack of trouble.

The Father Divine Movement

George Baker born 1878 (approx.)	Movement moves to New York City 1915		Trial for disturbing the peace 1931-32	Marries Mother Divine (Ritchings) 1946		Peoples Temple rebuffed at Woodman 1971	

1870–1885	1910–1925	1925–1940	1940–1955	1955–1970	1970–1985	1985–2000

| | 1912 Baker-Morris-Hawkins breakup | 1919 Sayville, Long Island, headquaters | | 1942 Move to Phildelphia; Mother Divine (Peninah) dies | | 1965 Father Divine dies |

At Valdosta, Georgia, in 1913, the Messenger was preaching the gospel in his own unique style. The townspeople were entranced and turned out in large numbers to hear the man who called himself God. While reports vary, there were some in the audience who were not impressed. Among the skeptics were a number of local pastors, who had the Messenger arrested and taken to court. The charge: Any person who believes himself or herself to be God must be of unsound mind.

For reasons best known to themselves, the jury upheld the charge, and the Messenger was declared insane. Instead of committing him to a mental institution, however, the court ordered him to leave the state of Georgia forthwith. He did so, and as far as we know, he never returned.

In spite of the resistance and harassment he met in the South, however, the Messenger did succeed in gaining converts. They were few, to be sure—probably not more than a dozen—but they were dedicated believers, and they would form the nucleus of his forthcoming religious organization. One person is worthy of particular mention: a stout, African American woman called Peninah, or Sister Penny. Before the group left the South, Sister Penny was reportedly the Messenger's chief angel.

The New York City Period

In 1915, the Messenger and his disciples arrived in New York City, undaunted by their troubles and apparently none the worse for wear. After a brief stay in Manhattan, the little group settled in Brooklyn. Starting in a rooming house, they began to develop the format for what would one day be a worldwide religious organization.

As they struggled to survive in the big city, the Messenger himself was in touch with his old friend and fellow deity, St. John the Vine Hickerson. Hickerson's own church—the Church of the Living God—had been fairly successful. The Messenger attended Hickerson's services, checked his methods, asked questions, and otherwise borrowed from St. John the Vine's repertoire.

Along with modest success, however, Hickerson was also having some difficulty. Like his mentor, Father Jehovia (Samuel Morris), St. John the Vine taught that God was not in heaven but within every person. This meant that although Hickerson could be God, there could be any number of auxiliary gods—and this is exactly what was happening. Wearing "gold" and "silver" crowns and royal purple robes, these deities clogged the path to Hickerson's church. There were Father Obey, Joe World, Elijah of the Fiery Chariot, Saint Peter, Father Paul, Steamboat Bill, Father Joshua, and many others. Later on there would be cult leaders and other exotic personalities, like Barnaby Bill, Sufi Abdul Hamid, and Daddy Grace. New York was fast becoming a religious maelstrom.

Before long, St. John the Vine's church fell under the weight of its own gods. Although he did not pass into oblivion like Samuel Morris, John Hickerson became a relatively obscure figure. Following World War I, he was heard from less and less.

The Messenger himself severed all connection with John Hickerson and never referred to him publicly again. The little group in Brooklyn, meanwhile, was holding its own—perhaps even growing a bit. A few of the original members had left, but new ones kept joining. The Messenger was a persuasive speaker, and his followers genuinely revered him. He ran a tight ship, however, and unlike St. John the Vine, permitted only one God—himself. He made all the rules and brooked no interference, and he followed that practice all his life.

As to its living arrangements, the group operated communally. The Messenger himself did no work outside the church—nor would he, ever again. Instead, he ran an employment service, supplying domestics and menial workers to those who were looking for honest, reliable help. Whether or not they got their jobs through his employment service, however, the Messenger's followers presumably turned their wages over to him. He then paid the rent, bought the food, and took care of the necessary bills.

Peninah was in charge of the actual household management—including shopping and food preparation—and from all accounts she was an indefatigable worker. In fact, some observers believe that the Messenger married her during this period, though others set the date much earlier. But whatever the date, the marriage was spiritual in nature. It may also have been legal—though no marriage license has been uncovered—but it was not sexual. Quite early in the movement, the Messenger declared that sex was unclean, a mark of depravity, and hence was forbidden. Neither he nor his followers have been known to violate the decree.

Name Game

During the New York period, another interesting phenomenon occurred: the Messenger underwent further name changes. The reason is not entirely clear, but presumably he felt the need for a more appropriate title. In any case, just as George Baker evolved into the Messenger, so the Messenger evolved into Major Jealous Devine, which was eventually shortened to M. J. Devine, and finally—over a period of years—*M. J. Devine* became *Father Divine*. These latter changes, though gradual, are a matter of record and are not really in dispute. The dispute arises over the earlier sequence: the transition from George Baker to the Messenger, and from the Messenger to Major Jealous Devine. These name changes, along with Father Divine's stubborn refusal to acknowledge his heritage, created a genuine mystery that did not unravel until years after his death.

The George Baker–Messenger–Father Divine story told in the preceding pages is most certainly not the account told by Father Divine's followers, or for that matter by Father Divine himself. Whenever he was asked when he was born, he might reply, "I wasn't born. I was combusted." He also answered queries about his birth with a scriptural, "Before Abraham was, I am."

Not all of his replies were nebulous, however. On one occasion, a radio news commentator stated in no uncertain terms that Father Divine's real name was George Baker. An excerpt from Father Divine's reply (by letter) follows:

> MY name is MAJOR J. DIVINE, better known as FATHER DIVINE. . . . MY name has never at any time been George Baker, as stated by you and many others who have filled the press and the air with radio broadcasts with false, erroneous and perjured testimonies endorsed as though they were true.[8]

Predictably, Father Divine's followers totally reject the George Baker story; indeed, they go out of their way to "set the record straight." Mother Divine, for example, recently wrote to the Library of Congress, requesting that their records be corrected. Their reply was as follows: "The Library of Congress heading created in 1936 for Father Divine under the spurious name 'George Baker' has been corrected. Our heading now reads: 'Father Divine.' The change . . . is being reflected on all records going into our new catalog."[9]

Sayville—The Turning Point

But let us pick up the chronological thread of our story. Starting in 1919, fortunately, the activities of Father Divine and his followers become

[8]Mother Divine, *The Peace Mission Movement* (Philadelphia: Imperial Press, 1982), pp. 106–7.
[9]Ibid., p. 108.

increasingly clear—and more and more a matter of record. During that year, he and his little group, numbering not more than two dozen, moved from Brooklyn to Sayville, Long Island. The house they moved to—an attractive, twelve-room dwelling at 72 Macon Street—still stands. It is used by the followers as a kind of shrine, for it was here that the movement first gained national and international recognition.

Things started off peacefully enough. The deed to the house was in the name of Major J. Devine and his wife, Peninah, and if the white community was less than enthusiastic at the prospect of blacks setting up in their midst, no overt reaction was apparent. In fact, for several years Sayville and its environs made good use of Father Divine's services. Operating an employment office—as he had in Brooklyn—Father Divine was able to supply reliable domestics for the many nearby estates.

From all accounts, Father Divine was a good neighbor. He kept 72 Macon Street spic-and-span. He worked in the garden. He was polite and friendly, with a ready smile. His followers did not inundate the neighborhood, as some had feared. The group did manage to grow in number—but slowly. They were not loud or unruly. There was no drinking. And there were never any sex problems.

Things went on this way for ten happy years.

Father Divine appeared to be consolidating his position. He was, in effect, learning how to combine the role of businessman with that of deity. On both counts, he was successful. As a businessman, he had the confidence and respect of the community—in spite of the general racial situation. And in his role as deity, he was superb.

African Americans of the 1920s were likely to be disadvantaged individuals. Faced with both social and economic discrimination, they often had a low level of aspiration and—more than occasionally—a feeling of hopelessness. Father Divine succeeded in imbuing his followers with a sense of hope and purpose.

He gave them economic security in the form of lodging, food, and employment. He encouraged self-respect by insisting that they give their employers an honest day's work for a day's pay. He forbade them to accept tips. He gave them a sense of self-discipline by prohibiting smoking, drinking, swearing, and "immodest behavior." And—above all else—he gave them spiritual security. For if he, Father Divine, was God Almighty, then his followers were assured of everlasting life.

To be sure, his followers had to make certain sacrifices. They had to renounce sex and marriage. They had to abide by Father Divine's rules and regulations, for he did not tolerate backsliders. And again, they presumably all turned their wages over to him. But these were small sacrifices compared to the economic and spiritual benefits involved.

Slowly but surely the fame of M. J. Devine—better known as Father Divine—spread. As the 1920s wore on, membership increased steadily. On Sundays, busloads of visitors would arrive at 72 Macon Street to see and hear God and partake of the mighty meals—thirty to forty courses every week, and all for free! No collection plate was ever passed; no request for donations was ever made. When—invariably—the question was asked, "But where does the money come from to pay for it all?" the answer was always the same: "It comes from God."

In 1930, the Sunday bus excursions were joined by private automobiles—first dozens, then hundreds. To local residents, it seemed like an endless caravan. The banquets also grew in size and vigor. There were testimonials and increasing reports of miraculous cures. (Father was clearly omnipotent.) Then came the songs and the clapping. And the sermon. And the hallelujahs. And so on. To the good citizens of Sayville, at least, things seemed to be getting out of hand. It was time that something was done.

At first there was police harassment. Many tickets for traffic and parking violations were issued in wholesale lots. When this tactic failed, the district attorney planted a female undercover agent at 72 Macon Street. Dressed as a poor African American working woman, the agent tried to verify rumors of sexual relations between Father Divine and his female followers. When this also failed, she tried to seduce Father Divine, but—by her own account—he ignored her. The only thing she could report was that everyone treated her with sympathy and kindness.

Next there were town meetings, with groups of angry residents demanding Father Divine's ouster. A committee of leading citizens was selected to visit 72 Macon Street and make their demands known. Father Divine received the group and listened patiently while they explained their point of view. Then he explained his. He and his followers were good citizens. They had broken no laws. He himself had helped Sayville economically by providing an employment service and by buying large quantities of food and supplies from local merchants. Furthermore, Father Divine pointed out, the Constitution guaranteed freedom of religion. So he was not going to leave Sayville. On the contrary, he was quite likely to expand his activities.

Father was polite, speaking in an even tone. But something in his manner told the committee that further discussion was futile, and they left. A short time later—during one of the Sunday services—police broke into 72 Macon Street and arrested Father Divine and eighty of his followers for disturbing the peace. The Sunday in question was November 15, 1931, a date that quite possibly marks the real beginning of the Father Divine movement. While the arrest itself was peaceful enough, the entire episode was a shot heard round the African American world.

Judge Lewis J. Smith   Despite the flimsiness of the case, Father Divine was indicted by the grand jury and held (on $1,500 bail) for trial. The black press—and a sizable segment of the white press as well—took up the cry of racial discrimination, and the fight was on. News stories made the front pages, and publicity grew by leaps and bounds. Within a few weeks, Father Divine had become a cause célèbre. He himself, though not visibly perturbed, vowed to fight the case—and, if necessary, to "rot in jail" rather than succumb to the forces of intolerance and bigotry.

John C. Thomas, an African American lawyer who had been an assistant U.S. district attorney, offered his services to Father Divine, who accepted. The presiding judge in the case was Lewis J. Smith, who was white, and who—the record would show—was clearly antagonistic in his attitude toward the defendant. One of the judge's first acts was to cancel Father Divine's bail and remand him to prison for the duration of the trial. This action, based on a legal technicality, set the tone for the entire trial.

The actual proceedings were fairly clear-cut. The prosecution contended that Father Divine and his followers had annoyed the neighbors, disturbed the peace, and obstructed traffic, and were a public nuisance. The defense naturally denied the allegations. Most of the witnesses were either neighbors (prosecution) or Father Divine's followers (defense). The only thing really noteworthy during the trial was the antagonism shown by Judge Smith toward several of the defense witnesses. It was easy to see where his sympathies lay.

Even in his charge to the jury, the judge showed partiality. He stated that Father Divine was a bad influence in the community, that his real name was not Father Divine but George Baker, that Mother Divine was not his legal wife, that he was not an ordained minister, and that he was able to induce others to turn their wages over to him.

After deliberating a short while, the jury—not unexpectedly—returned a verdict of guilty. They did, however, recommend leniency. Judge Smith adjourned the court for several days while he contemplated the sentence. The defendant, meanwhile, stayed in jail.

Public reaction was mixed. Some felt that Father Divine was in fact guilty as charged. Many fair-minded people, however, had come to the conclusion that he was innocent, a victim of unadulterated race prejudice.

Undaunted, Judge Smith reconvened the court and imposed the stiffest sentence the law allowed: one year in jail and a fine of five hundred dollars. Also undaunted, Father Divine went to jail, a quizzical expression on his face.

Three days later, Judge Lewis J. Smith was dead!

Only fifty years of age and apparently in good health, he reportedly had died of a heart attack.

When asked—in his cell—whether he had any comments regarding Judge Smith's demise, Father Divine replied, somewhat mournfully, "I hated to do it."[10]

---

[10]This statement has been reported countless times by various researchers, although Hoshor may have been the first (*God in a Rolls Royce*). Watts, in a more recent account, questions whether Father Divine ever "claimed direct responsibility for Smith's death" (*God, Harlem U.S.A.*; see her footnote 6, p. 211).

Afterward, the appellate court overturned Father Divine's conviction, basing its decision on the "prejudicial comments" voiced by (the late) trial judge. The fines levied against Father Divine and his codefendants were also rescinded.

Why They Joined

The death of Judge Smith had an overwhelming effect on large segments of the African American community. Although most white newspapers carried the story in routine fashion, the black press used banner headlines. In some neighborhoods, African Americans held parades and rallies. On June 26, 1932, for example—the day after Father Divine's release from prison—a "Monster Glory to Our Lord" rally was held at the Rockland Palace in Harlem. Lines started to form at five A.M., even though Father Divine wasn't scheduled to appear until noon. Over 7,000 persons jammed the auditorium, and thousands more were turned away.

Father Divine did not let his followers down. Shunning his usual figures of speech, he delivered one of the clearest talks of his career. Among other things, he said:

> You may not have seen my flesh for a few weeks, but I was with you just the same. I am just as operative in the mind as in the body. There were many who thought I had gone someplace, but I'm glad to say I did not go anywhere.
>
> I held the key to that jail all the time I was in it, and was with you every time you met. They can prosecute me or persecute me, or even send me to the electric chair, but they can never keep me from you or stop me from doing good![11]

When Father Divine finished his talk, the human explosion almost tore the roof off Rockland Palace. Eruptions of "Hallelujah!" "Sweet Savior!" "Father Divine is God Almighty!" rocked the auditorium. People jumped, screamed, shouted, shook, and whirled. Most were ecstatic, but some were overcome and wept. Harlem had never seen anything like it before.

After the waves of acclaim had passed, testimonials were heard. One woman had been cured of cancer through Father's intervention; another, of arthritis. A cripple had been healed and had thrown away his crutches. On and on they went, a spontaneous cascade of miracles.

Then the tone of the audience changed, and people began to complain not of their physical afflictions, but of their social oppression. They were poor and hungry. They lived in squalor and could not get jobs. They had no hope, no future. They needed help, and they needed it now—from God! Little by little, louder and louder, the chant was taken up: "Need you, Father! Need you! Need you! Need you!"[12]

[11]Harris, *Father Divine*, pp. 42–44.
[12]Harris, op. cit.

What were the sociological factors that accounted for this mass attraction? To answer the question in generalized terms is easy: the right person was in the right place at the right time—with the right people. A more specific answer would involve a number of points.

Manifest versus Latent Function   Sociologist Robert Merton first proposed the concept of **manifest** versus **latent function.** According to Merton, many social processes and institutions have a dual function: a conscious, deliberate, or "manifest" function, and an unconscious, unrealized, or "latent" function.

College fraternities and sororities, for example, have the manifest function of providing food, housing, and camaraderie for interested students. But there is also a latent function: the conferring of social status on those invited to membership. And so it was with the Father Divine movement. Men and women joined manifestly because they believed in the religious orientation of the group, but in a latent sense, the Divine movement provided them with certain rewards not otherwise attainable.

The nation was in the grips of the Great Depression, and as low persons on the economic totem pole, African Americans were the hardest hit. In many African American neighborhoods the housing was dreadful: run-down buildings, congestion, rats and roaches, three and four families sharing one toilet, no hot water, inadequate heat in the winter—year after year after year. Sickness, ill health, inadequate medical facilities, poor sanitary conditions, and a high death rate persisted, as did unemployment, desertion, drug addiction, and hopelessness. African Americans—particularly those in the lower class—did indeed need someone. And in the absence of a more appropriate candidate, it looked as though that someone might be Father Divine.

Of particular relevance here is the food factor. Social security, unemployment compensation, Medicare and Medicaid, Aid to Families with Dependent Children (AFDC), United Way, old-age assistance—such programs were still many years away. One of the first problems facing an unemployed person, therefore, was hunger. It is easy to see why Father Divine—whose daily services included huge quantities of free food—had such ready appeal. And whenever the question was asked, "But where does all the food come from—who pays for it?" the answer was always the same: "It comes from God, and God don't need money."

Indeed, the manifest reason most joined the movement was to be in God's inner circle. For many, the latent function was an escape from abject poverty.

The Racial Stereotype   The depression was not the only cause of African Americans' economic difficulties. Prejudice and discrimination were so widespread that even when jobs were available, African Americans were likely to be excluded. In the 1930s, even clerical and semiskilled occupations were generally closed to black applicants. One did not see black salesclerks in stores or black secretaries in offices. One did not see black bus drivers or mechanics or tradespeople.

In fact, in the 1930s, racial stereotyping was the order of the day. Originally defined as "pictures in the head," **stereotype** can best be described as an unreliable generalization about all members of a group that does not recognize individual differences within a group. Thus, the belief by whites that blacks were lazy or inferior is a typical racial stereotype. And while sociologists are well aware that stereotyping still occurs, it is probably not so prevalent as it was two or three generations ago. In the 1930s, certainly, it was commonly believed by prejudiced whites that blacks were listless, unreliable, happy-go-lucky, and largely incapable of holding a job.

Because so much of Father Divine's program was aimed at the elimination of racial stereotyping and job discrimination, it is easy to see why he had such an impact on the African American community. It is no accident that his appeal was greatest in those areas where congestion, unemployment, and discrimination were rampant: Brooklyn, Manhattan, Newark, Jersey City, Philadelphia.

Alienation   Things were so bad for African Americans in the 1930s that a feeling of alienation often prevailed. As used by sociologists, **alienation** is the condition of estrangement or dissociation from the surrounding society. Alienated persons feel that those in power have neglected them, and that there is nothing they can do about it. They believe that they have little or no control over their own destiny, and that—in effect—they have become dispensable.

More than any other leader of his time, it was Father Divine who fought against the spread of alienation, and he was a superb practitioner. He understood the masses. He could talk to them. He could engender feelings of self-respect, and he could play the role of God. Most important, he never lost sight of the two basics: food and jobs. These were the bedrock. As long as he was at the helm, Father Divine's followers would have ample food at little or no cost. And—through his employment service or within his own economic establishment—they would have jobs.

Food, jobs, and a joyous war against racism and alienation—no wonder large numbers of African Americans flocked to Father Divine's banner. Add to these his personal magnetism, his heavenly claims and obvious knowledge of the Bible, his penetrating voice and allegorical speech, his presumed healing powers, his spontaneous and vibrant manner, his intense concentration on goodness and fairness—for his followers, the result spelled God.

The Economic Structure

Over the years, there has been a good deal of misunderstanding regarding Father Divine's economic operations. His followers tended to believe that because he was God, he could "materialize" all the money he wanted, a notion that Father took no steps to dispel. The Internal Revenue Service, which had some genuine doubts about his deification, wondered why he never paid any income tax. After all, they reasoned, a man who wore expensive suits and diamond rings, who rode in Cadillac limousines and ate lavishly—such a man must also have a lavish income. Father Divine denied the imputation, and in a series of showdowns between "church and state," the state lost.

During his long career, Father Divine never paid a penny in income taxes. His critics contended that, under the mantle of the Lord, he used his workers' salaries to line his own heaven with gold. His supporters countered with the argument that Father Divine had never asked anyone for money in his life, and that even in his own churches there was no such thing as a collection plate.

Actually, Father Divine's economic operations were not so complicated—or so secretive—as his critics claimed. While much of the day-to-day procedure never became public knowledge, enough is known to permit a reasonable description. The basic economic principle was remarkably simple: to feed and house ten people communally did not cost ten times as much as it would cost to feed and house a single individual, especially if the ten were willing to let the Lord handle the fiscal details. This was the principle Father Divine (as the Messenger) had followed in Brooklyn during the World War I period, and he adhered to it throughout his entire career.

The Hotel Business   Of all the economic enterprises under the aegis of Father Divine—and there were many—none was more successful than the hotel business, the structural network around which the movement revolved. For example, although the organization had a number of churches, or missions, many of the meetings and rallies were held in the hotels. Communion banquet services, like the one described earlier, were held in the hotels.

When it came to labor, problems were minimal. Instead of being staffed by employees demanding union wages, the hotels would employ Father Divine's followers, who would work for no wages whatsoever. Instead, they received room and board and the eternal care of a loving God, whom they were privileged to serve on a regular basis. And, of course, because they served outsiders, the hotels were profitable. This in turn enabled the movement to feed thousands of needy people virtually free of charge. One further point should be mentioned. Father Divine and his followers did not build their hotels; they bought them. Often in run-down condition, the buildings were refurbished—with the help of the faithful—and then opened for business. Father Divine had a remarkable eye for real estate values, and much of his success stemmed from his uncanny ability to ferret out bargains. Once he made his intentions known, it was not difficult to find the necessary backers. Large urban hotels such as the Divine Tracy (Philadelphia), the Divine Hotel Riviera (Newark), the Divine Fairmount (Jersey City), and the Divine Lorraine (Philadelphia) were all acquired in this manner, and all were operated successfully initially, but only the Divine Tracy is still in operation today.

Father Divine was a strong believer in racial integration, and his hotels gave him the opportunity to practice what he preached. Blacks and whites not only worked together side by side but—as a matter of policy—were assigned to the same room. Father Divine said the hotels were his "demonstrators of democracy in action."

Employment Service   Father Divine first started his employment service during the New York period (1915–1919). He had an obvious knack for placing domestic workers, and throughout his career the employment service remained his most successful operation, with the possible exception of the hotels.

The reason for his success is that, as previously mentioned, Father Divine insisted on an honest day's work for a day's pay. Over the years, his workers' reputation—for honesty, reliability, and devoutness—grew. Indeed, as many housewives in the New York–New Jersey–Philadelphia area can attest, the demand for domestics was greater than the supply. Father Divine forbade his workers to accept tips or gifts. The following announcement was printed and reprinted in *New Day* hundreds of times:

To Whom It May Concern

A true follower of Mine does not want or desire a gift, or present, or anything of that type for Christmas or any holiday, and considers it to be unevangelical, unconstitutional, and not according to scripture. . . . MY true followers, as long as they receive just compensation for their labor, will not accept tips, gifts, or presents. . . .

This leaves ME Well, Healthy, Joyful, Peaceful, Lively, Loving, Successful, Prosperous and Happy in Spirit, Body and Mind, and in every organ, muscle, sinew, joint, limb, vein, and bone, and even in every ATOM, fiber, and cell of MY BODILY FORM.

Respectfully and Sincere, I AM
Rev. M. J. Divine
(Better known as *Father Divine*)

The ending is one that Father Divine used in his written communiqués. The message in the body of the letter is self-explanatory and is another example of how he could be crystal clear—when he wanted to be.

Father Divine's followers could work inside or outside the movement. If they worked inside—in a hotel, restaurant, or larger business establishment—they toiled in the service of the Lord, without wages. If they worked outside—as domestics, for example—what they did with their wages was up to them. Presumably, many of them did turn their wages over to the movement, but they were not forced to do so.

Social Organization and Nomenclature

All the groups discussed in the present volume are, in one way or another, outside the mainstream of American life. To help in their adaptation to the larger society, each of the groups has used certain techniques aimed at enhancing internal solidarity. The Father Divine movement has employed a combination of the sacred and the secular. Their churches, for instance, not only serve as places of worship but are designed to house and feed people.

Formerly known as "heavens," the churches and their branches are officially designated as "kingdoms, extensions, and connections," and many of the followers live in these buildings. Not all of the followers, to be sure: it is permissible to live at home. But the dedicated followers—sometimes called the "inner circle" or "holy family" of Father Divine—do live within the walls of the kingdoms. (It is from this group that the Rosebuds, Lilybuds, Crusaders, and secretaries have traditionally been drawn.)

Actually, the kingdoms, extensions, and connections are no more—and no less—than hotels, apartments, rooming houses, and other buildings used for all-purpose quarters by the faithful. Outsiders may also live in the kingdoms, but while they are on the premises, they are subject to the same strict rules of living as the followers. When the movement was at its peak—which is the historical present we are now discussing—there were over 175 kingdoms, extensions, and connections.

Followers who live in one of the kingdoms are closely knit and—like the Oneida Community discussed in Chapter 2—would comprise a genuine primary group. Describing an assembly of followers who were waiting for the appearance of Father and Mother Divine, Kenneth Burnham writes: "It was here that it was possible to experience the primary-group nature of the rank and file of the Movement. They have known each other from five to forty years. They have worked together, traveled together in the church cars, lived together in buildings they own jointly, and eaten together at Communion served by fellow believers, and in restaurants owned and staffed by 'brothers' and 'sisters.'"[13]

Dedicated followers are united in ways other than by living and working together. They also believe together. They are convinced that Father

[13]Burnham, *God Comes to America*, pp. 81–82.

Divine is God and that all his statements are literally true. They believe in the Bible, but for spiritual guidance they frequently turn to the community newsletter, which carries the sermons of Father Divine over and over again.

No Sex—No Marriage—No Family

Sociologists use the term **norm** to describe an established standard of behavior maintained by a society. In the Father Divine movement, the norm "It is better to be celibate than to marry" pervades the entire organization. True followers do not believe in sex, marriage, or family. Married couples can join, but if they live in one of the kingdoms, they must separate. (The usual procedure is for males to live on one floor, females on another.) If there are children, they must be reared separately.

With regard to family life, dedicated followers see themselves as children and Father and Mother Divine as parents, and they believe that this type of relationship is more gratifying—and more exalted—than normal family arrangements. Point seven of the Crusaders' "Declaration Concerning God" shows the intensity of their feelings:

> I believe that FATHER DIVINE is my Real FATHER, and that MOTHER DIVINE is my Real MOTHER, and that I never had another.

True followers also abstain from all sexual relationships. In fact, men and women have very little to do with one another. Before and after communion banquets, it is quite common to see the men talking among themselves and the women among themselves. There is no hostility or antagonism, merely a gentle avoidance.

The "International Modest Code," formulated by Father Divine, is the behavioral guide used by all dedicated followers. The code—in whole or in part—is prominently displayed in the various kingdoms, extensions, and connections. It was reprinted in issue after issue of *New Day* as follows:

International Modest Code
Established by Father Divine

*No Smoking * No Drinking * No Obscenity*
*No Vulgarity * No Profanity*
No Undue Mixing of the Sexes
No Receiving of Gifts, Presents,
Tips or Bribes

True followers adhere to the code, word for word, almost by second nature. But they seem to give special attention and credence to the section "no undue mixing of the sexes." Celibacy, virginity, purity, chastity, virtue—by whatever term, the followers seem almost to flaunt the idea of sexual abstinence.

The Rosebuds wear a white V (for virtue) on their jackets, and of their "Ten Commandments," number six reads, "We will endeavor to let our every deed and action express virginity." The Lilybuds' "Endeavor" says that they will "live pure, holy, virtuous, and clean." And the Crusaders pledge to "live a righteous, useful, consecrated Life which is devoted to holiness, purity, . . . self-denial."

The Rewards

The followers of Father Divine do not lead a completely sacrificial life. Far from it. They must renounce normal marital and familial relationships and abjure the profit motive, but the rewards—from their point of view— are far greater than the sacrifices.

Dedicated followers will never get rich, obviously, but then they have no need for riches. Their expenses are near zero. They have no family to support, no parents to look after. They pay no rent, have no mortgage or other expenses connected with a house. Their recreational and travel costs are minimal. They have no food bill. What need have these followers for wealth? The movement will care for their material needs as long as they live. And they in turn will provide the movement with a lifetime of dedicated service.

In the intangible sphere, dedicated followers' rewards are even greater. They have the day-to-day satisfaction of serving and being close to their God. They have the comfort of living and working with like-minded people. They are spared the worries of family living. They have no financial woes. They have peace of mind and a sense of spiritual well-being that outsiders often envy.

This latter point is perhaps the most important, for no one can be around the group very long without being intrigued by their spiritual outlook. They give the impression of inner security because they *understand*. Their love of God—Father Divine—is so great that it has given them an understanding, both of themselves and of the outside world.

Nowhere in Father Divine's teachings is any provision made for the hereafter, for the dedicated follower has everlasting life. Father Divine spoke literally, not symbolically, on this point. Over and over again, he promised his followers that if they adhered to his teachings faithfully, they would have perfect health and eternal life. On the basis of these pronouncements, followers refuse to buy insurance of any kind.

Goodwill toward all people, racial integration, righteous government, international modesty—all these things are desired *now*, in this world, not the next. It is on this premise that the plans, policies, and actions of the movement are based. And it is this "here and now" philosophy that gives true followers a sense of abiding satisfaction. They feel that if they can unashamedly express their love for Father, put his teachings into practice, and show that the system works, then human salvation will be at hand.

But is it really true that Father Divine's followers do not get sick or die? Of course not. Their morbidity and mortality rates seem to be the same as for the population at large. When followers do die, however, it is attributed to the fact that they somehow failed to live up to the principles set forth by Father. Had they abided by those principles, they would not have died.

Present-day followers are realistic on this point. They realize full well that their members die. The point they make, however, is that Father Divine's teachings represent a *goal,* and that while the goal is difficult, it is not impossible. Successful or not, the true follower is one who devotes his life to the attainment of that goal. Mother Divine writes as follows on the subject:

> In the Peace Mission Movement there are no funeral services. Followers of Father Divine believe in giving flowers to the living. . . .
>
> If a follower dies in the faith, the body is taken care of in a very simple, legal, unobtrusive way. Followers believe that the body returns to the dust from whence it came, and that the Spirit goes back to the GOD that gave it. HE will give it another body as it pleases HIM.
>
> A true follower who brings his body into complete subjection to the Law of the Spirit of Life that gave JESUS CHRIST the victory *will not die.* This goal of Perfection is something great to which to aspire, but nevertheless it is Jesus' command: "Be ye therefore perfect, even as your Father which is in heaven is perfect." (Matthew 5:48)[14]

Enemies and Defectors

Despite his phenomenal success as a religious leader, Father Divine experienced considerable opposition. Segments of the African American community have been scornful of the fact that one of their members had the audacity to play God. The popular press has often ridiculed the movement, and serious scholars—with some exceptions—have remained largely aloof.

In the early period, much of the opposition came from the outside clergy. There was, of course, St. John the Vine Hickerson, who contended that "God" was none other than little George Baker, from Baltimore. Daddy Grace was a more formidable opponent. Wearing colorful costumes and denouncing Father Divine as a false god, he set up "houses of prayer" along the East Coast and—at a dollar a head—performed special

[14]Mother Divine, *The Peace Mission Movement,* p. 51 (italics added).

baptismal rites on thousands of enthusiasts. He was apparently more adept at baptism than he was at filing his income tax, however, and after running afoul of the Internal Revenue Service, he fled to Cuba.

The next opponent was Bishop Lawson. Unlike so many of the others, Lawson was not an exotic or a cult leader, but a legitimate—and fairly well-known—African American minister. He denounced Father Divine in the press and on the radio, calling him an unscrupulous faker. On and on he railed, week after week, month after month. But in the end, the result was the same. He was forgotten, and Father Divine's followers increased by the thousands.

And so it was with all Father Divine's competitors. Decade after decade they sallied forth, only to be whirled back like pursuers before the Pillar of Fire. In retrospect, none of Father Divine's outside antagonists gave him much cause for concern. His real grief came from those who were within the gates. Of all his flock, however, Verinda Brown probably caused Father more trouble than all his other "problem children" combined.

An Apostate   All religions have to deal with **apostates**—people who have renounced their beliefs and allegiances. For faiths like Father Divine Peace Mission, apostates are a special challenge, since outsiders are more likely to believe the claims of an apostate of a faith generally viewed as marginal compared with more mainstream faiths, like Presbyterians and Roman Catholics. Verinda Brown had a respectable background. She had no vices, no jail record, no physical debilities. In fact, when she first met Father, she was a happily married woman. She and her husband, Thomas, worked as domestics for a wealthy New York family. They made good money, and one would not have expected them to join the celibate world of Father Divine. But join they did.

Somehow—they could never explain why—they were drawn to Father, and after attending several communion banquets, they were ready to accept him as God. To put aside temptations of lust, Thomas Brown relinquished his job and went to work in one of the kingdoms. Verinda Brown kept her outside job as a domestic.

A short while later they adopted new names: Thomas Brown became Onward Universe, and Verinda became Rebecca Grace. To show their allegiance to the movement, they began to convert their insurance, their building-and-loan holdings, and their real estate to cash. Some of the cash they gave to Father Divine outright. With the rest they bought him gifts. At least, that is what they said they did.

Then Father Divine began to treat them coolly. Apparently, he was not convinced that they had kept lustful thoughts out of their minds. At first Verinda Brown felt hurt, then resentful, then bitter. After thinking things over, she decided to leave the movement, and a short while later her husband followed suit.

But Verinda Brown was not finished. She had, in effect, given Father Divine nearly $5,000—and she wanted it back. She hired a lawyer and took the case to court. Father denied the claim, and produced a host of followers who swore that he never took money in any way, shape, or form. The judge ruled in favor of Verinda Brown, and Father Divine was ordered to pay the full amount plus court costs. Father refused and promptly appealed the case, but to no avail. The appeals court upheld the original verdict, and the decision stands to this day.

The decision stands legally, that is. Not morally: Father Divine refused to pay—not a dollar, not a dime, not a penny. Instead, he simply left New York, and in July 1942 moved his headquarters to Philadelphia, where it has been ever since. The only time he returned to New York was on Sundays, when, according to state law, process papers cannot be served.

Father Divine's refusal to obey the court order was strictly a matter of principle. Over and over, he proclaimed: "The charge was false. The decision was unjust. I would rather rot in jail before paying one cent." Even his lawyers were never able to get him to change his mind. It was their view that the $5,000 was little more than a nuisance claim, and that paying it was preferable to the onus of moving. But Father never budged from his position.

There is no doubt, however, that Father Divine was hurt by the court decision—in a number of ways. For one thing, adverse publicity always hurts, especially in the case of a religious movement. For another, the subsequent move to Philadelphia led to a noticeable decline in numbers, and while other factors were involved, the move itself was probably instrumental.[15] Many of the key personnel moved with their leader to Philadelphia. A number of the kingdoms, extensions, and connections closed down, and today only a handful remain in New York. (It was for these very practical reasons that Father Divine's attorneys advised him to pay the claim.)

But there is another side to the story, for if Father Divine was hurt, was not New York hurt even more? After all, as Weisbrot points out, "The stress on independence, honesty, and self-discipline all contributed to a dramatic lowering of the crime rate wherever new Peace Missions established themselves."[16] A number of judges and police officials attested to this fact.

In a similar vein, because of their honesty and reliability, true followers were in great demand as workers. Additionally, Father Divine was feeding tens of thousands of unemployed New Yorkers every year, virtually free of charge. And, of course, none of his followers were permitted to go on welfare or relief of any kind. In brief, he was saving New

[15]Weisbrot, *Father Divine,* p. 211.
[16]Ibid., p. 94.

York taxpayers a good sum of money on a more or less regular basis. Ironically enough, therefore, it looks as though New York's loss was Philadelphia's gain!

The Tommy Garcia Story   Tommy Garcia, at age fifteen, ran away from the Kingdom of Father Divine to find his natural father. Raised at Woodmont by Father and Mother Divine, Garcia believes he was being groomed to lead the Peace Mission Movement. When Father died in 1965 there was a power struggle in the church and Tommy was sent to a boarding school. Today, with his wife Lori, Garcia operates an equipment leasing business in Las Vegas, Nevada. The following is excerpted from a telephone interview conducted during October 1999:[17]

Zellner: How did you become part of Father Divine's family?
Garcia: I was born in Los Angeles in 1954. My birth mother, Georgia Garcia, was a photographer of some merit. My father, Tomas Garcia, is a legal immigrant from Mexico. Pop worked days in a music store and attended night school studying television technology. I had a sister, Susan, born in 1959.
Zellner: Philadelphia is a long way from Los Angeles.
Garcia: Yes it is. In 1962, my mother was taking pictures of me at a temple in Los Angeles. A woman named Louise Schell approached my mom and asked her if she would like to attend a meeting at Jefferson Mission, a Divine satellite.
Zellner: Did you go?
Garcia: Yes. I was very young, but I remember the first time well. People there were seated alternating black and white, men on one side, women on the other side. They were attentively listening to a voice recording of Father Divine. When I asked who was talking, I was told it was God—Father Divine. It didn't mean much to me at the time. I had been confirmed a Catholic when I was six years old, and the black man in the picture next to the tape recorder looked nothing like the God that existed in my mind's eye.
Zellner: How did you get from Jefferson Mission to Woodmont?
Garcia: Mom told pop that she wanted to take me and Susie to visit her family in New Hampshire. (By the way, it is very difficult for me to call her mom. She has disowned me in favor of the movement.) He gave us the car and cash for the trip. Louise went with us. When we got to Philadelphia, we went directly to the Divine Lorraine hotel. Susie and I were separated. I was escorted upstairs to a room where I stayed, alone, all night. The next morning I was delivered to Father Divine's study at Woodmont. It was there that he said the words that haunt me to this day.

[17]The Garcias maintain a Website: http://www.tommygarcia.com.

Zellner: And those words, Tommy?

Garcia: He said, "It has come to my attention, Tommy, that no one wants you. I want you. I care about you. If you agree, you will live with me here, and I will take care of you for the rest of your life."

Zellner: What were you thinking?

Garcia: I was thinking that there was something terribly wrong. In my mind's eye, I pictured the orphanages on the TV program *East Side Kids*. I feared going to a place like that. I looked at everything and everybody in the room. Then I looked back at Father Divine and said yes. He kept his word. From that time forward until his death, he treated me as his son.

Zellner: And Susie?

Garcia: I asked about her many times, and I was always told she had been taken to a different place. It was two years before I saw her again.

Susie was only three years old when she was put in that environment. I don't think she got the kind of nurturing young children need. She got what I call "disinterested caretaking." She was confused and hurt and her tragic death in 1993 may have brought her the only peace she would ever know.

Zellner: How did she die?

Garcia: She developed a drug habit and was thrown out of the extension when she was sixteen. She returned to Los Angeles where she went from the frying pan into the fire. She continued her addiction, and in 1993 she was raped and murdered on her way to a convenience store.

Zellner: That certainly is a tragic story.

Garcia: Her death is one of the reasons I feel obligated to tell my story. Many children ended up in the Peace Mission Movement, effectively abandoned by their parents. I don't know how much of this goes on today, but I understand that it still does. To the extent that it does, it is publicly supported kidnapping. People who patronize the movement's restaurants, hotels, and other businesses are contributing to criminal behavior and the personal enrichment of Mother Divine.

Zellner: Tell us more about being the *Son of God*.

Garcia: We traveled everywhere as a family unit. I saw enormous wealth. There was an abundance of everything. I witnessed firsthand that followers really believed that Father Divine was God.

Zellner: And what about you, Tom? Did you believe he was God.

Garcia: No! Father told me that he was not God. He told me, too, that it was not necessary to tell the followers that he wasn't. Why disappoint them? Father spoke to me privately and directly about the importance of kindness and generosity.

Zellner: What else did you observe?

Garcia: There were more women in the movement than men. And many were given positions of responsibility. I saw a man, Father Divine, who was adored by his followers. At banquets and other gatherings, women would sometimes "get into the spirit." It appeared to me as some sort of sexual gratification. When that happened, Mother Divine would gesture to a higher-up, and the woman would be taken away.

Zellner: What part did you play at the banquets?

Garcia: I was often asked to give testimony. I was given many gifts and made to feel special. I would simply thank Mother and Father for the most recent gift. For example, I had my own TV. It's quite common for children to have TV's in their rooms today, but it was a real rarity in the 1960s. I even had a go-cart and a tractor.

 I had every reason to feel special. I was the only person, other than Father and Mother Divine to have a chauffeur-valet-bodyguard.

Zellner: How do you account for your special treatment?

Garcia: I believe that Father Divine had tremendous foresight. He thought that some of the higher-ups had their own agendas. He was aware that many of the followers did not see Mother Divine as a Goddess.

 He knew he needed someone from outside the movement to be his successor. Just as Father Divine chose Mother Divine, he chose me. And, even at this time, if called, I will serve.

Indeed, there were many children raised in the Divine movement, but he was the only one raised at Woodmont. It was true, too, that he was given gifts and he was loved. But, Mother Divine insisted that he was not being groomed for a leadership role, stating that "No one would be groomed for that purpose. We are all striving to develop Christ from within. If there is any position of authority to be filled—at that time the person would be selected."[18] She went on to say that "He could do anything he made up his mind to do. People recognized early that he's a leader. I think he needs more opportunity to lead. I don't know what it would be."[19]

Scope and Operation of the Movement

Most of his followers worshiped Father Divine, and it seems that the closer they were to him, the greater was their reverence. Indeed, it is a tribute to his leadership that there were so few Verinda Browns. But how, specifically, did the organization operate? How did one go about joining? Was Father the sole executive and administrator, or did he have deputies and assistants? How large was the membership? In how many states and countries?

[18]Suzanne Gordon, "Life After Heaven," *Philadelphia Inquirer*, December 18, 1989.
[19]Ibid.

Some of the above questions are answerable; some are not. The most difficult ones are those pertaining to numbers, for membership lists were never kept, and neither Father nor Mother Divine has ever given any figures, even though they have been asked hundreds of times. The ban on published statistics extends to financial transactions, bank statements, tax returns, and other fiscal records.

The actual procedure for joining Father Divine's organization must have been extremely informal. Several years ago, when the movement was closer to its peak, a follower was asked how one went about joining. "Well," the man replied, "you come to the meetings and services, and show them you're really interested. You keep meeting people and, like, you give them a chance to size you up. Then if you want, you can stay on and try it for a while. It all works out. The wrong kind don't last long."

Actually, there are two classes of members: the true or dedicated followers, who live and work within the movement, and the adherents, who live at home. The latter group has always had varying degrees of affiliation and loyalty, and it is this group that has made it difficult to estimate numbers.

The magnitude of the Father Divine movement has likely been exaggerated. True, in its heyday, substantial numbers were involved. Standing-room-only crowds were in evidence almost every place that Father spoke, and there was often danger that fire laws were being broken. The demands on his time were such that he could scarcely keep up with his schedule.

But there was another side to the vociferation. Many of the standing-room-only crowds included quasi-members, or simply spectators who were eager to see what "God" looked like. On many occasions, busloads of Father's followers accompanied him from place to place, adding to the impression that there were followers everywhere.

To the press, also, God and His angels were good copy, and reporters constantly played up the movement's circuslike atmosphere. When Father Divine bought an airplane, one would have thought—according to the headlines—that he was taking off for heaven. Many of the newspaper stories, furthermore, were clearly inaccurate. Press reports that the movement numbered 15 to 20 million members represented a figure that was higher than the total African American population of the United States at that time.

Nevertheless, by World War II, traces of the movement could be found in some twenty-five states, although many of the organizations were short-lived. Although Father Divine himself continually stressed the international flavor of the organization, membership abroad never amounted to much numerically. A limited number of countries were involved— Australia, British West Indies, Canada, Switzerland, England, Germany, and Panama. Today, the foreign branches are defunct. The hub of the movement was always New York, New Jersey, and Philadelphia.

The peak period for the Father Divine movement came in the 1930s and 1940s. It was during these years that membership reached a maximum, that the movement became national and international in scope, and that Father Divine became a renowned religious leader. The organization remained moderately strong during the 1950s and early 1960s, although the vigor was clearly waning. After 1965, however—the year of Father's death—the movement seemed to go downhill rather sharply. Today the organization survives, reduced in both numbers and energy.

How large was the membership during the peak period? No one can say for sure. The number never approached the 22 million repeatedly claimed by Father Divine or the "millions" regularly headlined in the press. If the hangers-on and the spectators are excluded, it is doubtful whether the figure even ran to the hundreds of thousands. Membership probably could be counted in the tens of thousands, but only at the height of the movement. Today the number of followers is quite small, perhaps a few hundred dedicated believers, perhaps less.

Even when Schaefer visited the Woodmont estate in 2005 and would ask the Rosebuds present how many people were necessary to maintain the sprawling complex, they would respond, "we don't count our blessings." While estimates abound, there has been no real authoritative estimate of the Father Divine Movement, whether it was fifty years ago or today.

There have always been more blacks than whites in the movement. During the peak period, the black–white ratio was about 90:10 or 80:20. Also, females have always outnumbered males, by perhaps four or five to one. And—predictably—the movement has had more appeal to the middle- and older-age groups than to the young.

Leadership   Not too much can be said about the subject of leadership. Writing in the period when the movement was at its peak, Arthur H. Fauset contends that "in the Father Divine Movement, Father Divine *is* the organization. There are no assistant leaders, nor directors, vice-presidents, vice-chairmen, or elders. Whatever directive is carried out is assumed to have been issued by Father Divine."[20]

The contention is largely true. It was Father Divine—and no one else— who formulated policy, gave talks, bought property, established businesses (although not in his own name), counseled the followers, dealt with the public, made the major decisions, and otherwise controlled the destiny of the movement. None of the other religious leaders discussed in the present volume had anything like the authority vested in Father Divine.

Structurally, the movement encompasses five mother churches, all rendering allegiance to Father Divine. Some of the churches have branches,

[20]Arthur H. Fauset, *Black Gods of the Metropolis* (Philadelphia: University of Pennsylvania Press, 1944), p. 56.

although each church and each branch—in a legal sense—is independent. In fact, each of the five churches is incorporated, although the movement itself is not. And because the church buildings are designed to house and feed people, there are day-to-day management problems, paperwork, service details, and so forth, responsibility for which resides in duly elected officers and trustees.

Nominally, each church holds yearly meetings, at which time the officers are elected. Actually, it was an open secret that Father Divine made the selections, with the congregation joyously approving them. (*New Day* invariably carried the proceedings, and the same officers tended to be reelected year after year.) When he was alive, Father could count on a group of faithful lieutenants who assisted in local operations. In the years since his death, these individuals have often continued their local functions.

The Rosebuds, Lilybuds, Crusaders, and secretaries have generally been drawn from the inner circle of the movement, and—in terms of helping Father and Mother Divine—they can be counted on to do whatever has to be done. The secretaries (whose numbers have dwindled from a high of around twenty-five to a mere handful today) have always had high status in the movement. Their duties include handling appointments, greeting visiting dignitaries, taking care of correspondence and other paperwork, and, of course, recording and transcribing the various talks given by Father (and now by Mother) Divine.

This, then, is the leadership structure of the movement. On the one hand, there is no doubt that Father Divine had some much-needed help; after all, he was running an organization of thousands. On the other hand, when the movement was at its peak, there was scarcely a person in the organization who could make a significant move without prior approval from Father. This was the way he wanted it, and this was the way his followers wanted it.

The current leader of the movement is Mother Divine, who has proved to be a remarkable woman. Because she has always occupied a special place in the leadership structure, let us examine both her socio-historical and her present role.

Mother Divine

In spite of tribulations, the movement continued to grow and prosper all during the 1930s. Father Divine was emerging as a man to be reckoned with, and a variety of political figures—including the mayor of New York—courted his favor. But what of Sister Penny, Father's first wife? She was seen at his side less and less often. Finally, her appearances ceased altogether, and she was not heard from after 1940.

It was not until August 1946, however, that Father Divine broke the sad news to his followers. Peninah had died six years earlier. She had had a protracted illness, had grown old and weary in body, so—acceding to her wishes—Father Divine had permitted her to "pass." He had been reluctant to do so. He had also been reluctant to tell his followers the sad news and had waited until the right time to do so. But the right time had come, and on April 29 he had taken a new bride: Sweet Angel, one of his young, white secretaries. (As was previously noted, Father Divine's followers were not allowed to marry. Father felt he was the only one strong enough to marry and keep sexuality out of the bargain.)

As might be expected, the announcement of Father Divine's second marriage came as something of a shock, both to the public at large and to those within the movement. Most Americans in the 1940s were intolerant of interracial marriages. In sociological terminology, such marriages were against the *mores,* that is, those customs or beliefs about which the majority of people have strong emotional feelings.

In fact, at the time, interracial marriages were illegal in no fewer than thirty states. (It was not until 1967 that the Supreme Court declared such laws unconstitutional.) At any rate, the public was shocked and angered at Father Divine's action. Even for some of the followers, the announcement of Peninah's death plus the second marriage was too much. They simply left the movement.

After the first shock waves had passed, however, the new marriage proceeded to work out remarkably well. The public grew accustomed to seeing the couple together, true followers soon took Sweet Angel to their hearts, and Sweet Angel herself proved to be more of a help than even Father had foreseen.

So successful was the marriage that at the end of the first year a giant wedding anniversary banquet was held. From all accounts, it was something to behold. Indeed, it just may have been the most lavish ever given in the United States: 60 different kinds of meat, 54 vegetables, 20 relishes, 42 hors d'oeuvres, 21 different kinds of bread, 18 beverages, 23 salads, and 38 different desserts. All told, there were some 350 different kinds of food served, with the marathon meal lasting a full seven hours. Since then, the wedding anniversary celebrations have become one of the movement's most important yearly events, with followers attending from across the nation.

For the record, Mother Divine was born Edna Rose Ritchings, in Vancouver, Canada. Her father was a well-established florist, who would have been able to send Edna Rose to college. But her interest lay more in religion, particularly in Father Divine's brand. She became acquainted with the movement in Canada, and when she was twenty-one, she came to Father's headquarters in Philadelphia. A few weeks later, she was made one of the secretaries. At the time of her marriage, Sweet Angel had not yet reached her twenty-second birthday. She would eventually carry heavy responsibilities.[21]

According to the pronouncement made by Father Divine, Mother Divine was the reincarnation of Sister Penny, his first wife—and this is the view of all true followers today. But reincarnated or not, Mother Divine, formerly Sweet Angel, formerly Edna Rose Ritchings, has worked out very well indeed. When Father Divine was alive and in good health, she was at his side during virtually all the communion banquets, meetings, and interviews. During his declining years—roughly 1961 to 1965—she and the secretaries took over more and more of the movement's managerial duties.

Mother Divine has been more than a caretaker of a movement she inherited. In 1971 Jim Jones, the American leader of the People's Temple, came with two hundred of his followers to the Woodmont estate. It was clear that his intention was to gain the allegiance of all the Peace Mission followers at the headquarters and perhaps even begin to eventually take over the assets. Eventually leaving the grounds after several days, Jones contacted Father Devine's followers to try to persuade them to leave for his People's Temple. Only one member is documented to have left, and her appeals to Mother Devine were rejected to recognize Jones as the reincarnation of Father Devine. While little notice was made of these events by the general public, the world become aware of Jones' power over people when in 1978 he led to a mass suicide of hundreds of his followers who had followed him to Guyana.[22]

There is no doubt that the Peace Mission movement has been going downhill, a trend that at the moment appears irreversible. If it were not for the efforts of Mother Divine and a small group of followers who work closely with her, the entire organization might already have dissolved.

The Movement: Weaknesses and Strengths

Weaknesses   The basic weakness of the movement was that it developed as a one-person operation. Like the Oneida Community—but unlike the Jehovah's Witnesses and the Mormons—the movement made virtually no provision for succession. It was assumed that Father Divine would go

---

[21]The marriage proposal itself is of interest. Watts (*God, Harlem U.S.A.*, p. 168), writes that "one day while working with him, Sweet Angel boldly approached the minister and announced, 'I want to marry you because I know you are God.' Surprisingly, Sweet Angel's proposal did not offend him. He had observed the young woman as she worked and was impressed with her devotion to the movement. On April 29, 1946, he whisked Sweet Angel to Washington, D.C., and married her in a secret ceremony."

[22]Watts, *God, Harlem U.S.A.*, pp. 174–175.

on forever. Although present followers may deny it, his illness and death apparently decimated the movement. Father himself taught that true followers would not experience illness or death—and when he died, large-scale disaffection followed.

Granted, Father Divine's death would have created problems even if provisions for succession had been made. But the problems could have been solved. Other groups have faced and overcome similar obstacles. Oddly enough, however, the movement seems to be compounding the error in the case of Mother Divine: her death is not contemplated, and no successor has been designated. When the question of succession was raised with one of the followers, the answer was unmistakably clear: "But Mother Divine will always be with us, just as Father has always been with us . . ."

The movement's position on celibacy is related to their belief in immortality; that is, if dedicated followers live forever, there is no need for procreation. Of course, the fact that they do die means that the movement has no effective means of growth.

Exactly why Father Divine invoked the celibacy rule is not clear. Some writers feel that because the movement was interracial and because—at that time—attitudes toward miscegenation were decidedly negative, Father solved the problem neatly by prohibiting both sex and marriage. This explanation seems a little far-fetched. If he thought he was in the right, Father Divine would never have been deterred by public opinion. A more likely explanation is simply that he desired his followers to live the life of Christ, a position that was—and is—expressive of the very heart of the movement.

Irrespective of the reason, celibacy must be listed as one of the weaknesses of the organization. All groups grow by natural increase and/or by proselytizing. The Mormons have used both methods, and they have grown rapidly. The Amish have rejected all forms of birth control, and they have also shown rapid growth. Will celibacy lead to delcine, and is that fate in store for the Father Divine movement?

Strengths   The movement has already made some positive contributions. During the Great Depression, the various branches fed thousands of destitute people at little or no charge. The homeless were provided with a clean room at a dollar or two a week. Prostitutes, beggars, thieves—all were welcomed into the movement and given respectable jobs.

Once they joined, followers were taught the value of honesty and hard work, and the importance of building self-respect. They were forbidden to accept gifts or gratuities, and they were admonished to dress moderately, eschew vulgarity, and act kindly toward others.

In race relations, Father Divine was clearly a generation ahead of his time. The movement of the 1930s and 1940s was pressing for reforms that would not be enacted until the 1960s and 1970s: laws prohibiting segregation in schools and public places, establishing fair employment practices, removing "race or color" designation on personnel forms and official records, outlawing restrictive covenants in housing, and so on.

In the political field, also, Father Divine proved to be a seer, for many of the planks in his Righteous Government platform came into being in the decades following World War II: affirmative action programs, changes in welfare policy, changes in tariff schedules, expansion of civil service coverage, and the like.

It may be true that the various reforms would have come about with or without the assistance of Father Divine. But it is equally true that he spoke out in no uncertain terms when many others were silent. Without the impetus of the Father Divine movement, these reforms might have been slower in arriving.

One other feature of the movement should be mentioned: the great emphasis on peace. Father Divine probably desired peace as fervently as any other person who ever lived: peace between nations, peace between races, peace between ethnic groups, peace among people, and peace with oneself. This is what he stood for, and this is what he preached. He called his organization the Peace Mission movement, a name it is known by even today.

The Present Scene

The Peace Mission movement provided large numbers of blacks with an escape from the dismal reality of a white world. It gave them a sense of physical and spiritual well-being. And it tried to develop self-pride. On a societal level, the movement served as the tip of the spear, penetrating into the murky areas of civil rights and international peace. It also served as a reminder that Righteous Government principles could be adopted by persons other than politicians.

Yet today the Peace Mission movement is in trouble. Times change, and the 1930s are a far cry from today. The societal context has shifted, and a new set of societal problems has emerged. But the movement has not changed. Its goals, organization, and method of operation are much the same today as they were seventy years ago.

In the 1930s, the urban masses—both black and white—needed food, and Father gave it to them. During recent decades in the United States, fewer people suffered from starvation or lack of housing, and not many people sought the services of Father Divine's organization. Social service programs, however, suffered cutbacks during the 1980s and 1990s, and it is possible that there will again be a need for Divinite programs.

Affirmative action programs also suffered setbacks in the 1980s and 1990s, and there is evidence that racial discrimination is on the rise. Nevertheless, discriminatory levels today are not nearly as great as they were fifty years ago when blacks were excluded from hotels, restaurants, movies, and even organized sports. Although to some extent African Americans today are still handicapped by their color, they have better opportunities for getting a college education and making their mark in the business and professional worlds.

Eighty years ago, African Americans, particularly those in the lower classes, needed an inspirational leader who could stand up to the white world and show some results. And Father Divine filled that role. Today, leadership in the Peace Mission movement is white, and one suspects—given the temper of the times—that this fact may have a negative effect on black recruitment.

Sayville, Judge Lewis Smith, and the days of retribution are far behind. Father himself is no longer physically present to spark the membership and expand the organization. As a group, the followers are aging. Many have already died, and others have left the movement. The social climate that spawned the Peace Mission program has changed drastically. In brief, aside from self-perpetuation and the continuation of traditional rituals—such as publication of a newsletter, convocation of communion banquets, and the observance of holidays—there doesn't seem to be a great deal for the organization to do.

In some ways, the movement is still going. Thanks to Father Divine's perspicacity, the organization is well endowed financially and owns a number of valuable properties. True followers can still put on a spirited performance at their get-togethers. They are absolutely devoted to Mother and Father Divine, and to the movement itself. Inexorably, however, celibacy continues to block the main arteries of growth. New converts are hard to come by, and—numerically—the membership is at an all-time low.

This, then, is the present status of the movement. It is rapidly reaching the point—if it has not already—where the entire membership will consist of a small, spiritually elite group. One follower compared the present state of the movement with an earlier quiescent period of Christianity, the implication being that sooner or later there would be an inextinguishable resurgence for the Divinites.

All of which may be true. To an objective observer, however, there is nothing on the secular or spiritual horizon to suggest a rejuvenation. But whether there is or not, Father Divine will remain one of the indelible figures in the history of twentieth-century religious thought. He was—with the possible exception of Brigham Young—the most remarkable of all the leaders discussed in this book. He was also a person of infinite goodness.

KEY TERMS

Alienation, p. 180
Apostate, p. 187
Latent function, p. 179

Manifest function, p. 179
Norms, p. 184
Stereotype, p. 180

SOURCES ON THE WEB

www.libertynet.org/fdipmm/homepage.html
The official Web site of the Peace Mission Movement.

http://www.meta-religion.com/New_religious_groups/Groups/Christian/
peace_mission_movement.htm
Metareligion provides concise summaries of a vast array of religious groups including the Peace Mission of Father Devine.

SELECTED READINGS

Barnes, Roma. "Blessings Flowing Free: The Father Divine Peace Mission Movement in Harlem, New York City, 1932–1941." Ph.D. diss., University of York,
England, 1979.

Braden, Charles. *These Also Believe: A Study of Modern American Cults and Minority
Religious Movements*. New York: Macmillan, 1949.

Buehrer, Edwin. "Harlem's God." *Christian Century* 52 (December 11, 1935):
1590–93.

Burnham, Kenneth E. *God Comes to America: Father Divine and the Peace Mission
Movement*. Boston: Lambeth, 1979.

Calverton, V. F. *Where Angels Feared to Tread*. New York: Bobbs-Merrill, 1941.

Cavan, Ruth. "Communes: Historical and Contemporary." *International Review of
Modern Sociology* 6 (Spring 1976): 1–11.

Crumb, C. B. "Father Divine's Use of Colloquial and Original English." *American
Speech* 15 (October 1940): 327–37.

Fauset, Arthur H. *Black Gods of the Metropolis*. Philadelphia: University of Pennsylvania Press, 1944.

Galanter, Marc. *Cults: Faith, Healing, and Coercion*. New York: Oxford University
Press, 1989.

Gordon, Suzanne. "Life after Heaven." *Philadelphia Inquirer Magazine,* December
11, 1989, pp. 28ff.

Harkness, Gloria. "Father Divine's Righteous Government." *Christian Century* 82 (October 13, 1965): 1259–61.

Harris, Sarah. *Father Divine: Holy Husband.* 1953. Reprint. New York: Macmillan, 1971.

Higginbotham, A. Leon. *In the Matter of Color.* New York: Oxford University Press, 1980.

Hoshor, John. *God in a Rolls Royce: The Rise of Father Divine.* 1936. Reprint. Freeport, NY: Books for Libraries Press, 1971.

Hostetler, John. *Communitarian Societies.* New York: Holt, Rinehart and Winston, 1974.

Howell, Clarence. "Father Divine: Another View." *Christian Century* 53 (October 7, 1936): 1132–33.

Kelley, Hubert. "Heaven Incorporated." *American Magazine* 221 (January 1936): 40ff.

Kephart, William M. *The Family, Society, and the Individual.* Boston: Houghton Mifflin, 1981.

McKay, Claude. "Father Divine's Rebel Angel." *American Mercury* 51 (September, 1940): 73–80.

McKelway, St. Clair, and A. J. Liebling. "Who Is This King of Glory?" *New Yorker,* June 13, 1936, pp. 21ff; June 20, 1936, pp. 22ff.; June 27, 1936, pp. 22ff.

Moseley, J. R. *Manifest Victory.* New York: Harper & Row, 1941.

Mother Divine. *The Peace Mission Movement.* Philadelphia: Imperial Press, 1982.

Ottley, Roi. *New World A-Coming: Inside Black America.* Boston: Houghton Mifflin, 1943.

Parker, Robert Allerton. *The Incredible Messiah.* Boston: Little, Brown, 1937.

Shey, Thomas. "Why Communes Fail: A Comparative Analysis of the Viability of Danish and American Communes." *Journal of Marriage and Family* 39 (August 1977): 605–13.

Staples, Robert, ed. *The Black Family: Essays and Studies.* Belmont, CA: Wadsworth, 1978.

Stinnett, Nick, and C. W. Birdsong. *The Family and Alternative Life Styles.* Chicago: Nelson-Hall, 1978.

Washington, Joseph R. *Black Sects and Cults: The Power Axis in an Ethnic Ethic.* New York: Doubleday, 1973.

Watts, Jill. *God, Harlem U.S.A.: The Father Divine Story.* Berkeley: University of California Press, 1992.

Weisbrot, Robert. *Father Divine and the Struggle for Racial Equality.* Urbana: University of Illinois Press, 1983.

CHAPTER SIX

THE MORMONS

Of the nearly 1,200 different religions in the United States, none has had a more turbulent history than that of the Mormons. It would not be much exaggeration, in this respect, to say that the Mormons are in a class by themselves.[1] Born in controversy and vilified throughout most of the nineteenth century, they have nevertheless succeeded in establishing a socioreligious organization of unbelievable vitality.

The "Burned-Over" District

The groundwork and foundations of Mormonism were laid out in the 1820s in western New York State. The area came to be known as the "burned-over" district; that is, burned over by the fires of religious ardor. Never in our history has so much religious fervor been packed into one geographical area. Bibles, revelations, preachers, and prophets came (and went) with astonishing rapidity.

The Millerites proclaimed that the world was coming to an end. Ann Lee's Shakers renounced sex and marriage, and formed a nearby settlement.

---

[1]For recent accounts of the Mormon experience, see *Gordon B. Hinckley: Go Forward with Faith*, a biography of the current president of LDS, Sheri L. Dew (Salt Lake City: Deseret Books, 1996). Also see, *Growing Up in Zion: True Stories of Young Pioneers Building the Kingdom*, Susan Arrington Madson (Salt Lake City: Deseret Books, 1996); *Riding in the Shadows of Saints*, Jana Richman (New York: Crown, 2005); and *Mormon America: The Power and the Promise*, Richard N. Ostling and Joan K. Ostling (New York: HarperSanFrancisco, 1999). For reading fun, try Robert Kirby, *Best Loved Humor of the LDS People* (Salt Lake City: Deseret Books, 1999).

Jemima Wilkinson, ruling by revelation, built her colony of Jerusalem. John Humphrey Noyes started the Oneida Community. The Fox sisters, claiming to have communicated with the dead, founded the modern spiritualist movement. All of this occurred in western New York between, roughly, 1825 and 1850. Even the older denominations—Methodists, Baptists, Presbyterians—were torn by schism and dissent.

Into this religious maelstrom came Joseph Smith Sr. and his wife, Lucy. Lucy Smith consciously questioned many of the accepted faiths of her day such as the Baptists, Methodists, Roman Catholics, and decided that the Presbyterians would be the faith with which to align. Three of her eight children joined with her, but Joseph Jr. decided that he needed more time. In genuine perplexity, according to his own account, he turned to the Bible and was struck by the passage in James 1:5, namely: "If any of you lack wisdom, let him ask of God and it shall be given him."[2]

Accordingly, Joseph Smith entered the woods to ask God the all-important question. It was here that he had his first religious experience, for he was visited by both God the Father and His son Jesus Christ. Among other things, he was told that he was to join none of the existing sects, for "they were all wrong." Smith was only fifteen years old at the time, and the visitation remained engraved on him forever.

Smith made no attempt to hide the fact of his heavenly visitation. With the natural exuberance of a teenager, he divulged what had happened, but his story fell on deaf ears. "I soon found," he said, "that my telling the story had excited a great deal of prejudice . . . and though I was an obscure boy of only fifteen, yet men of high standing would take notice sufficient to excite the public mind against me, and create a bitter persecution."[3]

Although he could not know it at the time, Joseph Smith's persecutions would continue as long as he lived. In fact, they would accelerate. But despite the rising tide of troubled waters, he never once recanted or wavered in his spiritual beliefs. His alleged revelations and heavenly visitations continued right up to the day he died.

The Golden Plates   The next visitation came three years later (1823), when Smith was eighteen. This was the most noteworthy of all his religious experiences, because it involved the angel Moroni and the discovery of the golden plates. These plates, or tablets, form the very foundation of Mormonism, so let us read Joseph Smith's own account:

> After I had retired to my bed for the night, a personage appeared at my bedside, standing in the air, for his feet did not touch the floor. He had on a loose robe of most exquisite whiteness. . . .

[2]James Coates, *In Mormon Circles: Gentiles, Jack Mormons, and Latter-day Saints* (Reading, MA: Addison-Wesley, 1990).

[3]Joseph Smith, *Pearl of Great Price* (Salt Lake City: Church of Jesus Christ of Latter-day Saints, 1974), p. 49.

He called me by name, and said that he was a messenger from the presence of God, and that his name was Moroni; that God had work for me to do. . . .

He said that there was a book deposited, written upon gold plates. He said that the fullness of the everlasting Gospel was contained in it. Also, that there were two stones in silver bows—and these stones, fastened to a breastplate, constituted what is called the Urim and Thummim, and that God had prepared them for the purpose of translating the book.[4]

After several more visits—in which Moroni repeated his instructions—Joseph Smith was ready to unearth the plates. On the west side of the highest hill in the county, he came across a large stone. "Having removed the earth, I obtained a lever which I fixed under the edge of the stone, and with a little exertion raised it up. I looked in, and there indeed did I behold the plates, and the Urim and Thummim, as stated by the messenger."[5]

Eventually, Joseph Smith removed the plates from the hill (now known as Cumorah) and took them home. Each of the plates measured eight inches square, and since there were a number of them—the stack was six inches thick—the total weight must have been considerable. Yet young Joseph Smith experienced no difficulty in transporting them, or at least made no mention of the fact. He did, however, have trouble keeping them out of evil hands. "For no sooner was it known that I had them, than the most strenuous exertions were used to get them from me. But by the wisdom of God, they remained safe in my hands, until I had accomplished what was required."[6]

Although the golden plates were written in an ancient tongue, Joseph Smith—aided by the Urim and Thummim—translated them with relative ease. When he had finished, the angel Moroni came and took back both the original set of plates and the Urim and Thummim. The translation, of course, remained on earth and became known as the Book of Mormon.

Considering the theme of the book and the circumstances surrounding the writing, it is little wonder that the Book of Mormon has become a source of contention. Indeed, it is one of the most controversial books ever written. Its author, or translator—only twenty-three years old at the time—remains one of the most perplexing figures in American social history.

Joseph Smith—Man of Controversy

Joseph Smith was born in 1805 at Sharon, Vermont, of old New England stock. Whether any of his early activities foreshadowed other events is a matter of opinion. His grandfather claimed to have had heavenly visions

[4]Smith, op. cit., pp. 50–51.
[5]Ibid., p. 53.
[6]Ibid., p. 54.

and actually had his experiences published in book form. Joseph himself was fond of using a "peep-stone," a kind of native quartz or crystal, to locate hidden treasure. And while the digging never unearthed anything of value, the boy did show evidence of lively imagination and—quite important—the ability to lead people older than himself. Use of the peep-stone, incidentally, was a rather common practice of the period.

In a strictly religious vein, Joseph Smith was not precocious. He seemed neither more—nor less—attracted to the Lord than other children his age. Nor was he bookish or intellectual in any known sense. He could read and write, but his education, like that of most of his peers, was severely limited. He seems to have been a pleasant, likable young man, not significantly different from others of his age group—except, perhaps, for his preoccupation with treasure hunting.

Although the Smiths were never destitute, Joseph's father had some difficulty earning a living. When they moved to New York, their fortunes did not improve—and neither did young Joseph's luck with treasure hunting. How he would have fared in a competitive economy will never be known, for at an age when most young men were serving their apprenticeships, Joseph Smith was discovering and translating the golden plates. And at an age when most of his childhood acquaintances were starting up in business or agriculture, Joseph was founding a church.

The Mormons

		Brigham		Utah		Tenth	One
Joseph	Book of	Young		admitted		temple	hundredth
Smith	Mormon	arrives	BYU	as a		opens	temple opens
born	printed	in Utah	founded	state		(Los Angeles)	(Boston)
1805	1830	1847	1875	1896		1956	2000

1800–1825	1825–1850	1850–1875	1875–1900	1900–1925	1925–1950	1950–1975	1975–2000

1820	1844		1890	1923		1978
Smith	Joseph		Polygamy	First temple		Priesthood
receives	Smith		prohibited	outside U.S.		extended
first	killed			(Alberta, Canada)		to all males
vision						

The Book of Mormon   As transcribed by Joseph Smith, the Book of Mormon is a mammoth and fairly intricate work. The present edition runs to 531 double-column pages, divided into fifteen books—Nephi, Jacob, Enos, Jarom, Omni, and so forth. Each book is subdivided into chapter and verse, so that in style it is like the Bible; indeed, a number of Old and New Testament passages reappear verbatim.

The Book of Mormon tells the story of a family who left Jerusalem around 600 B.C. Lehi, the father, was a Jewish prophet who had been notified by God that the city was doomed to destruction. Under Lehi's direction, the family, together with some friends and neighbors, built a small ship and sailed eastward. Their probable route was the Arabian Sea, the Indian Ocean, and the South Pacific, for eventually they reached the western coast of America.

The little group established itself in this New World of promise and soon began to expand and multiply. When Lehi died, the group split into two factions, one following Nephi, the youngest son, the other following Laman, the eldest. The Nephites and the Lamanites eventually became hostile to one another, and fighting ensued.

Although there were exceptions on both sides, the Nephites were a more vigorous people than the Lamanites. The Nephites were industrious and well versed in the arts, and they prayed to God for guidance. The Lamanites were often in trouble and became slovenly and idolatrous. They incurred God's displeasure: as a result, their skins became dark, and they were reduced to savagery. They were, according to the Book of Mormon, forebears of the native Americans.

In brief, the Nephites advanced and the Lamanites declined, and while both groups had an Israelite background, it was no great surprise when Jesus appeared among the Nephites. Indeed, he taught the same things he had taught in Palestine and set up his church in much the same way. As the Nephites grew and prospered over the years, however, they tended to fall away from Christ's teachings. Prophets such as Mormon—who had kept a chronicle of the Nephites—exhorted them to mend their ways, but to no avail. God eventually lost patience with the Nephites and permitted their hereditary enemies, the Lamanites, to prevail.

The final battles took place around the hill Cumorah in A.D. 400, and the Nephites were destroyed as a nation. The last remaining Nephite was Mormon's son, Moroni, who took his father's chronicle, wrote the concluding portion, and buried the entire record—in the form of gold plates—on Cumorah. This was the same Moroni who, as a resurrected personage, divulged the hiding place to Joseph Smith.

The idea of a spiritual bridge between the Old World and the New had a natural appeal for people in the United States, especially since there was then much speculation about the origin of Native Americans. And while the account of the Nephites and the Lamanites represents but one small portion of the Book of Mormon, it does illustrate one of the central themes of the book: the cycle of good and evil. Humans follow the commandments of God; hence, they thrive and prosper. But prosperity leads to pride, and pride leads to selfishness and a rejection of God's ways—hence, humans fall. To rise again, they must repent and ask His forgiveness.

Over and over again, in a variety of different contexts and with a host of different peoples, the sequence is repeated: from goodness to prosperity, from prosperity to pride and selfishness, from pride and selfishness to downfall, from downfall to repentance. Repentance leads to goodness, and the cycle starts once more. There is little equivocation or obscurity in the Book of Mormon. Good and evil are portrayed with crystalline clarity. And as more than one commentator has pointed out, it is this clarity that adds to the appeal of the book.

Doubters and Believers   As was mentioned earlier, the golden plates—and the story inscribed thereon—provoked an avalanche of controversy. Critics denounced them as fakes, and Joseph Smith was decried as a mere yarn spinner. If scholars had difficulty with hieroglyphics, how could an uneducated twenty-three-year-old possibly have translated them? The Book of Mormon, furthermore, contains a number of internal errors. The steel sword of Laban is reported as existing in 600 B.C. (1 Nephi 4:9), long before steel was invented. Cows and oxen are reported in the New World about the same time (1 Nephi 18:25), although the first cattle were actually brought from the Old World by Columbus on his second voyage.

Some critics also question the Hebraic origin of these Native Americans, because archeological evidence indicates that the Native Americans (that is, American Indians) are a Mongoloid strain who reached the American continent via the Bering Strait. Some Mormons seem to have no idea that there is an alternative explanation outside the Book of Mormon for the peopling and history of the New World before the arrival of Columbus.[7]

Other critics see the Book of Mormon as a not-too-subtle attempt to paraphrase the Bible. They call attention to similarities in name-style and wording. The phrase "And it came to pass," for example, appears no fewer than 2,000 times.

Defenders of Mormonism reject all the above arguments in no uncertain terms. They believe that because Joseph Smith was a true prophet of God, he had no need of formal education to translate the golden plates. The Urim and Thummim, as instruments of the Almighty, were all that was necessary.

As for the plates themselves, Mormon supporters point out that eleven witnesses testified—by sworn statement—that they had actually seen the plates. A number of these witnesses later withdrew from the Mormon church and renounced their ties completely, but none ever repudiated their sworn testimony concerning the golden plates. To this day, every copy of the Book of Mormon contains a facsimile of the sworn statements, together with the eleven signatures.

As far as archeological evidence is concerned, Mormon defenders claim that it is unclear, that the authorities themselves have differing

[7]Mark Leone, *Roots of Modern Mormonism* (Cambridge, MA: Harvard University Press, 1979), p. 203.

interpretations, and that new discoveries are constantly being made. It is held that, when all the evidence is in, the account contained in the golden plates will be confirmed. The other criticisms—involving word meanings, grammar, and phraseology—are dismissed as inconsequential points that arise whenever a manuscript is processed for publication.

Most followers believe strongly that the Book of Mormon is an internally consistent document that has stood the test of time. They feel it is beautifully written, eternally instructive, and a true reflection of the word of God. They accept it—along with the Old and New Testaments—as Scripture. The net result, as Leone states, is that "Mormonism is not a part of traditional Christianity; it is a whole new version."[8]

The Early Years

On April 6, 1830, six young men gathered together not far from the hill Cumorah. In addition to Joseph Smith himself, there were his two brothers, Hyrum and Samuel, as well as Oliver Cowdery, Peter Whitmer, and David Whitmer. All had seen the golden plates—they had so testified— and all had been profoundly moved by the inscribed message. Indeed, they were gathered for the purpose of founding a church based on that message. The laws of New York State required a minimum of six members for incorporation, and these were the six. When the meeting opened, Joseph Smith announced that he had received a revelation from God which said, "Behold there should be a record kept among you: and in it thou shalt be called a seer, a translator, a prophet, an apostle of Jesus Christ, an elder of the church through the will of God."

By this revelation, and by the unanimous consent of the original six members, Joseph Smith was acknowledged to be a prophet of God and the undisputed leader of the church. Even today, in routine conversation, Mormons refer to him as the Prophet. However, the term *Mormon church* was never adopted, the original designation being simply the Church of Christ. (Outsiders referred to members as *Mormons* or *Mormonites*.) A few years later (1838), the present name was made official: the Church of Jesus Christ of Latter-day Saints. ("Latter-day" refers to the Western hemisphere period of scriptural history.) Members of the church do not mind being called Mormons. They use the name themselves. They are more likely, however, to use such terms as *Saints*, *Latter-day Saints*, or *LDS*.

The church grew rapidly—a thousand members in less than a year. It soon became apparent that, being American in both setting and theology,

---

[8]Leone, op. cit., p. 171.

LDS had a natural attraction for many people. Then, too, in this early period the church was blessed with a number of extremely able, vigorous leaders. In addition to Joseph Smith, a genuinely charismatic leader, there were Oliver Cowdery, Sidney Rigdon, and Parley Pratt. There was also a man named Brigham Young.

Mormon growth, however, was accompanied by prolonged and vicious persecution. In New York State, Joseph Smith was arrested several times for disturbing the peace. To escape harassment, the Prophet and his followers moved westward—to Ohio, Missouri, Illinois—but in each state they encountered real trouble. Raids, attacks by mobs, pitched battles—the trail of persecution seemed endless. Joseph Smith himself was assaulted, beaten, and jailed on a number of occasions.

The end came on June 27, 1844, when a mob stormed the jail at Carthage, Illinois, where four Mormon leaders were being held. Willard Richards and John Taylor managed to escape with their lives, but Joseph Smith and his brother Hyrum were brutally shot to death.

The Aftermath—And Brigham Young

The death of the Mormon leader shocked both the citizens of Illinois and the nation at large. Some of the public thought that the Latter-Day Saints would emerge to dominate the religious scene. Skeptics thought otherwise, questioning whether the faithful would survive the death of the Prophet.

As with many religious organizations, the death of the founder provoked a major crisis. The Twelve Apostles of the church prayed about a successor and announced they had received a revelation from God that a reluctant Brigham Young should be the second president of the church. Another group within the church created the *Reorganized Church of Jesus Christ of Latter Day Saints,* now known as the *Community of Christ.* The latter group's leadership was provided by Joseph Smith III and Emma Smith (the son and wife of the founder). More about this group later. Other smaller splinter groups broke away at this time, including the *Bickertonites,* the *Strangites,* and the *Church of Christ (Temple Lot),* some of which still function today.

In any event, the Church of Jesus Christ of Latter-day Saints not only survived but grew and prospered. The death of Joseph Smith did not result in a bankruptcy of leadership. On the contrary, LDS had any number of able and enthusiastic people. There was, of course, only one Brigham Young.

Born in 1801 at Whitingham, Vermont, Brigham Young reportedly came from the poorest family in town. Instead of going to school, he worked—with his hands. He became a skilled carpenter, painter, and glazier, and—on the side—learned to read and write. He evidenced no special religious leanings until he was twenty-two, when he became a Methodist. A few years later, after reading the Book of Mormon and becoming convinced of its authenticity, he converted to LDS.

In 1832 he met Joseph Smith, and the two had a long talk. From then on, Brigham Young was one of the Prophet's staunchest supporters—and one of Mormondom's most enthusiastic workers. As a carpenter, he helped build temples; as a planner, he laid out whole cities; as a missionary, he achieved a brilliant record in England. His rise within the church was rapid, and following Joseph Smith's death in 1844, he was the dominant figure in LDS for over thirty years. It is difficult to imagine what form Mormonism would have taken without his leadership.

After a short—and uneasy—truce, persecution of the Mormons was resumed. The alleged murderers of Joseph Smith were tried but were acquitted, and from then on things went from bad to worse. Mobs attacked Mormon families. LDS buildings were set afire. Attacks and counterattacks accelerated. At one time, both sides were using artillery pieces. By the end of 1845, it had become obvious that the Latter-day Saints would have to leave Illinois.

The exodus began on the morning of February 4, 1846, and the going was rough. It took the Saints nearly five months to reach Council Bluffs, Iowa, four hundred miles away. But the Rocky Mountains were still five hundred miles distant—and beyond the mountains was another stretch of a thousand miles, most of it unsettled land.

In the spring of 1847, an advance group of some 150 Mormons, headed by Brigham Young and Heber Kimball, set out to blaze a new path. Their success was startling. Known as the Mormon Trail, the new route was eventually followed by both the Union Pacific Railroad and U.S. Highway 30.

The trailblazers pushed on across the Rockies, and on the morning of July 24, 1847, Brigham Young caught his first sight of the Great Salt Lake Valley. He held up his hand and said, "It is far enough. This is the right place." His followers knew what he meant. Thenceforth, July 24 would be celebrated among the Mormons as Pioneer Day, their greatest holiday.

Miracle of the Gulls   One of the striking stories concerning early Mormon hardships is the so-called miracle of the gulls. The summer of 1849, thanks largely to innovative irrigation, was a good crop year. The vegetation was thick, and the leaves were lush. But just as the Saints were visualizing full storehouses for the winter, hordes of locusts swarmed over the plants and began to devour them. Horrified, the residents tried to beat the insects off with everything at their command. They also opened up the irrigation canals to try to drown the invaders. But for every 1,000 killed, 10,000 more appeared. Finally—after all human effort had failed—the Mormons knelt down beside their crops and prayed to God for help.

Suddenly, in the distance, a dark cloud appeared. It proved to be a large flock of gulls, and for a time the Mormons feared further crop destruction. But to their unbounded joy, the gulls began to devour the locusts, and soon the danger was over.

The story is a true one, and today there is a monument to the gulls in Salt Lake City. The gull is also the official state bird, and—understandably—is protected by Utah law.

Overseas Missions   It had always been Joseph Smith's feeling that Mormonism needed a strong overseas base, and as early as 1837 an LDS mission had been established in England. The actual flow of converts from Europe to America began shortly afterward, but not until Brigham Young took office did Mormon immigration flourish. During the thirty years of his presidency (1847–1877), tens of thousands of converts arrived in America, nearly all of whom remained loyal to the church.

The chief source of LDS immigration was England and Scandinavia, although some converts were also received from Germany and Switzerland. Mormon attempts in other countries—Italy, Spain, China— failed. There is no doubt, though, that much of Utah today is of Anglo-Scandinavian stock. As one writer puts it, "A summer day's walk down any street in Salt Lake City's business district shows a constant parade of blonds with blue eyes and skins tanned golden brown under the sun of the high desert."[9]

Polygamy

Once the Salt Lake region was consolidated, the Mormons experienced steady and rapid growth. Like all organizations, they had problems and conflicts. But there was one issue that dwarfed all the others, one issue that almost brought the edifice down. The issue was polygamy, and it is ironic that the very practice that came close to being fatal is the one that, in the public mind, seems interminably linked with Mormonism.

Strictly speaking, **polygamy** refers to plural spouses—husbands *or* wives—whereas polygyny includes only plural wives. However, writers of the period used the term *polygamy* when referring to the Mormons, and somehow the term has persisted. Accordingly, *polygamy* will be used throughout the present account.

How did the Latter-day Saints come to adopt polygamy in the first place? A number of explanations have been offered, most of them false. It

[9]Wallace Turner, *The Mormon Establishment* (Boston: Houghton Mifflin, 1966), p. 69.

has been suggested that plural marriage was used to take care of excess Mormon females. Census figures indicate, however, that—as in most of the West—the Utah area had an excess of males, not females.

It has also been suggested that polygamy was simply a convenient method of satisfying the high male sex drive, yet prurient interests can hardly have been paramount. Before a man could take a second wife, he was required to get the permission not only of his bishop but of his first wife. Only by so doing could he be assured of a sanctioned LDS marriage.

Some observers feel that plural marriage was a not-so-subtle attempt by the church to increase the Mormon birthrate. But this contention is not true either. Polygamous wives had, on the average, fewer children than did monogamous wives.

The Latter-day Saints adopted polygamy for one reason and one reason only. They were convinced that the practice had been ordained by God—as revealed through the Prophet Joseph Smith. Virtually all modern scholars are in agreement on this point.

Beginnings   While the history of Mormon polygamy contains numerous gaps, the following information has been fairly well documented. Joseph Smith reported that he had received a revelation from God prescribing polygamy. The date of the revelation is unclear. It was recorded, however, on July 12, 1843, for on that date the Prophet carefully dictated the lengthy revelation, later known as the Principle, to his clerk.

In the early period, polygamy was never publicly admitted; indeed, the revelation itself was locked in Brigham Young's desk for many years. Gradually, however, as more and more of the church hierarchy took plural wives, the element of secrecy was lost. When Orson Pratt and Brigham Young made the public announcement in 1852—based on the Prophet's earlier revelation—the Principle had become a more or less open secret.

By this time, of course, the Mormons had "escaped" from the East and the Midwest. Well beyond the Rocky Mountains, they were—or thought they were—safely ensconced in their territorial domain. Church leaders did not expect that the Principle would go unchallenged. They anticipated some intervention by the U.S. government, but thought that—in the interest of religious freedom—the courts would be on the side of LDS. This was an incorrect assessment.

Nevertheless, for a period of almost fifty years the Latter-day Saints not only practiced polygamy but did so with a fair amount of success. It may well be that this exercise in marital pluralism was the most unusual large-scale experiment in American social history.

The Operation of Polygamy   At the time, there were many misconceptions about Mormon polygamy, and some of them remain. According to the lurid accounts of the eastern newspapers, Mormon patriarchs were simply gobbling up unsuspecting girls in wholesale lots—for lewd and lascivious purposes. And while such charges were obvious nonsense, they did much to inflame public opinion.[10]

The "typical Mormon patriarch" was quite content to have but one wife, for in any group that permits polygamy, most people still practice monogamy. This is because at the marrying ages, males and females are roughly equal in numbers. When there is an excess of one sex, it is usually slight, so that—generally speaking—every plural spouse means that someone else is deprived of matrimony altogether.

What percentage of Mormons actually practiced polygamy? An accurate answer remains elusive. The figure doubtless varied over the years, peaking around 1860. The overall figure—the proportion of Mormon men who ever practiced the Principle—is estimated at 3 percent by LDS. Critics of Mormonism have placed the figure as high as 20 to 30 percent. When most scholarly calculations are considered, perhaps a fair estimate would be in the neighborhood of 10 to 15 percent. Whatever the figure, one very important fact is often overlooked: namely, that it was the upper-level Mormon men—especially those at the top of the church hierarchy—who were most likely to take plural wives.

Of those LDS men who were involved in polygamy, a clear majority had but one additional wife, which still ran counter to public impression. The misconception regarding numbers arose in part because of the prejudice of certain anti-Mormon elements. But it was also true that there were some church leaders who did indeed have a plurality of spouses. Orson Pratt had ten wives; his brother Parley had twelve. John D. Lee had eighteen wives and sixty-five children. Heber Kimball had forty-five wives and sixty-eight children. Brigham Young had twenty-seven wives and fifty-six children. And there were many others. Joseph Smith himself apparently had numerous wives, although the exact number remains in doubt.

A common polygamous practice was for the man to marry sets of sisters, the feeling being that such a procedure would reduce connubial tension. Whatever the reason, Joseph Smith is reported to have married three sets of sisters. Heber Kimball married four sets. John D. Lee married three sisters and also their mother! And so it went.

What about the economic aspect of plural marriage? Was having plural wives (and plural children) an asset or a liability? In many cases, it was a liability. True, an extra wife and children for a Mormon farmer meant that he would have additional help for the farm. But a fair number of Latter-day Saints were not farmers, and even among those who were, there was

[10]Kendall White, Jr., and Daryl White, "Polygamy and Mormon Identity," *Journal of American Culture* 28 (June), pp. 165–77.

a point of diminishing returns. A Mormon farmer with fifteen wives and forty-five children could hardly hope to keep them all productively engaged in farming. And with all those mouths to feed. . . .

Little wonder that so many Mormon polygamists were from the upper economic bracket. Poorer members could hardly afford the practice, a fact of life that was well understood by all concerned. Plural marriage held status advantages for Mormon women as well as for men. Polygamous wives held higher status by their association with the most influential men, and through the sense of serving as religious and social models for others. It wasn't unknown for a first wife to actively encourage her reluctant husband to take a plural wife so that they could both reach the highest state of exaltation in the afterlife.[11]

Celestial Marriage   One of the revelatory doctrines promulgated by Joseph Smith and practiced by LDS is **celestial marriage.** According to this concept, there are two distinct types of marriage: one for time and the other for eternity. The former is regarded as a secular marriage that is broken at the death of either husband or wife. Celestial marriage, on the other hand, serves to "seal" a man and woman not only for time but for all eternity. Such marriages are always solemnized in a Mormon temple and include rites and rituals that are never divulged to non-Mormons. Other types of ceremonies—civil or religious—are held to be valid only until death. (Marriages with non-Mormons run counter to LDS policy and are not performed in the temples.)

The point is that celestial marriage dovetailed nicely with polygamy. For example, if a man who had been sealed for time and eternity died before his wife, the latter could—if she desired—marry another man for time only. Some of the women married to Joseph Smith for time and eternity, later (after the Prophet's death) married Brigham Young for time only, even though they bore him children.

It was also possible to marry for eternity rather than time. A woman who had died without ever having married could be sealed for eternity to an LDS male—after her death. The fact that he might already have a legal wife would make no difference, because plural wives were perfectly acceptable.

Polygamous Households   Living arrangements varied among the polygamous families. In some instances, the wives lived with the husband under one roof. In the larger families, however, there were usually separate dwellings for the respective wives and their children. At any rate, a considerate husband was not supposed to show any favoritism. Hypothetically, at least, he was obligated to spend an equal amount of

[11]Lawrence Foster, *Religion and Sexuality* (New York: Oxford University Press, 1981), pp. 211–12.

time with (and money on) each wife. In some cases, evidently, the husband would practice "rotation": he would spend one night with each of his spouses.

The question is sometimes asked whether this sharing of love, as the **Gentiles** (non-Mormons) called it, did not have a sexually frustrating effect on the plural wives. In a strictly factual sense, there is very little information on a subject as sensitive as this. The fact that plural wives voiced no complaint along these lines suggests that the problem was not too significant.

During the nineteenth century, American women, both Mormon and non-Mormon, were regarded as having a procreative function. Birth control was by no means accepted in society at large and is still frowned on by the Mormon church. The point is that sexual intercourse was not considered by most females to be the pleasure-giving activity that it is today. On the contrary, it was more or less openly held to be a "wifely duty."

Sex was not the only problem associated with polygamy. Jealousies, economic disputes, child-rearing and in-law conflicts—these too were involved. In a monogamous pairing, for example, there are usually four in-laws, and the resultant problems are a well-known factor in marital discord. Where there were two or six or ten wives, the in-law problem must have indeed been formidable.

Conflicts over child rearing also occurred, especially when the wives and children all lived in one house. Children always knew who their real mother was, and they generally bowed to her authority. (The other wives were called aunts.) But with a half-dozen or so aunts in the house, such things as discipline, punishment, and lines of authority must have presented some real problems.

Instances of jealousy, also, were fairly common. It was only natural that there would be a certain amount of vying for the husband's attention—and for him to show total impartiality would have required superhuman effort. Conflict apparently occurred when a middle-aged husband took a young woman as an additional wife.

All things considered, it is remarkable that polygamous marriages worked as well as they did, for there is no doubt that some mighty problems existed. And it was the leadership that had to listen to the complaints. In 1860, Brigham Young told how he was often required to listen to accounts of sorrow associated with the institution that were, in his words, like "drinking a cup of wormwood."[12] The Prophet's problems aside, one of the best accounts of Mormon pluralism is by Kimball Young, a grandson of Brigham Young. Through personal interviews, as well as an

[12]B. Carmon Hardy, *Solemn Covenant: The Mormon Polygamous Passage* (Urbana: University of Illinois Press, 1992), p. 17.

examination of newspapers, journals, diaries, and autobiographies, Young estimated that about half the polygamous marriages were highly successful, a quarter were reasonably successful, and perhaps a quarter had considerable or severe conflict.

Although there is no satisfactory way to compare these figures with those of monogamous marriages, it does appear that Mormon pluralism frequently presented a stern challenge to the good ship of matrimony. According to Kimball Young, "The real problem was that the difficulties could not be easily settled, because the culture did not provide any standardized ways for handling these conflicts. For the most part, these people genuinely tried to live according to the Principle. But when they applied the rules of the game borrowed from monogamy, such as not controlling feelings of jealousy, they got into real trouble."[13]

The End of Plural Marriage

Mormon polygamists had their share of domestic discord—perhaps a bit more than their share. Given time, however, the system of plural marriage probably could have been made to work. The problems were not insurmountable, and the Saints were a dedicated people. Unfortunately for all concerned, the real difficulties were external rather than internal, and as time went on, the situation deteriorated. It soon became apparent that as far as the outside society was concerned, polygamy was creating a lesion of unhealable proportions.[14]

As portrayed in the Gentile (non-Mormon) press, Mormonism was a false religion—with many evil connotations. But the target attacked most was polygamy. Over and over and over again the traumas of plural marriage were emblazoned in bold headlines. Some of the stories were factual, but—given the nature of American newspapers—many were the products of reporters' imaginations.

Such stories clearly tended to inflame public opinion. And when that happens, political reaction is sure to follow. In 1862, President Lincoln

[13]Kimball Young, *Isn't One Wife Enough?* (New York: Holt, 1954), p. 209.

[14]By 1870, there were a small number of non-Mormons in Utah, who complained to the federal government about Mormon activities. Although plural marriage was the most publicized complaint, Cresswell writes that non-Mormon settlers also objected to "the church's economic and political domination of the territory." They further argued that "Utah was devoid of public nonsectarian schools; Utah had a wholly Mormon militia, intimately connected with the church; and the economic life of the territory was collectivist, directed by Mormon authorities. Elections were controlled rather thoroughly by the church hierarchy, and in short, Utah seemed to be an un-American theocracy" (Stephen Cresswell, *Mormons, Cowboys, Moonshiners and Klansmen* [Tuscaloosa: University of Alabama Press, 1991], p. 80).

signed a bill outlawing polygamy in the territories of the United States, and after the Civil War federal agents arrived in Utah. The difficulty was, however, that the agents could not always gain access to church marriage records. Also, Mormon polygamists became adept at scattering and hiding their wives, and—if necessary—themselves.

Brigham Young died in 1877 and was buried in a walnut casket he had designed himself. But even he had not escaped the long arm of the law, having been arrested and jailed on charges of polygamy. However, he was freed after an overnight confinement when he was able to convince the judge that in a *legal* sense, he had only one wife—the first.

After Brigham Young's death, things seemed to go downhill rapidly for the Saints. In 1879, the U.S. Supreme Court ruled in *Reynolds v. United States* that the free exercise of religion clause of the First Amendment did not protect the LDS practice of plural marriage. In 1882, a new federal law provided punishment for anyone found living in "lewd cohabitation," and Mormon leaders found themselves going to jail in droves. During a single year, 1887, some two hundred polygamists were imprisoned.

Still, the fight went on, with many Saints building secret passageways, hidden rooms, and underground tunnels between houses. Carmer writes that when federal officers appeared, "the 'cohabs' suddenly disappeared into church steeples, haystacks, cornfields, old cellars, or disguised themselves in women's dresses and sunbonnets. The whole countryside was playing a wild game of hide-and-seek."[15] John Taylor, Brigham Young's successor and a devout polygamist, was in office for ten years but had to spend practically all of it in hiding.

To many, it must have seemed as though the conflict between the "cohabs" and the "feds" was a standoff. On the one hand, no matter how many federal agents were sent in—and no matter how many polygamists were brought out—the Latter-day Saints continued to abide by the Principle. This was especially true of the leadership, practically all of whom remained steadfast in their beliefs. On the other hand, it had become clear that the government was prepared to take whatever steps were necessary to obliterate the remaining "relic of barbarism."

The year 1887 marked the beginning of the end of plural marriage, for in that year the Edmunds-Tucker Act was passed. This bill dissolved the church as a corporation and provided for the confiscation of church property. The cost to the Mormon church was over a million dollars, nearly half of it in cash. And the raids and imprisonments continued. In all, there were 573 convictions for polygamy.

---

[15]Carl Carmer, *The Farm Boy and the Angel* (Garden City, NY: Doubleday, 1970), p. 181. Also see Sarah Barringer Gordon, "The Mormon Question Polygamy and Constitutional Conflict in Nineteenth Century America," *Journal of Supreme Court History* 28 (March 2003): 14–29.

By this time, many Mormons had wearied of the struggle. Then too, LDS leaders—who remained resolute to the end—wanted statehood for Utah, a goal they realized was unattainable so long as polygamy was being practiced.

During 1887, John Taylor died (while still in hiding), and he was succeeded in the church presidency by Wilford Woodruff. In 1890, the Supreme Court upheld the Edmunds-Tucker Act as constitutional, a decision that marked the end of the line for plural marriage. Shortly after the decision was handed down, Woodruff made the following official pronouncement, known in subsequent years as the Manifesto (also called "The Great Accomodation").

> Inasmuch as laws have been enacted by Congress forbidding plural marriages, which laws have been pronounced constitutional by the court of last resort, I hereby declare my intention to submit to those laws, and to use my influence with the members of the church over which I preside to have them do likewise. . . .
>
> And I now publicly declare that my advice to the Latter-day Saints is to refrain from contracting any marriage forbidden by the law of the land.[16]

There is one extremely interesting footnote to the long-running battle over polygamy. The various statutes outlawing polygamy were generally ineffective until 1890, the year the Supreme Court upheld the Edmunds-Tucker Act. Note that it was not the Edmunds-Tucker Act itself, which was aimed at destroying the Mormon church, but the supporting Supreme Court decision that spelled doom for polygamy.

What has been almost entirely overlooked, however, is the fact that the Supreme Court ruling was based on a 5-4 decision. If a single justice had changed his vote, the Edmunds-Tucker Act would have been voided. And then what? Would polygamy—in one form or another—have continued? It is an intriguing question.

Although the Manifesto caused some internal resentment, both Mormons and non-Mormons were generally glad that the long battle was over. Woodruff's pronouncement was (and is) treated as a revelation. When asked about it, he replied simply, "I went before the Lord, and I wrote what the Lord told me to write." The pronouncement apparently ended the long conflict over plural marriage.

Or did it?

Woodruff's Manifesto put an end to the open practice of plural marriage, and President Benjamin Harrison granted a pardon to all the imprisoned polygamists. In 1896, Utah was admitted to the Union as the forty-fifth state. Nevertheless, for a decade or so following the Manifesto, a few Mormon leaders continued to take plural wives.

---

[16]Joseph Smith, *Doctrine and Covenants* (Salt Lake City: Church of Jesus Christ of Latter-day Saints, 1974), last section.

In 1902, Reed Smoot, an LDS official, was elected to the United States Senate. There was opposition to his being seated, however, and during lengthy hearings the facts concerning "secret" polygamy came to light. The Mormon church, while not condoning plural marriage, had taken no steps to remove those officials who were continuing the practice.

At the final Senate vote, Smoot was confirmed by a narrow margin, and political opposition to Mormon office seekers came to an end. In fact, over the years, any number of ranking government officials have been Mormons. After the highly publicized Smoot hearings, LDS adopted a policy of excommunicating any member known to practice polygamy, a policy that remains in effect today.

Interestingly, while Mormons no longer practice polygamy on earth, it is expected that polygamy is the norm for worthy male members in the afterlife. "Mormon men are taught that part of the reward that awaits them in the afterlife if they lead a 'pious' Mormon earth life is the opportunity to take on more than one wife after death so that they may become head of their own expansive patriarchies."[17]

Organization of LDS

The Mormons have one of the most complicated—and successful—clerical organizations in America. Every "worthy male" is expected to take his place in the hierarchical priesthood. There are now more than a million LDS priests, a figure that far surpasses the number of Roman Catholic priests in the entire world.

Although they are not professional in the sense of being seminarians or receiving pay for their work, members of the priesthood provide the leadership of present-day Mormonism. Within the priesthood there are two orders, or subdivisions: the Aaronic and Melchizedek. Both orders are subdivided into ranks, and these ranks, or gradations, form a kind of promotional ladder that the Mormon male ascends during his lifetime. Which rung he reaches depends largely on the effort he is willing to put forth in carrying out the Word.

A worthy male starts his priestly career at age twelve, when he is admitted to the Aaronic order with the rank of deacon. This is the lowest rank in the priesthood, usually attained a few years after baptism. Chief duties of the deacon include helping at church meetings, collecting fast offerings, and otherwise assisting the higher ranks.

After three years or so as deacon—if all goes well—the boy is promoted to the rank of teacher. This is a kind of apprenticeship, for while teachers do occasionally preach, their primary role is helping their su-

---

[17]"The Persistence of Polygamy." *New York Times Magazine*, March 21, 1999, Sec 6, p. 14.

periors. When he reaches eighteen or thereabouts, the boy advances to the highest rank in the Aaronic order, that of priest. The duties of the priest include preaching, teaching, baptizing, and administering the sacraments.

Assuming he has performed his duties in the Aaronic order satisfactorily, the boy is ready for the higher order, the Melchizedek, which also has three ranks—elder, seventy, and high priest. Elders are generally ordained in their early twenties and are invested with authority to take charge of meetings, to bestow certain blessings, and to officiate during rites when the high priest is unable to be present.

Seventies are essentially elders who have been chosen to be traveling missionaries, usually for a term of two years. Top rung in the ascending hierarchy is the rank of high priest. Once he has reached this level, there is no higher priestly rank a Latter-day Saint can aspire to. There are, however, any number of administrative and executive positions available—if he has the necessary qualifications. LDS is a huge operation, and its management requires immense effort.

Wards and Stakes   The Church of Jesus Christ of Latter-day Saints has two forms of administration, horizontal and vertical. Horizontal, in this context, refers to the various ward and stake organizations, whereas vertical refers to the overall administrative hierarchy of the church.

The basic horizontal or geographical unit of LDS is the ward, roughly corresponding to the Protestant congregation or the Catholic parish. Because Mormondom is growing, the number of wards is constantly increasing, the present figure reaching into the tens of thousands.

Although each **ward** contains both priesthood orders—with all the ranks thereof—the ward itself is administered by the bishop. It is he who baptizes and confirms, counsels members, receives contributions, conducts funerals, and so forth. He often gives a prodigious amount of his time, but neither he nor his assistants receive any pay for their work. All Mormons, incidentally, including those at the head of the church, must belong to some ward.

A **stake**—corresponding to the Catholic diocese—is made up of from five to ten wards. At the head is the stake president, who is assisted by two counselors. The president nominates the various ward bishops, holds conferences, and is generally responsible for the management of the wards under his jurisdiction. Although his is also an unpaid job, the stake president—like the ward bishop—spends an enormous amount of time on church-related activities.

The General Authorities   The vertical, or hierarchical, structure of LDS is more complicated than the horizontal. At the top of the Mormon establishment is the first president, also known as "prophet, seer, and revelator"—Joseph Smith's original title.[18] The first president holds office for life.

Because his mantle of authority is believed to be inherited from the Prophet himself, and as his title "revelator" signifies, the first president is the only member of the church empowered to voice revelations. "He is the one who receives inspiration for all of Mormonism, though he is not prone to impose his views forcefully without substantial support from other apostles."[19] The system is theocratic, and authority comes from the top. Indeed, some observers believe that the first president holds more power than any other church leader except the pope.

In addition to two presidential assistants, there is an executive council of twelve apostles, also appointed for life. "Position in the *Quorum of Apostles* is by seniority: once selected as an apostle, one is at the bottom of the ladder."[20] As apostles die, there is movement up the ladder. On the death of the first president, the senior apostle succeeds to the presidency.

Participatory Involvement   To outsiders, at least, the participatory involvement of Mormons is staggering. There are ward activities and stake activities and temple ceremonies. There are constant family visitations by teachers and bishops. Streams of missionaries flow to faraway places, and the conversion rate is high. There are annual and semiannual conferences and visits by the apostles. There are sealings for time and eternity. New religious tracts and publications are constantly being issued. There are weekly social events and Mormon holiday celebrations. There are recreational and musical activities and sporting events. There are a host of subsidiary organizations: women's relief society, young men's and young women's mutual improvement associations, scout troops, the Sunday school union, the genealogical society, the church welfare plan, the Tabernacle Choir, and so on. LDS even has a department of education, which, among other things, administers a series of institutes and seminaries. The church also maintains Brigham Young University, founded in 1875.

From the outside, LDS gives the appearance of being a beehive of activity—which in fact it is. It is no accident that a figure of the beehive, prominently displayed on so many LDS buildings, was chosen to be the state symbol for Mormon Utah. Both literally and figuratively, Mormons

---

[18]The first president of LDS has two counselors. Both are referred to as president. It is possible to be introduced to President Gordon Hinckley and his first counselor, President Thomas S. Monson.

[19]Philip L. Barlow, *Mormons and the Bible: The Place of the Latter-day Saints in American Religion* (New York: Oxford University Press, 1991), p. xxviii.

[20]Barlow, op. cit.

are always on the move. In fact, the Latter-day Saints themselves good-naturedly define a Mormon as "one who is on his way to a meeting, at a meeting, or returning from a meeting."

In addition to the meetings, there are always new jobs to do, new conversions to make, new challenges to meet. And while the personnel requirements are enormous—it takes hundreds of thousands of dedicated workers to staff the various organizations—the church has never had any recruitment difficulties.

This is not to say that all Latter-day Saints are dedicated. Some young men are considered unworthy and are not accepted into the priesthood. Some adults of both sexes are only moderately active, and others (called Jack Mormons) are inactive. But somewhere between one-half and two-thirds of LDS members are not only active, but hyperactive. This participatory involvement—this hyperactivity—is one of the distinguishing marks of Mormonism.[21]

Vitality of the Family

Another feature of Mormon social organization is the strong emphasis placed on family relations. Whether the family member is young, middle-aged, or old—or even deceased—he or she is assured a meaningful place in the kin system. Conversely, Latter-day Saints are against those things that they feel are harmful to family life. Premarital and extramarital sex are frowned upon, along with abortion, masturbation, indecent language, immodest behavior, birth control, and divorce. While the church mounts no special campaign against these practices, most Mormons seem to have little difficulty abiding by the rules.

There are lapses, to be sure. Some young Mormons do engage in premarital sex, though the incidence is much lower than for non-Mormons.[22] Some LDS marrieds do practice birth control, and in fact the Mormon

[21] Apparently, the hyperactivity is difficult for some Mormons. A number of self-help books written specifically for Mormons have appeared. For examples see John C. Turpin, *The New Stress Reduction for Mormons* (Covenant, 1991); Ron Schow, Wayne Schow, and Marybeth Raynes, eds., *Peculiar People: Mormons and Same-Sex Orientation* (Salt Lake City: Signature Books, 1991); and Carroll Hofeling Morris, *"If the Gospel Is True, Why Do I Hurt So Much?": Help for Dysfunctional Latter-day Saint Families* (Salt Lake City: Deseret, 1991).

[22] Scott H. Beck, Judith A. Hammond, and Bettie S. Cole ("Religious Heritage and Premarital Sex: Evidence from a National Sample of Young Adults," *Journal for the Scientific Study of Religion* 30[2] [June 1991]: 173–80) conducted a study and reported that "both female and male, white non-Hispanics whose religious heritage was classified as 'Institutionalized Sect' were less likely to engage in premarital sex, even with controls for other factors." The authors included both Mormons and Jehovah's Witnesses in their study groupings as members of institutionalized sects.

birthrate has fallen somewhat. However, it is still twice as high as for society at large. Mormons take the Biblical injunction to "multiply and replenish the earth" very literally and seriously.[23] Predictably, Latter-day Saints have comparatively few divorces, and the Utah abortion rate is the lowest of any state.

The familistic orientation of LDS is revealed in a variety of other ways. Whereas most Americans are accustomed to pursuing individualized interests, hobbies, and activities, Mormons tend to participate as families. Their social life is largely a function of church and family. Ward dances, parties, outings, and sporting events are all attended by families and are designed to encourage the intermingling of different age groups.

Another example: Monday evening is designated as home evening. On this occasion, all members of the household stay home and devote themselves to family recreation, such as singing, games, instrumental music, and dramatics. Surveys indicate that nearly seven of ten LDS families observe the tradition.[24]

The Kin Family Network   In view of the stress on family, it is understandable why kinship plays such an important role throughout Mormondom. Brothers and sisters, aunts and uncles, nieces and nephews, grandparents, cousins, in-laws—all maintain an active and enthusiastic kin relationship. During reunions of the kin family network—one of the Saints' favorite summer pastimes—it is not uncommon to see several hundred people in attendance! Special consideration is often shown to direct descendants of pioneer Mormon families, particularly those whose forebears had direct contact with Joseph Smith or Brigham Young.

However, their emphasis on family and kinship does not fragment the Mormon community. On the contrary, every effort is made to extend and apply familistic feelings to the community at large. One has but to attend any of the ward activities to see the closeness and camaraderie involved. The entire social fabric of Mormonism is designed so that "no one feels left out." And in their routine dealings with one another, this same type of in-group feeling is evident.[25]

Search for the Dead   Before leaving the subject of family, one final observation is in order: the Latter-day Saints' predilection for extending their range of kinship to those long dead. The basic problem is simple.

[23]Bruce Campbell and Eugene Campbell, "The Mormon Family," in Charles Mindel, Robert Habenstein, and Roosevelt Wright, Jr., eds., *Ethnic Families in America* (New York: Elsevier, 1988), p. 483.

[24]Debbi Willgoren, "For Mormons, No Place Like Home: Monday Night Gatherings Are a Mainstay of Family Life," *Washington Post,* July 8, 1996, p. B1.

[25]Robert Mullen, *The Latter-day Saints: The Mormons Yesterday and Today* (Garden City, NY: Doubleday, 1966), pp. 27–28.

Mormons believe that they themselves are following God's word, as re-vealed to the Prophet Joseph Smith. But what about those who died with-out ever hearing the Prophet's revelations?

The answer is also simple. Ancestors who died before the religion was founded in 1830 may be baptized or sealed by proxy. That is, the living person stands in for the deceased during a baptismal or sealing ceremony. The ceremony itself takes place in a Mormon temple, and the deceased is accorded full rites.

Difficulty arises from the fact that, as one goes back in time, (1) the number of ancestors becomes enormous, and (2) they become exceedingly difficult to track down. LDS does not do things halfway, however, with the result that the search for ancestry has become one of the major func-tions of the church.

The Mormon Genealogical Society, an administrative arm of LDS, is lo-cated in downtown Salt Lake City. Additional Family History Centers are maintained throughout the United States and abroad. The amount of ge-nealogical research undertaken at the various branches is staggering. Vital statistics, census materials, church records, poll books, official documents of all kinds—such things are constantly being microfilmed for use by Mormon (and non-Mormon) researchers. And now there is www.family-search.org, a Web site opened by LDS in May 1999. At its inception, it at-tracted more traffic than its server could handle. Open to Mormons and non-Mormons alike, the site has a catalog of millions of names. It expects to increase the number by more millions in the near future. The Mormons have records on more than 600 million deceased people.[26]

In recent years, medical researchers have taken an interest in Mormon family histories. According to Ray White, cochairperson of genetics at the University of Utah: "The million or so Mormons here—some of whom have thousands of members of their extended families living nearby—are mostly descendants of about 20,000 pioneers."[27] In Utah, scientists have been able to identify dozens of kin-groups with extensive bloodlines.

Geneticists have determined, by comparing Mormon genealogical records with cancer treatment records, that clustering exists in colon, prostate, lung, cervix, and stomach cancers. At this time, a responsible and trackable gene has not been identified. If the gene can be flagged, those with hereditary predispositions to these illnesses could be periodi-cally tested, affording them the opportunity for early treatment.

Ancestral baptism is not without its detractors by non-Mormons. After protests, Jewish leaders reached agreement with LDS that the names of

[26]Cf. Kristen Moulten, "Mormon Church Puts Its Genealogy Data Online," AP, Allentown Morning Call, Allentown, PA, May 24, 1999, Sec A, p. 1, and www.familysearch.org.
[27]Quoted in Michael Waldholz, "The Mormons' Genetic Legacy," Saturday Evening Post, November 1988, p. 52.

380,000 Holocaust victims be removed from the Geneological Institute's lists and that the proxy baptisms of Holocaust victims be halted immediately. Ten years later, representatives of the Jewish community again protested the efforts to baptize by proxy other deceased Jews, but the LDS responded that they would not guarantee that this would not occur.[28]

Distinctive Mormon Customs

"To us, the greatest day of all time is today." These words, spoken by a former Mormon leader, exemplify LDS philosophy. Few other groups are as present-oriented as the Latter-day Saints. It is not that they disregard or play down the significance of the hereafter. Their emphasis on genealogy, ancestral baptism, and sealing for time and eternity shows the importance they attach to the next world. But the way they prepare for the next world is to keep religiously active in the present one.

Group Identification   Mormons place great stress on cultural and recreational activities, but in both instances the emphasis is on group, rather than individual, participation. Team sports, organized recreation, dancing and ballet, orchestral music, choir work, theater—all such activities are felt to have a religious base in the sense that *they enhance in-group identification.* **In-group** is defined as any group or category to which people feel they belong. Simply put, it comprises everyone who is regarded as "we" or "us."

The in-group may be as narrow as a teenage clique or as a broad as an entire society—say the United States immediately after September 11, 2001. The very existence of an in-group implies that there is an entire out-group that is viewed as "they" or "them." An **out-group** is a group or category to which people feel they do not belong. So, for most LDS members, they see the Church as an in-group and nonmembers, Gentiles, as the out-group. This does not necessarily mean they feel antagonistic to Gentiles, just that they feel apart from them.

Devout Mormons never forget that they are Mormons. The fact that they are helping to carry out God's word reinforces group identification. Even their *individual* involvements—baptism, tithing, prayer, genealogical research, and certain temple investitures—serve as reinforcement factors.

One of the more interesting of the latter is the issuance of special undergarments. These derive from one of the temple ceremonies called the endowments. When they receive their endowments, Mormons are issued a special set of underwear, which they are supposed to wear at all times.

---

[28]"LDS Proxy Baptism of Jews Still's an Issue." *USA Today,* April 11, 2005, p. 7D.

Originally the temple garments, as they were called, gave the appearance of a union suit. They were made of knit material and covered the body from ankle to neck. Although they are still worn by devout Mormons of both sexes, the undergarments themselves have been shortened in length and modified in appearance. They still contain the embroidered symbols that remind the wearers of their temple obligations.

Word of Wisdom   It is a common observation that Mormons do not drink alcohol or smoke, a proscription that derives from one of Joseph Smith's revelations:

> That inasmuch as any man drinketh wine or strong drink among you, behold it is not good. . . .
> And again, strong drinks are not for the belly, but for the washing of your bodies.
> And again, tobacco is not for the body, neither for the belly, and is not good for man, but is an herb for bruises and all sick cattle. . . .
> And again, hot drinks are not for the body or belly.[29]

The revelation is known throughout Mormondom as the Word of Wisdom. Included in the prohibition are tobacco in any form, alcoholic beverages of any kind (including wine and beer), tea, and coffee. LDS has even substituted water for wine in the Sunday communion service.

Although they themselves abstain, Mormons have no objection to drinking or smoking on the part of visitors or outsiders. At the same time, however, the Word of Wisdom makes Mormons uncomfortable at cocktail parties, coffee breaks, and other such gatherings that serve the rest of American society as important occasions for social interaction.[30]

In any case, the Latter-day Saints are convinced they are right, and point to the fact that LDS prohibited smoking long before the surgeon general of the United States and the Royal College of Surgeons affirmed that tobacco was a cancer-causing agent. Mormons are permitted to drink hot chocolate, lemonade, fruit juice, and a variety of other nonalcoholic beverages.

But does the membership really abstain, abiding by the Word of Wisdom? The answer is yes, *all worthy* Mormons do abstain. Indeed, abstinence is one of the traits most clearly separating the true believer from the Jack Mormon. The Word of Wisdom is looked upon as a commandment. Those who disobey are not considered to be worthy Mormons and are denied admission to the temple—which means that they cannot participate in ceremonies involving sealing, baptism of the dead, endowments, and the like.

[29]Smith, *Doctrine and Covenants*, sec. 89, p. 5.
[30]Dean L. May, "Mormons," in Stephan Thernstrom, ed., *Harvard Encyclopedia of American Ethnic Groups* (Cambridge, MA: Harvard University Press, 1980), p. 730.

Legislating Morality   While Mormons do not drink, and they are not strictly opposed to those outside the faith drinking, they do attempt to control the drinking habits of others. There are more than a thousand bars, restaurants, and clubs serving alcoholic beverages, generating $124 million a year. There are five members on the Utah Alcoholic Beverage Control Commission, on which teetotaling Mormons are well-represented.[31]

During May 1999, LDS purchased a downtown park from Salt Lake City for $8.1 million dollars, provided that the park remain open twenty-four hours a day to the public. Shortly afterward, the church laid down a myriad of rules, which include: no smoking, sunbathing, music, speech-making, cursing, or begging. The ACLU is challenging the LDS decision to enforce such rules.[32]

LDS is often criticized for the influence it exerts over life in Utah, where 71 percent of the population is Mormon. But is this not true of life in any part of the country in which one religious perspective is clearly dominant? For example, the polity of the South clearly reflects the influence of the Southern Baptist Convention. There is also evidence that the Mormons' spirituality may serve to restore the fervor of the non-LDS in Utah. Sociologists Rodney Stark and Roger Finke found that Utah Protestants such as Lutherans, Presbyterians, and Methodists attend church more and contributed more to their church than their non-Utah counterparts.

Tithing   In addition to their adherence to the Word of Wisdom, Latter-day Saints have two other customs that should be mentioned. One is tithing; the other is missionary work. Taking them in order, **tithing** comes from *tithe*, meaning "one-tenth." And in simplest terms, this is exactly what LDS expects: 10 percent of one's income "for the support of the Lord's work." Authority for the tithe comes from another revelation of Joseph Smith, this one in 1838.

> Those who have been tithed shall pay one-tenth of all their interest annually; and this shall be a standing law unto them forever . . . and all those who gather unto the land of Zion . . . shall observe this law, or they shall not be found worthy to abide among you.[33]

The 10-percent figure is not based on the income that remains after normal living expenses have been deducted; it is a flat 10 percent "off the

[31]Drummond Ayres, Jr., "Sober Reality in Utah: Mormons Fulfill Role," *New York Times,* July 22, 1998, Sec. A, p. 2.

[32]"Rights Group Challenges a Church's Restrictions," *New York Times,* May 7, 1999, Sec. A, p. 20; Michael B. Toney, Chalon Keller, and Lori M. Hunter, "Regional Cultures, Persistence and Change: A Case Study of the Mormon Culture Region," *Social Science Journal* 40 (2003): 431–45; and Rodney Stark and Roger Finke, "Religion in Context: The Response of Non-Mormon Faiths in Utah," *Review of Religious Research* 45 (2004, No. 3): 293–98.

[33]Smith, *Doctrine and Covenants,* sec. 119.

top." Tithes are collected by the ward bishops and forwarded directly to the general authorities in Salt Lake City, a procedure that also stems from one of the Prophet's revelations.

The membership does not ask—and the general authorities do not disclose—exactly how much money is collected or what happens to it. However, the two major expenditures are for missionary work and education, including the support of Brigham Young University.

It is true that all Mormons are not full-tithers. Occasionally, members are permitted to give less than 10 percent and still remain in good standing. Others—the inactive group—may give little or nothing. The typical Mormon, however, not only gives his or her 10 percent but is quite happy to do so. By being worthy members, Mormons maintain their place in the Mormon community, are assured of full temple privileges for themselves and their families, and have the inner security that comes from carrying out the word of the Lord as revealed to the Prophet Joseph Smith.

Missionary Activity   As Wallace Turner aptly points out, "It is foolish to pick any *one* aspect of this remarkable religion and assert that 'this is its strength.' Yet the temptation is strong . . . to select the missionary program."[34]

Like so many other aspects of their religion, the Mormon missionary program is considerably different from that of other groups. It is larger, more vigorous, more youthful, more systematic—and more successful. Latter-day Saints consider it an honor to be missionaries, and many young Mormons look forward to the time when they will be selected. The selection is made by the ward bishop, who forwards a detailed application to the missionary committee in Salt Lake City. The applicant must be young (nineteen or twenty), of good character, and worthy in the eyes of the church. Also he or she (or his or her family) must be able to afford the cost, for the expenses incurred during the fieldwork are not borne by LDS.

In 1990, James Coates reflected on the costs that many parents willingly bear while their children serve the church in the field. At that time, estimates placed the cost to the family of keeping a young missionary in the field at $350 per month or $8,400 for a typical two-year mission.[35]

Either sex may apply, although males outnumber females by a margin of about four to one. If an applicant is accepted by the committee, he or she receives a "call," a letter with a territorial assignment. This may be in any one of the fifty states or abroad, but in either case the young missionary is expected to stay for the stipulated period of time, usually one and a half or two years. Before departing for his or her post, the missionary spends four to eleven weeks in Salt Lake City attending a training course.

[34]Turner, *Mormon Establishment*, p. 89.
[35]Coates, *In Mormon Circles*, p. 138.

Those who have been approached by Mormon missionaries may have wondered how these young people manage to learn so much about Mormonism in so short a time. But the fact is that they have been trained in Mormonism all their lives. The short intellectual period in Salt Lake City is merely to explain the operational details.

Once they have reached their assigned areas, the young emissaries work hard. It is not at all uncommon for them to put in eight to ten hours a day, seven days a week. They operate in pairs, living together and visiting the homes of potential converts together. They have strict rules of conduct and are not permitted to date during the missionary assignment.

When they discuss Mormonism with potential converts, the missionaries are sincere but not insistent. They patiently and systematically explain their point of view in accordance with a routine mapped out by LDS authorities. They leave pamphlets and other literature, and often make return visits to the same home. The work is occasionally tiring and—like all door-to-door efforts—more than occasionally discouraging. Nevertheless, most missionaries are happy in their assignments. There are close to 60,000 of them in the field at any one time, up from 30,000 a decade ago, and when their tour is over, memories of their experience will undoubtedly remain with them for the rest of their lives.

Coates observes that "statistics show just how dramatically the missionary experience influences Mormons in general. Of the 6.7 million church members on the rolls in 1990, no fewer than 826,000 of them had served two years as missionaries sometime since 1960. . . . Another particularly telling statistic illustrates that between 1976 and 1980 the average missionary was bringing in seven recruits in the course of a two-year tour."[36]

In recent years, LDS began using self-supporting senior citizens as missionaries. Today, there are more than 1,500 couples in the field. They do not go door-to-door, spreading the word, as do their younger counterparts. Often they work as tour guides at LDS historical sites, as genealogical researchers, in campus ministries, or in foreign missions. Many are retired married couples. Singles who volunteer are assigned same-sex partners and sent into the field.

Hard work aside, is the missionary effort successful? Indeed it is. First, the conversion rate is fantastically high. The number of yearly converts is reported to be in the neighborhood of 300,000. This is what accounts for much of the phenomenal growth of LDS. Second, Mormon missionary efforts have been so successful that in many parts of the world permanent missions have been established. In fact, in Hawaii, Canada, Brazil, England, South Korea, Switzerland, New Zealand, the

[36]Ibid., p. 141.

Philippines, Guatemala, Peru, Germany, South Africa, Sweden—and many other countries—Mormon temples have been erected or are under construction.

Due in part to effective proselytizing, the Church of Latter-day Saints is now a "world" church. Nevertheless, the church per se does not have a pilgrimage program. There is no doubt, however, that all of Utah benefits from visits made by Mormon converts to holy sites within the state—yet another positive latent function of the missionary effort. As evidence of the effect of tourism, Hudman and Jackson note that "more than two million Mormons visit Temple Square yearly, combining the elements of the pilgrim's devotion with modern tourism for pleasure."[37]

Sociologist Anson Shupe observes yet another interesting latent function of Mormon missionary efforts. "Both the Federal Bureau of Investigation and Central Intelligence Agency eagerly recruit Latter-day Saints. Overseas missions have provided many male missionaries with valuable foreign-language experience and contacts."[38] Shupe goes on to say that, apart from their language skills, Mormon recruits are valued for their sobriety, patriotism, and respect for authority. Mormon attorney Reed Slack notes how patriotism is fostered by church doctrine. "Modern prophets, modern scriptures, and modern revelation proclaim that the Constitution was divinely inspired. . . . The answer to why the Constitution was inspired lies in the Mormon belief that the Americas are the site of the New Jerusalem, the land of Zion. . . . The divine inspiration for the Constitution came through the foreordination of the Framers and through the influence of the Light of Christ acting upon them."[39]

Not a Job for an Amateur   Until the summer of 1996, Ronald Rasband was president of Huntsman Chemical Corporation, the largest privately held chemical company in the United States. At forty-four, master of the multi-million-dollar deal, he was comfortable, self-confident, and respected. Nevertheless, he took a leave of absence from his job.

For several years, Rasband will direct the activities of some two hundred young missionaries in New York City. He is doing it because he was asked to. A direct descendant of ancestors who crossed the continent to Utah with Brigham Young, Rasband feels an obligation to apply his administrative skills in organizing the missionary effort. His experience should help. In 1970, he was a young missionary pounding the same streets.

David Gonzales notes, "Other executives might be content to write a check with lots of zeros and feel, rightfully, that they had contributed to

[37]Lloyd E. Hudman and Richard Jackson, "Morman Pilgrimage and Tourism," *Annals of Tourism and Research* v19 (1992): 120.

[38]Anson Shupe, *The Darker Side of Virtue* (Buffalo, NY: Prometheus Books, 1991), pp. 124–25.

[39]Reed D. Slack, "The Mormon Belief of an Inspired Constitution," *Journal of Church and State* 36 (1994), pp. 37, 39.

society. Mr. Rasband said it was his duty to heed the request made by officials of his church who rely on unpaid clergy members and missionaries to carry out its aggressive campaign of evangelization."[40]

Rasbad did not remain an amateur for long. In 2000, he became a full-time leader, and then in 2005 he was named to serve as a member of the Presidency of the Seventy, which serves as the principal representative of the LDS president.

Some Mormon Challenges

All large organizations have their problems, and LDS is no exception. In fact, in a historical sense, the Mormons have probably had more than their share. That they have managed to solve most of them is due to good management, plus—always—the conviction that God is with them. Of the problem areas that remain, seven seem to merit particular attention.

The Intellectuals   In view of the origin and nature of Mormonism, the church has a special problem with the intellectual element. That is to say, intellectuals are by definition challengers. They challenge accepted beliefs and try to apply a so-called rationality to various issues. Through their critical insights, they are able to provide concepts—new ways of looking at things—not obtainable from other sources.

The Mormon church, on the other hand, is based on revelation. It is active rather than contemplative; it maintains a set of long-cherished beliefs; and, of course, it holds to the view that the Book of Mormon and the Bible (correctly translated) are literally true. As a result, disagreements between LDS and the intellectual members of the church crop up every now and then.

Academics and women, especially academic women, are fueling fires of discontent within the Mormon community. For example, two Brigham Young University (BYU) professors failed their tenure reviews in 1993, apparently because their views conflicted with church teachings. Celia Konchar Farr, a specialist in feminist literary theory, was reprimanded for speaking at pro-choice rallies. Rebuked by university officials for her political position on abortion, Farr was refused tenure because her scholarship did not have "sufficient academic standing." Farr's supporters argue that her work showed greater scholarship than that of many who were approved for tenure, and "insufficient academic standing" was used as an excuse.

Anthropologist David Knowlton was also denied tenure. He was accused of attacking the church, though he contends he never intended to. "He says he was threatened with excommunication after he gave a talk

---

[40]David Gonzales, "Financial Star Is a Recruiter for His Faith," *New York Times*, September 4, 1996, p. B12.

suggesting that terrorists attacked Mormon churches in Latin America because they saw them as a symbol of American imperialism. He never expounded that belief himself, he said."[41]

New language has been added to BYU's employee conduct policy. Employees must "refrain from behavior or expression that seriously and adversely affects the Church. They must also show the university that they are 'temple worthy'—meaning that every year they must demonstrate to local ecclesiastical leaders that they attend church, are devoted Mormons, and give 10 percent of their income to the church."[42] This policy, in essence, gives a measure of community control over BYU faculty.

In 1996, the new language was used to deny tenure to Gail Houston, an assistant professor of English. Her letter of denial said in part that she was a good teacher, scholar, and person, but there were times when she contradicted church teachings. For instance, she advocated praying to "Heavenly Mother."[43] Interestingly, Mormonism accepts both a male and female deity as parents of humankind. In a 1991 speech, President Hinckley did not deny a "Holy Mother," but said all prayers should be directed to "Our Father."[44]

Maxine Hanks, editor of *Women and Authority: Re-emerging Mormon Feminism* (1992), writes, "Excommunication was a small price to pay for my voice. It didn't take away my theology or my spirituality, which the church does not control. God's spirit cannot be homogenized, mass-produced and marketed by blue-suited septuagenarians from a high-rise in downtown Salt Lake City."[45]

Differences between intellectuals and the church are not to be aired in public. Lavina Fielding Anderson was excommunicated in 1993 for publication of a paper detailing church leaders' conflicts with Mormon intellectuals and feminists.

If the church is to change, the change will be slow. Boyd Packer, a church leader, told a Mormon conference in 1991, "feminists pose a serious threat to the faith, along with homosexuals, and so-called intellectuals and scholars."[46] He urged local leaders to deal with the problems. Women, in response, are protesting the "phallic" structure of the church in a variety of ways, such as publishing a newsletter they call *Neanderthal Watch.*[47]

---

[41]Carolyn J. Mooney, "Conservative Brigham Young U. Contends with Small but Growing Movement for Change," *Chronicle of Higher Education* 39 (June 30, 1993): A13.

[42]Ibid.

[43]Kit Lively, "Brigham Young Denies Tenure to Scholar for Contradicting Mormon Views," *Chronicle of Higher Education* 42 (June 21, 1996): 15.

[44]Dirk Johnson, "As Mormon Church Grows, So Does Dissent from Feminists and Scholars," *New York Times,* October 2, 1993, p. 1.

[45]Maxine Hanks, "A Struggle to Reclaim Authority," *Los Angeles Times,* July 10, 1994, p. M7.

[46]Johnson, "As Mormon Church Grows," p. 1.

[47]Lynn Smith, "Protesting Patriarchy," *Los Angeles Times,* May 16, 1993, p. E1.

National survey data seem to indicate that religiosity tends to decrease as education increases. For most intellectuals, religious beliefs are unable to stand in the face of challenges generated by modern science and higher education. Not so with the Mormons. Brigham Young University sociologist Stan Albrecht, in a study of Mormon religiosity and higher education, found the following:

> In stark contrast to the pattern evident in these national survey data, our studies of Latter-day Saint samples demonstrate a strong positive relationship between level of education and religiosity. . . . For men in the sample, weekly attendance at Sunday services goes from a low of 34 percent for those with only a grade school education to 80 percent for those with postgraduate experience. For women, the results are the same except for a modest drop-off in attendance for women with post-baccalaureate experience.[48]

Women's Role   LDS does not prohibit its female members from joining the labor force, and Mormon women are to be found in all walks of life, including the professions. At the same time, there is no doubt—in terms of priorities—that the church leaders feel that "woman's place is in the home." President Hinckley noted in October 1996, "It is well-nigh impossible to be a full-time homemaker and a full-time employee. To you [women] I say do the very best you can. I hope that if you are employed full time you are doing it to ensure that basic needs are met and not simply to indulge a taste for an elaborate home, fancy cars and other luxuries."[49]

For the first time in the state's history the Utah fertility rate is declining. Although the birthrate has dropped—from 3.2 to 2.5 births per woman— it is still considerably higher than the national average of 1.8. Women are postponing the birth of their first child. The average woman in Utah now bears her first child when she is 23.3, up from 22.2 at the close of the 1980s. When women delay childbearing, they have fewer children. Demographers attribute the decline in fertility to economic necessity—women having to work to make ends meet.

Although they have their own organization within the church, women are not permitted to ascend in the LDS hierarchy. All Mormon leaders, from ward bishop to church president, are—and always have been— male. Some Mormon women have resented their exclusion and have complained. A few have even been excommunicated for "preaching false doctrine, and undermining church leadership because of their public statements."

---

[48]Stan L. Albrecht, "The Consequential Dimension of Mormon Religiosity," essay presented as the BYU Distinguished Faculty Lecture, February 15, 1989, p. 103.

[49]Vern Anderson, "Mormon President Says Moms Should Stay Home with Kids," *Associated Press*, October 7, 1996.

This, then, is the problem: although the large majority of Mormon women seem to be quite satisfied with the role accorded them by the church, some are clearly dissatisfied. There is no denying that the women's movement has had some impact on Mormon women, and it is equally apparent that it has had some impact on the church. During 1990, in a rare revision of the endowments, the church dropped wording that required women to pledge to obey their husbands; now, like the men, they must only vow to obey God.[50] It would be an exaggeration to say, however, that the women's movement has had a critical impact on either Mormon women or the church.

African Americans at one time held a similar position vis-à-vis the church; that is, while they were welcomed into church membership, they were not eligible for the ranks of the priesthood. It took a revelation—reported by church president Spencer W. Kimball on June 9, 1978—to change the rules. Whether a similar change might someday occur regarding the role of women is problematical.

All that can be said is that since Joseph Smith's death, revelations have been announced by the church in only three instances: once by Brigham Young when he was guided to Utah; once by Wilford Woodruff when he was commanded to put an end to plural marriage; and once by Spencer W. Kimball, whose revelation indicated that "all worthy male members of the church may be ordained to the priesthood without regard for race or color."

The Race Question   Mormon's have a mixed history with people of color, to say the least. First, their settlement of Utah was marked by violent confrontations with tribal people—ironic given the Prophet Joseph Smith's teachings of Jesus' appearance among the indigenous peoples of North America.

Second, the Church banned black men from the priesthood beginning in 1852. Brigham Young's pronouncement came from his teaching the "curse of Cain," that God marked the descendants of Cain with black skin and were persecuted forever. The Book of Mormon implies in several places that white skin is pure and black skin is vile. Church President Spencer Kimball's revelation from God led to dropping the racial ban in June 1978. The pronouncement also brought the church in line, using its past rulings of granting priesthood to black people in the Pacific who were not of African descent.

The LDS reversal on race can be viewed as a belated recognition of racial equality, but it also can be seen as reflective of a community, family-oriented faith—values that resonate with many members of racial and

---

[50]The endowment ceremony is a Mormon prerequisite for living in the highest level of heaven. It has remained mostly intact since Smith's revelations. In the same 1990 revision, LDS made another interesting compromise with the world. Clergy of other religions are no longer portrayed in the ritual as paid agents of Satan.

ethnic minorities. It also made sense given the LDS' success in developing countries, as represented by Brazil with its racially mixed population. By 2000, non-English-speaking members became the majority worldwide.

The history of past exclusion weighs heavily, and racist doctrine still is to be found in Mormon historical texts used today by church leaders, but efforts to have them to officially repudiated have been ignored. African Americans number a miniscule 10,000 today. Blacks (and Latinos) wield little influence in the church's upper achievement. LDS members are still discouraged from crossing "racial lines in dating and marriage," although this is supposed to be for reasons of compatibility and not a scriptural commandment. Outside the United States, Latinos and non-whites have become very visible among the LDS.

Mormons are hardly unique among Christian faiths in the United States, having a racist legacy that echoes in the present in all-white nature of most mainstream Protestant congregations. Yet the LDS failure to repudiate the past in its totality serves to separate it from major Protestant faiths.[51]

Inflexible Process of Succession   LDS presidents serve for life, most followers believing that they are chosen by God. At death they are replaced by the senior apostle from the quorum of twelve. The twelve are the only members who cannot retire. This process guarantees a gerontocracy, or rule by elders. Critics argue that by the time these leaders come to office, they are too old to serve.

Ezra Taft Benson assumed the presidency at age eighty-six in 1985. He died May 30, 1994, at ninety-six. Benson served as secretary of agriculture during the Eisenhower administration. During his lifetime, he was at the forefront of many conservative causes. A vibrant man until he suffered a stroke, Benson served more than half his presidency severely incapacitated, barely able to communicate.

Steve Benson, a Pulitzer prize–winning cartoonist, is Benson's grandson. During a visit in 1993, he said his grandfather said "virtually nothing" to him.[52] He further said that despite their close relationship, "my grandfather looked at me quizzically, as if he were examining me."[53]

Steve Benson resigned from the church because it appeared to him that church hierarchy was projecting a false image that his grandfather was capable of governance. In response to Benson's condition, Gordon Hinckley, then first counselor to the president, assured the public that there was no

[51]Richard N. Ostling and Joan K. Ostling, *Moron America: The Power and The Promise*, (San Francisco; HarperCollins, 2000), pp. 99–112; and Margaret Ramirez, "Mormons' New-Time Believers" *Chicago Tribune*, July 24, 2005, pp. 1, 17.

[52]"Mormons' Inflexible Process of Succession Questioned," *Associated Press, Saturday Oklahoman and Times*, July 31, 1993, p. 12.

[53]Ibid.

leadership problem in the church, that "the apostles all possess priesthood power to be prophets, seers and revelators, but only the president has the authority to receive revelations from God for the church."[54] He went on to say that "when the president is ill or not able to function fully . . . his two counselors together comprise a Quorum of the First Presidency."[55]

On the day after Ezra Taft Benson's death, LDS publicly heard the voice of a living prophet for the first time in five years. Senior apostle Howard Hunter was named president. A much less visible man than Benson, a scholarly type, it appeared that he was "ready to lead a church more tolerant of dissent."[56] In apparent reference to feminists and scholars, he asked that "Mormons treat each other with more kindness, more courtesy, more humility and patience and forgiveness."[57] He wanted them back in the fold. Hunter, eighty-eight when he assumed the presidency, was not to see his hope come to fruition. He died March 3, 1995, having served only nine months.

Little more than a week later, Gordon Hinckley became the fifteenth president of the Church of Latter-day Saints. An experienced administrator, Hinckley had served three presidents as counselor and had often acted as the voice of the church in the absence of these presidents. Hinckley, however, was ninety-six years old in 2006.

The Apostates   Over the years, LDS has had its share of trouble with apostates—those who have left the fold. During the nineteenth century, much of the anti-Mormon propaganda could be traced to disgruntled Mormons. Some of the apostates were simply individuals who had become dissatisfied with certain policies of the church. Much more serious, however, were those who, finding themselves unable to accept church doctrine, defected as a group to pursue their own set of religious beliefs.

A number of such withdrawals occurred after polygamy was officially proclaimed in 1852. The most significant was that of the Josephites, who rejected not only the doctrine of plural marriage but also the leadership of Brigham Young. The Josephites held that church leadership should have followed a hereditary line, and that the rightful heir, following Joseph Smith's death, was his son Joseph Smith III.

Organized in 1852, the Josephites grew steadily, if not spectacularly, and at the end of the decade proclaimed themselves the Reorganized Church of Jesus Christ of Latter Day Saints, with Joseph Smith III as head. Today it is a large, active organization, with some quarter-million members. In 2001, the church took on the new name of Community of Christ.

[54]Ibid.
[55]Ibid.
[56]"At Day's End: Mormons," *Economist* (April 9, 1994): A30.
[57]"The Prophet's Mantle," *Economist* (June 11, 1994): A24.

The relationship between LDS and the Community of Christ is amicable enough. Indeed, the two groups have much in common, including their founder, Joseph Smith. Like LDS, the Community hierarchy includes a president, twelve apostles, and a quorum of the seventy. The church likewise relies on the nonsalaried services of elders and priests for the handling of their local congregations. Most important, perhaps, both accept the Book of Mormon as divinely inspired. The original manuscript, dictated by Joseph Smith from the controversial golden plates and written in longhand by Oliver Cowdery, is owned by the Community of Christ church and kept in a temperature-and-humidity-controlled bank vault in Kansas City.

On the other hand, there is little likelihood that LDS and the Community of Christ will bury their differences and unite; the division is too pronounced. In addition to the leadership factor just mentioned, the Community of Christ does not maintain a volunteer missionary system. Also, they have no secret temple rites of any kind, no endowments, no special undergarments, no sealings, and no celestial marriage. The temples—and the meetings—are open to the public. In recent years they have allowed women to be priests.

Although members of the Community of Christ do tithe, their 10 percent is not "off the top" but is figured after normal living expenses have been deducted. The difference between the two kinds of tithes is substantial and goes a long way toward explaining why LDS has grown so much faster than the Community of Christ.

The Fundamentalists   Just as the official adoption of polygamy created a number of schisms within the Mormon church, the Manifesto announcing an *end* to plural marriage had the same effect. Small groups of Mormons—or more accurately, ex-Mormons—have continued to practice plural marriage, even though it is against both the law and the tenets of LDS. These "Fundamentalists," as they are called, have had the unfortunate effect of prolonging the association between Mormonism and polygamy. Hence, it is little wonder that they are denounced by LDS.

After the Manifesto was proclaimed, some of the fundamentalists migrated to Mexico, but others stayed in the United States—mainly in remote areas of Arizona, Utah, and California—where they have continued their polygamous practices.

Exactly how many fundamentalists there are is not known, because their operations are generally underground. Estimates from the 1970s through 2006 of plural marriage have edged upward, placing the number between 30 and 50 thousand people. These estimates can be variously viewed as very small compared with the millions involved in the various mainstream Mormon faiths; it can also be viewed in absolute numbers as a very large number of faithful engaged in an illegal activity. Regardless, there may well be more living in plural marriage now than 120 years ago when it was practiced legally in Utah.[58]

A number of observers—including, perhaps, most LDS members—look upon the fundamentalists as deviants, and of lower socioeconomic status. Fundamentalists themselves say that they come from all walks of life. They also claim to be devout rather than deviant. In point of fact, they seem to be both.

Fundamentalists contend that just before he died in 1887, First President John Taylor (Brigham Young's successor) called together five of his followers and told them that the practice of polygamy must, at all cost, be retained. His message had great impact on the five men for two reasons: (1) in defense of the Principle, he himself had spent the last years of his life in hiding, and (2) because he was president of the church at the time, the five men felt that his counsel was based on revelation.

Whatever the rationale, there is no denying that the spark of polygamy is still very much alive—despite the fact that the pluralists have long since been cut off from the Mormon church. The fundamentalists may have some sort of clandestine organization, although not too much is known about it. From time to time they publish and distribute literature, and every so often the popular press runs an exposé of their plural marriages. But responsible information is hard to come by.

The reason for our dearth of knowledge is twofold. In the first place, despite their agreement on the Principle, the fundamentalists are not united or organized into one cohesive organization. They are spread over several states and Mexico, and their geographical area encompasses thousands of square miles. A number of different sects are involved, most of them quite small. Indeed, many of those who adhere to the Principle do so as individuals; that is, they have no connection with *any* group or organization.

The second reason for the lack of information is that polygamy is illegal, and those involved never know when the authorities will crack down. To circumvent possible court action, most polygamists take but one *legal* wife. Subsequent marriages—and some polygamists are reported to have as many as eleven wives—are performed by some sort of religious officiant, and do not involve a marriage license.[59] Utah, in turn, has made cohabitation a felony—provable merely by the presence of children. (In retaliation, fundamentalists have reportedly planted spies in both LDS and the police departments to warn of impending raids.)

Actually, authorities have been increasingly reluctant to take legal action against the polygamists. For one thing, cohabitation is far from uncommon

[58]Melissa Merrill, *Polygamist's Wife* (Salt Lake City: Olympus, 1975), p. 116; and Elise Soukup, "Polygamists, Unite!" *Newsweek*, March 20, 2006, p. 52.

[59]James Brooke, "Utah Struggles with Revival of Poligamy," *New York Times*, August 23, 1998, Sec 1, p. 107.

in society at large, with the public apparently taking a rather tolerant position. For another, there is the welfare problem. If a polygamist is prosecuted and sent to prison, his wives and children can—and do—go on welfare. And local governments may not have budgetary provisions necessary to handle such cases.

Plural marriage with its sensational aspects continues to fascinate the media and the public. National television from the Oprah Winfrey show to the Jerry Springer show devotes programs to it. While the LDS denial of any relationship to such arrangements is regularly noted, the embarrassment to the church is apparent. Recently the national spotlight was shown on it when a disaffected Mormon who proclaimed his vision as polygamist snatched fifteen-year-old Elizabeth Smart from her Salt Lake City home. The last thing the Mormons want is to continue to be associated with plural marriage. But as long as fundamentalism exists, that association seems inevitable.[60]

Mormonism Today

Irrespective of what criteria are employed—total membership, rate of growth, wealth, devoutness, education, vigor—the Church of Jesus Christ of Latter-day Saints has an extraordinary record. There is no evidence, furthermore, that its various activities are diminishing, either in scope or tempo. On the contrary . . .

Business and Financial Interests To say that the Mormon church is wealthy would be a clear understatement. A number of observers, including *Time* magazine, believe that on a per capita basis, LDS is the richest church in the world. For example, the church carries hundreds of millionaires on its rolls. Apart from individual wealth, the church has enormous organizational wealth.[61]

Time estimates that the Mormon church is an empire worth at least $30 billion. Among their holdings is the 312 thousand-acre Deseret Cattle and Citrus Ranch near Orlando, Florida. Apart from the income it generates as the top beef ranch in the United States, the real estate is valued at nearly $900 million. As part of their agribusiness complex, the church also owns fifty other farms.[62]

[60]White and White, "Polygamy and Mormon Identity." While legal intevention is infrequent, the polygamy question has sparked the formation of two interesting self-help groups, *Tapestry Against Polygamy* (www.polygamy.org) and *The Women's Religious Liberty Union*. Tapestry is a self-help group that seeks to free women from polygamy, while the Union's aim is to deter those who would interfere with the happiness of women involved in polygamous marriages.

[61]Cf. David Van Biema, "Kingdom Come," *Time*, August 4, 1999, vol. 150, no. 5, pp. 50–54.

[62]Ibid.

Their real estate holdings include much of the property around church headquarters in downtown Salt Lake City. The Polynesian Cultural Center, the number one visitor attraction in Hawaii, generates revenues of up to $40 million a year for the church. They own Brigham Young University in Provo, Utah, and several smaller educational institutions.[63]

Then there are the church's media holdings. Again according to *Time*, they own sixteen radio stations and one TV station that, combined, generated $162 million in 1996. They own Deseret Books, a publishing house with thirty chain outlets in Utah. Their newspaper, *Deseret News*, has a circulation of 65,000.[64] The church has a stock portfolio of more than $1 billion. They own choice hotels and motels, department stores, insurance companies, and skyscrapers in New York and Salt Lake City. The list could be extended.

While the church generates $600 million a year from its investments, this sum is dwarfed by the $5.3 billion in tithes and offerings given by its members and there is no doubt that the church hierarchy is aware of the importance of the tithe. President Gordon Hinckley, in a State of the Church address delivered in 1991, said: "We have a few income-producing business properties, but the return from these would keep the Church going only for a very brief time. Tithing is the Lord's law of finance. There is no other financial law like it. It is a principle given with a promise, spoken by the Lord Himself for the blessing of His children . . . . The only real wealth of the Church is in the faith of its people."[65]

The Mormon church has been powerfully successful. This is a safe statement, despite the fact that no yearly financial statements are released. The economic prosperity of LDS stems from a generous and enthusiastic tithing system, plus sound business practices. The money generated is used for the maintenance and continued expansion of the church.

Welfare   All Mormons are not rich, naturally. Most of them belong to the broad middle class. And, of course, there are some at the lower end of the economic ladder. LDS, however, takes care of its own needy, and the latter seldom have to depend on public relief. The system employed is most effective, for it permits those in need to be helped without drawing on general church revenue.

The program has two main features. First, each stake has one particular welfare project. Some stakes have farms, others have orchards, others have canneries or factories, others raise cattle, and so on. All project labor is performed without charge by LDS members. Each stake has a quota, and the interchange of commodities takes place on the basis of administrative conferences.

---

[63]Ibid.
[64]Ibid.
[65]Gordon B. Hinckley, "The State of the Church," *Ensign*, May 1991, p. 51.

Turner, who studied the distribution system, shows how extensive the program is: "Peanut butter comes from Houston; tuna from San Diego; macaroni from Utah; raisins from Fresno; prunes from Santa Rosa, California; soup from Utah; gelatine from Kansas City; toothpaste and shaving cream from Chicago; orange juice from Los Angeles; grapefruit juice from Phoenix and Mesa; sugar from Idaho."[66]

The second half of the welfare program involves "fast money" contributed by LDS members. On the first Sunday of the month, each Mormon family skips two meals. The estimated price of the meals is then given as a welfare contribution, most of the money being used for items not obtainable from the exchange program, such as clothing, razor blades, light bulbs, and so forth. Although the fast money collected from each family may not seem like much—perhaps fifteen to twenty dollars a month—the LDS welfare program takes in millions of dollars every year by this method.

All the welfare items, both produced and purchased, are stocked in the various bishops' storehouses scattered throughout Mormondom. The storehouses—some 150 of them—resemble fair-sized supermarkets, except that no money changes hands. The needy simply present a written order from the ward bishop, whereupon the necessary supplies are dispensed. (If money is needed, there is a special bishop's fund available.)

Some contend that no Mormon ever goes on public relief, and while this may be true in some wards, it is probably not true in all. Also, in spite of the obvious success of its welfare program, it is doubtful whether LDS could handle the need that would arise, say, in the event of a major depression. But then, neither could most other groups. All in all, the Mormon welfare program is one of LDS's more successful undertakings.

Education   For some reason, the general public seems unaware that LDS places great stress on education. But the fact is that the Mormons founded both the University of Utah—the oldest university west of the Mississippi—and Brigham Young University.

One of the two major educational efforts of the Latter-day Saints is their system of seminaries and institutes. The seminaries are programs held as supplements to high school, and the institutes are socioreligious centers for Mormon college students. There are well over 2,000 institutes and seminaries in the United States and abroad, and at any one time some 100,000 Mormon youth attend them. These programs are used "to bridge

---

[66]Turner, *Mormon Establishment,* p. 123.

the critical period of life when young Mormons must make the transition from the blind faith of their childhood to the reasoned acceptance of the faith the church hopes they will achieve."[67]

The second major thrust of the Mormon educational program is in higher education itself. Utah leads the country both in the percentage of college enrollees and in the percentage of college graduates. Latter-day Saints are justifiably proud of this accomplishment, and of the fact that they have supplied the presidents for many colleges and universities outside Utah. (The number of eminent people who have been Mormons—corporation heads, scientists, engineers, governors, senators, presidential cabinet members—is too great to attempt even a partial listing.)[68]

Brigham Young University (BYU), of course, is the capstone of the Mormon educational effort. The buildings and campus are magnificent, and—in terms of physical plant—would probably rank at or near the top of U.S. colleges and universities.

In the last fifty years, enrollment has gone from roughly 5,000 to well over 28,000, making it, as mentioned earlier, the largest church-related university in the nation. The fact that it is church-related, however, does not signify any curtailment in extracurricular activities. In fact, 1984–1985 was a banner school year for BYU. The football team was ranked number one in the country;[69] and Sharlene Wells, a twenty-year-old Brigham Young student, was crowned Miss America at the Atlantic City pageant.

Tuition at BYU is low—just a little more than $3,600 a year. (For non-LDS, the tuition is $7,200.) And although the university receives no federal aid of any kind, building and other expenses present little problem. As elsewhere in Mormondom, tithing supplies fuel for the educational machinery.

BYU is primarily an undergraduate institute, although it does offer the doctorate in 25 fields. The large majority, about 98 percent, of the student body are Mormons, and they come from all fifty states as well as over 120 foreign countries.

Why the stress on education? The impetus can be traced to a revelation of Joseph Smith's in 1833: "The Glory of God is intelligence, or, in other words, light and truth." This motto, encircling the figure of a beehive, can be seen on university literature and letterheads.

---

[67]Turner, *Mormon Establishment*, p. 123.

[68]Besides the well-known Mormon professional baseball players listed in the next footnote, Mormon celebrities include Stephen Covey (founder and head of a management and leadership company), Richard Paul Evans (author of *The Christmas Box*), former Massachusetts governor Mitt Romney, football quarterback Steve Young, and professional golfer Johnny Miller.

[69]Mormons seem to do well in professional sports. A must for baseball buffs is Jim Ison's *Mormons in the Major Leagues: Career Histories of Forty-Four LDS Players* (Cincinnati, OH: Action Sports, 1991). The best of the past are sluggers Harmon Killebrew and Dale Murphy and pitchers Vernon Law and Jack Morris. More recent players include Dennis Eckersley and Wally Joyner.

While BYU is a major university in every sense of the word, it is still a *Mormon educational institution*. The campus is organized into wards and stakes, as is Mormondom at large. Also, student attire and behavior are conservative, in keeping with the tenets of the church. The men, for example, are not permitted to wear beards, while for women "the no-bra look is unacceptable." The BYU Web site proudly notes *The Princeton Review* consistently ranks the university as the most "stone-cold sober" school in the United States.

The Outlook

During World War I, LDS membership stood at approximately half a million. At the outbreak of World War II, the number had risen to around a million. Today, total membership is more than 12 million! Clearly, church membership is not only growing but accelerating.

In 1980, there were thirteen temples (for rituals such as the endowments, baptisms, and sealings) in the United States and six temples in other countries, increasing over the years to forty-four worldwide. By the beginning of 2007, there were 124 temples. There are now wards and stakes in all fifty states. LDS membership is also increasing sharply in a number of foreign countries. In fact, nearly half of LDS membership now lives in foreign countries, with the greatest conversion increase in South America.[70]

There is nothing secret about this phenomenal rate of increase. The Mormon church grows because it wants to grow. The Latter-day Saints have not only a high birthrate but a low death rate. On the average, they live several years longer than other Americans. (This they attribute to their prohibitions against alcohol, caffeine, and tobacco.)

As mentioned earlier, the Mormons have a high conversion rate. This, coupled with their high birthrate and low death rate, has led to astounding growth. For example, it was reported in the fourth edition of *Extraordinary Groups* that in 1987 church membership was 6,440,000. In the fifth edition membership exceeded 8,000,000. As of 2005, this figure exceeded 12,000,000, with 5,500,000 in the United States alone.

The same avenues of growth are open to other groups but are seldom used in conjunction with one another. The Old Order Amish, for instance, have exceptionally high birthrates, but their conversion figures are near zero. True, not all LDS members are active, but the ratio of active to inactive is probably higher than in most other denominations.

---

[70]Bernard Wysocki, "Worldly Blessings: Utah's Economy Goes Global, Thanks in Part to Role of Missionaries," *Wall Street Journal*, March 28, 1996, p. A1.

Mormonism emerged into the national limelight in an unusual way in 2007. Former Massachusetts Governor Mitt Romney announced his plans to run for the Republican nomination for the 2008 presidential race. As with any presidential hopeful, the candidate's policy positions came under close scrutiny, but in this so did his religion. Romney was a lifelong Mormon. National surveys showed that many of the public would not consider a Mormon for president, even if the candidate were qualified. In some respects, his campaign served to educate the general public about the Mormon faith, as John F. Kennedy did about Roman Catholicism in 1960 and Joe Lieberman did about his Orthodox Judaism in 2000 during his vice-presidential campaign.

The Latter-day Saints have had more than their share of challenges. They have been criticized for not assimilating, for not caring enough about the larger community. They have been troubled by apostates and plagued by polygamy. They have been rebuked because of their position on women. And they have been condemned by other denominations for stealing their members.

In the early days, of course, persecution was rampant. Time after time, in state after state, entire Mormon settlements were forced to flee. LDS leaders were jailed, and substantial amounts of church property were confiscated. Despite the many problems, however, both old and new, the long-term vitality of the movement has remained unimpaired. If anything, the tempo has increased. The fact is that Mormonism is more than a religion or a set of theological beliefs. For most of its members, it is a whole way of life.

KEY TERMS

Celestial Marriage, p. 215
Gentiles, p. 216
In-group, p. 226
Out-group, p. 226

Polygamy, p. 212
Stake, p. 221
Tithing, p. 228
Ward, p. 221

SELECTED READINGS

Albrecht, Stan, Howard Bahr, and Bruce Chadwick. "Changing Family and Sex Roles: An Assessment of Age Differences." *Journal of Marriage and the Family* 41 (February 1979): 41–50.

Alexander, Thomas, and Jessie Embry, eds. *After 150 Years.* Midvale, UT: Charles Redd Center for Western Studies, 1983.

Arrington, Leonard. *Brigham Young: American Moses.* New York: Knopf, 1985.

Baer, Hans. "Sex Roles in a Mormon Schismatic Group: The Levites of Utah." In *Sex Roles in Contemporary American Communes,* edited by John P. Wagner, pp. 111–54. Bloomington: Indiana University Press, 1982.

Barlow, Philip L. *Mormons and the Bible: The Place of the Latter-day Saints in American Religion.* New York: Oxford University Press, 1991.

Campbell, Bruce, and Eugene Campbell. "The Mormon Family." In *Ethnic Families in America,* edited by Charles Mindel, Robert Habenstein, and Roosevelt Wright Jr., pp. 456–94. New York: Elsevier, 1988.

Campbell, Eugene. "Foreword." In *The Essential Brigham Young.* Salt Lake City: Signature Books, 1992.

Carmer, Carl. *The Farm Boy and the Angel.* Garden City, NY: Doubleday, 1970.

Clark, Annie Turner. *A Mormon Mother: An Autobiography.* Salt Lake City: University of Utah Press, 1969.

Coates, James. *In Mormon Circles: Gentiles, Jack Mormons, and Latter-Day Saints.* Reading, MA: Addison-Wesley, 1990.

Cresswell, Stephen. *Mormons, Cowboys, Moonshiners and Klansmen: Federal Law Enforcement in the South and West, 1870–1893.* Tuscaloosa: University of Alabama Press, 1991.

Decker, Ed. *What You Need to Know about Mormons: Conversations with Cults.* Eugene, OR: Harvest House, 1990.

Dew, Sheri L. *Gordon B. Hinckley: Go Forward with Faith.* Salt Lake City: Deseret Books, 1996.

Foster, Lawrence. *Religion and Sexuality.* New York: Oxford University Press, 1981.
———. *Women, Family, and Utopia: Communal Experiments of the Shakers, the Oneida Community, and the Mormons.* Syracuse, NY: Syracuse University Press, 1991.

Gates, Susa Young. *The Life Story of Brigham Young.* New York: Macmillan, 1930.

Givens, Terry L. "The Church of Jesus Christ of Latter-Day Saints." In *Introduction to New and Alternative Religion in America,* edited by Eugene V. Gallagher and W. Michael Ashcraft, vol. 2, pp. 19–37. Westport, CT: Greenwood Press, 2006.

Hardy, B. Carmon. *Solemn Covenant: The Mormon Polygamous Passage.* Urbana: University of Illinois Press, 1992.

Hartman, Moshe, and Harriet Hartman. "Sex-Role Attitudes of Mormons vs. Non-Mormons in Utah." *Journal of Marriage and the Family* 45 (November 1983): 897–902.

Heinerman, John, and Anson Shupe. *The Mormon Corporate Empire.* Boston, MA: Beacon Press, 1985.

Homer, Michael. "Children in New Religious Movements; The Mormon Experience." In *Introduction to New and Alternative Religion in America,* edited by Eugene V. Gallagher and W. Michael Ashcraft, vol. 1, pp. 224–42. Westport, CT: Greenwood Press, 2006.

Ison, Jim. *Mormons in the Major Leagues: Career Histories of Forty-Four LDS Players.* Cincinnati, OH: Action Sports, 1991.

Krakauer, John. *Under the Banner of Heaven: A Study of Violent Faith.* New York: Doubleday, 2003.

Leone, Mark. *Roots of Modern Mormonism.* Cambridge, MA: Harvard University Press, 1979.

Madson, Susan Arrington. *Growing Up in Zion: True Stories of Young Pioneers Building the Kingdom.* Salt Lake City: Deseret Books, 1996.

May, Dean L. "Mormons." In *Harvard Encyclopedia of American Ethnic Groups,* edited by Stephan Thernstrom, pp. 720–31. Cambridge, MA: Harvard University Press, 1980.

Merrill, Melissa. *Polygamist's Wife.* Salt Lake City: Olympus, 1975.

Morris, Carroll Hofeling. *"If the Gospel Is True, Why Do I Hurt So Much?": Help for Dysfunctional Latter-day Saint Families.* Salt Lake City: Deseret, 1992.

Mullen, Robert. *The Latter-day Saints: The Mormons Yesterday and Today.* Garden City, NY: Doubleday, 1966.

Nibley, Hugh. *Tinkling Cymbals and Sounding Brass.* Salt Lake City: Deseret, 1991.

Ostling, Richard N., and Joan K. Ostling. *Mormon America: The Power and the Promise.* San Francisco: HarperCollins, 2000.

Porter, Blaine. *Selected Readings in the Latter-day Saint Family.* Dubuque, IA: Brown, 1963.

Schow, Ron, Wayne Schow, and Marybeth Raynes, eds. *Peculiar People: Mormons and Same-Sex Orientation.* Salt Lake City: Signature Books, 1991.

Shupe, Anson. *The Darker Side of Virtue.* Buffalo, NY: Prometheus Books, 1991.

Stark, Rodney. *The Rise of Mormonism.* Edited by Reid L. Neilson. New York: Columbia University Press, 2005.

Stegner, Wallace. *The Gathering of Zion.* New York: McGraw-Hill, 1964.

Thornton, Arland. "Religion and Fertility: The Case of Mormonism." *Journal of Marriage and the Family* 41 (February 1979): 131–42.

Tobler, Douglas F., and Nelson B. Wadsworth. *The History of the Mormons in Photographs and Text: 1830 to the Present.* New York: St. Martin's, 1989.

Turner, Wallace. *The Mormon Establishment.* Boston: Houghton Mifflin, 1966.

Turpin, John C. *The New Stress Reduction for Mormons.* Covenant, 1991.

West, Ray B., Jr. *Kingdom of the Saints.* New York: Viking, 1957.

Whalen, William. *The Latter-day Saints in the Modern-Day World.* New York: Day, 1964.

Whipple, Maurine. *This Is the Place: Utah.* New York: Knopf, 1945.

White, Jr., Kendall, and Daryl White, "Polygamy and Mormon Identity," *Journal of American Culture* 28 (June 2005): 165–77.

Wilkinson, M., and W. Tanner. "The Influence of Family Size, Interaction, and Religiosity on Family Affection in a Mormon Sample." *Journal of Marriage and the Family* 42 (May 1980): 297–304.

Young, Kimball. *Isn't One Wife Enough?* New York: Holt, 1954.

GOD'S WORD
OLY BI
THE WATCHTOWER
ANNOUNCING JEHOVAH'S KINGDOM
Truth or Tradition WHICH?

CHAPTER SEVEN

THE JEHOVAH'S WITNESSES

Most Americans in the twenty-first century separate their religious and secular lives, and there is relatively little condemnation of competing religious ideologies. But there are certain religious groups that are often thought of as being beyond the pale.

One such group is the Society of Jehovah's Witnesses, now numbering 1 million in the United States and worldwide another 5 million. Americans exhibit a range of attitudes toward the Witnesses from indifference to derision to occasional hostility. Yet the group continues to grow and prosper, not only through natural increase but also through proselytizing.

Why have they been so successful? To answer this question, it is necessary to know the group's history, understand their belief system, and examine the "supports of faith" that bind them together.[1]

---

[1]Because Witness ideology conflicts in many ways with the ideologies of mainstream Christianity, it is difficult to find unbiased accounts of Jehovah's Kingdom. The most recent literature is much like past literature. Writers interested in the Witnesses tend to focus on interpretations of Scriptures. Some, mostly Witnesses, argue the correct posture of the Watchtower Bible and Tract Society; others, often apostates, argue the opposite. Membership estimates are drawn from Eileen W. Linder, *Yearbook of American and Canadian Churches 2005* (Nashville: Abingdon Press, 2005), Table 2, and *2005 Yearbook of Jehovah's Witnesses* (Brooklyn: Watchtower Bible and Tract Society, 2005), pp. 38–39.

Included in the apostate literature is *In Search of Christian Freedom* by Raymond Franz (Atlanta: Commentary Press, 1991), a former member of the governing body of Jehovah's Witnesses, and a nephew of Frederick Franz, immediate past president of the Society. Also, see David A. Reed, ed., *Index of Watchtower Errors*, comp. Steve Huntoon and John Cornell King

Millenarian Movement

The Jehovah's Witnesses are an example of a millenarian movement. A **millenarian movement** is a group of people who anticipate a dramatic change when everything will be perfect. Obviously, such beliefs have their own biases about what constitutes a perfect future.

Typically, millenarian movements are associated with a prophecy about this imminent change, which is frequently delivered by a charismatic individual. Millenarian movements have included the Ghost Dance practiced by the Plains Indians and the cargo cult of the South Pacific. While many religions speak about a better future at some vague point in time in the future, millenarian movements may also describe a remaking of society and can be very specific about when this prophecy will occur, as we will see with the Jehovah's Witness.

Charles Russell

Charles Russell, founder of the Jehovah's Witnesses, was born in 1852 in Allegheny, Pennsylvania, now a part of Pittsburgh. Both his parents, Joseph L. and Eliza Russell, were of Scottish-Irish descent. The Russells were religious people, members of the Presbyterian church. Eliza Russell died when Charles was nine, so it is difficult to know how much religious influence she had on her precocious child. As to child and father, it is probable, at least in a religious sense, that the son had greater influence on the father than the father on the son.

An exact date does not appear in Witness literature, but sometime during his adolescence, young Charles left the Presbyterian church and joined a Congregational church, ostensibly because its attitudes were more liberal.

Joseph Russell, a haberdasher, owned a chain of five shops. After only a few years of formal education, Charles joined his father in business. By day, Charles sold shirts; at night, he studied the Bible. He was most interested in the prophetical books, particularly Daniel. By the time he was fourteen, he was on the streets with colored chalk writing Scriptures on the sidewalk. Nevertheless, at age seventeen, Russell encountered a spiritual crisis. He found himself no longer able to accept the concepts of eternal punishment and predestination. Surely, he believed, a good and just God would offer a plan of salvation for all of humankind. And certainly a

(Grand Rapids, MI: Baker Book House, 1990). For commentary, see Matthew Alfs, *The Evocative Religion of Jehovah's Witnesses: An Analysis of a Present-Day Phenomenon* (Minneapolis, MN: Old Theology Book House, 1991) and Andrew Holden *Jehovah's Witness: Portrait of a Contemporary Religious Movement* (London: Routledge, 2002).

loving God would not eternally damn even the worst of his children. For a period of time he rejected religion.

During Russell's youth, there was an industrial depression. Foreseeing a revolution on the horizon, he declared that "the old order of things must pass away, and the new must supersede it. . . . The change will be violently opposed by those advantaged by the present order."[2] Russell wrote: "Revolution world-wide would be the outcome, resulting in the final destruction of the old order and the introduction and establishment of the new."[3] His words share the tone of the *Communist Manifesto,* but there is no evidence that he ever read Karl Marx.

During his religious renunciation, which lasted about a year, Russell stated: "I'm just going to forget the whole thing and give all my attention to business. If I make some money, I can use that to help suffering humanity, even though I cannot help do them any good spiritually."[4] By the time he was thirty, he had accumulated $300,000, a fortune in the 1880s. There is no indication that any of this money was used to aid humanity in a secular sense. Russell soon showed, however, that he was quite willing to use his fortune when it came to the expansion of his religious beliefs.

The Millerites   Russell's return to faith came as a result of his contact with the Second Adventists, or Millerites, a group founded by William Miller in 1829. Millerite membership was, for the most part, confined to the middle Atlantic states, and most followers were economically disadvantaged. Miller preached that the Second Coming of Christ would occur in the 1840s, thus making it a millenarian movement. The failure of this prophecy, of course, was already evident by the time Russell encountered the group. Russell believed the Millerites were "called of God," but had miscalculated the date for the Messiah's return. The Millerites were the only religious group Charles Russell did not denounce during his lifetime.

After Miller's death, his followers recalculated and decided Christ's Second Coming would occur in 1873 or 1874. In 1870, Russell organized a Bible study group in Pittsburgh. He and his group—there were only six members—determined that the Second Coming would occur later, and that Christ's return would be invisible. To set the record straight, Russell published, at his own expense, 50,000 copies of a booklet entitled *The Object and Manner of the Lord's Return.* An early convert was his father, Joseph, who lent Charles both emotional and financial support.

Russell's following began to grow, and in 1879 he began publication of a periodical called *Zion's Watch Tower and Herald of Christ's Presence.* The

---

[2]Quoted in Barbara Grizzuti Harrison, *Visions of Glory* (New York: Simon & Schuster, 1978), p. 43.

[3]Ibid.

[4]*Yearbook of Jehovah's Witnesses* (New York: Watchtower Bible and Tract Society of New York).

new magazine had an impact. By 1880, some thirty congregations were established in seven states. Also, in 1881, the Zion's Watch Tower Tract Society was organized as an unincorporated body in Pittsburgh. Stipulated in the organization's charter was the intent to "disseminate Bible truths in various languages by means of publication of tracts, pamphlets, papers, and other religious documents." Society pamphlets sold for five cents, books for twenty-five cents. Potential converts with no money were given the literature free. This practice has not changed.[5]

By 1909, the organization had grown so large that it was decided to move its headquarters to Brooklyn, New York. The original building on the site was the home of the noted abolitionist Henry Ward Beecher.

Personal Characteristics   Charles Russell was a small, thin man with an ascetic demeanor. A spellbinding speaker, he possessed charm and appeared to enjoy meeting people. He welcomed the press and photographers, and a large pictorial account exists of his ministry. He studied the Bible, and quoted Scripture readily in support of his beliefs. In his later years, his long white beard gave him the appearance of a sage patriarch. He was, indeed, a genuinely charismatic leader.

Russell was a workaholic. It is estimated that in the forty years of his ministry, he traveled a million miles, delivered 30,000 sermons, and wrote more than 150,000 pages of biblical exposition. While doing this, he managed a worldwide evangelistic ministry that employed more than seven hundred speakers.

Hints of Scandal   The Witnesses had to overcome several scandals during their formative years, but none was as far-reaching and caused as much disruption as Russell's marital difficulties. In 1879, Charles Russell married Maria Ackley. No children were born to the union. In the early years of the marriage, Maria Russell worked side by side with her ambitious husband, answering correspondence and addressing women's groups in his stead. But by 1909, the marriage had deteriorated to such a point that she sued for divorce, alleging, among other complaints, that Pastor Russell, as he had become known, had sexual relations with female members of the congregation. Russell always denied these charges, but the divorce was granted.

During his ministry, two serious scandals, apart from his marital difficulties, received much press attention and caused some loss of Society

[5]The Jehovah's Witnesses until 2000 were officially incorporated as Watch Tower Bible and Tract Society of New York, Watch Tower Bible and Tract Society of Pennsylvania, and International Bible Students Association, Brooklyn. Now the organization's work is conducted by the Christian Congregation of Jehovah's Witness (to supervise educational activities), Religious Order of Jehovah's Witness (to manage staff in full-time service), and Kingdom Support Services (to administer building construction and maintenance).

membership. In his Brooklyn congregation, Russell sold bushels of a western wheat that was alleged to have marvelous properties. The wheat sold for sixty dollars a bushel. Grandiose claims for the magic grain brought vigorous press attacks, particularly from the *Brooklyn Eagle,* a popular local newspaper of the period. Pressure from the press finally forced the preacher out of the wheat business. Russell sued the *Eagle* for $100,000, but lost.

A similar episode involved Russell's endorsement and sale of a cancer cure, a compound of chloride of zinc, which may have sped some of his followers to an early reward. The caustic paste was not only ineffective as a cure but also damaging to those who used it. Although the cancer paste and wheat did not have marvelous properties, there is no reason to suggest that Russell himself did not believe in the products. It is often said that no one is easier to sell than a salesperson; Russell, a superb salesperson, may have been sold on the usefulness of these products—he even offered to return the purchase price of the merchandise to anyone who was dissatisfied.

Russell was often sued and was quick to use the courts in retaliation. He had unshakable faith in the invincibility of his own rightness. Because he was quick to attack Christians of every denomination, it is not surprising that those he denounced were often eager to attack him. His belief that only he understood the Bible made him anathema to most religionists of his time. On October 31, 1916, the stormy life of Charles Russell came to an end. While on a nationwide lecture tour, he died unexpectedly of heart failure in a Pullman car near Pampa, Texas.

Charles Russell, the moving, dynamic organizer of the Jehovah's Witnesses, is now but a footnote in the history of the organization. Today, the faith, which is heavily involved in publishing, does not even reprint his works. When a knowledgeable elder was asked how it all began, he answered, "It began in Pennsylvania when a group of Bible students wanted to learn the 'real truth.' They studied the Bible just as we are studying." Then, as though it were an afterthought, he added, "One of them, Charles Russell, was probably a little more prominent than the others."

Witnesses and the Federal Government

Judge Joseph Rutherford (1869–1942) was elected president of the Jehovah's Witnesses shortly after Russell's death. Within a few months of Rutherford's election, his convictions were tested. At the beginning of World War I, there was much pro-war sentiment in the United States. The Witnesses do not believe in war for any reason; also they do not believe in silence when secular beliefs conflict with the Witness worldview.

In 1917, Rutherford and seven other Witness leaders were indicted for violation of the Espionage Act. The Witnesses were charged in federal

The Jehovah s Witnesses

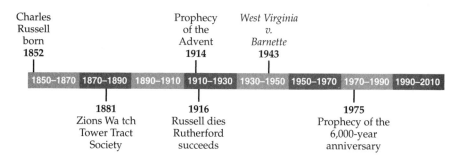

Charles Russell born 1852

Prophecy of the Advent 1914

West Virginia v. Barnette 1943

| 1850–1870 | 1870–1890 | 1890–1910 | 1910–1930 | 1930–1950 | 1950–1970 | 1970–1990 | 1990–2010 |

1881
Zions Wa tch
Tower Tract
Society

1916
Russell dies
Rutherford
succeeds

1975
Prophecy of the
6,000-year
anniversary

court with "the offense of unlawfully, feloniously and willfully causing insubordination, disloyalty and refusal of duty in the military . . . by personal solicitations, letters, public speeches, distributing and publicly circulating throughout the United States of America various publications."[6] The Witnesses argued that they owed allegiance to no person, flag, or nation; they owed allegiance only to Jehovah. They were "of another world."

Rutherford and his followers were convicted, and all but one was sentenced to serve twenty years in the federal penitentiary at Leavenworth, Kansas; the seventh man received a ten-year sentence. The Witnesses began serving their sentences in June 1918. A petition for a new trial was filed, and in March 1919, all of the jailed Witnesses were released on bail. By then the war was over, and the government chose not to retry the case. Many people considered the jailing of the Witnesses a travesty of justice, and Society membership grew rapidly in the decade that followed.

Rutherford, like Russell, was a prolific writer. He proclaimed the group's name to be henceforth "Jehovah's Witnesses" and the use of the name "Jehovah" as the personal name of God as a major point of doctrine and faith.

Despite the central roles of Miller and Rutherford, the Witnesses, however, de-emphasize individuality and stress the importance of the "group." Since the death of Rutherford in 1942, none of their publications bears an author's signature. When knowledgeable Witnesses are asked about authorship, the usual response is that the article in question was probably written by a committee of Bible scholars.

Following Rutherford's death, Nathan Knorr (1905–1977) was elected third president of the Society. He, too, had to stand up for Witness pacifist beliefs in the face of a draft. During the First World War, Witness leaders

[6]Alfs, *Evocative Religion of Jehovah's Witnesses*, p. 17.

had been jailed; the government took a different tack during the Second World War. Instead of jailing a few leaders, more than 4,000 of the rank and file were arrested and jailed for failure to comply with draft laws. The Witness argument continued to be that they were "of another world."

Harassment of Witnesses on other issues was evident as well. During the war, Witness children were targeted in public school systems. Harrison, an ex-Witness, describes in her book, *Visions of Glory,* a grade school experience: "Having to remain seated . . . during flag salute at school assembly was an act of defiance from which I inwardly recoiled. . . . Not saluting the flag, being the only child in my school who did not contribute to the Red Cross, . . . and not bringing in tinfoil balls for the War Drive did not endear me to my classmates. I wanted to please everybody—my teachers, my spiritual overseers, my mother; and, of course, I could not."[7]

Many Witness children were expelled from public schools for failing to conform to the system's expectations, and the Witnesses brought court suits in response to the expulsions. A 1940 Supreme Court decision, *Minersville v. Gobitas,* held that children who did not salute the flag were subject to expulsion. In 1943, the issue was returned to the Supreme Court in *West Virginia v. Barnette.* The Court ruled that the previous case had been "wrongly decided," and it was a Fourteenth Amendment violation to force children to salute the flag.

Following Knorr's death in 1977, Frederick Franz was elected president. Little conflict existed between the Witnesses and the outside world during his leadership. However, no draft occurred during his tenure as president, and no attempt was made to bring the flag-saluting incident back into court. The Witnesses have not changed their minds on these issues.

For several years, Franz, who died in December 1992 at the age of ninety-nine, was incapable of fully participating in the day-to-day affairs of the Society. The Witnesses believe, however, that all major decisions should be the consequence of a committee process, and because all the members of the governing committee are considered competent Bible scholars, it matters little if one committee member—even the president—requires a reduced workload.

Witnesses and Other Governments   Jehovah's Witnesses have been the victims of prejudice and discrimination in a number of countries. Part of Hitler's pogrom, before and during World War II, Witnesses were sent to death camps along with Gypsies (Roma), gays and lesbians, and Jews. About 3,200 Witnesses were sent to concentration camps for their refusal to sign a document renouncing their faith.

Currently in Russia, prosecutors are trying to prohibit the Witnesses from practicing their religion "under a law that gives the courts the right

[7]Harrison, *Visions of Glory.*

to ban religious groups found guilty of inciting hatred or intolerant be-havior."[8] Charged with making a decision, a panel of experts has been ap-pointed to review Witness literature.

Organization

During the early years, the Society's work was carried on by a board of di-rectors. Anyone who donated ten dollars to the Society was eligible to cast one vote at board elections. Contributors could cast one additional vote for each ten-dollar increment contributed above a minimum donation. During his lifetime, Russell was the Society's unquestioned leader, and voting for the presidency was perfunctory.

In 1944, the Society's charter was amended to remove monetary contri-butions as a means of access to the governing body. Today, a governing body made up of eighteen men meets weekly in Brooklyn, New York, to make both secular and religious decisions. In 1976, to assist the governing body, the following standing committees were formed: Service Commit-tee, Writing Committee, Publishing Committee, Teaching Committee, and Chairman's Committee, with the term of appointment to any committee not to exceed one year.

At the next echelon are district and circuit overseers. Charged with the responsibility of visiting each congregation twice each year, these men (there are no women overseers) often accompany local Witnesses on home visits, ostensibly to help them with proselytizing techniques. When leadership positions open, all baptized male Witnesses over age twenty are eligible for consideration.

At the head of each local congregation is a presiding overseer chosen from among the elders. This is a rotating position, the appointment not to exceed one year. The transience of the position fortifies the authority of the New York Society, emphasizing that no one man at the local level is in-dispensable.

Headquarters   The Witness headquarters complex in Brooklyn is called Bethel (House of God). Residents at Bethel, including married couples, live two to a room. Baths and toilets are shared. Most of the needs of the Bethelites are met within the confines of the complex, which includes its own barber shop, tailor shop, laundry, and bakery. Food and housekeep-ing services are provided. The rooms are pleasant and the food is good. Staff members, including the president of the Society, receive a monthly stipend of ninety dollars for personal needs. A few Witness detractors

---

[8]Arin Gencer, "Jehovah Witness Tells L.A. Audience of Defying Nazis," *Los Angeles Times*, May 26, 2006, p. 133, and Terence Neilan, "World Briefing," *New York Times*, June 29, 1999, Sec. A, p. 6.

make much of the fact that headquarters personnel travel first class when on tour. It would seem, though, that Witness leaders move about in no greater style than leaders of other religious organizations.

The Society also owns and operates a number of farms, including a 1,698-acre farm near Wallkill, New York, which provides most of the food required by the more than 3,500 headquarters workers. Witness farmworkers produce a large vegetable crop, maintain a herd of beef cattle, raise broiler chickens and laying hens, and milk a dairy herd. They also process what they produce. Eight hundred workers are required to operate the farm, processing facilities, and the two large printeries located on the farm.

Printeries   The printing operation at Wallkill produces the magazines *Watchtower* and *Awake!* The farmworkers and printing-plant workers are classified as minister-volunteers and live a dormitory lifestyle similar to the Bethelites. They, too, receive a ninety-dollar-per-month stipend.

It is difficult to know just how much printed material is produced by the Jehovah's Witnesses. *Awake!* in the 1990s claimed an average printing of 18,350,000 copies. Similarly, *Watchtower* reported an average printing of 20,980,000 copies. Each magazine is produced semimonthly. The printeries at Wallkill, which produce the magazines, are not nearly as large as the Bethel printeries, which produce books and pamphlets, where six of the ten multistory buildings are devoted to production of the written word.

Until recently, *Watchtower* and *Awake!* issues sold for twenty-five cents each, a standard Bible for four dollars, and a deluxe version for seven dollars. No book was overpriced, based on materials and labor costs. Nevertheless, in April 1990, the Society began giving away its literature, or merely asking for donations. Based on an interview with a Witness leader, *Christianity Today* reported that the reason was "probably due to a Supreme Court decision that ruled religious literature sold by [televangelist] Jimmy Swaggart's Louisiana-based organization was liable for sales taxes in other states."[9]

A fair portion of Society literature was given away even before the Society mandate. Individual ministers, in carrying out the work of the Society, prepaid the printing costs of tracts, books, and magazines needed in their daily work. When encountering people open to their views, many ministers often left literature with such potential converts and did not ask for payment.

Patterson Farm   In 1984, the Witnesses bought a 670-acre dairy farm in Patterson, New York, to build an educational center. According to a spokesman, the facility was 99-percent complete in January 1997.[10] The campus is the major educational institution for the church's missionaries

[9]*Christianity Today,* October 22, 1990, p. 52.

[10]In January 1997, Zellner called the Patterson facility to request some information. A spokesman politely gave the author all the information he asked for. The spokesman would not give his name, however, preferring, as Witnesses often do, to remain anonymous.

and staff. It is equipped to teach, feed, and house 1,600 people at a time. Presently, there are about 1,300 on the campus.

The school was built the Jehovah's Witness way. During the building process, an estimated five hundred workers plied their trades, from engineers to architects, carpenters, draftsmen, concrete workers, plumbers, electricians, and laborers—all volunteers. These workers, from every part of the United States, received the same ninety-dollar-per-month stipend as the headquarters' workers.

Today, there are six apartment houses two to five stories high with more than six hundred apartments, garage space for eight hundred cars, a 144-room motel, and a kitchen big enough to serve 1,600 people at one sitting. There is an office building, a classroom building, and several service buildings.

Church officials estimate the cost of construction when completed at $50 million above the low-cost labor. The complex is valued at about $130 million.[11]

Finances

Each year, the Society places a notice in an issue of the *Watchtower* soliciting contributions. To facilitate planning, the notice asks contributors to specify how much the Society can expect to receive and when contributions will be made. Collections are not taken at the Kingdom Halls, and the elders do not solicit money from the pulpit.[12] Every Hall has a contribution box, but contributions from this source seem to be few and far between. Most donations come from self-imposed tithes.

Classified as a charitable religious organization, the Society is not required to make public its financial statements. Many denominations, similarly exempt, choose to make public disclosures of income and assets; that the Witnesses do not may be linked to past problems with tax collectors. The most notable of these occurred in 1971, when the state of New York enacted a law permitting taxation of property not exclusively used for religious purposes. The Society paid $2 million, under protest, to the city of New York. On July 11, 1974, tax exemption was restored to the Society by the New York State Court of Appeals. The court's written decision stipulated that the Society was organized exclusively for religious purposes within the meaning of the statute.

---

[11]Harold Faber, "Jehovah's Witnesses Build Center on Dairy Farm," *New York Times,* April 4, 1991, p. 28. See also, Mary McAleer Vizard, "Watchtower Project Grows in Patterson," *New York Times,* April 18, 1993, p. R9.

[12]Kingdom Halls are places for education and worship. Witnesses do not use the term *church.* A body of believers is termed a *congregation.*

The Witnesses are trying to be good neighbors at the new Patterson facility. The church voluntarily put the Patterson Motel on the tax rolls. Witnesses have about twenty houses in the community, all on the tax rolls. When the church built five-story structures on the Patterson campus, the fire department said they could not provide services because they did not have the equipment to fight fires in tall buildings. The Witnesses responded by buying them a new truck.[13]

Charity   Members of other faiths, legislators, and the public in general do not understand the Witness position on charity. There are no charitable entities within Witness organizational structure: no hospitals, no clinics, no food programs. The Society believes that the last days are so near that all available funds must be spent on the "promulgation of the truth" (spreading Jehovah's word).

The edict to be charitable permeates Society literature. Charity is up to the individual, however; it is not viewed as an organizational responsibility. Aid usually involves services such as baby-sitting, shopping or providing transportation for the elderly, and reading Scriptures to the infirm. It is difficult to know the private transactions of the Witness "in-group," but it is probable that they help each other financially as well.

Building Construction   Erecting new buildings is not a problem for most Witness congregations, which are willing to expend their own time and energy. For example, a Minnesota congregation has a new Kingdom Hall, built almost entirely by the members, many of whom are skilled laborers. Nothing was spent for outside help. When they had difficulty planning and installing the electrical system, a call for assistance was sent to nearby congregations, and the problem was resolved quickly. When the building was dedicated, members of the congregations who lent assistance were honored. Great pride was felt in the accomplishment. An investment of time and labor is apparently more rewarding than a monetary contribution.

Financing construction of Kingdom Halls is a relatively simple matter. Congregations need only finance the cost of building materials; there are no labor costs. The elimination of labor costs creates built-in equity for the lender. For example, a Kingdom Hall valued at $100,000, minus the cost of labor, may necessitate only a $50,000 loan. There is almost no risk for the lender. The parent Society maintains a list of bankers and institutional investors eager to invest in Kingdom Halls.

Witness congregations save money in many ways. For example, they do not hire janitors. In most congregations, janitorial and maintenance duties

---

[13]Vizard, "Watchtower Project Grows," p. R9.

are assigned to Bible study groups on a rotating basis. Most Witnesses are skilled or semiskilled laborers, so maintenance is never a problem for them, and thus, the Kingdom Halls are well cared for.

What Witnesses Believe

In the Beginning   Before earth there was heaven and in heaven was God (Jehovah) and he was alone. His first creation was a son, the Archangel Michael. Michael "was used by Jehovah in creating all other things."[14] Michael's first creations were other spirit sons for God, angels numbering in the millions. Among these sons was Lucifer, who would later be called Satan, which means "Resister."

After creating the earth, Jehovah said to Michael, "Let us make man in our image."[15] Their purpose was to create a perfect paradise (Eden), for a perfect man (Adam) and woman (Eve). Adam and Eve, in turn, were expected to bear perfect children, who would live according to Jehovah's laws and glorify him.

The Fall   It was Jehovah's intent that humans should live in perfect harmony with their environment and never die. Lucifer was put in charge of Eden. Jealous of Jehovah, he wanted followers who would adore him. To accomplish this, he had to alienate Adam and Eve from God. While Jehovah rested at the beginning of the seventh day (Genesis 2:2), Lucifer found the fatal flaw in Adam and Eve.[16]

Jehovah had given Adam a single prohibition: Do not eat the fruit of the tree of knowledge of good and evil, or you will die. Satan, using a snake as a medium, convinced Eve to eat the fruit. She then seduced Adam, and he, too, ate the fruit. Jehovah's punishment was death to Adam and Eve, and death for all of their kind yet to come.

Witnesses do not attribute the Fall to the sex act. Interestingly, original sin is tied to intellectual freedom. Eve's act led to freedom of choice, which didn't exist before the forbidden fruit was eaten. Before the Fall, Adam simply obeyed Jehovah's laws, as he had been commanded: "The woman was the first human sinner. Her temptation by God's adversary . . . was not through an open appeal to immorality of a sensual nature. Rather, it paraded as an appeal to the desire for supposed intellectual elevation and freedom. . . . He [the snake] asserted that eating the

---

[14]*Insight on the Scriptures,* vol. 1 (New York: Watchtower Bible and Tract Society of New York, 1988), p. 527.

[15]Ibid.

[16]All biblical references are from the *New World Translation of the Holy Scriptures* (New York: Watchtower Bible and Tract Society of New York, 1971).

fruit from the proscribed tree would result, not in death, but in enlightenment and godlike ability to determine for oneself whether a thing was good or bad."[17]

The Ransom   Jehovah loved Adam despite his failure, and chose to release Adam's children from the death penalty. Viewed by the Society as the head of a theocratic legal system, even Jehovah must act according to law. Humankind could be released from the certainty of death, but only through a legal ransom. Witnesses define *ransom* as an exact corresponding price. Adam was a perfect man, therefore a perfect man had to be sacrificed to redeem humankind.

Witnesses reject the concept of a Holy Trinity—the idea that Father, Son, and Holy Spirit are one. Jesus is believed to be God's first son, the Archangel Michael. Because Adam was human, Michael was sent to earth in human form. As Jesus, he was capable of sin, but to pay Adam's "ransom," he had to live a sinless life. After the Resurrection, he was restored to a spiritual being.

Prophecy Failure   The most important date in early Witness chronology is 1914. Witnesses believe that on October 4 or 5 of that year, Christ fought the devil in heaven, won the battle, then hurled Satan and his demons to earth. Russell and early Witnesses thought that Christ would establish his earthly kingdom in that same year. When Christ did not make a visible appearance, the date for his advent was recalculated to 1918. Despite the recalculation and Russell's charisma, there was some decrease in Society membership in the years that followed.

Judge Rutherford, Russell's successor, studied the Scriptures and concluded that the Society had erred. It was decided that Christ had established his "invisible heavenly kingdom" in 1914 but that he would not establish his "earthly kingdom" until after a "generation had passed." A generation was defined as the life span of all those living in 1914 who were old enough to understand the horrors of that year. The Society cites the beginning of World War I, along with other disasters that occurred in that year, as proof that an angered Satan, cast out of heaven, was displaying his wrath.

Witnesses believed that an infant would not have understood the horrors of 1914 but, perhaps, a precocious child of three or four years would. If there was to be a second prophecy failure, it could not occur until the Witnesses were convinced that all those who understood the events of 1914 were dead.

---

[17]*Insight on the Scriptures,* vol. 2 (New York: Watchtower Bible and Tract Society of New York, 1988), p. 963.

[18]Kenneth L. Woodward and Joel P. Engardio, "Apocalypse Later: Jehovah's Witnesses Decide the End Is Fluid," *Newsweek,* December 18, 1995, p. 59.

With the generation that was alive in 1914 rapidly disappearing, the *Watchtower* magazine reported in November 1995 that all timetables pinpointing exactly when Armageddon would take place were merely speculative. Jesus said that "no one knows the day or the hour."

Kenneth Woodward observes, "The year 1914 still marks the beginning of the last days [for the Witnesses]. But those who hoped to witness the battle of Armageddon and the establishment of God's kingdom on earth will have to wait. Henceforth, any generation that experiences such calamities as war and plagues like AIDS could be the one to witness the end times. In short, the increasingly middle-class Witnesses would do well to buy life insurance."[18]

Eschatology   **Eschatology** is a part of theology that refers to the final events of the world. Often referred as "end of the world" predictions, eschatology, when practiced, proclaims the coming of a new world, a new life. Christian eschatology is concerned with the Second Coming of Christ, the resurrection of the dead, the last judgment, and the effect of human existence on the completion of history.

Russell's final dispensation, "The World to Come," begins with the "Millennial Age." Christ, and those already in heaven, are waiting to begin the battle of Armageddon—the final, decisive battle between good and evil. Satan will be defeated in the battle and cast into an abyss for a thousand years, a millennium.

Witnesses believe that only 144,000 people "have the heavenly hope" (Revelation 14:1), to rule with Jesus in heaven. Along with Witnesses eligible for heavenly service are the prophets David, Abraham, Moses, and Noah. All who will serve have already been chosen, and only a handful of those, known as the "remnant," remain on earth.

Witnesses do not believe in a fiery hell. Most of the billions of people who will die before the battle of Armageddon will be turned to dust, from which they will be resurrected. The few who will not return are those who in life were "willfully wicked." Witnesses view the "willfully wicked" as those who knew the will of Jehovah but defied Him. There appears to be no consensus among Witness rank and file as to who had been "willfully wicked," but the number is deemed small. Adam and Eve, Judas, and Nimrod are certain to remain in dust. All others returned from the dust will live in an earthly paradise ruled by Jehovah.

Since the failed prophecy of 1914, leaders of Jehovah's Witnesses have become involved in the failed prophecy. In 1966, the Governing Body issued a major proclamation that traced the history of humankind beginning with the creation of Adam and that the 6,000-year anniversary

---

[18]Kenneth L. Woodward and Joel P. Engardio, "Apocalypse Later: Jehovah's Witnesses Decide the End Is Fluid," *Newsweek*, December 18, 1995, p. 59.

would come in 1974. The proclamation continued on "how appropriate" it would be for the Jehovah God to make this point the "jubilee" and proclaim liberty throughout the world.

While not specific a declaration of another prophecy, many Witnesses interpreted it this way and began to treat 1975 the way Witnesses two generations earlier had treated 1914. Faithful reported doing everything from selling property to avoiding having children as the year approach. When 1975 came and went, membership dropped significantly and evangelistic efforts enjoyed little success. Since these events, the leadership of the Witnesses has avoided statements that could be interpreted as yet another prophecy.[19]

Paradise   By the end of the millennium, humankind will have reached a perfected state; vice, disease, corruption, and death will disappear from the earth. But at the end of the millennium, Satan will be freed from his bondage. He will gather demons around him, and together they will try to persuade humankind to follow them. Witnesses believe that few will. After experiencing paradise, how could humankind want to lead an immoral and degrading life? Satan's small army will be defeated, and a second judgment day will follow.

Jehovah's first judgment, after Adam's failure, was against all of humankind. The final judgment, following the destruction of Satan, will be of individuals. All those deemed unworthy will be condemned to eternal dust. Even this untoward group will not have to suffer the agonies of a tormenting hell.

After the millennium, Christ will return a perfected earth to Jehovah. Jehovah will become an active king in his theocratic system. Survivors of the final judgment will live in harmony with their creator in paradise for eternity. There is little speculation as to what life will be like in "the Ages to Come." Most Witnesses simply believe that it is beyond the power of mortals to comprehend all the goodness Jehovah has in store for them.

Social Characteristics

Voting Behavior   Most Jehovah's Witnesses do not vote. Those who do ordinarily confine their ballots to local issues such as zoning, taxes, and school board elections. At a group meeting in Minnesota, an elder was

[19]Andrew Holden, *Jehovah's Witnesses: Portrait of a Contemporary Religious Movement.* (London: Routledge, 2002), p. 98, and David L. Weddle, "Jehovah's Witnesses." In *Introductions to New and Alternative Religions in America*, Vol. 2, pp. 69–70. Edited by Eugene V. Gallagher and W. Michael Ashcraft. Westport, CT: Greenwood Press, 2006.

asked if he didn't think it was in the interest of the Society for members to vote for national candidates who might best represent Witnesses' moral convictions. His response was that it didn't make much difference who was elected, because nothing would change. Satan's evil plan would be followed until Jehovah establishes his kingdom on earth. The wife of the congregation's presiding elder ended the conversation when she asked the interviewer, "If you were a citizen of France, would you expect to vote in Great Britain's elections?" The interviewer said he would not. "Well," she continued, "we are citizens of Jehovah's Kingdom. Not only should we not want to vote, we really don't have the right to vote."[20]

Sexual Attitudes   Witnesses do not consider sex to have been the downfall of Adam and Eve. But this has not led to "liberated" sexual attitudes. Masturbation is considered self-love, and most Witness children are told early and often about the Scriptures that forbid the practice of self-adoration. Witness children are warned that masturbation can inhibit a happy marriage, noting that it is a man's responsibility to ensure that his wife derives pleasure from the sex act. If a habit of premarital masturbation develops, one thinks only of oneself, and it becomes difficult to satisfy a partner. Witnesses take the position that masturbation can lead to homosexuality. Homosexual behavior is considered an unnatural abomination and is grounds for disfellowship. Homosexuals are counseled before action is taken against them.

The Witness term for excommunication is **disfellowship.** During a two-year study of Minnesota congregations, Zellner found that two young women were disfellowshipped from one of the congregations, each deemed guilty of fornication; both were living unwed with a male friend. On several occasions, "brothers" visited and counseled the errant "sisters." Members of the congregation all felt the sisters were censured fairly, but all hoped the women would repent: Society doors are opened to repentant sinners.

Note, the brothers counseled the women. Sisters are considered the weaker vessel; their position in the Society is one of support. In the Minnesota study, a rather stable, seemingly strong young woman was asked if she resented the secondary role assigned women by the Society, if she didn't think it was unjust that she couldn't counsel, in an official way, those who faltered, or that she couldn't hold a leadership position in the church. "Oh, no!" she replied, and looked at the interviewer with a somewhat puzzled expression. "Women are not emotionally strong enough to handle those kinds of things."[21]

---

[20]William Zellner, "Of Another World: The Jehovah's Witnesses" (Ph.D. diss., South Dakota State University, 1981), pp. 60–61. (All subsequent references to the "Minnesota study" were extracted from this thesis.)

[21]Zellner, "Of Another World," p. 62.

Witnesses recognize Jehovah's biblical commandment to be fruitful and multiply. Members are, however, permitted to practice birth control. Witnesses are opposed to abortion, so birth control must not include the use of intrauterine devices (IUDs), on the grounds that these devices act to abort the egg after fertilization has occurred. Such methods as the pill, a diaphragm, or prophylactics may be used at the discretion of the individual. There are no available statistics on average Witness family size. Most members, however, are blue-collar workers, a group with a higher birthrate than middle-class families.

The Society suggests that young Witnesses consider singleness—celibate singleness—as a viable alternative to marriage. Missionaries are particularly encouraged to give extra thought before marrying. The Society warns that marriage could limit their ability to carry out their duties properly. The Society further makes the point that, with Armageddon so near, there is no need to hurry parenting; it might be better to wait and bring children into a perfected world.

Marriage and Family   Idyllically, the Witness marriage is the kind of marriage that was supposed to have existed in the United States before the sexual revolution of the 1960s. The husband is responsible for meeting the family's economic needs, whereas the wife is responsible for maintaining and caring for the home. A good wife defers to her husband on all matters of importance. Many Witness texts, however, such as *Happiness, How to Find It*, suggest that the husband—to promote marital happiness— give in to the wife on unimportant matters.

In practice, the familistic orientation of the Witnesses is very similar to that of the Mormons. Families are encouraged to do things together or with other Witness families. Congregational functions are to be attended by all members of the family, and families are encouraged to work together, play together, and worship together. There are no separatist bodies within the Society—no men's groups or women's groups.

The Society does, however, recognize that some married couples are so mismatched that it is impossible for them to live together. Charles and Marie Russell were such a mismatch. In such cases, separation is condoned, but divorce is permissible only on the scriptural ground of adultery.

The Society recommends that women whose husbands live outside the Kingdom defer to their spouse on all matters except those that contradict Jehovah's teachings. It is thought that if a wife continues to exhibit a "sweet nature," the husband may eventually mature.

Integrated Community   The Witnesses evidently do not practice racial discrimination, and Society literature clearly denounces the practice. On several occasions during the Minnesota study, an observer attended meetings (they are never called services) in a racially mixed urban neighborhood. The congregation reflected the makeup of the larger community. Intermarriage is quite common, and it is not unusual to see a white grandparent making a fuss over a black grandchild. The interactions within this congregation clearly showed that racial harmony is the norm. Male African American Witnesses are eligible for, and do attain, leadership roles in the organization's hierarchy.

Medicine   Based on their interpretation of a number of Scriptures, for example Acts 15:29 (that Christians abstain from things offered to idols, from blood, from things strangled, and from sexual immorality), Jehovah's Witnesses do not accept blood transfusions, regardless of medically defined need.

The Witnesses refuse blood transfusions, but this does not mean they categorically reject the medical profession. The Society does not object to the use of medicinal drugs, inoculations, internal medicines, or necessary surgery, provided blood transfusion can be avoided. The ban against the use of blood is also based on Leviticus 17:10: "God told Noah that every living creature should be meat unto him; but that he must not eat blood, because the life is in the blood." Witnesses cite the current AIDS epidemic as proving this long-held belief to be correct.

The proclamation of blood transfusions has been advanced since 1945, and since 1961, members who accept a transfusion are subject to being banished from the faith. Kidney dialysis is permitted as long as the blood continually circulates, and hemophiliacs are allowed certain specific blood treatment.

Some hospitals recognize the Witnesses' position and beginning about 2005, the American Medical Association urged medical personnel to consider alternative forms of care when treating Witnesses that normally would require transfusions. Nonetheless, cases involving minor children or pregnant women in danger of placing the fetus in peril occasionally reach courts, where the emotional matter is settled on a case-by-case basis.[22]

Witnesses do not believe in faith healers. Such individuals are considered absolute frauds. The Society acknowledges that a select few, prior to Christ, had the ability to heal, as did Christ and the apostles, but the gift was lost with the death of the last apostle.

Education   At one district convention, a Witness speaker encouraged young people of ability to attend trade schools and stay away from colleges, insisting that college instruction contradicts Jehovah's teachings. Society literature directs the Witness father to train his sons to use their hands. When he repairs his car, his son should be allowed to help. Daughters should be trained by their mothers and taught to sew, cook, and maintain a clean house. At one Bible study, a well-attired young man had

[22]David L. Weddle, pp. 79–80.

the floor. "No, you won't find much of man's education in this room," he said. "You won't find no bachelor's degrees, no master's degrees. This is not what we seek. Our education is of God's word."[23]

Witnesses place little value in insights beyond the scope of their religion. One need only have reading skills sufficient for comprehending the Bible and Witness publications. Witness apostate David Reed, formerly a Society overseer, writes that "although most outsiders are unaware of such a restriction, Jehovah's Witnesses know well that they are forbidden to read the literature of other religious organizations. They have been told that 'it would be foolhardy, as well as a waste of valuable time, for Jehovah's Witnesses to accept and expose themselves to false religious literature that is designed to deceive.' And they have been taught that 'reading apostate publications' is 'similar to reading pornographic literature.'"[24]

Holidays The "Memorial of Christ's Death," the observance of the death of Christ, is the only Witness holiday (occurring on Passover eve annually). It is not a festive occasion, but a very solemn meal of unleavened bread and wine. There is no thought of the bread and wine as symbolic of the body and blood of Christ. Only those who are convinced that they are part of the "remnant" (those still living who will ultimately rule in heaven with Christ) actually partake of the meal; all others simply pass the bread and cup. When members are asked how they know they are part of the "remnant," the response is always, "You just feel it." Only two persons in a Kingdom Hall in Minnesota, where an observer regularly attended meetings, felt justified in eating the meal.

The Witnesses find reasons for not celebrating other holidays. The Easter rabbit and Easter eggs are pagan symbols of fertility; New Year's celebrations are debaucheries; Halloween is associated with Catholicism's celebration of the dead; secular holidays, such as Labor Day, Independence Day, and Columbus Day, glorify humans. In *Reasoning from the Scriptures*, the Society debunks Christmas and birthday celebrations in a single paragraph:

> Suppose a crowd comes to a gentleman's home saying they are there to celebrate his birthday. He does not favor the celebration of birthdays. He does not like to see people overeat or get drunk or engage in loose conduct. But some of them do all those things, and they bring presents for everyone there except him! On top of that they pick the birthday of one of the man's enemies as the date for the celebration. How would the man feel? This is exactly what is being done by Christmas celebrations.[25]

[23]Zellner, "Of Another World," p. 66.
[24]Reed, *Index of Watchtower Errors*. The author quotes two *Watchtower* sources: May 1, 1984, p. 31, and March 15, 1986, p. 14.
[25]*Reasoning from the Scriptures* (New York: Watchtower Bible and Tract Society of New York, 1985), p. 179.

Witnesses do not celebrate their own birthdays. They contend that the only birthday celebrations mentioned in the Bible (a pharaoh of Egypt and the Roman ruler Herod) ended in misery. While the birth of Christ may be a joyful occasion, Witnesses do not partake in the celebration since they contend we do not know the precise day and, anyway, Christmas has been overtaken by secular images.

Media Relations   In the decades following Russell's leadership, press coverage of Witness events had not been encouraged. Witness positions were simply Witness positions, and the Society exhibited no concern for public image. At a Minnesota district convention attended by author Zellner, there was a pressroom set up and staffed by elders who could quote Scripture in support of any Witness viewpoint. The existence of the press center may have been significant, evidencing a sensitivity to the "other world," a sensitivity that has not existed in the past.

When one of the elders was asked by an observer why a press center had been established, he said that the Society had taken positions against draft registration and the Equal Rights Amendment, and they wanted the public to understand that their views were based on Scripture.

There were many chairs in the large pressroom; half were occupied by elders, half were empty. There were press releases, books, and pamphlets. The only thing missing was the press.

Gaining Converts and Maintaining the Faith

Why people join and maintain membership in a group that is often deprecated is an interesting question. The answer has remained somewhat elusive. Witnesses themselves are often less than cooperative. The few studies we do have contain little more than demographic data. The important issues, such as how members of the Society come to agree on rules, definitions, and values, are not addressed.

In the Minnesota study, Zellner went beyond collecting demographic data, and chose, instead, to observe Witnesses as they function in the day-to-day world. He attended meetings and participated in a home Bible study. Questions were asked in a conversational way and recorded later. Often, the questions did not have to be asked. Witness converts, like most other religious converts, have a penchant for comparing their former unfulfilling lifestyles to their new, much-improved life situation. The questionnaire that follows contains typical answers. The respondent was a forty-nine-year-old white female identified by the pseudonym Kate Williams.

Q. What is your marital status?
A. Widow.

Q. Do you have any children?

A. Eight.

Q. Are they members of the group?

A. Three participate fully. Five are, at this time, living outside of Jehovah's Kingdom. It is difficult to raise children in Satan's world. They are sent to school and taught by teachers who know nothing about Jehovah, or have rejected him. Then when they get a job, they are surrounded by more people who either don't know or won't accept Jehovah's word. It is my sincerest hope that all my children will eventually enter Jehovah's Kingdom.

Q. What kind of work do you do?

A. Material sorter.

Q. How long have you been a member of the Jehovah's Witnesses?

A. Twenty-six years.

Q. How did you first encounter the group?

A. They came to the door when we were living in California. I wasn't at home the first time they came, but I remember my husband was very excited about their visit. We studied over the literature for many hours.

Q. Were the Jehovah's Witnesses any different in California than they are here [Minnesota]?

A. Jehovah's people are Jehovah's people wherever you meet them.

Q. Were you at a time in your life when you were experiencing some sort of unusual strain?

A. We had not been living in California very long, and we were having some difficulty getting adjusted to that way of life. We felt we were surrounded by godless people.

Q. Do you feel that a pattern for life is important?

A. Everyone should have direction in life. My husband and I both felt that need.

Q. Did your becoming a Jehovah's Witness fulfill that need?

A. Most definitely.

Q. Did you believe in the existence of God before encountering the Jehovah's Witnesses or would you have considered yourself an agnostic or atheist?

A. My husband and I both believed in God. We went to a Lutheran church before moving to California.

Q. Before attending formal group [Witness] meetings, did you form a close tie with one or more of the Witnesses?

A. We liked the people who came to our house, and we began attending meetings right away. We went to the Kingdom Hall and met people who wanted to live according to God's will. It was very different from what we had previously experienced in California.

Q. Did your becoming a Witness cause a strain between you and other family members?

A. All of my family was alienated; so was my husband's.

Q. Did your joining the group strain relationships between you and your friends?

A. We had no friends to speak of in California. But when we got back to Minnesota, I lost a friend who was like a mother to me. I still feel bad about that.

Q. Has being a Witness caused you any problems in your work situation?

A. No. Most of the people I work with are very nice. I do feel sorry for them, though. They search and search and what they are looking for is right under their noses. Jehovah has laid out his plan for us all.

Q. How many hours a week do you spend in organizational activity?

A. Twenty-two to twenty-three hours a week. [This included attending meetings and proselytizing.]

Q. How long was it before you moved from verbal agreement with the group to commitment, attending regular meetings, and so on?

A. We began right away.

Q. Do you seek to gain new members for the group? How?

A. Of course. We are obligated to spread the word. When I feel that I can talk to someone at work, or someone in the neighborhood, I talk to them about Jehovah. Also, I go door-to-door like all Witnesses who are able.

Q. Do you subscribe totally to the belief system of the Jehovah's Witnesses or do you have some doubts or disagreements?

A. I believe totally.

Q. Do you consider membership in the group the most important aspect of your life?

A. Yes, I do. I have brought at least ten people into the "new system." If my life wasn't fully committed, I couldn't have done that.

Kate Williams is an extremely pleasant woman and her claim of conversions is probably accurate. Most Witnesses are not nearly so successful at bringing new members into the group despite their dedicated activity.

There are more than five million Witnesses worldwide, and their further growth is more or less guaranteed by the process of natural increase. Witnesses, however, are not content with only that kind of growth. Because they believe that the end is near, the Society has defined its mission as bringing as many as possible into the "new system" before Armageddon.

On three occasions, Zellner spent half a day proselytizing with a Jehovah's Witness. He was not convinced that the Witness liked the idea of his tagging along. Because Zellner had not completed his home Bible study, the elder felt Zellner's training was inadequate to the task. It was only after Zellner assured the elder that he would be friendly, but leave the Bible talk to him, that the elder reluctantly allowed him to go along.

Two of the trips were to working-class neighborhoods, the other to a middle- to upper-middle-class area. Very few doors were opened to the pair, and what little success they did have was in the working-class neighborhoods. The Witness making the calls was employed by a janitorial service. When he got his foot in a door, he not only talked about the Bible, but about his family and job as well. He had much in common with most of the working-class people to whom he spoke—shared backgrounds, experiences, and problems.

Not surprisingly, a proselytizing butcher does not attract a college student; rather, he or she tends to attract a carpenter or a plumber. A working-class housewife is more likely to develop rapport with a widow working in a school lunchroom than she is with a banker. As a group, Jehovah's Witnesses have similar social-class backgrounds, one of the consequences of the proselytizing process.[26]

Bonding   Forming an "affective bond" (an emotional relationship) with one or more members of the group is the keystone to conversion for most Witnesses. Kate Williams's response to the survey question "Before attending formal group meetings, did you form a close tie with one or more of the Witnesses?" was typical. Thirteen of the eighteen Witnesses interviewed had their first encounter with the Society when Witnesses called on them at their homes. All of the Witnesses interviewed reported having formed an affective bond with one or more Witnesses before becoming active in the group.

Bonding is more important than dogma. The differences between Witness dogma and conventional Christian dogma are not emphasized in the proselytizing process. What is emphasized are the similarities. Zellner made the following observations concerning his home Bible study program:[27]

> It was several months before my instructor revealed that Christ was not God incarnate, long after an affective social bond, under ordinary circumstances, would have been formed. It would have been very difficult to break a strong interactive bond based on that one bit of information. The dogma comes in bits and pieces.
>
> I was never lied to, but when I did not initiate the "hard" questions associated with doctrinal differences between the Witnesses and normative Protestant denominations, the differences were not revealed until my instructor thought I was ready for the "truth."[28]

There are no half-hearted Witnesses. The price for not buying wholeheartedly into the belief system, after a reasonable length of time, is possible loss of interaction and the cutting of affective bonds. The potential convert must accept Society teachings or risk losing interaction in the form of primary-group relationships.

Meaningful bonds are apparently formed very quickly. Kate Williams responded to the survey question "How long was it before you moved

[26]There are notable exceptions. Rock star Michael Jackson was a Jehovah's Witness, as was Mickey Spillane, the creator of the fictional detective Mike Hammer, and President Dwight D. Eisenhower. Teenage tennis stars Venus and Serena Williams are active Witnesses. Other members with differing levels of activity include the singer Prince, the late singer Selena, actor Terrance Howard (*Crash*), the Wayans brothers and sisters, and supermodel Naomi Campbell.

[27]Zellner was working as a Pinkerton security guard during the course of his "participant observation" of the Jehovah's Witnesses. He did not reveal to the Witnesses that he was a sociologist.

[28]Zellner, "Of Another World," pp. 101–2.

from verbal agreement with the group to commitment, attending regular meetings, and so on?" that she and her husband began attending meetings right away. This was not an unusual response. Of the eighteen Witnesses interviewed, most became active in a period varying from a few weeks to a few months; only one held out as long as six months.

Need for Certitude   A "need for certitude" is a necessary, but not sufficient, condition for conversion to the Jehovah's Witnesses. All eighteen converts felt that their lives lacked direction before encountering the group, all felt that a pattern for life was important, and all felt that their conversion satisfied this need. The Witness belief system is conformity-demanding.

Prescriptions for action cover every situation. Converts are told exactly what is required of them in family situations or job situations, and how to act in the presence of nonbelievers. The Society provides a way to cope with the suffering and inequities of Satan's world. The plan meets the human need for certitude, provides light beyond death, and becomes the convert's *raison d'être.*

Anomie   First used by Émile Durkheim and now a part of the standard sociological vocabulary, **anomie** refers to a sense of powerlessness or worthlessness, leading eventually to a feeling of alienation. An anomic person feels left out of the mainstream of society, and because of this state of normlessness, an individual's survival comes into question. At least, this was Durkheim's belief.

As applied to people who join the Jehovah's Witnesses, *anomie* is perhaps too strong a term. Note, however, that five of the eighteen converts had just moved to a new community where they had no family and few or no friends. Four had weak or nonexistent family ties even before they encountered the Jehovah's Witnesses. Family ties, in most cases, suffer further strains after conversions. For those who feel a need for primary-group relations, the Society offers access to such relationships with like-minded people.

Shared Values before Conversion   The convert must accept new religious dogma, but most share similar social values before conversion. Society literature merely confirms and refines what most converts already believed about the world.

Also, most converts share many of the Society's social values before encountering the group. For example, the Society generally rejects voting; only two of the Witnesses interviewed voted before joining the group. Most were fundamentalists, and believed the Bible should be taken literally. All believed that the male should be dominant in the family unit. The Society emphasizes that people should work with their hands and strongly denounces higher education; all the converts worked with their hands before joining the group. The Society provides support for those who, for whatever reason, are not well educated in the traditional sense. Joining the Society adds group affirmation and justification for a lifestyle already chosen.

The Religious Perspective

Sociologists recognize three major problem-solving perspectives: religious, psychological, and political. Most people employ all three in their efforts to resolve life's problems. There are those, however, who tend to rely on only one perspective. Members of a radical political party emphasize a political problem-solving ideology, whereas people who buy self-help books from supermarket shelves tend to use the psychological perspective. Devoutly religious people almost exclusively answer life's questions with religious explanations. All eighteen Witnesses interviewed believed strongly in God and had a religious problem-solving perspective before joining the movement.

House Calls   Conversionist religious groups do not convert atheists or agnostics. Any door-to-door vacuum cleaner salesperson can relate to this argument. Rarely does a salesperson knock on a door to have it opened by someone who shouts, "Hey! That's just what I was looking for!" Salespeople must knock on many doors; when they find one open, they must sell first themselves and then the sweeper. For the vacuum cleaner salesperson to have a chance, the potential customer must have a rug. For the Witness proselytizer, the customer's rug must be a religious problem-solving perspective.

Jehovah's Witnesses are believers; there is no doubt about that. Zellner discusses the rejection Witnesses encounter when seeking converts door-to-door: "I will never forget the few field trips I made with a Witness proselytizer. Next to no-one-at-home, I considered polite indifference a good call. After the Witness introduced himself, the occupant usually said, 'I'm a Presbyterian, Catholic, Jew, or whatever.' What the prospect meant was 'I'm not open to a new religious outlook,' and doors closed to us very quickly."[29]

Proselytizing and perceived persecution are important "supports of faith." The Witnesses uniformly perceive the rejection they encounter in their missionary work as persecution; this common feeling creates internal cohesion and a strong we-feeling. They are convinced that the world is on the brink of the millennium, the time when Satan's strength is on the increase. They talk endlessly about those they meet who are in poor spiritual condition, and the many good people deceived by Satan.

---

[29]Zellner, "Of Another World," p. 106.

Past Relationships   Most Jehovah's Witnesses more or less sever relations with the outside world; meaningful relationships occur only within the microcosm. In response to the survey question "Did your becoming a Witness cause a strain between you and other family members?" only two of the eighteen converts reported any degree of normality in family relationships, and both felt there was room for improvement. Many had tried to convert relatives but had given up. All hoped their relatives would someday understand "the truth."

In response to the question "Did your joining the group strain relationships between you and your friends?" all eighteen Witnesses reported changing friends after joining the Society; a few reported having few or no friends before membership. The new friends were, of course, Jehovah's Witnesses.

Alienation   Eleven converts reported that they had, at one time or another, been chided at their workplace because of their beliefs. Through interaction, Witnesses share common definitions of situations, and all felt sorry for their tormentors. For the convert, religion is a matter to be taken seriously and never joked about. There is no question that Witnesses are alienated in most situations outside of the microcosm, yet it is alienation with hope—not hope that they will someday fit in, but a hope that someday the rest of the world will join them.

Group Membership   As previously noted, the Society effectively promotes primary-group relationships. When the Sunday meetings are over, Witnesses do not leave their religion at the Kingdom Hall. They consider themselves "of another world," and spend as much time as possible in their self-created microcosm. In many ways, they are social isolates: most are alienated from their families, and most have few friends outside the group. What they do have is each other, and they interact much like an extended family.

The Meetings

In general, Witnesses consider group membership the most important aspect of their lives. Most spend as much time as possible in organizational activity. The structure of these meetings is not left to local congregations; a printed format outlining what is to be done during the entire year is sent from the Society in New York, and local congregations must not deviate from the plan. Only meeting hours may vary from one congregation to the next.

Witnesses have five formal meetings each week, and each represents an important support of faith. All Witnesses are expected to attend as many meetings as possible. Sickness and secular employment are acceptable excuses for missing, but if too many meetings are missed, a flagging Witness can expect a visit from a group of brothers.

The first hour each Sunday is labeled a "Bible Educational Talk." The talks range from denouncing "the evils of the United Nations" to "how to communicate within one's family." The speaker, an elder, always relates his topic to Scripture. In urban areas, the speaker is sometimes a visiting elder from another congregation in the city; rural congregations as well will occasionally exchange speakers.

The second hour of the Sunday meeting is spent reading the current issue of the *Watchtower*. After a reader has read a paragraph from the text, the congregation is asked to respond to a question printed at the bottom of the page. The questions are numbered and correspond to the numbered paragraph in the *Watchtower* containing the answer. Many hands are raised. Ushers, usually teenage and always males, carry microphones on metal poles, and when the reader calls on one of the congregation to respond, an usher extends his pole down the aisle so the responder can read back the paragraph that has just been read. When a question appears easy enough, the reader will occasionally call on one of the children in the congregation to answer. If the child responds correctly, everyone beams approvingly.

This process of question and response is an important "support of faith," and often takes the form of friendly competition. Many Witnesses preread the questions and then underline what they think is the appropriate response. No abstract thinking is required. The following is from the *Watchtower:*

6   Do the scriptures speak of Peter as living in the "last days" of something away back there? Yes! Those particular "last days" began with the baptism of Jesus by John the Baptiser. . . . (Acts 10:37, 38).

Question at the bottom of the page:

6   When did the "last days" in which Peter was living begin?[30]

Pioneers and Publishers   To be a Jehovah's Witness is to surrender one's self to the group. Proselytizing—Witnessing for Jehovah—is expected, and almost every Witness is involved in the activity. Proselytizers are divided into four categories: special pioneers, pioneers, auxiliary pioneers, and publishers.

Special pioneers obligate themselves to a minimum of 150 hours each month in active fieldwork. Those in this category receive ninety dollars per month from the Society, the same as Bethel workers. This, of course, does not begin to cover their expenses. Special pioneers are often retired

[30]"'In the Last Days,' Since When?" *Watchtower*, October 1, 1980, p. 20.

or are the wives of working men who can economically support the activity. There were four such persons in the Minnesota congregation where Zellner regularly attended meetings.

There were four pioneers in the congregation, obligated to a minimum of ninety hours per month in the field. There were also four auxiliary pioneers working sixty hours per month. During the winter, there had been eighteen in the latter category. When the presiding elder of the congregation was asked about the drop in numbers, he winked and said, "The numbers will improve again when cold weather sets in. Many Witnesses have lawns and gardens to take care of."[31] Witnesses who dropped from the rank of auxiliary pioneer for the summer, of course, did not stop proselytizing altogether; they became publishers.

There were 120 publishers in the Minnesota congregation, each obligated to ten to fifteen hours per month in the field. Almost every member of every congregation is in this category. Most male Witnesses work at low-income blue-collar jobs, and many have working wives. It is difficult for these people to attend all the Witness functions and also make field calls, but they do remarkably well.

Jehovah's Witnesses do not maintain formal membership rolls at either the national or local level; however, at any given time, they have more than just a vague idea as to their numbers. Each congregation maintains a territorial map, and a record is kept for each fieldworker. Because almost every Witness is an active proselytizer, a membership count is relatively simple. The Minneapolis congregation had 131 active fieldworkers. There were about 20 members who did fieldwork irregularly, mostly aged Witnesses, and 4 in Bible study. By simply adding categories, it can be deduced that there were about 150 adult Witnesses in the congregation.

Argot

Argot is the special language peculiar to a group. The Witness microcosm has a special language, uniquely its own, which adds to the desired feeling of separation of "us" from "them." Only a few examples need be cited to illustrate the depth and richness of this language.

Witnesses always refer to God as Jehovah, in the belief that he would prefer his people call him by his name. They note that "Jehovah"—not "God"—appears 6,961 times in the original Hebrew Scriptures.

"Sheep and goats" are commonly used argots. A sheep is a person receptive to a Witness proselytizer, a goat is not. Biblical justification for this usage rests in Matthew 24:32: "And all the nations will be gathered about Him, and He will separate the sheep from the goats."

[31]Zellner, "Of Another World," pp. 103–4.

"In the truth" is another common argot. This means an understanding of Jehovah's plan, and a willingness to live by it. A Baptist or Pentecostal might ask, "Are you saved?" A Witness would ask, "Are you in the truth?"

The 144,000 who will serve in heaven with Christ are referred to as the "mystery class" or the "little flock." Christ told his disciples that this group would "know" the "mysteries" of the Kingdom of Heaven. More commonly, the 144,000 are called the "little flock," derived from Luke 12:32, in which Christ said, "Have no fear, little flock, because your Father has approved of giving you the kingdom."

Jehovah's Witnesses believe that they will survive Armageddon, should they be alive when the battle takes place. They refer to this survivor-class as "Jonadabs" or "other sheep." It is thought that this group, along with Witnesses returned from the dust, will be the leaders and teachers in the "new system." The "new system" is defined as Jehovah's kingdom on earth under theocratic law.

Armageddon

Adult Witnesses are convinced that their religion is the only true religion, and salvation is possible only through Jehovah's plan as revealed by the Society. All other religions are false religions, and the Witnesses do not want their children associated with nonbelievers. But they have no choice. The Society does not maintain schools of its own, and Witness parents are required by law to send their children to secular schools. At a tender age, their young are forced out of the microcosm and into Satan's world.

Nevertheless, the Witnesses do everything possible to isolate their children from the contaminating effects of a public education. Their children are not allowed to salute the flag, vote in school elections, run for class office, or sing the national anthem or school songs. They are not allowed to celebrate holidays, participate in extracurricular activities, date, attend school dances, or join school clubs. The Society has published a thirty-two-page booklet, *School and Jehovah's Witnesses*, setting out what their children can and cannot do in school. Witness children are instructed to give the publication to their teachers.

Despite efforts to isolate their offspring from mainsteam activities, children do not always share the religious zeal of their parents. But while the Society does lose some of its children, membership loss appears to be small. The Witness "socialization" process is effective, and although some do stray, it is usually only for a short time. Children raised in a close-knit social group often come to find life outside the group intolerable.

Kate Williams responded to the survey question "Are they [your children] members of the group?" that she was concerned for her children; she may well have been overly concerned. Although five of her eight children were living outside of the Kingdom, this does not mean that they had joined other religious organizations. To be fully part of the "new system" means that meetings must be attended regularly and field commitments met. Young people sometimes find it difficult to meet these obligations. The best guess is that Kate Williams's children will return to full-time Witness activity.

The Society is an established sect. Witnesses are "of another world," and it appears that they will remain so. The believers are uncompromising; they refuse to acknowledge the legitimacy of any other religious organization, and believe the direction that they have taken is the only path to salvation. The Society continues to grow, because the members work long and hard, with Matthew 24:14 always in mind: "And this good news of the kingdom will be preached in all the inhabited earth for a witness to all the nations; and then the end will come."

KEY TERMS

Argot, p. 276
Anomie, p. 272
Disfellowship, p. 264

Eschatology, p. 262
Millenarian movement, p. 250

SOURCES ON THE WEB

www.watchtower.org
The official Web site of the Watchtower Society, the publication arm of The Jehovah's Witnesses.

www.religioustolerance.org/witness5.htm
www.cesnur.org/testi/se_geova.htm
Two sources of relatively objective information about this faith and its symbols, history, belief, and practices.

SELECTED READINGS

Alfs, Matthew. *The Evocative Religion of Jehovah's Witnesses: An Analysis of a Present-Day Phenomenon.* Minneapolis: Old Theology Book House, 1991.
Beckford, James A. *Trumpet of Prophecy.* New York: Wiley, 1975.

Blackwell, Victor V. *O'er the Ramparts They Watched.* New York: Hearthstone, 1976.

Bowman, Robert M., Jr. *Understanding Jehovah's Witnesses: Why They Read the Bible the Way They Do.* Grand Rapids, MI: Baker Book House, 1991.

Franz, Raymond. *In Search of Christian Freedom.* Atlanta: Commentary Press, 1991.

Gaylin, Willard. *In the Service of Their Country: War Resisters in Prison.* New York: Viking, 1970.

Harrison, Barbara Grizzuti. *Visions of Glory.* New York: Simon & Schuster, 1978.

Hoekema, Anthony A. *Jehovah's Witnesses.* Grand Rapids, MI: Eerdmans, 1974.

Holden, Andrew. *Jehovah's Witnesses: Portrait of a Contemporary Religious Movement.* London: Routledge, 2002.

Insight on the Scriptures, vol. 1. New York: Watchtower Bible and Tract Society of New York, 1988.

Insight on the Scriptures, vol. 2. New York: Watchtower Bible and Tract Society of New York, 1988.

Manwaring, David R. *Render unto Caesar: The Flag Salute Controversy.* Chicago: University of Chicago Press, 1962.

Penton, M. James. *Apocalypse Delayed: The Story of Jehovah's Witnesses.* Toronto: University of Toronto Press, 1985.

Pike, Edgar Royston. *Jehovah's Witnesses: Who They Are, What They Teach, What They Do.* New York: Philosophical Press, 1954.

Reasoning from the Scriptures. New York: Watchtower Bible and Tract Society of New York, 1985.

Reed, David A., ed. *Index of Watchtower Errors,* comp. Steve Huntoon and John Cornell. Grand Rapids, MI: Baker Book House, 1990.

Rogerson, Alan. *Millions Now Living Will Never Die: A Study of Jehovah's Witnesses.* London: Constable, 1969.

Sterling, Chandler. *The Witnesses: One God, One Victory.* Chicago: Regency, 1975.

Stevens, Leonard A. *Salute! The Case of the Bible vs. the Flag.* New York: Coward, McCann & Geoghegan, 1973.

Stroup, Herbert Hewitt. *The Jehovah's Witnesses.* New York: Columbia University Press, 1945.

Weddle, David L. "Jehovah's Witnesses." In *Introduction to New and Alternative Religion in America,* edited by Eugene V. Gallagher and W. Michael Ashcraft, vol. 2, pp. 62–88. Westport, CT: Greenwood Press, 2006.

White, Timothy. *A People for His Name: A History of Jehovah's Witnesses and an Evaluation.* New York: Vantage Press, 1968.

Your Youth: Getting the Best Out of It. New York: Watchtower Bible and Tract Society of New York, 1976.

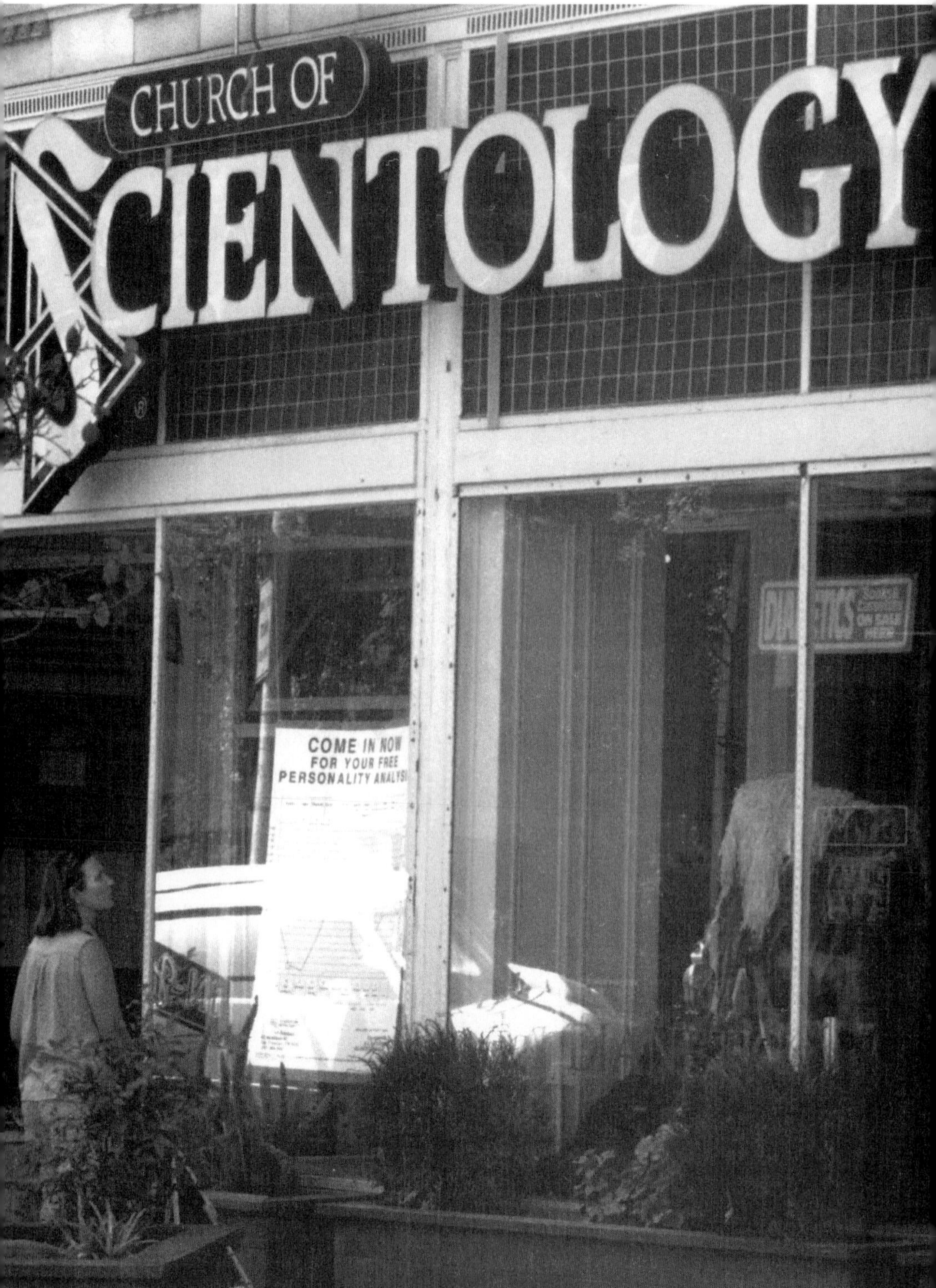
CHURCH OF
COME IN NOW
FOR YOUR FREE

CHAPTER EIGHT

CHURCH OF SCIENTOLOGY

- L. Ron Hubbard
- David Miscavige
- Scientologists: By the Numbers
- Dianetics: An Overview
- Scientology as a Religion
- Social Positions

- Scientology Enemy No. 1: The Government
- The Death of Lisa McPherson
- Hollywood Connections
- The Last Words

Although all contemporary faiths have their unique aspects, the Church of Scientology is in a class by itself. Its roots are in a self-help therapy that was developed by a science fiction writer. The Church of Scientology has little, if any, relationship to any other organized religious group, historically or ideologically. Indeed, its detractors, and there are many as we will see, question whether it even deserves to be referred to as a religion; some say the label "religious cult" would be more accurate.

Despite enjoying a devoted following of hundreds of thousands, if not millions, worldwide, the Church of Scientology has been sharply criticized and has been a continuing subject of derision, humor, and ridicule. Another characteristic that distinguishes Scientology from other religions is that popular awareness of Scientology is based mainly on either its Hollywood celebrity adherents or the name of its founder. Let's first consider the remarkable life of L. Ron Hubbard, the founder.[1]

---

[1] The core publication of the Church of Scientology is L. Ron Hubbard's *Dianetics* (Los Angeles: Bridge Publications, 1991). Depending upon the printing, this book carries the subtitle "The Modern Science of Mental Health" or "A Handbook of Dianetics Procedure." The companion book is Hubbard, *What Is Scientology?* (Los Angeles: Bridge, 1998). Although the latter formally bears Hubbard's name as the sole author and states it is "based on the works of L. Ron Hubbard," it is obviously a composite volume because it covers Hubbard's death and developments in the organization of the Church of Scientology following the founder's death. Relatively speaking, the most objective book on the Church of Scientology is sociologist J. Gordon Melton's *The Church of Scientology* (Toreno, Italy: Signature Books, 2000). However, many critics of the Church of Scientology see Melton as an apologist and prefer more critical treatments. There is no lack of sharp criticism, ranging from a *Penthouse* magazine interview (June 1983) with the founder's eldest son to a cover story in *Time* (May 6, 1991).

L. Ron Hubbard

Lafayette Robert Hubbard, the founder of the Church of Scientology, was born in Tilden, Nebraska, in 1911. The town of 1,000 population takes pride in its location on the Cowboy Trail but makes no effort to acknowledge its being the birthplace of a religious founder. Indeed, former Philadelphia baseball player Richie Ashburn, born sixteen years after Hubbard, was recognized with his name on a park and a small museum in a local pharmacy; plans to similarly honor Hubbard went unrealized.

In 1997 a group of Scientologists donated $50,000 to Tilden to build a park in Hubbard's honor. As park plans grew grander, Scientologists pledged another $800,000. The City Council gratefully accepted the offer until they became aware of public perceptions of the Church of Scientology. The money was returned and the park was not built. The Tilden link is forgotten except by historians of Scientology.[2]

Early Life   Tilden was not an important part of Hubbard's development. His father was a naval officer, and his family moved often; they left Tilden while Hubbard was an infant. As far as can be determined, he never returned. His youth was spent on the move, including two trips to Guam when he was a teenager to visit his father, who was stationed there.

Hubbard's life is difficult to describe in a simple narrative because so many conflicting versions exist. For example, Hubbard himself and, after his death, the Church of Scientology, gave great significance to his travels as a young man to Asia. These accounts speak of encounters with Chinese magicians and Buddhist monks that involved an openness not usually available to foreigners. This exposure to Eastern religion and mysticism is said to have sparked the young Hubbard with thinking about new ways of exploring one's inner self. However, detractors of the faith point to documentation that they believe shows that Hubbard spent little time in Asia; these detractors argue that they have uncovered notes of the young man speaking very disparagingly of the Chinese in particular.[3]

Book-length critiques by former Scientologists include those by famed novelist William S. Burroughs (*Ali's Smile: Naked Scientology* [Bonn, Germany: Expanded Media Editions, 1991]) and Jon Atack (*A Piece of Blue Sky: Scientology, Dianetics and L. Ron Hubbard Exposed* [New York: Lyle Stuart, 1990]). The general absence of serious treatment of this important movement in spiritual thought was the subject of a scholarly paper by Douglas E. Cowan, "Researching Scientology: Academic Premises, Promises and Problematics" (paper presented at the Annual Conference of the Center for Studies on New Religions, Waco, TX, 2004). The Church of Scientology is said to be the most demonized cult on the Internet, according to Massimo Introvigne, "So Many Evil Things" (paper presented at the Annual Meeting of the Association for Sociology of Religion, Chicago, August 5, 1999).

[2]Mike Wilson, "Tilden, Nebraska: Scientology Crooks Thrown Out of Town," *St. Petersburg Times*, May 11, 1997.

[3]Jon Atack, *A Piece of Blue Sky: Scientology, Dianetics and L. Ron Hubbard Exposed*, Chapter Two, "Hubbard in the East," (New York: Lyle Stuart, 1990).

There does appear to be consensus that Hubbard graduated from Woodward School for Boys near Washington, D.C. He then attended George Washington University while at the same time serving a brief stint in the Marine Corps Reserve. In college, he had poor grades and left after two years while on academic probation. Nonetheless, Scientology publications sometimes referred to him as a civil engineer. More commonly they assert Hubbard was frustrated with formal learning and that the academics and scientists failed to appreciate his scientific experiments and the understandings he had gained earlier from "Philippine pygmies" and "shamans of Borneo."[4]

Writing Career   In the 1930s Hubbard's writings began to emerge in fiction magazines with titles like "Final Blackout" depicting war-ravaged, disease-infested Europe in the future and a psychological horror story, "Fear."[5] These and his other writings were enormously popular and created a ready audience for Hubbard's output.

In 1933, at the age of twenty-two, Hubbard married Margaret "Polly" Grubb in Washington State. Soon their two children were born (L. Ron Jr. in 1934 and Katherine May in 1936). Hubbard would later have two other wives. Mary Sue Hubbard, his third wife, played a significant role as the First Lady of Scientology from the beginning of their marriage in 1952.

With American involvement in World War II approaching, Hubbard joined the U.S. Navy in June 1941, continuing on active duty until 1945. As with his youthful sojourns to Asia, there remain parallel yet different accounts of his military service; they range from the depiction of constant reassignments due to quarrelling with superiors to the Church of Scientology's account of his playing a critical role in naval hospitals helping unresponsive patients get past "mental blocks" that were impeding their recovery.[6]

In 1949, Hubbard says he wrote to the American Psychological Association about his process *narcosynthesis*. This process involves helping a patient recall repressed memories and emotional traumas. This controversial and disputed technique has advocates independent of Hubbard or the Church of Scientology. Undeterred by critics of the technique, Hubbard, then thirty-nine, made his views public in the popular magazine *Astounding Science-Fiction* in 1950. The article described Dianetics, a system of thought (described in a later section of the chapter), and the

[4]L. Ron Hubbard, *What Is Scientology?* (Los Angeles: Bridge Publications, 1998), pp. 34–38.
[5]L. Ron Hubbard, *Final Blackout* (Hollywood: Galaxy Books, 2005 [1940]), and *Fear* (Los Angeles: Bridge, 1991).
[6]Atack, *A Piece of Blue Sky;* Hubbard, *Handbook of Scientology;* and Melton, *The Church of Scientology,* p. 2.

next year the religion's foundation text *Dianetics: The Modern Science of Mental Health* was published.[7]

Church of Scientology

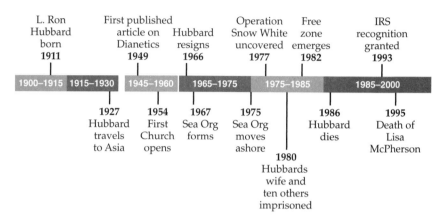

Hubbard became a popular lecturer as people wanted to learn more about a do-it-yourself way to improve mental health. By all accounts he was a charismatic individual, attracting people to his message much like Joseph Smith and Father Divine.[8]

In contrast to the psychology establishment in general and psychotherapy in particular, Dianetics was more accessible, according to Hubbard, to the average man and woman. Indeed, Hubbard told his audiences that users of Dianetics could then become practitioners helping others.

By 1954, Hubbard oversaw the establishment of the first Church of Scientology, although what was to be referred to as the Founding Church of Scientology was opened in 1955 in Washington, D.C. Hubbard had clearly taken the position that Dianetics was no longer just a secular self-help therapy but was religious-based counseling.

L. Ron Hubbard passed away on January 24, 1986. Mystery surrounded his death as it did the last ten years of his life, which was spent in reclusion in a series of homes in rural parts of Southern California. Hubbard had signed a statement forbidding an autopsy for religious reasons, which is binding in California. So when he died at age seventy-four, the

---

[7]Hubbard had privately published *The Original Thesis* in 1948 and then expanded these ideas about Dianetics for the limited audience of *The Explorers Club Journal* ("Terra Incognita: The Mind," Winter/Spring 1948) of New York City. Therefore, the newsstand appearance of "Dianetics: The Evolution of a Science," *Astounding Science-Fiction* 45 (No. 3), 1950, pp. 43–87, is considered the unveiling of Dianetics. The successive publication of *Dianetics* and Hubbard's many other writings is now overseen by the Church of Scientology's publication arm, Bridge Publications of Los Angeles.

[8]Simon Locke, "Charisma and the Iron Cage: Rationalization, Science and Scientology," *Social Compass* 51 (No. 1): 111–31, 2004.

sheriff's office photographed his body and took fingerprints to confirm his identity. Shortly thereafter his ashes were "scattered at sea," according to the Church of Scientology.[9]

Hubbard never claimed to be a divine figure nor does the Church of Scientology today view him that way.[10] He is regarded by the faithful as an extraordinary man who has no successor. There is no expectation of any future prophetic clarifications, rather it is the prolific writings of Hubbard to which Scientologists continue to turn for understanding and inspiration.

David Miscavige, at age twenty-six, was named the head of the Church shortly after Hubbard's death, a position he continued to hold as of 2007.

David Miscavige

L. Ron Hubbard is the founder, the definer, and the ideologue of Scientology, but David Miscavige has been the driving force behind the Church of Scientology for the past two decades. Although the Church explicitly states that Miscavige is not an official spokesperson, he publicly represents the faith on special occasions. He is the person who typically answers for the Church of Scientology in rare public interviews. Miscavige's biography and speeches are second only to Hubbard's in dominating the official Scientology Web site.[11]

Miscavige's official title is Chairman of the Board of the Religious Technology Center (RTC), a nonprofit organization aimed at maintaining and promoting Scientology. He is acknowledged as the ultimate ecclesiastical authority regarding the standard and pure application of L. Ron Hubbard's religious theories.[12]

Miscavige was raised a Roman Catholic in New Jersey but followed his father's encouragement to become a Scientologist. The elder Miscavige had struggled with asthma and credits the faith with ending the symptoms. Shortly thereafter his father's conversion, the family moved to the Church of Scientology's retreat in England. By age twelve, David Miscavige was introducing others to Scientology through a process called auditing (described later in the chapter).

[9]Associated Press, "L. Ron Hubbard, 74, Founder of Scientology Church Dies," *New York Times*, January 28, 1986, and Robert Lindsey, "L. Ron Hubbard Dies of Stroke; Founder of Church of Scientology," *New York Times*, January 29, 1986.

[10]Cowan and Bromley, "The Church of Scientology," p. 172.

[11]Since 1982 to the present, the president of the Church of Scientology International is Heber C. Jentzsch. Born in Utah, raised a Mormon, Jentzsch was caught up in the Snow White scandal and sentenced to prison, but he continuously held the title of President. See "Heber C. Jentzsch," accessed January 14, 2007, at www.scientology.org/scnnews/jentzsch.htm, and CNN, "Larry King Live: Guest, the Reverend Heber Jentzsch," December 20, 1993.

[12]Church of Scientology, "David Miscavige," posted at www.scientology.org/scnnews/miscavige.htm and accessed on January 11, 2007.

Miscavige dropped out of high school in 1976 at the age of sixteen, joining the elite branch of Scientology known as the Sea Org (discussed later in the chapter). He became an assistant to Hubbard, who was then sixty-six. The young Miscavige, called Misc (pronounced "Misk") by his friends, quickly became known as skilled in developing film recordings of Scientology activities. Miscavige rose within the organization while handling legal, financial, and public affairs. He began efforts, that continue to the present, to have the Church of Scientology hold the copyright to all of Hubbard's voluminous nonliterary writings.[13] By the mid 1970s, he was the most significant figure in Scientology except for Hubbard and his wife.

Controversies over Scientology teachings and the Church's efforts to squelch government investigations in the late 1970s sent Hubbard into reclusion and his wife to prison. Miscavige became the organizational rock that got the Church of Scientology through the embarrassments.[14]

Scientologists: By the Numbers

Counting followers of a faith is a difficult task. First, it must be acknowledged that some "members" of a religion rarely have any relationship to the organization or even to other members. Second, the number is subject to fluctuation especially during times of growth and decline. Third, and most important, given the absence of external counts in a census, it is the organization itself that offers the "official number."

In the case of the Church of Scientology, the Church does not make official announcements of members other than broad announcements. Independent national surveys show less than 50,000 members, but even Scientology critics agree that many people are reluctant to indicate, even to a researcher, their attachment to a faith so stigmatized in the media. From survey estimates (or perhaps "guesstimates" is a better term), membership ranges somewhere between 3 million and 9 million. Understandably both Scientologists and its strongest critics benefit from a large estimate.

Moving to global estimates is even more difficult, especially given, as we will see later, that in some countries the Church of Scientology experiences significant governmental criticism. Worldwide membership estimates range from 5.6 million to 10 million.

It is probably accurate to say that the largest following of the Church of Scientology is in the United States, and that both in North America and worldwide the religion is growing rapidly.[15]

---

[13]The fiction writings are handled by an independent outlet, Galaxy Press in Hollywood, a few blocks from the Church of Scientology Celebrity Centre.

[14]Thomas Tobin, "The Man behind Scientology," *St. Petersburg Times*, October 25, 1998.

[15]The estimate ranges come from the respected, independent Internet resource Adherents.com as of January 7, 2007; Religious Tolerance, "Religious Affiliations: Comparing the U.S. and the World," posted December 23, 2005, accessed January 7, 2007, at www.religioustolerance.org.

Where do these new members come from? The Church of Scientology makes effective use of distributing its publications and maintaining an informative Web site. The publicity it receives, whether positive or critical, keeps it before the public.

The Church of Scientology, like many other religious organizations, mounts significant social outreach, especially in campaigns aimed at drug abuse, illiteracy, and human rights.[16] As with so much of Scientology, none of this is without controversy. The Church of Scientology is proud of its efforts to help people free themselves of drugs. But its Narconon Program, founded in 1966, has been critiqued by those who argue for better external verification of its effectiveness despite personal statements of assistance by such celebrities as actress Kirstie Alley, a former cocaine abuser.[17]

Scientology "volunteer ministers" are often available at disaster sites around the world. The Church of Scientology is proud of the ministers' role at Ground Zero in New York City following 9/11 assisting recovery workers. Their assistance is not always welcomed, especially in cultures suspicious of new religions. The volunteer ministers were in South Asia following the 2005 tsunami, but they were asked to leave when their techniques of counseling survivors were seen as too religious in nature.[18]

Despite the criticism, the Church of Scientology's nonreligious outreach activities attracted attention, curiosity and, eventually, adherents to the faith. Also, as with most religions, family and friends have supplied an important source of converts. According to the Church of Scientology, family and friends introductions account for half of the new adherents. According to Church data, 56 percent of members in the early 1990s joined the Church when they were between the ages of twenty-one and thirty. Hence Scientology is able to present a more youthful image than many other established faiths.[19]

Dianetics: An Overview

The Church of Scientology is based on the writings of L. Ron Hubbard. By some estimates, he has written 40 million words and has had more than 3,000 lectures transcribed. In addition he wrote more than 500 novels and

[16]Melton, *The Church of Scientology*, pp. 44–46; Church of Scientology, "This Is Scientology," DVD, Golden Era Productions for the Church of Scientology, 2004; and Religious Tolerance, "About the Church of Scientology," accessed January 7, 2007, at www.religioustolerance.org/scientol2.htm.

[17]Joel Sappell and Robert W. Welkos, "The Courting of Celebrities," *Los Angeles Times*, June 25, 1990, p. A18.

[18]Peter S. Goodman, "For Tsunami Survivors, a Touch of Scientology," *Washington Post*, January 28, 2005.

[19]Bromley and Bracey, Jr., "The Church of Scientology: A Quasi-Religion." In *Sects, Cults, and Spiritual Communities: A Sociologial Analysis*, edited by William W. Zellner and Marc Petrowsky, pp. 151–52. Westport, CT: Praeger, 1968.

short stories. Although the teachings do not explicitly exclude following other belief systems, typically Scientologists do not perceive themselves as being both a Scientologist and, say, a Lutheran or Buddhist, at the same time.[20]

Scientology affirms the existence of a Supreme Being but does not describe a divinity figure or specify the relationship to man or woman. Hence, one cannot approach Scientology by building upon even the basic elements of any other faith. It is truly a unique dogma.

Dianetics strives to have the individual achieve a heightened, positive state. The word *Dianetics* comes from Greek words meaning "through" and "soul." It is a method to alleviate unwanted emotions, irrational fears, and psychosomatic illnesses.

The word *Scientology* did not appear in the initial presentations of Dianetics by L. Ron Hubbard. Dianetics was first advanced by Hubbard as a means to gain control of one's life. While Dianetics outlined the process and philosophy behind the Church of Scientology, Hubbard later started using the word publicly in 1952 and a few years after that came to view Scientology as a religion. Critics then and now argue that claims by the Church of Scientology to be a religion were no more than a marketing device to make money and to avoid federal taxes.[21] The Church presents the word *Scientology* as literally meaning "the study of truth." The term reflects Hubbard's efforts to bring scientific-type devices or strategies to resolve philosophical and personal issues.

Auditing   Essential to Dianetics is the process known as **auditing.** This is usually the first step one takes to become a Scientologist. It is a form of personal counseling in which the auditor, always a church member, measures a person's mental state using an Electropsychometer, or E-Meter, a device developed by Hubbard. This desktop device uses low voltage to measure the person's emotional state by registering skin conductivity (or galvanic responses). A dial with a fluctuating pointer registers "rises" and "falls" of emotional change and is said to assist the auditor to help the person heighten his or her ability to think clearly. The recipient of this audit is referred to as a *Preclear* because he or she is on the way to becoming a *Clear*.[22]

---

[20]The presentation of Dianetics is based on Hubbard, *Dianetics,* and Hubbard, *What Is Scientology?* A significant amount of detail has been set aside here; it is impossible to summarize an entire religious doctrine in a couple of pages.

[21]Stephen A. Kent, "Scientology—Is This a Religion?" *Marburg Journal of Religion* 4 (July 1999). Accessed February 11, 2007, at web.uni-marburg.de/religionswissenschaft/journal/mjr/frenschkowski.html.

[22]Capitalization of terms like *Clear, Preclear,* and *Thetan* is inconsistent in Scientology writings. They are capitalized throughout this chapter to bring attention to the reader of their special usages and definitions of the Church of Scientology.

The **Clear** is the highly valued state within the Church of Scientology. It is only attainable through Dianetics. The **Preclear** is no longer a victim of stimulus-response of the mind, but now takes control. During the audit, the Preclear has gained awareness and has begun to overcome any fear he or she may have of the **engram.**

Dianetics describes the *engram* as a particular type of mental image. A Clear is free of any engram. To lay people the auditing process seems akin to some type of psychoanalysis, but the Church of Scientology observes that the auditors never evaluate what the Preclear says. Preclears are guided but their responses are not placed in any context; for example, any role played by their early upbringing, dreams, or sexual fantasies does not come into play. Auditing bears no relationship to psychology and the Church of Scientology typically is critical of psychological therapies or treatments, with or without prescriptive drugs. Furthermore, Dianetics and auditing are accessible to anyone; in time, anyone could become a practitioner, an auditor. This, of course, contrasts with the long training involved in becoming a psychotherapist.

The antagonism that Scientology shows toward psychiatry gained national attention when devotee Tom Cruise appeared on national television in 2005 proclaiming psychiatry to be a "pseudoscience" and criticized actress Brooke Shields for taking Paxil, a prescribed antidepressant, to treat her postpartum depression after the birth of her daughter in 2003. Cruise claimed there is no such thing as chemical imbalances and saw the drug as masking a more underlying problem; he said she should take vitamins, exercise, and "various things." Many watchers took Cruise to be espousing Scientology over accepted medical treatment programs.[23]

The auditing process has been critiqued not only because it stands apart from traditionally accepted methods of therapy, but also because of the expense to the individual. Although additional audits may be free, the Church of Scientology charges for most of the auditing process, which can run into hundreds if not thousands of dollars. Auditors, typically full-time employees of the Church of Scientology, collect these fees. Indigent Preclears are provided for through some form of assistance, but most pay for the sessions over the length of the auditing process.

Some scholars have likened auditing to multilevel sales organizations like Amway and Herbalife. Preclears pay for auditing, but in time can become practitioners themselves and be employed by the Church.

[23]NBC Television, "Today Show," June 24, 2005; American Psychiatric Association, "APA Responds to Tom Cruise's Today Show Interview," News Release, June 27, 2005; and Brooke Shields, "War of Words," *New York Times,* July 1, 2005. Cruise was introduced to Scientology during his marriage to Mimi Rogers (1987–1990) and credits Dianetics with helping him overcome his dyslexia.

Accounts appear in the media of people mortgaging all they own to continue with the audit sessions they want—claims the Church of Scientology say are exaggerated or downright false.[24]

Another important part of Scientology in addition to auditing is the training that comes later as one moves beyond being Preclear. Training involves learning the laws of life as written by Hubbard to maintain the freedom said to be gained through auditing. The training process is displayed in a Scientology chart called "The Bridge to Total Freedom," subtitled a "classification and gradation chart," and becomes a lifelong process. This chart outlines the steps a Scientologist takes to reach the state of Clear, as first presented by Hubbard in 1965 and since refined.[25]

According to the Church of Scientology, there were already 750 groups by 1950 applying the techniques described here. Hubbard read their reports of Preclears reporting previous lives or incarnations. Drawing upon these reports, he advanced the discovery of the "Thetan."

The Thetan   *Thetan* is the Church of Scientology term for the immortal spiritual being similar to a soul. Scientologists see the soul as independent from oneself, therefore the **Thetan** has an existence apart for one's body. But unlike the usual concept of a soul, a Thetan can be associated with more than one person over the millennium. By becoming one with a Thetan, Scientology believes that a person crosses a chasm and moves to a brighter, happier world.

By becoming Clear, one reaches the Operating Thetan (OT) level, which means literally you truly are able to act. To be OT does not mean you become God; it means to Scientologists that you become wholly one. To be OT is a significant step for a Scientologist, worthy of personal celebration, and the Church of Scientology allows one to acknowledge it by wearing an OT bracelet.

As we will discuss later, the introduction of Thetan moves Dianetics from therapy closer to the spiritual teachings that come to define a religion. As Hubbard postulated publicly about Thetan during the 1950s, critics characterized him not as insightful but self-promotional and out for financial gain. As criticism of his religious activities mounted and drowned out appreciation for him as a literature writer, Hubbard moved several times during this period. In 1966 he resigned his organizational leadership positions, passing his authority to trusted associates, to immerse himself further in his research and writing.

The Sea Org   Shortly after Hubbard set aside the day-to-day operations of the Church of Scientology bureaucracy, he founded in 1967 an elite

---

[24]Richard Behar, "The Thriving Cult of Green and Power," *Time* 171 (May 6, 1991), and Cristina Gutiérrez, "Religious Aspects of Multilevel Sales Organizations," paper presented at the Annual Conference of the Center for Studies on New Religions, London, 2001.

[25]The "Bridge to Total Freedom" can be accessed at www.scientology.org.

branch within Scientology called the Sea Organization, or simply Sea Org. This branch is staffed by advanced, dedicated members of the Church who pledged to work full-time.[26]

The name *Sea Organization* comes from the fact that the unit initially was housed on three oceangoing ships, in one of which Hubbard lived for a short time. In 1975, the Sea Org moved onshore to Clearwater, Florida. Hubbard continued to become less involved with any aspect of the Church of Scientology's functioning and by 1980 withdrew entirely from public life until his death in 1986. Therefore, the Church of Scientology is built upon the writings and speeches made by L. Ron Hubbard primarily between 1950 and the early 1980s. As noted before, the Church of Scientology does not add to the doctrine of Dianetics or Scientology as outlined by Hubbard but continues to be inspired by it.

The Sea Org remains the dedicated community of Scientologists headquartered in Church complexes around the world. Scientologists entering this community sign what has come to be known as the "billion-year contract." One agrees to enter full-time employment and go where one is needed by the Sea Org "for the next billion years."

Members of the Sea Org have some similarities to a community of monks or nuns. Life revolves around the faith. There are married couples but typically if they have children they move to staff positions. When members' children reach age six, they may return to the Sea Org, with their children being schooled at the Church of Scientology Cadet School.[27]

Rehabilitation Project Force   In any religion, people's dedication often wanes. They become disenchanted and may return to reassert their commitment. Typically this pattern common to all faiths occurs informally and with little fanfare and virtually unnoticed by the religion's hierarchy. For Sea Org members, disenchantment with the faith is totally different.

The Church of Scientology began in 1974 the Rehabilitation Project Force (RPF) in 1974 to address members of the Sea Org who perform unsatisfactorily. Just exactly what this means and what the RPF does to rehabilitate members is the subject of fierce debate between skeptics and followers of Scientology. There appears to be consensus that theft and lying within the Church may bring one to the attention of the RPF for discipline, but matters for the RPF can also include more major violations such as adultery and severe derelictions of duty by members of the Sea Org. Officially the Church sees RPF review as a means of spiritual recovery for members of the Sea Org who have signed the pledge to eternal service. Intense daily

[26]J. Gordon Melton, "A Contemporary Ordered Religious Community: The Sea Organization," paper presented at the Annual Conference for the Center for Studies on New Religions, London, 2001.

[27]According to Private Schools Report the Cadet School had 169 students ranging from third through tenth grades. See http://schools.privateschoolsreport.com accessed January 14, 2007.

counseling and isolation from others are techniques used by the RPF to address this "burn out" in the Sea Org.

Critics contend that the RPF processes amount to forced labor and describe people identified by the RPF as inmates. Some people going through rehabilitation choose to leave the Sea Org or are dismissed from the faith altogether.[28]

MEST   The existence of Thetans—the spiritual essence—goes back trillions of years, according to the Church of Scientology. This spirit of collective Thetans is responsible for the material universe—matter, energy, space, and time, commonly referred to by Scientologists with the acronym MEST.

Since one's Thetan extends well beyond a single lifetime, a person needs to confront engrams suppressed not only from his or her life but from previous lifetimes of the Thetan. The Thetan has been embodied many, many times—a belief commonly called reincarnation. Scientologists avoid using this term and do not believe, as do some believers of reincarnation, in transmigration. That is, Scientologists do not believe the Thetan takes any animal form other than human.

How do Scientologists believe that we can be affected by something we ourselves have not experienced in *our* lifetime?

Scientologists illustrate this with "a pinch test." Early in the auditing process the practitioner will lightly pinch the Preclear. The E-Meter records this response, which the Church of Scientology interprets as measuring the engram created by the pinch. At a later point or even at another session, the practitioner will ask the Preclear if he or she recalls the pinch. The E-Meter records the same response even though the Preclear was not touched.

Engrams generated by past events more traumatic than a mild pinch may be at the root, according to Hubbard, of diseases ranging from arthritis to measles to tuberculosis as well as kidney trouble, the common cold, high blood pressure, and underdeveloped genital organs. A key concept in Dianetics is that engrams may predate one's own lifetime and that auditing raises one's consciousness to deal with them effectively.[29]

Once a Scientologist recognizes the engram from the pinch, the event will no longer produce the negative impact. It will be remembered in the traditional notion of memory, but this engram will be cleared.

Auditing is an ongoing, lifetime process to be cleared of engrams. At some point a person assumes control for his or her own audit; it is at this

---

[28]Cowan and Bromley, "The Church of Scientology"; Kent, "Scientology–Is This a Religion?"; and "What Is the Rehabilitation Task Force?" accessed January 13, 2007, at www.scientology.org.

[29]Hubbard, *Dianetics*, pp. 123–147.

point that the person is said to have attained the level of Clear. This status is reported to the Church in a manner analogous to a Christian being "born again": the Clear makes joyous pronouncements and looks forward to future enlightenment.

Scientologists contend they can eliminate engrams and increase their survival ability. This survival proceeds across eight dynamic stages, beginning with individual survival and proceeding up through infinity. At this culmination, one unites with the universe. At this stage, does the person become a god? We, as humans, according to the Church of Scientology, are not advanced enough to know that or to truly describe what God or the deity is truly like.

Scientologists are engaged in a quest. They seek to move from Preclear to Clear. With this enhanced spiritual development, Scientologists are more self-determined, less vulnerable to engrams. By 1995, the Church reported 50,000 practitioners had reached a state of Clear. In time, the Church of Scientology believes, as more people reach this state, global problems such as pollution, drugs, crime, and war will be eliminated. Scientology is presented literally as a bridge to a better life, for the individual, for all.

Scientology as a Religion

At the outset, we noted that many outsiders refuse to view Scientology as a religion. Later we will consider the legal skirmishes the Church of Scientology has had with governments concerning whether this official status has been granted, but first we want to consider its status as a religion within the scholarly community.

The Church of Scientology is upfront in its defense as a religion. It contends that it is "the only major new religion to emerge" in the twentieth century.[30] Scientology presents itself as not unlike Judeo-Christian religions and Eastern religions, particularly Buddhism. Skeptics find this far-fetched, but the Church of Scientology sees the doctrine of Thetan as similar to the concept of the soul. Scientologists are quick to acknowledge the differences that distinguish Thetan, such as that a Thetan is believed to live through many lifetimes in what is referred to as a "time track," and that some of these earlier experiences become increasingly obscured and must be identified through auditing.

However, because an organization declares its doctrine to be a religion does not make it so. Some scholars straddle the fence and place the Church of Scientology in the category of a **quasi-religion**. This category has been created to include organizations that may see themselves as religious but

[30]Hubbard, *What Is Scientology?*, p. 561.

are seen as "sort-of religious" by others. Included in this classification system are New Age movements and Transcendental Meditation as advanced by Maharishi Mahesh Yogi and introduced in 1958.[31]

Academic scholarship related to the Church of Scientology, admittedly limited, is moving toward accepting Scientology as a religion. This does not mean scholars regard Scientology as presenting an accurate worldview, any more than religious studies scholars call such diverse doctrines as those of Episcopalians or Hindus as "accurate" and the "last word." Organizationally many religion scholars find problematic Scientology's method of financing operations. Most religions seek voluntary contributions and payment for services (e.g., child care programs and youth activities) as secondary to the doctrine. In the Church of Scientology, the doctrine speaks of "reciprocity" and expects people to pay for the spiritual benefits they receive through auditing and training.

Scientology can be viewed as a religion because it has a body of beliefs as expressed in *Dianetics*, offers an explanation of the world and a purpose for humankind, and addresses issues like salvation and afterlife.[32]

Let's consider aspects of Scientology to see how they may, or may not, resemble those of more conventional religious organizations.

Doctrine   Salvation is a common religious theme, but in Scientology it is more immediate as one proceeds through auditing. The process for this auditing occurs in "the scripture," as the Church of Scientology sometimes refers to the writings of L. Ron Hubbard.[33]

Within Scientology you do not find the general membership offering new interpretations of Hubbard's teachings. Rather his message is accepted and the only public interpretation is how one may apply it to one's own existence.

Worship   Members of many religions gather together to worship. Do Scientologists gather? Scientology contends it does *not* mandate a particular relationship with God. Whereas prayer may be logical for others, it is not appropriate for Scientologists.

"Auditing and training are the two central religious services of the Scientology faith."[34] This declaration may be hard to get past for those accustomed to clergy addressing groups of people. Yet Scientology is a community of believers, even if they do not gather in sizeable collective groups on regular, scheduled basis.

---

[31]A. Greil and D. Rudy, "On the Margins of the Sacred," in T. Robbins and D. Anthony, eds., *In Gods We Trust* (New Brunswick, NJ: Transaction, 1990), p. 221.

[32]David G. Bromley and Mitchell L. Bracey, Jr., "The Church of Scientology," op. cit., p. 142, and Melton, *The Church of Scientology.*

[33]Hubbard, *What Is Scientology?*, p. 562.

[34]Ibid., p. 563.

Although ceremonies of birth, marriage, and death (funerals) are outlined in Scientology, it is auditing and training that are the core services.

There are Sunday services in the Church of Scientology but they are not critical to one's self-identification as a Scientologist. At the service, principles of Scientology are read and an audio lecture by L. Ron Hubbard is played. Those in attendance may ask questions or engage in a discussion.

The Church of Scientology has naming ceremonies akin to baptism and funeral rites that are not unlike mainstream Protestant ceremonies. However, of course, no Biblical references are made. Rather, the naming ceremony is described by the Church of Scientology to help orient the Thetan; the funeral bids farewell to the deceased and then believers present invite the Thetan to take up another body.

Ceremonies   There are also ordination ceremonies for Church of Scientology ministers that take place after an examination of the potential minister's knowledge of the organization and Dianetic beliefs.[35]

The identifiable high points of the Church of Scientology's calendar are the Scientology holidays; these include L. Ron Hubbard's birthday on March 13 and the Auditor's Day celebration on the second Sunday of September. Celebrants at local churches may see prerecorded or live broadcasts prepared at one of the main centers of Scientology, such as those in Los Angeles or Clearwater, Florida. Hubbard's birthday is an opportunity for devotees to pay tribute to their founder and usually involves Church statements speaking in positive terms about the organization's future.[36]

The second red-letter day, Auditor's Day, is a tribute to the hard work of the thousands of auditors. Because this event tends to be celebrated as a part of Sunday service, opponents of Scientology often use the occasion to mount protests or information pickets outside Church of Scientology's buildings.

The Free Zone   Despite being a relatively new organization, the Church of Scientology already has had to denounce splinter groups, including sects that claim to practice Dianetics complete with E-Meters independent of the Church. Members of the sects refer to themselves as the "Free Zone." The sects appear to have emerged over disagreements beginning in 1982 with the operations of the Religious Technology Center, the arm of the Church of Scientology headed by David Miscavige.

---

[35]Régis Dericquebourg, "Are the Ceremonies of the Church of Scientology Really Important?" paper presented at the International Conference of the Center for the Study of New Religions, Palermo, Italy, 2005.

[36]For example, see David Miscavige, "Opening Address in Honor of L. Rom Hubbard's Birthday," March 2002. Posted at www.lronhubbard.org.

Early in its history, people attracted to Dianetics came and went, of course, some returning to their traditional faiths and others striking out on their own. Most notable among these was Werner Erhard. He was a Scientologist in the 1960s and went on to create Est (Erhard Seminars Training) in 1971, which itself became to many a quasi-religion.

These splinter groups, while embracing some of Hubbard's writings or worldview, have developed their own principles. Especially significant among the Free Zone are the thoughts of William "Captain Bill" Robertson, who broke from the Sea Org and the Church of Scientology hierarchy in 1983. Although the size of the splinter groups is difficult to assess, especially since Robertson's death in 1991, the Free Zone appears to be most active in Europe, especially in Germany, and relatively insignificant in North America.

The very existence of break-away organizations reflects that Scientology is moving into a more mature stage.[37]

Social Positions

The Church of Scientology's positions on social issues are neither consistently conservative nor consistently liberal. As with any spiritual faith, devotees conform and deviate from accepted practices, but we can consider the Church of Scientology's official position in several areas.

Gay Marriage and Homosexuality

Scientologists recognize marriage as a part of the second of eight dynamics of existence. The second dynamic includes all creative activity, including sex, procreation, and child rearing. The Scientology marriage ceremony is traditional and addresses a union between a man and a woman. However, the present-day Church of Scientology has not specifically precluded gays and lesbians seeking to legalize their relationships as same-sex couples.

Initially homosexuality was placed in the same category of "sexual perversions" as sexual sadism. However, Hubbard cautions that punishment of gays and lesbians is as bad as acceptance. Homosexuality is regarded as an illness that must be overcome; the Church teaches that people with preference for same-sex partners need therapy through Dianetics.

Hubbard's early pronouncements came at a time when professional psychiatry still saw homosexuality as a disease. As new research and conclusions emerged, Hubbard, to his credit, renounced his earlier positions. In 1967, he declared that it was not his intention to regulate people's private

---

[37]"Free Zone Association," accessed January 14, 2007, at www.freezone.org; "Ron's Org," accessed January 14, 2007, at www.ronsorg.org; and "Larry King Live," op. cit.

lives and therefore "all former rules, regulations and policies relating to the sexual activities of Scientologists are cancelled."[38]

Abortion   As described in *Dianetics*, abortion and attempted abortion can traumatize the mother and unborn child physically and spiritually. Scientologists believe the fetus to have already been occupied by a spiritual being. Hubbard dramatically writes of the aborted child condemned to a "life" with "murderers." In some instances, abortion might be chosen because of health concerns of the mother or other personal factors.

Birth Control   Procreation and child rearing are considered part of one of the eight dynamics of existence. Couples are free to decide the size of their families, and do so by determining the greatest good across the dynamics. Personal and social circumstances, profession, and income are part of this decision, as with members of any faith.

Afterlife   Scientologists believe the Thetan (spirit) has lived lifetime after lifetime. An individual experiences in his next lifetime the civilization he had a part in creating today. With this knowledge comes more responsibility to help make that tomorrow a good one to return to.[39]

Scientology Enemy No. 1: The Government

Religions often engage in adversarial relationships with central government. In the United States, for example, organized religions are in conflict with the government over display of sacred symbols such as nativity scenes in public areas or in engaging in business that competes with the private sector.

In the context of these typical secular–sacred tensions, the confrontational experiences of the Church of Scientology in its short history with many governments are unprecedented in modern times.

Healing Under Attack   *Dianetics* first appeared in book form in 1951, and by 1958 the Food and Drug Administration (FDA) was investigating Scientology concerning its healing practices. The FDA seized quantities of Dianazene tablets, which the Church of Scientology marketed as a means to prevent and treat radiation sickness. The E-Meters were seized because the FDA felt that they were being presented as treatments for physical ailments.

---

[38]Hubbard, *Dianetics*; "About Scientology," *St. Petersburg Times*, July 18, 2004; and Religious Tolerance, "The Church of Scientology and Homosexuality," posted December 2006 and accessed January 7, 2007, at www.religioustolerance.org.
[39]"About Scientology," *St. Petersburg Times*, July 18, 2004.

After appealing the actions, the Church of Scientology agreed to make such items available only for religious practices and agreed to carry labels stating they were *not* effective at preventing or treating physical illnesses.[40]

Operation Snow White   The adversarial relationship between the Church of Scientology and the government is reflected in an episode that has come to be known as Operation Snow White.

Acting under suspicions that Scientologists were trying to infiltrate federal agencies to uncover and remove reports unfavorable to the Church, the FBI raided Scientology offices in 1977. Specifically they raided the Guardian Office, which had been created in 1966 to monitor antichurch actions being taken by governments worldwide. They uncovered an elaborate espionage plan called the Snow White program.

Hubbard himself was named an unindicted coconspirator. The exact extent of his knowledge of the undercover program could not be proven. However, a number of high-ranking officials, including his wife, Mary Sue Hubbard, were convicted of conspiracy against the U.S. federal government and actually served prison time.

Needless to say this was a very embarrassing event in the history of the Church of Scientology. Typically when officials mention the events, it is usually asserted they were set up by the government or others trying to destroy the faith. The leaders who were imprisoned have been effectively written out of Scientology. Mary Sue Hubbard, once the First Lady of Scientology, was removed from all Church positions while her husband was still alive. They were separated at the time of her ouster. Eventually her name was removed as coauthor of publications she wrote with L. Ron Hubbard.[41]

U.S. Milestone: Recognition   Although Scientology has never been banned in the United States, the government for decades questioned its legal status as a religion when it came to tax matters and official consideration as a charity. The Internal Revenue Service (IRS) recognized it as a tax-exempt charity as far back as 1957 but this status was revoked in 1967, at least in California.

---

[40]Current official publications of the Church of Scientology carry this disclaimer of Dianetics as a spiritual healing technology: "It is presented to the reader as a record of observations and research into the human mind and spirit and not as a statement of claims by the author [Hubbard]. The benefits and goals of Dianetics technology can be attained only by the dedicated efforts to the reader." The Hubbard Electrometer (or E-Meter) carries the disclaimer: "In itself, the E-Meter does nothing. It is not intended or effective for the diagnosis, treatment or prevention of any disease, or for the improvement of health or any bodily function." Source: L. Ron Hubbard, *Dianetics*, p. vi.

[41]Cowan and Bromley, "The Church of Scientology," pp. 185–86; and Melton, *The Church of Scientology*, pp. 19–20.

After much legal action, in 1993 the IRS granted the Church of Scientology full status recognizing that it was organized and operated exclusively for religious and charitable purposes. As a part of this announcement, the Church of Scientology agreed to pay the IRS $12.5 million in settlement of disputes over payroll, income, and estate taxes. Although this was a significant amount of money, the Church of Scientology was exceedingly pleased with the outcome. David Miscavige took the podium at the Los Angeles Sports Arena and announced in his two-and-a-half-hour speech that, "The war is over!" The Church of Scientology was officially a tax-exempt church, at least in the United States.[42]

A World Religion   Government hassles have not been limited to the United States. Typically countries have been reluctant to grant the Church of Scientology legal status equal to that of religions such as Presbyterian or Islam. Church authorities have to make legal arguments that can be very protracted; some continue into the present.

After actually being banned from Australia, the Church was granted religious status in 1982. Other countries have granted status as a religion including South Africa, Sweden, and relatively recently, Italy in 2000, New Zealand in 2002, and Taiwan in 2003. Scientology still has no official recognition in Canada, and Great Britain continues to reject its application to be considered a charity.

The most official opposition is in France and Germany. Since 2001, France has officially designated the Church of Scientology as an "aggressive cult." Earlier during the 1990s, several of Germany's states labeled Scientology as a threat to the constitution. For a period of time Scientologists were prohibited from elected office and from entering into government contracts. Belgium and Austria have also created official lists of suspect religious groups that include the Church of Scientology.

This animosity between governments and the Church of Scientology has led to a long-time involvement related to global human rights. Scientologists cite Article 18 of the Universal Declaration of Human Rights from the Charter of the United Nations that guarantees freedom of thought, conscience, and religion. They argue that the attempts to curtail their organization are no different from the hostility that Communist countries today and in the past have shown to religions. Beginning in 2003, the Church of Scientology opened its International European Office of Public Affairs and Human Rights in Brussels, Belgium, home of the European Parliament. Scientology leaders are increasingly active in allying themselves with the broad issue of religious freedom. For example, they

---

[42]Derek H. Davis, "The Church of Scientology: In Pursuit of Legal Recognition," paper presented at Center for Studies on New Religions, Waco, TX, 2004; Douglas Frantz, "The Shadowy Story Behind Scientology's Tax-Exempt Status," *New York Times,* March 9, 1997.

point to the persecution they experience in some European countries as similar to that experienced by Muslims.[43]

The Death of Lisa McPherson

Reflecting upon Operation Snow White and being labeled a cult by the French government, it may be surprising that the most difficult controversy for the Church of Scientology revolved around a car accident.

Fort Harrison Hotel   Long-time Scientologist (after a Baptist upbringing) Lisa McPherson, age thirty-six, was involved in a relatively minor automobile accident on November 18, 1995. At the accident scene, paramedics observed signs of mental disorder in McPherson; she also voluntarily removed all of her clothes. They took her to a nearby hospital for psychiatric evaluation.

Church officials soon removed McPherson from the hospital and took her to the Fort Harrison Hotel, the Church of Scientology's headquarters in Clearwater. While there, her physical condition deteriorated and she died seventeen days after the accident. She never saw a licensed physician during this time and was allegedly force-fed vitamins, herbal remedies, and sedatives. The official cause of death was a blood clot that developed as a result of "severe dehydration" and "bed rest." At the time the Church of Scientology called the "circumstances" of her death "unfortunate," and contended that the Church had no "intent to do any harm" to its member.[44]

The Church was charged with practicing medicine without a license and criminal neglect. Two years later, McPherson's estate joined in a wrongful death suit. For nearly ten years, Scientology nationally and worldwide, and particularly in Clearwater, Florida, came to be defined in the media by the criminal and civil cases surrounding the death of Lisa McPherson.

Clearwater, Florida   Clearwater, Florida, may seem like an unlikely city for this drama to play out, but actually it is not. With more than 100,000 people, Clearwater is a part of the larger Tampa Bay metro area of 2.6 million. Sun and surf are the attractions for residents and tourists alike. However, it is not too much of an overstatement to refer to Clearwater as the capital, if not Mecca, of the Church of Scientology.

[43]Davis, "The Church of Scientology"; John Lichfield, "Churches in France Oppose Anti-Cult Law, *The Independent* (London), June 25, 2000; and Robert A. Seiple, "Discrimination on the Basis of Religion and Belief in Western Europe," testimony before the House International Relations Committee, U.S. House of Representatives, June 14, 2000.

[44]Richard Leiby, "The Life and Death of a Scientologist," *Washington Post,* December 6, 1998, p. F1.

For reasons that are unclear and may not be particularly spiritually important, L. Ron Hubbard was attracted to the Tampa Bay area. In 1975, the land base of the Scientology Organization (the Sea Org) was located here and when much of those operations were moved ashore, growth of the Church of Scientology infrastructure in the deteriorating old downtown area of Clearwater exploded. Dozens of buildings now make up the Church of Scientology official presence and a 2004 estimate placed at two hundred the number of stores, restaurants, service operations, and small businesses owned by Scientologists in Clearwater.

One proud devotee declared, "You can't separate Salt Lake City and the Mormons and you can't separate Clearwater and Scientology." Indeed, today the Church of Scientology officially proclaims Clearwater as the "spiritual headquarters" of the faith. Church employees number at least 1,200, and estimates of numbers of followers in this city of 100,000 range from 7,000 to 12,000. No city in the world has such a high proportion of Scientologists.

Clearwater has economically benefited from Scientology. However, like Linden, Nebraska, birthplace of L. Ron Hubbard, this Florida city does not publicize its role in the contemporary Church of Scientology. Indeed, careful perusal of any official literature of the history or attractions of this Florida city will mention it as the birthplace of the Hooters Restaurant chain in 1983 but no mention is made of it as a virtual pilgrimage destination for Church of Scientology elites.[45]

As the months and years dragged on, the McPherson death started to take on the aura of street theater. Memorial vigils occurred on the anniversary of her death. As the legal process ground on, critics of Scientology would picket Fort Harrison carrying signs saying "Scientology Kills." In one of the Clearwater mayoral races, an incumbent mayor supportive of the prosecution fought off an opponent backed by Scientologists.

A Legal Resolution   In this climate, how was the tragic death of Lisa McPherson resolved? Ultimately, the outcome of the criminal case was anticlimactic. The county medical examiner's records on this case were so poorly maintained that criminal prosecution had to be dropped.

Eventually, in 2004, the Church offered $20,000 to McPherson's estate as a settlement in the civil case. The estate countered with a demand for $80 million. The suit was settled before it went to trial with the amount remaining undisclosed by mutual agreement of the parties involved.[46]

[45]"Scientology in Clearwater," accessed January 7, 2007, at http://Scientology.fso.org; and Robert Forley, "Scientology's Town," *St. Petersburg Times,* July 18, 2004.

[46]Douglas Frantz, "Distrust in Clearwater," *New York Times,* December 1, 1997; Richard Leiby, "The Life and Death of a Scientologist," *Washington Post,* December 6, 1998, p. F1; and *New York Times,* "Scientologists Settle Lawsuit," May 30, 2004, p. 25. An anti-Scientology Web page is still maintained at www.lisamcpherson.org.

Although the McPherson death is viewed generally as a dark moment in recent Scientology history, it also reflects a connection to more accepted religious faiths. To Scientologists, their intervention with ill devotees is no different than prayer as a supplement to, or even a replacement for, accepted medical treatment. The Church's relationship to the medical establishment is similar to that of the Christian Scientists, who also prefer that believers follow a more spiritual route to healing. Scientologists see the auditing process as promoting spiritual growth and they believe that physical enhancements may be a by-product of the process.

The medical establishment often scorns Scientology practices, but the Church contends that if the word *Dianetics* were to be replaced with the word *faith*, or *auditing* with *prayer*, the Church of Scientology would deserve the same benign skepticism given by medicine to other religions. To date, scientific studies of the impact of prayer on physical health are mixed and no independent researcher has published findings on Scientology's practices on health—either mental or physical.[47]

Hollywood Connections

Scientology's visibility is heightened by its connections with celebrities. Although this celebrity connection may not have been predictable, Hubbard was a creative person who showed a passion for artistic expression. The faith's strength in Los Angeles and its being apart from established religions made it attractive to those alienated from more conventional worldviews. Numerous Hollywood celebrities were attracted to new religious movements, most notably The Beatles with Transcendental Meditation beginning in 1967.

Several celebrities who are identified as adherents of Scientology are very willing to express their support for the faith against its critics. Among those active proponents are actors Kirstie Alley, John Travolta, and Kelly Preston—all of whom lend their name to the faith.[48]

Notable in his support was the famed African American songwriter and musician Isaac Hayes. In 2006 he publicly and bitterly left the television show *South Park* after nine years of voicing the role of Chef in the popular Comedy Central animated adult series. He broke with the series over the November 16, 2005, episode, "Trapped in the Closet," which included a highly satirized synopsis of Scientology beliefs and sarcastic attacks on Tom Cruise, John Travolta, and others. Although some embraced his

---

[47]Religioustolerance.org, "Prayer as a supplement to, or a replacement for medical treatment," accessed January 7, 2007, at www.religioustolerance.org/medical.htm.

[48] Among other notable Scientologists are Nancy Cartwright (voice of "Bart Simpson"), singer Chaka Khan, jazzman Chick Corea, skateboarder Jason Lee, actor Mimi Rogers, singer Lisa Marie Presley, actress Priscilla Presley, FOX-TV personality Greta Van Sustern, and the late singer and congressman Sonny Bono.

taking the "high road," others noted that he seemed to have no problem with the show's ridicule of Jesus, Muslims, Mormons, Roman Catholics, Jews, and gays.[49]

Celebrity Centres   L. Ron Hubbard, himself a celebrity independent of Scientology, understood the creative spirit. Therefore, in 1969 he created the Church of Scientology Celebrity Centre to utilize the full body of Dianetics and Scientology on behalf of the creative individual.

Another of the Church of Scientology alliances with Hollywood was through the Warner Brothers production in 2000 of *Battlefield Earth*. The motion picture based on the L. Ron Hubbard 1982 novel of the same name is set in the year 3000 and follows the actions of enslaved earthlings trying to break free of the tyrant Psychlos, played by Scientologist John Travolta. Although the motion picture plot does not embrace Scientology teachings, anti-Scientologists were quick to find parallels. In any event, this cinematic treatment of Hubbard's writing was a failure both among film critics and at the box office.[50]

The Scientology Wedding   Weddings are important events and most religions take them seriously, attaching devotional readings and significant statements of commitment by the two involved. However, Scientology, as it often has, faced worldwide scrutiny when Scientologist Tom Cruise married Katie Holmes. Before considering "TomKat," as the celebrity press came to call the couple, let's consider the role of weddings within Scientology.

Scientology provides for weddings conducted by an ordained Scientology minister. Marriage is viewed as essential to the life of a Scientologist as is procreation and the raising of children.

Scientology marriage ceremonies, as in other religions, can vary in their degree of formality. Although marriage and weddings are fundamental to the Church of Scientology, the Church does not require that nonbelieving partners convert. Scientology weddings may include traditional rituals such as those involving rings and statements of commitment, and the Church does not prohibit customs from other religious faiths at their weddings.[51]

Cruise–Holmes   The most famous Scientology wedding was between Tom Cruise and Katie Holmes on November 18, 2006, in Italy. Although it may seem frivolous to focus on such an event when considering an extraordinary group, this wedding for much of the world brought Scientology to the front page.

[49]Ben Sisario, "Citing Religion, Isaac Hayes is Leaving South Park," *New York Times*, March 14, 2006.

[50]Rick Lyman, "'Battlefield Earth': Film Doggedly Links to Scientology Founder," *New York Times*, May 11, 2000.

[51]Nadine Brozan, "For Mrs. Cruise, Perhaps a Cat," *New York Times*, November 12, 2006.

Cruise, twice divorced, and the Roman Catholic Katie Holmes gave birth in April 2005 to a girl, Suri Cruise, and then announced their engagement in June 2005. The significance of Scientology to Cruise was underscored by his selection of David Miscavige, head of the Church of Scientology since the death of L. Ron Hubbard, as his best man. (Matron of honor to Holmes was her sister.)

A Scientology minister officiated at the Italy ceremony. Was this legal in Italy? The issue is mute because the couple reportedly made their marriage official in Los Angeles prior to heading for Italy.[52]

The Last Words

Scientology, despite its apparent success and growing membership, is not popular. One 1995 national survey of born-again Christians found that 81 percent felt that Scientology has a negative impact compared to 92 percent who felt the same way about atheism.[53]

Perhaps even more distressing to Scientologists than the low esteem with which the general public holds their faith, is that it continues to be ridiculed and parodied. In October 2006, a French acting troupe staged the off-Broadway play *A Very Merry Unauthorized Children's Scientology Pageant*, complete with a depiction of Katie Holmes as a sock puppet on the hand of an actor playing Tom Cruise. The Church of Scientology was not pleased to say the least.[54]

All religions are subjected to criticism and humor, but what makes the Church of Scientology different is that virtually all popular media treatments of any aspect of the Church of Scientology are critical. Despite this social context, the Church of Scientology remains supremely confident of what it has to offer the individual and what its adherents collectively can offer society.

Given his voluminous literary output, it is appropriate to close with the words of L. Ron Hubbard, which are often used as a part of weddings. "Happiness and strength endure only in the absence of hate. To hate alone is the road to disaster. To love is the road to strength. To love in spite of all is the secret of greatness. And may well be the greatest secret in this universe."[55]

[52]"Tom Cruise and Katie Holmes Marry," People.com, posted November 19, 2006.

[53]The 1995 Barna Research survey is reported at Religious Tolerance, "Prejudice of Americans towards various religions," accessed January 7, 2007, at www.religioustolerance.org/amer_intol.htm.

[54]Ben Brantley, "A Guided Tour of Hell, With an Appearance by Satan," *New York Times*, October 14, 2006; and "A Very Merry Unauthorized Children's Scientology Pageant," *New York Times*, December 15, 2006.

[55]Religious Tolerance, "Interesting Quotes: On Topics from Justice to Morality," accessed January 17, 2007, at www.religioustolerance.org/quotes1.htm.

KEY TERMS

Auditing, p. 288
Clear, p. 289
Engram, p. 289

Preclear, p. 289
Quasi-religion, p. 293
Thetan, p. 290

SOURCES ON THE WEB

www.scientology.org
The official site for the Church of Scientology.

www.religioustolerance.org/scientol1.htm
www.cesnur.org/testi/se_scientology.htm
Two sources of relatively objective information about this faith and its symbols, history, belief, and practices.

www.xenu.net
A major anti-Scientology site, with extensive news articles, analyses, and criticism of the faith, Dianetics, and L. Ron Hubbard.

www.lisamcpherson.org
www.lisamcpherson.com
Sites highly critical of the Church of Scientology surrounding the death of Lisa McPherson.

SELECTED READINGS

Bromley, David G., and Mitchell L. Bracey, Jr. "The Church of Scientology: A Quasi-Religion." In *Sects, Cults, and Spiritual Communities: A Sociological Analysis,* edited by William W. Zellner and Marc Petrowsky, pp. 141–56. Westport CT: Praeger, 1998.

Burroughs, William S. *Ali's Smile, Naked Scientology.* Bonn, Germany: Expanded Media, 1985.

Cooper, Paulette. *The Scandal of Scientology.* New York: Tower Publications, 1971.

Cowan, Douglas E., and David G. Bromley. "The Church of Scientology." In *Introduction to New and Alternative Religions in America,* vol. 5, edited by Eugene V. Gallagher and W. Michael Ashcraft, pp. 169–96. Westport, CT: Greenwood Press, 2006.

Frenschkowski, Marco. "L. Ron Hubbard and Scientology: An Annotated Bibliographical Survey of Primary and Selected Secondary Literature." *Marburg Journal of Religion* 4 (July 1999). Accessed February 11, 2007, at web.uni-marburg.de/religionswissenschaft/journal/mjr/frenschkowski.html.

Hubbard, L. Ron. *Dianetics.* Hollywood, CA: Bridge Publications, 1950.

———. *Scientology: The Fundamentals of Thought.* Hollywood, CA: Bridge Publications, 1997. {Comp: set these "author" lines same as in other chapters.}

———. *What Is Scientology?* Hollywood, CA: Bridge Publications, 1998.

———. *The Modern Science of Mental Health.* 1995.

———. *Scientology: A New Slant on Life.* Hollywood, CA: Bridge Publications, 1997.

Kin, L. *Scientology—More Than a Cult.* Wiesbaden, Germany: Edition Scien Terra, 1991.

Melton, J. Gordon. *The Church of Scientology.* Torino, Italy: Signature Books, Center for Studies on New Religions, 2000.

Wallis, Roy. *The Road to Total Freedom: A Sociological Analysis of Scientology.* New York: Columbia University Press, 1977.

Whitehead, Harriet. *Renunciation and Reformation: A Study of Conversion in an American Sect.* Ithaca NY: Cornell University Press, 1987.

GLOSSARY

Alienation The condition of estrangement or dissociation from the surrounding society.

Anomie A sense of powerlessness or worthlessness, leading eventually to a feeling of alienation.

Apostate A person who has renounced his or her belief in and allegiance to a religion.

Argot A special language peculiar to a group.

Ascending fellowship The Oneidan practice in which older godly male members in a special group called the Central Committee could pick a virgin at about the age fourteen for whom they were spiritually responsible.

Assimilation The process through which a person forsakes his or her own cultural tradition to become part of a different culture.

Auditing A form of personal counseling that is the first step one takes to become a Scientologist.

Bori In Rom culture, a new wife who lives with her husband's family and comes under the supervision of her mother-in-law.

Celestial marriage A Mormon marriage ceremony that serves to "seal" a man and woman not only for time, but also for all eternity.

Charismatic authority Power made legitimate by a leader's exceptional personal or emotional appeal to his or her followers.

Clear The most highly valued state within the Church of Scientology.

Commune A form of cooperative living where community assets are shared and individual ownership is discouraged.

Complex marriage A communal circumstance in which every man and every woman is married to each other. They could engage in sexual intercourse, but are not attached to one another as couples.

Conspicuous consumption The tendency to gain attention through the overt display of one's wealth.

Counterculture Any group behavioral pattern that arises in opposition to the prevailing culture.

Cult Generally a small, secretive religion or major innovation of an existing faith.

Culture The totality of learned, socially transmitted customs, knowledge, material objects, and behavior.

Cultural relativism The tendency to view people's behavior from the perspective of one's own culture.

Daro The traditional Rom payment by the groom's family to the bride's family in a marriage arrangement.

Definition of the situation A concept referring to the idea that a social situation is whatever it is defined to be by the participants.

Denomination A large, organized religion that is not officially linked with the state or government.

Disfellowshipped The Witness term for excommunicated.

Ecclesia A religious organization that claims to include most or all members of a society and is recognized as the national or official religion.

English (or Englishers) Non-Amish, as defined by the Amish.

Engram A particular type of mental image, as described by Dianetics.

Eschatology A part of theology that refers to the final events of the world.

Established sect A religious group that is the outgrowth of a sect, yet remains isolated from society.

Ethnocentrism The tendency to assume that one's own culture and way of life represent the norm or are superior to all others.

Eugenics The study of human genetics and of methods to improve inherited characteristics.

Familia The functional extended family that is the essential nucleus of Rom social organization.

Familiyi Plural of **Famlia.**

Formal social control Social control carried out by authorized agents, such as police officers, judges, school administrators, and employers.

Gadje Romani word for non-Gypsies.

Gentiles Non-Mormons, as defined by Mormons.

Ideal type A model for evaluating specific types, enabling the sociologist to compare an actual situation with a conceptualized ideal.

In-group A group or category to which people feel they belong.

Informal social control Social control that is carried out casually by ordinary people through such means as laughter, smiles, and rituals.

Kris The Rom system of law and justice.

Latent function The unconscious, unrealized function of a social institution or process.

Male continence The method of birth control practiced by the Oneidans, in which the male willingly refrains from ejaculation.

Manifest function The conscious, deliberate function of a social institution or process.

Marimé The Romani word for defilement or pollution, used both as an object and a concept.

Meidung The shunning or avoidance of excommunicated members in the Amish community.

Melalo The Romani word for *dirty*, as opposed to marimé, or *polluted*.

Millenarian Movement A movement made up of people who anticipate a dramatic change that will bring about a perfect future.

Mutual criticism The uniquely Oneidan practice in which a member who was being reprimanded was taken in front of either a committee or sometimes the whole community to be criticized for his or her action.

Natsiyi The Rom word for nations. There are four: the Lowara, Machwaya, Kalderasha, and Churara.

Norms Established standards of behavior maintained by a society.

Out-group A group or category to which people feel they do not belong.

Perfectionism The doctrine that, given the proper environment, people can lead perfect, or sinless, lives.

Polygamy The practice of taking multiple spouses; in the Mormon tradition, the practice of taking multiple wives.

Preclear A member of the Church of Scientology who has received an audit but has not yet attained Clear status.

Primary group Groups characterized by intimate, face-to-face association and cooperation, such as the family.

Quasi-religion A category of organizations that may see themselves as religious but are seen as "sort-of religious" by others.

Relative deprivation The idea that people feel aggrieved not because of what they are deprived of in any absolute sense, but because of what they are deprived of in terms of their reference group.

Romaniya The Gypsy way of life and view of the world, embracing their moral codes, traditions, customs, rituals, and rules of behavior.

Rum springa A period of discovery during which Amish youth often test their subculture's boundaries. The term literally means "running around."

Sanction A reward or punishment employed by a group to bring about desired behavior on the part of its members.

Secondary group A formal, impersonal group in which there is little social intimacy or mutual understanding, such as a large corporation.

Sects A relatively small religious group that has broken away from some other religious organization to renew what it considers the original vision of the faith.

Social control Techniques and strategies for preventing deviant human behavior in any society.

Stake LDS geographical unit made up of five to ten **wards.**

Stereotype An unreliable generalization about all members of a group that does not recognize individual differences within that group.

Stirpiculture The selective breeding method employed for the biological improvement of the Oneida Community.

Subculture A segment of society that shares a distinctive pattern of mores, folkways, and values that differs from the pattern of the larger society.

Thetan The Church of Scientology term for the immortal spiritual being or soul.

Tithing The LDS custom of members giving one-tenth of their incomes annually "for the support of the Lord's work."

Value The collective conception of what is considered good, desirable, and proper—or bad, undesirable, and improper—in a culture.

Vitsa A Rom unit of identity, or kin group, made up of a number of familiyi.

Ward The basic horizontal or geographical unit of LDS, roughly corresponding to Protestant congregation or the Catholic parish.

INDEX